MANAGING CHANGE
IN THE
NEW PUBLIC SECTOR

Forthcoming titles in the public sector management series

Accruals accounting in the public sector by V Archibald

Purchasing in Government by P Behan

Strategic management and planning in the public sector by R Smith

Marketing in the new public sector by L Titman

Managing change
in the new public sector

edited by
Roger Lovell

Published by Longman in association with
The Civil Service College.

MANAGING CHANGE IN THE NEW PUBLIC SECTOR

Published by Longman Information and Reference, Longman Group Limited, 6th floor, Westgate House, The High, Harlow Essex CM20 IYR, England and Associated Companies throughout the world.

A catalogue record for this book is available from The British Library.

ISBN 0-582-23893-5

Contents

Series foreword

The Longman/Civil Service College series of texts on Management in the Public Sector covers many of the most important topics on the current management agenda, in central government and in the public sector as a whole. In the past many of these topics may have been the preserve of specialists. Finance was for the Finance Division, human resource issues were for the Personnel Group, contracts were for the Contracts Branch. Increasingly all managers, at senior, middle and junior management levels, find themselves drawn into these, previously specialist, topics. With flatter management structures and increased delegation, all managers need a broad understanding of a range of management topics. This series of books has been produced with their needs in mind.

The texts are intended to be straightforward and easily understood, to provide a good summary of current understanding and best practice, and to illustrate the key points with examples from the public sector. There will still be room for the specialist, but these texts should enable every manager to talk intelligently with the specialist and understand him or her better.

In the past people may have thought that the public sector, particularly central Government was protected from or perhaps immune to change. It is doubtful whether many people would argue such a case today. The pressure of and for change is felt just about everywhere. It runs through organisations from top to bottom, with implications for all staff from Permanent Secretaries and Chief Executives, to middle managers, to supervisors, to those delivering services directly to members of the public. It is hoped that this book will contain something for all such people, helping them to identify the issues which they personally need to think about.

Robert J. Smith

August 1994

Author's foreword

This book blends theory and practice to provide an understanding of the management of change which has taken place in the public sector during the past few years and is written by people who have had direct experience of managing these changes. While it tends to focus on change in the Civil Service, there are examples of work in other parts of the public sector, which, in general, have followed similar trends. It will be of interest therefore to managers, students and academics who have an interest in the public sector at large.

In view of the benefit of such practical experience, the book recognises that, unlike many systematic packaged approaches, there are no universal panaceas. In truth different situations require different solutions and no situation is ever repeated in its entirety. It therefore endeavours to provide managers with an understanding of the underlying issues involved and in particular the inter-relationship between them. Above all, it is not a 'cook book' designed with 'menu management' in mind. Instead, in understanding the culture, constraints and complexities facing managers with responsibility to achieve the new public management, it provides a comprehensive guide for turning ideas into action.

From a personal point of view, during more than thirty years in the public service, I am indebted to so many people who have encouraged and influenced me and shown me good practice. Above all I am grateful to those who have demonstrated the soul of management and exhibited it in its art form. I would particularly like to thank my fellow authors for their contributions, and copyright holders for their permission to use material, all of which have been given so willingly.

I am especially grateful to Mahen Tampoe without whose encouragement I would not have made the transition from practitioner to commentator. I am also greatly indebted to Archie Cameron, Ian Hiscutt and Chris Eling for their support. Of many colleagues at the College who have been so supportive, I have particularly to thank Peter Tebby, Lionel Titman, Laurence Cranmer, Jane Tatum and Tony Povey for their enlightenment during my time in their company. I am also extremely grateful to Robert Smith for his help and encouragement and to Bob Pike and Kieran Bright for their work in preparing the text and diagrams.

Last, but no means least, I would like to express my gratitude to my wife, Aileen, and my children, David and Victoria, who have been so supportive to me over the years in indulging me in my thirst for learning.

Roger Lovell
Sunningdale

Copyright Acknowledgements

The author and publisher wish to thank particularly the following for permission to reproduce copyright material:

Addison-Wesley for Figure 4.1

Bolknap for figure 12.1

Brain Books for Figure 5.5

Consulting Psychologists Press for Figure 5. 2

Element Books for Chapter 7

European Foundation for Quality Management for Figure 22.4

Jossey-Bass for Figure 4.3

Kogan Page for Figure 11.5

MIT for Figures 12.2 and 12.4

McMillan for Figure 6.1

PA Consulting for Figures 22.5 and 22.6

Peforrest Aegis Group for Figures 22.9 and 22.10

Pfeiffer & Co for Figures 1.1 and 4.6

Prado for Figures 5.3 and 5.4

Prentice-Hall for Figure 4.3

Process Management International for Figure 12.3.

TMS (UK) Ltd for Figures 5.3 and 5.4.

Part 1 — Managing Change

Chapter 1 - The environment for change

Roger Lovell

'We live in a world where the only certainty is change.'

How often has such a statement been used over the centuries? Undoubtedly the feelings could have been expressed with some passion in the 1790s as the Industrial Revolution was beginning. Indeed, there may never have been a period when people felt they were living in stability at the time. Such notions tend to emerge only after the event in fits of nostalgia. It is also fair to say that the human race, by and large, does not actively relish discontinuity. The only person who appears to like change is a wet baby!

What is it therefore that gives the opening statement particular credibility in the 1990s? Whilst the move from the domestic to the industrial system was a fundamental shift, requiring a different way of viewing the world, it took place over a considerable time span and affected local communities at different times. Our move, from the Industrial to the Information Revolution, is taking place not only at a phenomenally faster pace but also on a global basis. In other words, the speed and size of change are greater than many can cope with and are producing tremendous strain, with virtually the whole community affected by it in some way.

As far as the workplace is concerned, it is interesting how much more easily people can cope with new technology at home than at work. Generally people cannot wait to buy the latest labour saving, or leisure giving, gadget for the house, since they have some control over whether or not to take part. At work however, they seem more fearful and reluctant since their level of control and choice is usually limited.

Types of change

Before looking at the reasons to change at this particular time, it is worth looking briefly at the four types of change shown in Figure 1.1 (Ferguson, in Pfeiffer, 1990) on the following page.

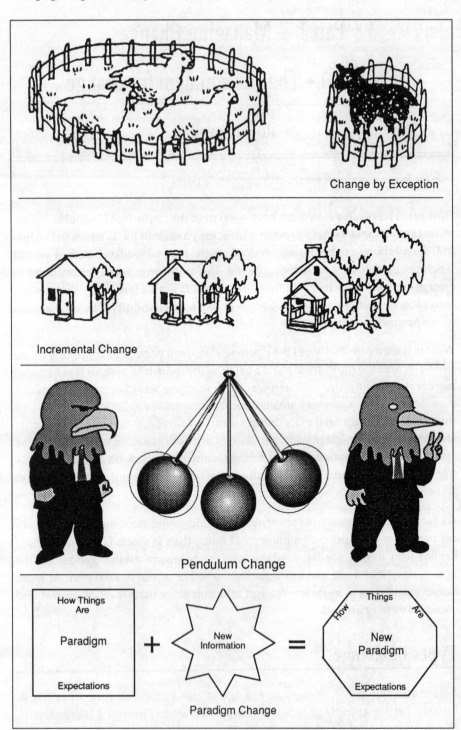

Figure 1.1 Four types of change (Ferguson, in Pfeiffer, 1990).

❑ Change by exception

Change by exception is usually handled by setting up a project to manage its implementation. It has a distinct beginning and end where success can be relatively easily measured. It will often have little impact on the way the remainder of the organisation works, hence it can be seen as the black sheep at the time. A good example of this type of change in recent years has been relocation projects, where posts have been moved, generally away from the South East. The movement causes a temporary discontinuity to the system but the business carries on and eventually settles down to business as usual once the move has been completed.

Another example of exceptional change is the way legislation is implemented. This is especially true of changes resulting from the Budget. The ability to introduce a new policy within an existing system in a remarkably short space of time has always been a considerable strength of the public sector.

❑ Incremental change

By far the most usual type of change is that which occurs in an evolutionary way, often without the participants realising that it has happened. In the picture, for example, people only occasionally notice that the trees have grown. This is often demonstrated by making an inventory of changes over say the past three years. The precise amount of change which has actually taken place often surprises staff, since many may well believe that they have been in a relatively steady state situation.

Ironically the degree of stability is the key to this. In practice most changes are in themselves small. By far the vast majority of operations remain the same but publicity for 'the change' usually far exceeds mention of what is not changing. Staff often believe that the status quo is threatened more than it actually is. In fact people can often only change with any confidence if they do so from a basis of some security. Stability needs therefore to be talked up rather than forgotten as it frequently is. We need to recognise what is good about the past, not simply to preserve it but to use it as a springboard for even better performance in future.

Another strength of the public sector has been its ability to change almost seamlessly over the years to accommodate circumstances as they evolve.

❑ Pendulum change

Pendulum change is often associated with fashion. In other words, the change swings from side to side of a spectrum as moods change. An obvious example is the fashion for centralisation or decentralisation. Another is the movement back towards work measurement and performance pay which was in fashion in the 1960s.

3

❏ Paradigm shift

By far the most important type of change in the present environment is paradigm shift. A paradigm is a way of viewing the world, or the values which underpin our viewpoint. Many would argue that a paradigm shift is taking place in public administration at the moment. The period following the implementation of the Northcote Trevelyan reforms of 1870 looked to keep the public sector honest and fair. Practices arising in the post-war period also tended to concentrate on ensuring administration was robust and resilient, often to the extent of having duplicate systems in place. The new public management tends to emphasise keeping administration lean and purposeful (Hood,1991).

We will return to the theme of the new public management below. In the meantime, it is important to identify why such a swing is needed.

Why change?

In the private sector, increased competition as a result of global production and world recession has required a fundamental reappraisal of working practices in order to gain, or retain, competitive advantage. This has shown itself through:

- changes in the way of working as a result of new technology
- restructuring businesses in order to reduce levels of hierarchy which are not seen as adding sufficient value to the business for them to be retained
- re-examination of the way work is processed
- changing the managerial culture where control is carried out by a team itself and managers adopt the role of coach.

These and many other changes in working practice have been taking place over the past 15 years with varying degrees of success. Why however should they now be considered relevant to the public sector? What types of change are required and how might these be brought about?

❏ Supply and demand

From the Second World War until the oil crisis of the early 1970s, public expenditure tended to grow along with the economy. For example, public expenditure at the turn of the century as a proportion of Gross Domestic Product was 10%. After the Second World War it was 35% and by the mid-seventies nearly 50%. The world recession that followed meant that such growth was no longer possible. Not only did the size of public expenditure need to contract, but also the demand for its services has increased.

Apart from temporary pressures such as unemployment benefit in times of recession, the increasing longevity of the population is placing a greater demand on social and health services, to say nothing of the increasing cost of more sophisticated treatments. In addition, all of this needs to be financed from a shrinking working population. For example, the most recent projections from the Office of Population and Censuses, (1992), show an increase in the overall population of England and Wales of 8% over the next thirty years. Projected increases in older age groups however are as follows:

Age Group	Percentage Increase
45 - 59	11
60 - 74	49
75 - 84	51
85 and over	126

The increasing awareness of quality products in our private lives is also being transferred to demands for value for money from the taxpayer. In other words, if services are to endeavour to keep pace with demand, more must be delivered at less cost while still satisfying the customer.

❏ Technology

The move from the 'industrial' to the 'information' age has brought in its wake fundamentally different ways of organising and managing work. With the increase in technology has come greater complexity. Gone are the days when a manager was expected to know more about the job than the subordinate. The 'local knowledge' held by staff represents a significant movement of power away from managers towards those nearer the customer. This is especially so where the person is involved in a function critical to the success of the work. To this end, managers will increasingly be forced into the role of coach, rather than controller. In other words, their role will be to help and facilitate others to make decisions.

Unattractiveness of working in London, amongst other things, has led to a large dispersal of civil service jobs away from the South-East. In 1979 about 230,000 civil servants worked in the South-East; now only 187,000 remain (Oughton,1993). The fact that such redeployment has taken place in a seamless fashion, where a call to London can be answered by a person in Glasgow without the customer being aware of the change, has been largely due to the ability to transfer information and data considerably more easily as a result of advances in technology. Indeed, increases in the capability of remote, and particularly home or 'tele,' working during the coming years will also bring about further changes in the manager/staff relationship with a need for greater trust and increased dependence on managing outcomes.

❏ Changes in work perceptions

The psychological contract of employment is an unwritten agreement between individuals and the organisation of which they are members. It describes certain expectations that the organisation has of the individual and the individual's expectations of the organisation. From the perspective of both employee and employer this is changing.

From the viewpoint of the employee, the increased specialisation and knowledge of staff, together with a general reduction in deference from the younger generation, has undermined the control style of management. Despite the obvious need for money to be able to maintain a basic standard of living, the three highest motivators for staff now are often felt to be respect, information and involvement. In other words, they want to be respected for who they are and the skills that they bring to the job. They want to be informed of the reasons behind a decision so that they can understand its logic and how it fits the wider picture. They wish to have some input into deciding what should be done through participating in the decision making process.

From the employer's point of view, whilst, as the Oughton report points out (1993), the statement that civil servants invariably have a job for life is incorrect, most civil servants have undoubtedly viewed the relationship in parent/child terms for a considerable number of years. Block (1991) describes this as a type of patriarchal contract, whereby when we join the organisation we sign on to submit to authority and deny our self-expression, in return for a belief that we will be looked after in the future and that the organisation will treat us justly.

This relationship, as with many white collar workers in the private sector, tends to be breaking down. Instead, the concept of mutuality is being encouraged. This depends more on a relationship between adults, where reward is given for work today without expectation of the future. In return, the acquisition of greater knowledge and skills by employees are seen to make them more marketable and, as such, they are left to manage their own careers either within, or outwith, the sector. With this lack of dependence also comes a greater desire to be involved and have more control over your own destiny.

❏ Dissatisfaction with bureaucracy

Two fundamental schools of thought have developed over recent years as to how to improve public administration i.e. the public choice and the managerialist. Both agree that the pre-1983 modus operandi of the bureaucracy was inefficient and ineffective. In brief, public choice theorists are concerned at the apparent lack of control over the bureaucracy and wish to see greater constraint imposed upon it by elected representatives. Those belonging to the 'managerialist' school, however, believe that in order to reach their objectives, bureaucracies need to institute management practices which allow this to be done. In other words, they believe that it should move from 'administration', which is an adherence to formalised processes and procedures, to 'management' which is concerned with the use of resources to achieve results. As such, managerial techniques similar to those used in the private sector should be applied to the public (Aucoin,1990). This in turn requires more leadership which is to do with inspiration, motivation, communication and coaching, as opposed to the more traditional management skills of planning, organising, directing, co-ordinating and controlling.

This book is concerned with implementation of the changes resulting from the 'managerialist' school which have provided the main thrust of developments over the past 15 years and loosely can be termed the 'new public management.'

New public management

The new public management has evolved over a number of years and is by no means restricted to the United Kingdom. While it does not have a specific international definition, its principles have been summed up by Hood (1991) as follows:

- a focus on management not policy, and on performance appraisal and efficiency
- the disaggregation of public bureaucracies into agencies which deal with each other on a user-pay basis
- the use of quasi-markets and contracting out to foster competition
- cost-cutting
- a style of management which emphasises, amongst other things, output targets, limited term contracts, monetary incentives and freedom to manage.

This definition is consistent with the view of the future as stated by Richard Mottram, the Permanent Secretary at the Office of Public Service and Science, in a speech at York University in September 1993 (Oughton,1993):

> What will the Civil Service of the future look like? Let me offer some guesses and goals, not prescriptions in headline form. Numbers will fall to new lows since the war. The central departments will concentrate on strategic issues; there will be a minimum framework of prescribed rules concentrated on 'ethical' standards and effective accountability; for the rest, they will work by facilitating and disseminating best practice. Operational management will be delegated to departments and agencies. Departments will be restructured with, at their centre, smaller staffs concentrating on policy making, strategic management, and target

setting and monitoring contracts or agreements for services supplied by a mix of public and private sector providers. A still bigger proportion of the Civil Service than now will work in a changing constellation of executive agencies.

There will be greater emphasis on leadership and on management and professional skills in picking and developing managers and more interchange with the rest of the economy.

These sentiments are in line with the recent white paper on the Civil Service, *Continuity and Change* (Cm 2627). What does this mean in practice?

❏ Policy

Traditionally, the preparation of legislation and its administration have been carried out by public sector employees. While the ultimate responsibility for policy implementation still remains with Ministers, it is no longer felt that the work itself needs to be carried out solely in the public sector. In other words, the centre is seen as setting the general direction i.e. providing the steer, while others are left to implement the policy i.e. row.

This approach is also analogous with the concept of managing by outcomes rather than inputs. For years concentration has been on resource costs, rather than the actual result of the expenditure. For example, if one gives a speech, it is only right that its success is judged on its outcome i.e. whether it had the desired effect of changing behaviour, rather than the way in which the speech was prepared. While economy and value for money of course remain necessary, the split between clients and contractors allows the clients to specify the outcome of the service required and the contractors to deliver that outcome in the way they consider most effective.

❏ Structure

The split between purchaser and provider can be seen in the establishment of Executive Agencies under the Next Steps initiative. To this end, not only is the distinction between steering and rowing made explicit but also clearer lines of responsibility and accountability are drawn and invested in chief executive officers to deliver.

❏ Customer focus

Identification of the 'customer' has never been easy in the public sector. Indeed many instances exist where competing demands appear to be taking place within the same organisation. While the establishment of agencies provided the internal mechanism for greater focus on customer needs, the Citizen's Charter has endeavoured to direct attention to the ultimate end-user of services i.e. the general public. In turn this has underlined the importance of providing those nearest the customer with greater power to satisfy a dissatisfied customer as quickly and effectively as possible, in other words, greater freedom to manage.

Achieving the new public management

Approaches to achieving the new public management can broadly be divided into two categories:

* contract management;
* improving the current organisation.

This is illustrated in more detail in Figure 1.2

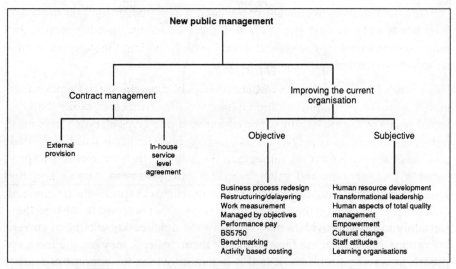

Figure 1.2. Ways of achieving the new public management.

❏ Contract management

Under contract management, services will be provided either by an external contractor or an in-house team who have successfully won a competition against other bidders to supply a specified service for a contracted period. The primary initiative for the exercise is the 'Competing for Quality' White Paper, 1991 (Cm 1730).

If in-house staff are to compete successfully with external suppliers they must be able to change their view of the world and see things from a wider perspective. In other words, they need to be able to see things from the mind set of the other bidders. Figures 1.3 and 1.4, adapted from Argyris (Kolb et al, 1991) represent the dilemma.

9

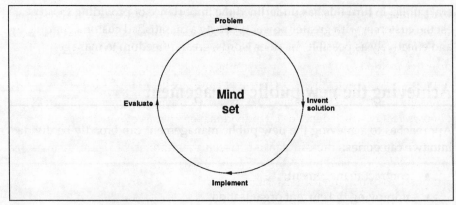

Figure 1.3. Single loop learning.

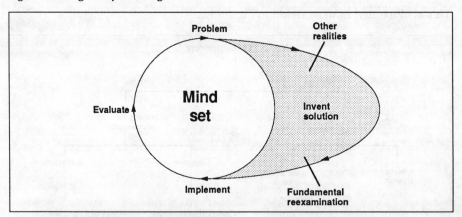

Figure 1.4. Double loop learning.

Certainly external providers may not have the detailed knowledge of current operations, but neither are they bound by them. Instead, they bring a fresh approach to solving problems. It is this ingenuity which the concept of market testing wishes to capture, in other words, to be able to move from the bounded thinking with the single loop in Figure 1.3, to the more fundamental examination, or double loop, of Figure 1.4. in which realities outside the mind set are considered. In other words, organisations need to move from first order changes which are mutations of the current strategy to a second order transformation, to an entirely new way of behaving, (Bate, 1994). It is difficult however to change long established mind sets.

❑ Improving the current organisation

Another way of achieving the overall objective is to improve the current public sector organisation. In this regard two main thrusts of management thinking can be seen i.e. the objective, or scientific stream, and the subjective, or art form.

In distinguishing between the two, much depends on how we view reality. Objective forms of management technique tend to work from the belief that the social world exists externally, and that its properties can, and should, be measured through objective methods, rather than inferred subjectively through sensation, reflection or intuition. Subjective methods, on the other hand, are based on the belief that reality is socially constructed rather than objectively determined. In other words, we create our own reality which depends on individual perceptions of how things are.

Hunt (1986) defines the difference between the rational, or scientific management style propagated by Taylor in the early part of the century, and the behavioural styles of management as follows:

> The rational model of management is about order, structure, defined strategy, management by objectives etc. The behavioural model is about creativity, innovation, gut feel, emotion and feeling.

In recent years there has been a return to some of the concepts of the rationalist style. These can be seen in terms of:

- performance pay
- the setting of targets
- work measurement
- business process redesign
- structural delayering
- formal control systems such as BS 5750.

Alongside these are the more subjective influences. These are seen in the move away from the rather narrow thinking of personnel to the more all embracing notion of human resource development, the need to change styles of leadership in order to transform organisations, and in such movements as empowerment and the human relations aspects of Total Quality Management which, amongst other things, are directed towards changing attitudes and behaviour within the culture in which people work.

Under scientific management, staff are often seen as individual units responding directly to some fairly simple incentives and punishments (Pollitt, 1992). This tends to overlook the complexity of human behaviour. The subjective approach therefore concerns itself with understanding the people and, if necessary, endeavouring to change the culture within which the work is being carried out in order to release the creative energy within the staff.

Management styles and techniques of themselves are not panaceas for all ills. Just as it is important to counsel against the 'tick box' approach to some scientific management techniques, it is also necessary to warn against the 'quality' movement. As Pollitt points out (1992), *'the use of quality as a term has become quite promiscuous.'* We all wish to see quality service. Attaining it however requires far more than the articulation of being a Total Quality organisation. Indeed, as we will discover in the book, the very people who are closest to that state are usually those who admit how difficult it is and are often reluctant to admit their success.

Format of the book

Managing change is a complex process under most circumstances. As noted above, the increased pace and scale of change to which the public sector is now being subjected makes it even more complicated. Added to this, all changes are highly idiosyncratic and are not therefore susceptible to definitive formulae of success. Endeavouring to establish a scientific path through this maze, in what is often an art form, merely adds to the confusion, particularly in trying to rationalise what are often intuitive processes. Frequently in this area we can only learn from our own experience and the experience of others.

This book therefore offers an account of the thoughts and experiences of a range of people from different backgrounds, all fully aware of what is happening in their various areas and with extensive experience of managing change. It is divided into three parts looking at the process of managing change, instruments for change, and case studies of recent changes that have taken place, and is designed to allow readers to dip into topics without having to read it sequentially.

❏ Part 1

Part 1 looks at concepts, tools and techniques in order to manage change successfully and is based around the model in Figure 1.5. Before embarking on a programme of change it is important to understand the environment and need for change which we have discussed above. You then need to articulate what you wish to achieve as a result of the change and compare this against the current situation. This will both establish the gap between what you wish to attain and where you are starting from. It will also allow some understanding of the likely impact of the change. Chapter 2 considers ways of establishing this strategy. Having identified the gap between where you wish to go and the current position, it is then possible to commence the transformation process. Chapter 3 considers how this might be organised, planned and monitored, taking account of some of the methods of project management which may help. Most change programmes fail because of a lack of support from people capable of bringing about the change. Chapter 4 examines how the political environment surrounding a change can be managed and support gained.

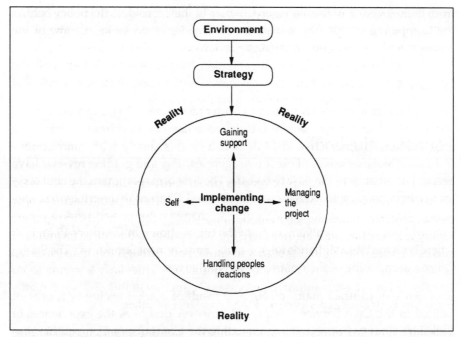

Figure 1.5 Model for change.

Bringing about change requires an understanding of people and how they are likely to react, communicating the change, dealing with resistance to the change, counselling those who find it difficult to change, and understanding the effects of stress on both those being changed and those endeavouring to bring about the change. These topics are considered in Chapters 5 to 9 respectively.

❑ Part 2

Having looked at processes for carrying out change, Part 2 looks at some of the instruments currently popular for bringing this about. It is divided into two sections. The first provides suggestions on how to bring about a more customer focused organisation. Chapter 10 considers achieving service excellence by looking at how the public service establishes a service strategy and its consequent effects on the people, processes and practices of organisations. Chapter 11 examines the concept of empowerment and provides a means by which this might be utilised in a controlled and gradual manner to improve the overall effectiveness of the organisation. Chapter 12 provides an explanation of how total quality management can assist in transforming an organisation.

The second section looks in more detail at two of the latest central initiatives i.e. the Citizen's Charter and Competing for Quality. Chapter 13 considers the Charter from the viewpoint of the manager. Chapter 14 then considers the policy behind the Competing for Quality initiative, whilst Chapter 15 looks at some of the management issues in out-sourcing a service.

❑ Part 3

Part 3 provides a series of case studies from practitioners. A strong theme of any initiative to change organisations is the need to have support from the top of the organisation. Chapters 16 and 17 demonstrate this clearly with contributions from two chief executives of executive agencies. Pay and grading reviews have become popular over the past two years. The first organisation in the civil service to carry out such an exercise was HMSO and Chapter 18 describes the experience. The fallacy that it is not possible to change cultures and working practices without direct involvement from the top is shown in Chapters 19 and 20, where both the West Midlands Region of the Employment Service and The Stamp Office outline some of their management initiatives.

Experience of contract management as a result of market testing is at present limited in the Civil Service. Chapter 21 however describes the experiences of Berkshire County Council in implementing the Compulsory Competitive Tendering initiative. An example of a civil service organisation preparing itself for contract management however is given in Chapter 22 where the Department of Employment describe their endeavours to establish a Contracts Branch. Finally, publicising the rights and standards of customer entitlements in a charter is one thing, delivering a quality service to match those promises is another. Chapter 23 gives a brief description of some research into the implementation of the Patient's Charter in looking at how six hospitals varied in their approach and performance to the Charter.

About the author

Roger Lovell is a historian with an MSc in Organisational Development and a principal lecturer at the Civil Service College. As a civil servant for over 30 years, he has extensive experience of managing change as a practitioner, lecturer or researcher in all of the recent management initiatives from the FMI, through Next Steps and the Citizen's Charter to market testing. He was previously head of establishments at the Intervention Board and prior to that was a member of the FMI team in the Ministry of Agriculture.

References and suggested reading

Aucoin, P. (1990) Administrative reform in public management: paradigms, principles, paradoxes and pendulums *Governance* - Vol 3 No 2 - April

Bate, P. (1994) *Strategies for Cultural Change* Oxford, Butterworth-Heinemann

Block, P. (1993) *The empowered manager* Oxford, Jossey-Bass

Butler, Sir R. (1993) *McLaren Lecture* Aston University - 12 October

Cm 2627 (1994) *The Civil Service: Continuity and Change* London, HMSO

Easterby-Smith, M., Thorpe, R. and Lowe, A. (1993) *Management Research - 5th Edition* London, Sage

Gill, J and Whittle, S. (1992) Management by panacea: accounting for transience *Journal of Management Studies* - 30:2 March pp 281 - 295

Handy, C. (1994) *The empty raincoat* London, Hutchinson

Harrison, A. (1993) *From hierarchy to contract* Newbury, Policy Journals

Hood, C. (1991) A public management for all seasons *Public Administration* - 69:1 Spring - pp 3 - 19

Hunt, J. (1986) *Managing people at work* London, McGraw-Hill

Kanter, R. (1983) *The change masters* London, Unwin

Kolb, D., Rubin, I., and Osland, J. (1991) *The organisation behaviour reader* 5th Edition Englewood Cliffs NJ, Prentice-Hall

Mottram, R. (1993) *Developments in the Public Sector* Speech delivered to the Joint University Council at York University - 7 September

OPSS (1992) *Monitoring of national population projections* London, HMSO

Osborne, D and Gaebler, T. (1992) *Reinventing government* Reading MA, Addison-Wesley

Oughton, J. (1993) *Career management and succession planning study* London, HMSO

Pfeiffer, J. (1991) *Theories and Models in Applied Behavioural Science* Vol 4-San Diego CA, Pfeiffer and Co.

Pollitt, C. (1992) *Managerialism and the Public Services* Second Edition - Oxford, Blackwell

Chapter 2

Setting strategy

Robert Smith

A wise man will make more opportunities than he finds.
(Bacon Essays 52 'Of Ceremonies and Respects')

There are some people who have moved house so many times that they seem able to treat the process almost as a matter of routine. To others, though, moving house is a traumatic experience and stands amongst the most significant changes which affect their domestic lives. Indeed, to some the prospect of moving house is so daunting that, on changing jobs, they choose long distance commuting in preference to a domestic move. The process of deciding on a move, familiar to so many, does serve to illustrate some of the general principles of choosing strategies for change, even if the process in most families is likely to be less formalised than it might be in a business situation.

Moving house may be something which is required because of external circumstances, usually a change of job, or it may be desired for internal reasons, such as a preference for a newer, more peaceful, or larger property. Whether the reasons are internal or external the starting point in deciding where to move is, in effect, the current situation. Take the situation where the cause is a change in job. In deciding what type of property might be suitable, consideration will be given to many aspects of the present circumstances. Examples might be:

employment - are other members of the family in employment, if so what type of employment, and how important is this employment to the family finances;

schooling - are there children at school, if so, what age are they, will they soon need to change school anyway, or will they shortly be taking important examinations;

leisure interests - what activities do the family most enjoy in their leisure time, to what extent are these dependent on the nature or location of the property;

transport - are some members of the family heavily dependent on the availability of public transport;

| wider family | - do members of the family or friends frequently wish to come and stay; |
| finances | - is the present mortgage a serious burden on the family finances? |

Some of these circumstances may themselves change anyway, because of the move, so the next consideration is what these changes might be. For example, if the move takes one nearer to the wider family they may no longer need to stay overnight; alternatively the move may take one further away and make spare bedrooms a necessity. If the move will generate an increase in income and permit the purchase of a second car the dependence on public transport may ease.

Once the present circumstances and likely changes to those circumstances have been considered, the stage has been reached to draw up a statement of the characteristics of the desired new property. This may cover aspects such as:

- price range
- number of bedrooms
- size of garden
- preferred locations
- proximity to specific amenities
- availability of mains services.

This specification will help estate agents to decide which properties to suggest, act as a guide for the final choice of a property, and set criteria against which the ultimate success of the move can be judged.

Once the 'final destination' has been specified, more work will be required to determine how the chosen changes will actually be achieved. Decisions will have to be made about;

- who will take responsibility for particular changes, such as arranging the actual removal, organising the conveyancing, enroling the children in new schools
- dates by which particular actions need to have been completed
- how certain aspects of the process will be organised, for example, should the existing furniture, carpets and curtains be taken or left?

In the case of setting the strategy for organisational change, the same basic processes are necessary as in moving house, namely:

- analysing the present situation

- reviewing the impact of external developments
- specifying the desired future
- organising the transition.

Analysing the present situation

The starting point in developing a strategy for change is to establish where and why change is necessary. Looking at the present, where are present performance and practices in some sense unsatisfactory? What needs to be done differently?

A key principle at this stage is to ensure objectivity in the analysis. It is not sufficient for senior management alone to consider where change is required. They can only too easily both be remote from important operational practices and also impose their own views of what they feel customers should want rather than establishing what customers really do desire. After attention is drawn to SWOT analysis, an approach to stimulating ideas and summarising conclusions which is familiar to many, a good deal of emphasis is placed on the use of focus groups and benchmarking in order to facilitate objectivity. Finally attention is drawn to one or two other strategic analysis techniques which could prove helpful. All of these techniques are covered, with full references, in a further book in the current series (Smith 1994).

❏ SWOT analysis

Many managers will already have participated in a SWOT exercise, on a management course if not in the workplace. The mnenonic stands for:

S	trengths
W	eaknesses
O	pportunities
T	hreats

Those participating are asked to look at the organisation and list its internal strengths and weaknesses, and the external opportunities and threats facing it. There are many different ways in which the ideas can be generated:

- a group working together, brainstorming, each member contributing ideas in a team session
- individuals generating ideas on their own and pooling the results
- individuals working on their own and posting their ideas on charts around a room, where they are immediately visible to others who can then add to them.

Another question at this stage concerns who should be involved in the SWOT analysis. In some cases it is done by the management team alone, but the strong recommendation, as explained below when discussing focus groups, is that a good cross-section of staff should participate, to ensure a wide perspective.

Where a cross-section of people is used care needs to be exercised to ensure that the approach adopted to generating and recording the ideas does not inhibit any individual from contributing freely and honestly. The presence of a senior manager who is known to have particular strong views can be extremely inhibiting!

Sometimes SWOT analysis is used on its own, but it can be particularly powerful when used in combination with, indeed after, other techniques. For example, benchmarking can help to identify strengths and weaknesses, PEST analysis can help to identify opportunities and threats. A SWOT analysis can then be the place where all the ideas generated can be brought together and added to, and where the messages and implications can be deduced.

SWOT analysis looks both internally and externally, strengths and weaknesses being internal, opportunities and threats external. In practice it is sometimes difficult to distinguish whether a particular item is a strength or an opportunity, internal or external. Time should not be spent worrying over the classification of the item! The important thing is that it should be identified rather than where it should be classified. The strength of SWOT analysis is that it forces people systematically to address each of the four categories. It sometimes appears that a particular item is both a strength and a weakness or both an opportunity and a threat. This too should not be of concern, it should be recorded as both. An example might be the dedication of the staff to their present work. This is a strength but can also be a weakness, making them traditional in approach and reluctant to look for better ways of doing things. The dedication of some professional groups is good for the technical quality of their work but can result in a lack of responsiveness to the needs of stakeholders or customers. The agenda of change embraced by the new public management may be seen by some groups as a threat, by others as an opportunity, and by others as both.

A danger of SWOT analysis is that it can be very inward looking. It will only contain the thoughts and perspectives of those involved in the exercise. It is therefore wise to involve as wide a group as possible, perhaps through focus groups.

❑ Focus groups

The origin of the term 'focus group' is fairly obviously that it should be a group of people with a particular 'focus'. In applying this to analysis of the present situation, when setting a strategy for change, the important point is the need to obtain ideas from people who together cover the full range of perspectives The groups may themselves be asked to undertake a SWOT analysis or they may simply be asked to join in a discussion, the record of which will then be used to identify points to be added to the strengths, weaknesses, opportunities or threats. The discussion could be structured, with a set agenda, or free ranging. It is normally advisable to strike a balance between the two. If a discussion is left too free ranging it may be difficult to identify many relevant points, on the other hand the danger with a structure is that the organisation setting up the group will set its own agenda. At the extreme this may result in a conclusion that everything it does is done well, with the group having no opportunity to tell the organisation what really matters, which is that it is doing the wrong things.

Focus groups should certainly embrace staff at all levels from within the organisation. However hard management try, it is difficult for them to be sure that they really understand what people are thinking, how they perceive their jobs and the organisation, the problems which they can see in the way in which things are done currently. It is now widely recognised that the people who have to deal directly with customers are in the best position to see what most pleases or annoys the customer and that they are willing, when given the opportunity, to use this knowledge and their experience of operating practices to suggest where change could be most effective. As emphasised earlier, when discussing SWOT analysis, it is important that those involved in focus groups should not feel inhibited in contributing to the discussion. It may be wise to employ an outside consultant to facilitate the discussion to encourage people to speak freely, it is certainly important that participants are assured that remarks critical of the organisation and management will not be held against them. This needs to be reinforced by supportive behaviour after the event or the whole exercise will be undermined.

If staff are involved in focus groups which help to identify where change is necessary, there is also the potential benefit that they will be more committed to the need for change and to the actual changes chosen. There may then be less need to deal with some of the human issues addressed in subsequent chapters of this book. However, management may ultimately need to decide on some changes which remain unwelcome to staff, perhaps because there are important stakeholders whose influence is not fully recognised by middle management and more junior staff. Raising false hopes through focus groups can, of course, make the subsequent task of managing change more demanding!

Focus groups involving customers and key stakeholders should certainly be considered when analysing the present situation and current performance. These people are ultimately key players in determining whether an organisation has been successful or not. It is very easy for both management and other staff to build up their own perception of what satisfies customers, to monitor performance against that perception, and to miss the fact that customer requirements are changing. Focus groups involving customers and stakeholders can help to avoid that situation.

An alternative to setting up focus groups is to use questionnaires to seek views. This can be every effective in obtaining data in a structured form which makes analysis relatively straightforward. The problem is that designing the questionnaire sets the agenda, the organisation will only receive answers to the questions which it specifically asks. There is the danger that it will fail to receive the feedback that the dimensions of quality described there are not what really matters.

The purpose of focus groups is to obtain objective information about strengths, weaknesses, opportunities and threats from key players and knowledgeable players. A further approach to seeking objective information about performance is to employ the technique known as benchmarking.

❏ Benchmarking

Benchmarking is currently very much in vogue in the field of strategic management and planning. Essentially it involves making comparisons with others. In the industrial field a manufacturer may undertake detailed analysis of a competitor's product, to identify where it is superior to its own. This will identify a weakness to be put right. Alternatively where the product is superior to that of the competitor, the strength is one which needs to be maintained! This idea can be extended into areas of activity other than the direct production process, for example, distribution, marketing, and overheads.

In the public sector some organisations may face the situation where others are doing very much the same type of work as themselves. Examples would be individual social security offices, individual courts, public libraries or hospitals. Where this is not the case, other organisations may have to undertake at least some of the same activities, for example, maintaining buildings, paying staff, catering and so on. At the very broadest level, it is possible to compare approaches to customer service, staff management, public relations and so on with organisations recognised as leaders in the field. Any of these comparisons may be with other organisations from either the public or the private sector. Using such comparisons is a way of ensuring that the information fed into a SWOT analysis is objective and is not confined to the perceptions of those within the organisation as to what is possible. A demonstration of how the technique is being used in the Department of Employment is shown in Chapter 22.

❏ Other techniques

The range of techniques associated with strategic management and planning is substantial, and any of them may have some contribution to make in analysing the present situation to determine where change might be necessary. Two which immediately spring to mind are value chain analysis and process modelling.

Value chain analysis involves looking closely and objectively at which elements of an organisation's activities or processes really add value for the organisation. This value may come from a major contribution to customer satisfaction or from an important source of competitive advantage, the two inevitably being related. Process modelling requires the organisation to describe, in diagrammatic form, how it actually does things. This in itself is often useful in identifying opportunities for change. For example, it may reveal how often papers are passed from one person to another and suggest that there ought to be ways of streamlining the process to reduce delays and the possibility of error caused by misunderstanding between the many parties involved.

Reviewing the impact of external developments

When undertaking a SWOT analysis, the opportunities and threats cannot strictly be confined to the present. There are many opportunities or threats which are likely to arise in the future and which need to be addressed immediately if they are to be seized or countered. It may sometimes be easier to manage change when a crisis has arisen, because the need for change is then widely recognised. However, it is generally wiser to make changes so that the organisation is ready to make the best of the opportunities when they arise and to avoid the threats. This means looking to the future, reviewing what might happen and incorporating the findings into the SWOT analysis. There may be occasions when quantitative methods can be helpful in identifying trends and projecting them into the future, but in most cases it is necessary to use 'softer' methods, relying on drawing together a range of experience and views in as structured a manner as possible. Two particular approaches suggested here are PEST analysis and Delphi techniques.

❏ PEST

PEST is another mnemonic, which stands for:

P olitical

E conomic

S ocial

T echnological

It is a way of ensuring that each of these important elements is discussed, nothing really more sophisticated than that. As in SWOT analysis the boundaries between each category are not really important; time should not be spent worrying about whether a particular item should be classified as political or economic. The important point is that no important factor should be missed.

When an organisation wishes to review future trends and developments the first step should be to ask whether the factors represented by the initial letters of PEST are the right ones. It could well be that other items could be added or one or two dropped. Then sufficient time should be left for each one of the key elements to be fully discussed, with a view to reaching agreement on what is most likely to happen, which developments could happen and need to be guarded against, and which possibilities can to all intents and purposes be ignored.

Points made earlier about participation in the SWOT analysis apply equally to PEST. If discussion is restricted to the organisation's management team the perspective could be very limited. A wide range of the organisation's own staff could probably make a useful contribution and a stakeholder and customer perspective is likely to be valuable. There may also be market research available which could contribute to the debate; for example, there are a number of such studies of trends in management training which are helpful to the Civil Service College.

❑ Delphi

Delphi is an approach to managing the discussion and could therefore be combined with, rather than being an alternative to, a PEST analysis. The basic aim of a Delphi approach is to ensure that all views are heard but that there is ultimately a degree of convergence of view. Different facilitators are likely to operate in slightly different ways. The starting point, however, is likely to be that individuals are asked to express their own particular views on a particular subject or question. These views are then collected together, without attribution, and presented to the full group. There may then be a general discussion about the range of views and the thinking behind them. In the light of the understanding now gained the group may be asked to submit their views anonymously again, before a final attempt is made to draw conclusions together in a full session. Readers may recognise this approach as bearing a resemblance to the way interview panels often work.

Specifying a desired future

After deciding what needs to change to meet the present situation and likely future developments, the next stage is to draw up a clear picture of what form the change should take. It is usually helpful to express this in some form of statement of what the desired future state should look like. This can be done in a number of ways, for example:

- a mission statement
- a vision statement
- a values statement
- strategic objectives

The distinctions between these are often extremely blurred.

❏ Mission statements

At one extreme, a mission statement may be a single sentence or even just a phrase. It may be lofty:

> to be known as the best operation of our type in the world.

Or it may be suitably aspirational but more mundane:

> to provide a high quality of service to all of our customers with due regard to value for money.

The second example is probably the most familiar within the public sector. Mission statements of this type are not likely to be particularly valuable as statements of the desired future to help in setting a strategy for change. However, there are examples of mission statements which are a good deal lengthier, as explained by Campbell and Young (1990).

Longer mission statements are likely to include separate statements on each of a number of aspects of performance, such as:

- levels of customer service
- levels of efficiency
- treatment of staff and working environment
- citizenship i.e. attitude to the local community
- behaviour of staff to each other
- behaviour of staff towards customers.

Such mission statements can be helpful in clarifying to all concerned what changes are required and how the success of the proposed changes will be judged. To serve that purpose the statements must be reasonably specific, in explaining what type of behaviour is required, how efficiency is defined, and so on. At this point the distinction between a mission statement and a set of objectives will be somewhat blurred.

❏ Vision statements

The distinction between a longer type of mission statement and a vision statement is not easy to draw. If a distinction has to be made, the vision statement may put more emphasis on how the organisation is perceived, regarded and positioned relative to others. It may include phrases along the lines of:

- seen as the leading provider of this type of service in the UK
- accepted as near the top of the league for efficiency gains in the 1990s
- a favoured employer
- an asset to the town.

If such phrases as these are to be effective in setting strategy for change, there has to be a common understanding among those concerned as to how they could tell that the desired status had been achieved.

❏ Values statements

Both mission and vision statements may include some description of the values to which the organisation will operate. If the changes desired concentrate on the culture of the organisation and on the way in which people behave, it is possible to rely heavily on a statement of the desired values. The Benefits Agency is an example of an organisation which has leaned heavily on a simple statement of core values. This is described in Chapter 17.

❏ Objectives

A statement of objectives would normally tend to be more specific than a mission or vision statement in defining what is meant by the desired state. One would normally expect to be clear as to how one could assess whether an objective had been achieved or not. On the other hand a mission or vision statement which left it completely unclear as to how success would be assessed would not really give the clarity of direction desired. Objectives might include phrases along the lines of:

- achieve a high level of customer satisfaction in the annual customer survey
- reduce costs per case in real terms
- reduce staff turnover

- increase levels of delegation
- refurbish the headquarters building.

The choice of whether to use a mission statement, a vision statement, a values statement or a set of strategic objectives will depend heavily on which is felt to be most likely to encourage people to respond to and achieve the desired changes. A decision on this may well be influenced by feedback from the consultations with staff at the stage of analysing the current situation.

Organising the transition

The desired state will not just happen. A description of it helps but specific actions and measures will be necessary. Continuing interest and encouragement from the top will be essential, encouragement in the positive sense of exhortation and example, but also encouragement in the form of disappointment, or even anger, if progress is not made. In many respects managing the transition is similar to managing projects and this aspect of managing change is covered in the next chapter.

At this point, when talking about setting strategy, suffice it to say that it will be critical to:

- identify leaders
- establish key tasks, mini-projects or initiatives to bring about elements of the desired changes
- clarify who will be responsible for satisfactory completion of each task, project or initiative
- agree on key milestones for the tasks, projects and initiatives and on arrangements for monitoring progress.

Ultimately the vision of setting the strategy has to be combined with the discipline of project management, described in Chapter 3, if change is to be successfully achieved.

About the author

Robert Smith is Director of Studies at the Civil Service College. He has over twenty years of experience of working in the civil service and nationalised industries, mostly in the areas of transport and environment. Virtually all of his posts have included responsibilities for planning and strategy.

References and Suggested reading

Campbell, A and Young, D. (1990) *Do You Need a Mission Statement?* London, Economist Publications

Smith, R J. (1994) *Strategic Management and Planning in the Public Sector* Harlow, Longman

Chapter 3

Managing the project

Terry Whittles and Roger Lovell

'Would you tell me, please, which way I ought to go from here?'

'That depends a good deal on where you want to get to' said the cat.

'I don't much care where' said Alice.

'Then it doesn't matter which way you go' said the cat. *Lewis Carrol.*

Chapter 2 has examined some of the ways to establish the strategy for change by comparing the desired future state with the current position and thereby establishing the gap between the two. Achieving change is about managing the transition in closing the gap. The remainder of the first part of the book looks at ways of turning the idea into action. In this chapter we examine how to organise, plan and control the change process. In doing this we look at some of the techniques of project management.

A project is often described as a set of activities delivering a specified outcome over a finite time. As was shown in looking at various types of change in Chapter 1, not all change in the new public sector easily fits into this definition. This is particularly so in areas demanding continuous change, such as many total quality management initiatives. Even in such cases, however, the general principles of project management may well be used to advantage in ensuring an orderly and successful achievement of the goals. For example, we still need to define what we wish to achieve, organise and plan how we will do so, execute the work and review progress.

Definition

Chapter 2 has looked at defining what needs to be changed. A major reason for the failure of many projects is a misunderstanding by those involved of what the project is aiming to achieve. This is seen also in the relationships of people during the change. Most start on a friendly helpful basis all round with enthusiasm and trust high. The actual desired state shines like a beacon and all are keen to set out on the journey to arrive. All too often there are as many beacons as there are players with everyone having their own view of the future reality. Unless time is spent at the outset in clarifying what is to be achieved, the divergence of expectations will quickly start to emerge and disillusionment and acrimony will set in.

Project management is not a new discipline. It has been carried out in the construction industry for at least three thousand years since the building of the pyramids. In recent times, however, the numbers of projects undertaken and the speed of their completion have increased dramatically. While similar techniques can be used, they need to be adapted to take account of the particular change and its setting. This is especially so in clarifying objectives and involving the people who will ultimately need to live with the change, otherwise known as users.

❑ Clarity of objectives

Figure 3.1 looks at how precisely it is possible to define objectives at the outset of a change, and the degree of involvement of users in deciding what will be done as the project progresses. While all projects will have some idea of their objectives and a degree of contact with users, these will vary between high and low according to the type of project concerned.

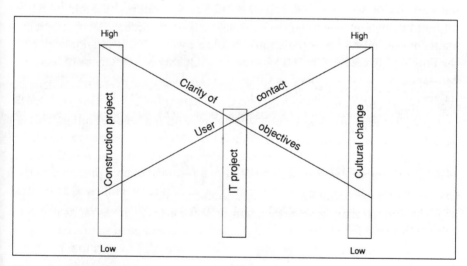

Figure 3.1 Clarity of objectives and user contact.

Traditional projects

The more traditional projects, like construction and mechanical engineering, are able to fix objectives fairly clearly at the outset. For example, the design of a building is drawn by the architect and approved by the customer. Plans are then drawn up on the basis of the drawings and the project executed. During the process very little contact will be had with the users who ultimately will arrive to inhabit the building once it is completed to satisfaction.

Information technology projects

In projects like information technology, over the years there has been an increasing involvement of users as the project evolves. This has been necessary in order to be able to control expectations as the project has developed. In the early days of computing the perceptions of the systems analyst as to what was required held sway. Understandably, the eventual outcome more often than not failed to match up to the user's expectations and changes were costly. With the increase in computer literacy of users, systems are now developed in greater partnership with the obvious improvement in results.

Culture change projects

Recent trends, such as changing organisation cultures, often start from an ill defined vision and involve gradual movement in a general direction. The approach is often iterative where progress is considered as it unfolds and new initiatives started and old ones abandoned as they go. Morgan, in his latest book on the use of metaphor in understanding organisations, *Imaginization* (1993), likens this approach to the way termites build their nests, in that they start building various piles which appear half completed and abandoned; the termites later return to them, joining up the nests through a series of arches. An excellent example of this in practice is the approach taken by the West Midlands region of the Employment Service in introducing Total Quality Management to their organisation, which is described in Chapter 19. While within such projects it is no longer possible to be totally clear of objectives as the project is being formed, it is still possible to control them as closely as possible at every stage. A vehicle to achieve this is a project definition workshop.

❏ Project definition workshop

Ideally the project definition workshop should be attended by all people with an interest in the change, since the main objective is to ensure as far as possible agreement on what is to be achieved. The added advantage of such a meeting is that it provides an opportunity for personal relationships to start to form.

Objectives

Precise definition of the objectives of the change may be reached very quickly, perhaps building on earlier work, or alternatively there may be a great deal of confusion. In the latter case, it is often best to proceed to the next stage before returning, since the most important part of the exercise is setting the scope of the project.

Scoping

In defining what is included in the scope of a project, it may be better to start by deciding what is excluded. It is at this stage where disagreements and misunderstandings quickly appear. Hardly surprisingly, users frequently believe that more is included in the project than do those delivering it. Lengthy discussion at this stage however is never wasted. Having defined in more precise terms what is included, it is often useful to return to the objectives to confirm that they are still coherent with what has been decided.

How far you can go during a project definition workshop in deciding on how the project will be organised, resourced, planned and controlled will depend on its size, complexity and the circumstances. If not possible at the time, such areas will need to be considered as quickly as possible to get the project under way.

Organisation

How the project is organised will depend upon a variety of factors according to the structure of the organisation and the type of change involved. For example, an organisation which is highly bureaucratic and used to fairly stable routine business will be more inclined to treat a change as exceptional than will a business where normal day to day business is more flexible.

❏ Size and impact of change

One way to distinguish how a change is managed is to look at its size and impact. Figure 3.2 demonstrates this. If both the size and impact of the change are small, it may be possible to implement it as part of normal day to day business. If the size is small but the impact significant, it may be sensible to appoint a project co-ordinator from within the line management chain to keep an eye on matters. If the size is significant and the impact low, a project manager working

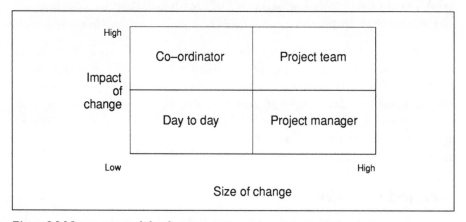

Figure 3.2 Management of the change.

alone, but outside the line command, may be the best approach. When both the size and impact of the change is large, a dedicated project team may be the best way forward. While this may result in better control of the design of the change, care needs to be taken that those affected by the change are not isolated from developments as they occur.

❏ Matrix management

Changes undertaking a project management approach rarely fit easily into the normal structures of an organisation. If the project is to be managed successfully, it is necessary to set up an organisation structure solely for the purposes of the project. This often involves commitment from a range of locations within the organisational matrix. The notion of matrix management is therefore common to project work, requiring staff to work for periods outside their normal reporting and management lines. This can often result in a conflict of loyalties, priorities and career interests. If the project organisation is not clearly established, it is easy for this work to be seen as of secondary importance to routine operational work.

If matrix management is to work it is crucial for the project manager to enter into a contract with the line manager to guarantee use of resources at particular times. It is also important to provide regular feedback to line managers on the quality of the project work being undertaken, since, all too often, those out of sight are out of mind.

❏ Project board

For changes spanning a variety of commands, it is important to establish a board with overall direction of the project. This board should represent each part of the organisation which is involved in the change and which by taking, or failing to take, a decision or by failing to provide information or resources, can jeopardise the success of the project.

The board must have sufficient seniority to be able to take clear and unequivocal decisions. The level of seniority will also send important messages to the remainder of the organisation as regards the esteem and importance with which the change is viewed within the organisation. Great care needs to be taken, however, to ensure that the board is not overlarge. Its prime concern is that of directing the project, too often it can turn into a talking shop where any decisions taken are, at best, unclear.

❏ Project manager

While the project board will provide overall direction for the change, implementation will be in the hands of the project manager. In this respect, the manager becomes the main agent of change. Comment on the type of person most suited to this role is made in Chapter 5. In the meantime, suffice it to say that care needs to be taken that the person will have sufficient ability and authority to be able to bring about the changes.

In dealing with more senior people, the manager must be able to command respect and gain commitment. In terms of the people needing to change, he or she must be aware of the impact of change upon them and how they are likely to respond. To this end it is important to become pro-active and anticipate behaviour as much as possible beforehand. As will be shown in Chapter 4, he or she will also need to know when to fight for the needs of their project and when to succumb for the corporate good. Failure to achieve the former will place increasing pressure on the project team and stop them from achieving their tasks, while failure to acknowledge the latter could result in being ignored by those in power.

❑ Project team

Rarely in the public sector do project managers have the opportunity of selecting their team, although the project should be resourced with the specific staff and skills to deliver the change. From the point of view of the project manager it is often necessary to match the job to the person. In other words, identify individual strengths and play to these, supplementing skills that are absent by training or recruitment.

Nothing succeeds like success. It is therefore vital to ensure that the team quickly achieves a target, however small, in order to build an atmosphere of confidence and self esteem. This can best be achieved by involving staff in drawing up the plans since they are the best people to appreciate what needs to be done and how long it will take.

Planning

It is clearly impossible to control any activity which has not first been planned. It is also impossible to monitor and control events with a degree of resolution finer than that which has been applied to planning. The project planner's task, and the project manager should certainly be involved if not wholly responsible, is to work out the sequence, timing, dependencies and resource requirements of these activities. In doing so, he or she will establish management expectations and intentions for the project and allow it to be controlled to a successful conclusion.

❑ Initial planning

The creation of the best available plan as early as possible in a project, to provide a starting point for comparison and control, is more important than any amount of spurious certainty in that plan. The estimating and planning process will identify the level of uncertainty and the sources of risk in a project from which a strategy can be developed to minimise their effect. The success of any project will depend directly on the clarity and realism of the project plans. These will be in direct proportion to the effort which is applied to the estimating and planning tasks involved. Failure to recognise and act on these simple principles is another main cause of project failure.

❏ Product identification

The first planning task is to consider what needs to be delivered at the end of the project i.e. the technical components. The establishment of these differs from the more traditional approach of first identifying the major activities that need to be undertaken and then specifying the deliverables that should result. It helps ensure that a firm project boundary is established and focuses attention on required outputs throughout the project life. An ideal time to consider the required outputs may well be the project definition workshop mentioned earlier as all concerned should be present and this is an ideal vehicle for stating the scope of this project. An example of a technical component would be the supply of appropriate accommodation for a relocation project.

Taking the example of a house move from Chapter 2, if it had been decided to accomplish the move by means of a single project, the initial thoughts of the strategy team could act as a project brief for the project team who would then need to consider the issues in greater detail. But what are the outputs from the project? The obvious output is a 'moved family' (such a simple statement in itself can be a major achievement as it concentrates minds from the outset on the eventual goal). Diagramming techniques can be used to help identify the outcomes, as illustrated in Figure 3.3.

Constantly ask the question 'what does this consist of ?' This quickly offers a good picture of the real scope of the undertaking. It should be noted that, at this stage, no consideration is given to time or sequence.

❏ Activity planning

Having described the project in terms of deliverables, (and there will always be deliverables, cognitive activities result in some form of report or recorded decision,) we can now consider the activities required to produce the deliverables, their order and timing.

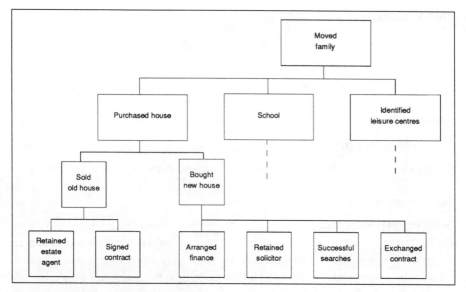

Figure 3.3 Diagramming – moving house

For the product 'arranged finance' in Figure 3.3 typical activities may be:

- consider amount needed
- decide on source of finance
- apply for loan.

A natural sequence will begin to fall from this by asking the following questions:

- what do I want to know
- what can I do at the same time
- what must be done before I can do this
- what must be done after this has been done?

❑ Estimating

Having established the sequence of activities we need to estimate their duration in order to compose a meaningful plan against which to measure progress. This is one of the most difficult areas of planning, particularly if embarking on a new type of project for the first time.

An estimate is nothing more than a probabilistic assessment, it is *not* a quote. Great care should be taken to produce an honest estimate, it is easy to produce a plan showing any activity to any timescale, whether the plan is a true or political statement will quickly be discovered when the project begins.

Things to beware of are:

- estimate = answer which management demanded
- estimate = answer which management demanded plus negotiated addition.

These are political statements; we are estimating, not bartering.

- Recorded slippage = anticipated future time saving

is also a common approach to problems, but we are managers, not ostriches.

How to estimate

Some industries keep measures and figures of past performance which prove very useful, but in a change management project you are unlikely to have access to such figures. If possible, however, you should try to identify a similar, successful project. This can be a powerful estimating technique as long as the analogous project is truly analogous and actual performance was accurately and fully recorded.

Should a similar project not be found, you may have to rely on expert judgement (sometimes called the MSTM, my stomach tells me, method!) If so, bear in mind that people tend to be 30% too optimistic about their own ability to deliver. The effect of this can be lessened by asking others to estimate independently or by using the Delphi technique as described in Chapter 2, (but be careful not simply to end up with an average or paying too much attention to the most powerful personality).

Estimates should be produced from at least two different approaches. If the final results are similar, then the estimate may be relatively good. If they are not, ask why and try again. If there are no other methods available, try at least a top down estimate, (how big do I think it is in its entirety) and bottom up, (add together the statements for each of the individual components).

❏ Stages and milestones

Having established sequence and timescales, the final plan can be produced. While those carrying out the work will require detailed plans to element level, (an element being about ten days work for one person,) at the other end the project board will require no more than an overall plan of events. From such plans more detail will be added as the project progresses and greater understanding emerges. To this end, it is often helpful to divide the project into stages and within the stages to adopt a system of milestones, or points where progress can be assessed against plan.

In more complex projects, once the logical sequence of activities has been worked out and estimated times added, the use of critical path analysis will help identify which tasks are crucial, in terms of time available, to the change. Nowadays this area of project planning is supported by a wide range of software tools.

Execution

Plans provide an effective means for the comparison of actual progress against what is expected to be achieved during execution of the project.

❏ Management controls

Management controls monitor progress and expenditure. Primarily this is done on the basis of 'management by exception' using tolerances, whereby concern is drawn to the next level only when the tolerance is likely to be exceeded. For example, it would obviously be counter-productive for the project manager to call exceptional meetings of the project board every time a particular element exceeded the planned time. It is more realistic to provide the person with a tolerance, then so long as the project remains within certain limits of time and resource it is for the manager to decide how to control the work. Having raised an exception, however, it is crucial that it is considered and acted upon in a controlled manner.

❏ Technical controls

In addition to managing the activity, it is also necessary to control the boundary of the project by agreeing procedures as to how changes might be made. The first step is to recognise that something is a change in the first place. As the project progresses, many people will be struck with ideas of the ' wouldn't it be nice if.....' variety. Such creativity is to be encouraged, but in the enthusiasm of the moment it is easy to include new ideas without sufficient thought to their impact on time, cost and the main objectives of the project. Once this clarity is lost, projects quickly develop into 'runaways', over budget, over time and not achieving the intended outcome. Likewise it is also important to monitor issues. A problem can arise in a management line and be solved within that line. An issue is a problem which cannot be solved in the line and therefore needs to be considered elsewhere. Unless these are identified and controlled, it is possible for them to be forgotten about until they cause damage to the project.

❏ Quality control

Finally, in terms of execution, it is important that quality is maintained. Time spent early in the project ensuring that the early deliverables such as plans, the scoping document, the definition of requirement are as error free as possible is never wasted. A detailed, formal check of a document may take two weeks and there will be great pressure to remove this check from the plan to save time. This rarely, if ever, works. The penalty is paid downstream when problems begin to surface. The Japanese company, RICOH, found that finding and correcting a fault in one of their photocopiers cost $368 at the design stage, $17,000 before shipment and $590,000 once the product had reached the customer. That is an extreme example from manufacturing industry perhaps, but how often do we take the line that 'we don't have time to do it properly now, but we'll have time to fix it later'? Increasingly quality control is achieved by peer group assessment, as opposed to more imposed methods. The advantage of the former is that it is carried out by people more familiar with what should be done. Secondly, if sufficient commitment to the project has been achieved the more committed will the staff be to ensuring that the output is fit for purpose.

Review

By definition a project has a finish. Completion of the project is therefore capable of being measured along with an assessment of its success. As has been noted at the start, much change being managed nowadays is of a continuous nature. It is not therefore as easy to measure progress and success. In any change of behaviour, however, it is crucial not only to review but also to reinforce the change. This can be done through auditing progress by survey, interview or observation and assessing its success.

Even if change is implemented on project lines, it is vital to chart carefully the implementation of the change when it is handed over to those directly affected by it. Sometimes this is done by parallel running, sometimes different elements are phased in over a period, whilst at other times a big bang 'all or nothing' approach is adopted. Whichever way it is implemented it is important to spend time with those affected to encourage them to start to own the change. This can be achieved more easily the more they have been involved as the project develops.

Many of the techniques used in project management are also applicable to other management situations. As a composite set, however, they are particularly geared to the successful delivery of an outcome (usually a product of some kind) over a finite time span.

This chapter is not an exhaustive study of project management, but only an introduction. There are many books available on the subject as well as a number of proprietary and non-proprietary project management methods (e.g. PRINCE) which advocate particular approaches to the organising, planning and controlling of projects. For those with limited time, Obeng's book, *All Change: the Project Leader's Secret Handbook,* is both educational and highly entertaining.

Finally, the tools and techniques of project management can be invaluable in the implementation of change. Any project is at the end of the day only as good as the people involved in it. While the systems are of considerable use, it is only by their sensible application that results can be obtained. We need to look next therefore at how such support may be gained.

About the author

Terry Whittles is a senior lecturer at the Civil Service College with particular responsibility for courses in the management of information systems projects. He has been involved in project management for over 10 years, mainly in the delivery of IT systems, but also other administrative areas. Recent training and consultancy assignments have included work in Eastern Europe.

References and suggested reading

Bergen, S. (1986) *Project Management* Oxford, Blackwells

Morgan , G. (1993) *Imaginization* London, Sage

Loch, D. (1992) *Project Management* Aldershot, Gower

Obeng, E. (1994) *All Change: the Project Leader's Secret Handbook* London, Pitmam

Reiss, G. (1992) *Project Management Demystified* London, E and F N Spon

Turner, J. (1993) *The Handbook of Project-Based Management* Maidenhead, McGraw-Hill

Chapter 4
Gaining support

Roger Lovell

'May you have a brilliant idea and not be able to convince others.'

An Old Rumanian Curse

Endeavours to change may easily fail because of an inability to attract support and manage the internal political environment surrounding the change. Occasionally changes are so welcomed by all sides and their benefit so apparent that support is automatic. In organisational life, however, this is rarely the case and support needs to be worked for and managed. This chapter is about how the change agent may go about gaining support to help implement change. It needs to be read in conjunction with Chapters 5 to 9 which consider handling reaction to change through understanding people, communications, counselling and stress management. In this chapter we concentrate on power and influence and their implication for gaining support for change.

Power is used constantly but rarely discussed. It depends as much on perception as actual usage. Its strength is rarely identical to hierarchies and legitimate authority. It encompasses force and manipulation as much as the delicacy of persuasion and influence. It is not always necessary to gain commitment in order to change behaviour, but in order to change attitudes, it is. Ideally, power makes you behave in the way I wish without you realising it.

To gain support, the change agent must:

- identify where power lies
- determine whose support is most important.

Having considered each of these subjects, we then look at how to gain support for changes externally imposed and internally generated.

Where does power lie?

Before being able to identify who needs to be influenced and how, it is necessary to understand where power lies in the organisation. This will obviously be easier for internal agents of change, since they will be familiar with the day to day working of the organisation. While legitimate authority may appear to flow from the organisation chart, it would be a mistake to believe that this always reflects the actual use of power within the organisation. It is important therefore to understand at least the following power bases:

- legitimate authority
- control of resources
- expert power
- reward and punishment
- personal power
- departmental power
- the power of networks.

❏ Legitimate authority

Traditionally the power of bureaucracies has been exerted through the hierarchy by setting standards and objectives against which to measure performance. Authority is top-down and utilises formal, usually vertical, communication channels. Power is therefore vested in position and status, rather than the person as such.

❏ Control of resources

Control of resources will often be linked to legitimate authority but particular groups, such as planning, finance or personnel, may exert strong influence. However, this power is changing. Increased delegation of authorities and activities into the line command is altering the balance of power, since finance, personnel and even information technology departments are tending to be seen in the role of adviser, rather than provider.

❏ Expert power

The power of expertise on the other hand is increasing. Over the past twenty years the use of the term 'knowledge workers' has tended to refer to professionals such as scientists or computer experts. It was always a misnomer to believe that subordinates had no power and did as they were told, since the power of managers actually comes from their staff rather than above. The increasing complexity of working life however means that staff at lower levels are themselves becoming more expert in their knowledge. The increased focus on customer service is also providing staff closest to the customer, who tend to be more junior, with more power.

❑ Reward and punishment

Reward and punishment have always been dubious practices upon which to base power, this is amply demonstrated by Kohn (1986 and 1994). For a start they have a tolerance. In either case in order to achieve the desired change in behaviour you need constantly to increase the dosage required. The ability to make financial reward is only open to those in legitimate authority. Having said that, the greatest power a manager possesses is the power of 'psychic' reward, which is of course open to all. In other words, a positive reinforcement of 'thanks' and encouragement at the time the behaviour occurred. Sadly the opposite is often the case where a blame culture is created, mistakes punished and 'management by embarrassment' is the order of the day, where league tables are used to spur the 'lower' performers to greater efforts. The result of such behaviour is usually grudging compliance and a loss of creativity and commitment. It is also in this area where the genuine support for change is identified. Unless the espoused values of managers are matched by a change in their behaviour which supports the change, their efforts will be undermined.

❑ Personal power

Many Executive Agencies have been blessed with dynamic and charismatic chief executives, specially selected to drive change through their organisations. Undoubtedly support for change from above is highly desirable. Unless this support is reinforced further down the organisation however it is unlikely to permeate or consolidate. Nevertheless, the power of personality should not be underestimated, since, at the end of the day, it is the ability to persuade which is vital in achieving support.

❑ Departmental power

Factional support must also be identified by the change agent. This arises where one part of the organisation believes that it is more powerful and important than another. As time goes by there is a tendency for the department to see its goals as more important than the corporate objectives. This often comes to the fore during the allocation of resources. Like many senior managers in their fear of change, those with most to lose are often least likely to desire a change which they themselves have not inspired.

❑ Networks

Networks can be both official e.g. Trade Unions, or unofficial e.g. grapevines. The power resulting from the ability to be able to operate horizontally across organisations should never be underestimated. Used in a conscious manner it can be an invaluable source of information and dissemination. Loss of influence within it can equally undo the best laid plans.

Whom to influence

Once the relative strengths and weaknesses of the various power bases within an organisation are understood, the next stage is to identify who needs to be influenced in order to gain support for the change. We therefore look at support from above, from peers and staff.

❏ Support from above

To the change agent, top management support is extremely important if not crucial, particularly when the change affects the whole organisation or when increased resources are necessary. A champion of change at the highest level can not only represent your interest at senior management meetings but also send signals throughout the organisation about the status and importance of your particular change. To this end, much will depend on the strength of the champion within the senior management environment, especially since organisation charts rarely portray the strength of power bases within organisations. The secret is to understand which manager's support is needed.

The model in Figure 4.1 by Greiner and V. Schein (1988), is used to demonstrate relationships at Board level. The same principles apply though at any level of management above the change agent.

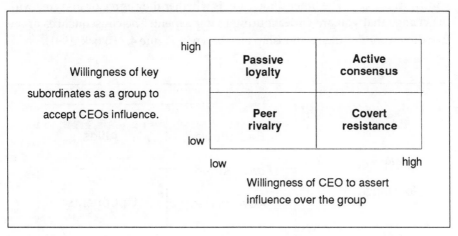

Figure 4.1. Political resolutions in top management (Greiner and V. Schein, 1988).

In identifying a champion, much will depend upon the willingness of the Chief Executive to assert his or her influence over senior colleagues and the willingness of them to accept that influence. For example, if the CEO is highly assertive and the management team are positively willing to accept that leadership, active consensus will occur in decision making and, from the change agent's viewpoint, the success of the change will need the CEO on board. If, on the other hand, the CEO wills it but senior managers are against it, covert resistance may well take place where an impression that it is happening is given but the change is being undermined in practice.

At the same time, if the CEO is less willing to assert influence in the area, the identification of the most powerful senior manager will be extremely useful to champion the change, since peer group rivalry is likely to exist if the team are less than willing to go along with the CEO. If that person happens to be your boss this is fortunate. If not, it will be important to find ways to discuss the change with that person and endeavour to gain support. If neither the CEO nor the senior managers are that interested there may be passive acceptance but little support will appear if things go wrong.

❏ Peer group support

Often the greatest skill is to influence your peers, and yet, like power itself, little is written on the subject and it is rarely spoken about. This is even more so in the public sector with its strong emphasis on the equality of power within a particular grade.

Fundamentally, relationships with peers often revolve around the question of trust and, in particular, the degree of trust you have with one another during your working day. The other dimension is whether they agree or disagree with the change that you are endeavouring to implement. The consequences of the two dimensions of the relationship are shown in Figure 4.2 (Block, 1991).

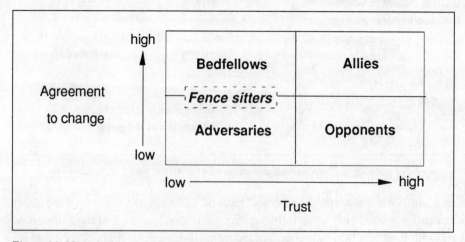

Figure 4.2. Negotiating agreement and trust (Block, 1991).

Allies

If you normally trust a peer and he or she is in agreement over the change, they are 'allies' and, as such, will be vital to you in promoting the change.

Opponents

If you normally trust them but on this particular occasion they do not agree with you, they are 'opponents.' The crucial thing here is that you normally enjoy a good relationship and, presumably, will do so in the future. Such people are most likely to be open to persuasion and may be brought around to supporting the change. If this is asking too much and they remain opposed, because you normally trust each other they are unlikely to do you immense damage in implementing the change.

Bedfellows

In any change situation there will be people who would not normally be 'in your camp' but on this particular occasion are willing to support you for a variety of reasons but probably because it suits their selfish interests. They are 'bedfellows,' willing to join you on this occasion but not to be relied upon in future.

For example, consider two people who do not particularly like or trust each other but who find themselves abseiling together. One will have to rely on the other to hold the rope. In that situation both can trust and support each other. Their behaviour does not affect the way that they generally feel about each other, nor does it change their relationship thereafter.

Fence sitters

Less reliable than bedfellows are 'fence sitters.' These are the people who waiver until it becomes obvious which way the change is going and that it is in their interest to come along. They will undoubtedly be there when the 51% mark is reached in support. Such people cannot be relied upon at any time. So long as the change agent is fully aware of their leanings however, they form an often vital component in providing the ballast for change.

Adversaries

Finally, there are those who not only oppose this particular change but also have a less than trusting relationship with the change agent normally. Such 'adversaries' are unlikely to respond to persuasion unless it can be shown that there is in fact 'something in it for them,' in which case they become bedfellows seeking their own self interest. More likely, they will continue to oppose the change and all the agent can do is to minimise the damage that they can cause.

In practice, allies can be used to share our anxieties about the change and talk through difficult issues. They are also available to attract support from those who would not normally be so willing to help us. In view of the normal trusting relationship we have with our opponents, they are in many ways the most useful people since the honesty of our dealings will allow both of us to articulate and explore our varying concerns about the change. To this end, opponents will help us refine our ideas and test them out for audiences who require more logical convincing.

The fact that we do not normally trust bedfellows means that we will tend to be guarded in what we tell them, especially about our fears. On the other hand it will be useful to endeavour to mend fences from the past and seek to understand how we can remain allies for the future. The best means of bringing fence sitters on board is to identify whose opinions they respect and endeavour to influence that person. As for adversaries, it is probable that they reflect the shadow side of ourselves. In other words, if we believe strongly in participative management, they are likely to prefer strong centralised control. To that end, we understand their position but find it difficult to accommodate. They likewise will no doubt feel the same way. Unless care is taken and time spent on trying to understand these differences, it is likely that the poor relationship will continue with attitudes becoming more entrenched than ever. The tactic is to endeavour to identify and surface these concerns. Sadly so often we are unable ourselves to come even half way because of our own deep seated suspicion.

❏ Team support

Change managers frequently concentrate on influencing upwards and sideways in their endeavours to get resources and support, without appreciating the huge pay-off in mobilising support from below. A prime reason for enrolling the support of a project team is to give them a stake in drawing up the plans upon which they are due to work. So often plans and schedules are imposed from above in answer to a senior management deadline, which has little understanding of the actual work involved. Involvement of those who are expected to carry out the change not only makes sense in setting realistic objectives, but also immediately starts the task of building a commitment to change.

In order to achieve change, it is important to identify where staff are in terms of their support for the change. Figure 4.3 from Mintzberg (1983) shows a useful spectrum for this.

Obviously greatest use can be made of those with a natural identification for the change. Recruitment and promotion boards can be used to select people with affinity with the change. Much influence in gaining support for change comes

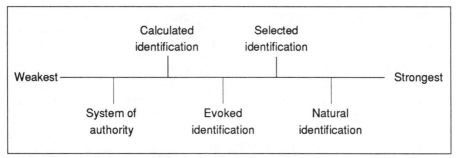

Figure 4.3. Orientations towards change (Mintzberg, 1983).

through the use of official communication channels. These are reinforced by publications such as in-house magazines. This evokes an identification with the change through propaganda.

For those who remain unconvinced, despite all efforts at communication or persuasion, there is a serious choice between going or staying. In the public sector to date, with its relatively secure employment base, the choice to go has been mainly amongst the younger staff, or those who have sufficient knowledge to market elsewhere. Those who stay make a calculated decision to do so. They may appear on the surface to go along with it but their performance is unlikely to be first class. For those still unwilling to change, as a last resort, authority and discipline might need to be used.

❏ Force field analysis

In order to be able to work out a strategy of how to gain support from the various stakeholders i.e. all those interested in or affected by the change, we need to be able to identify not only who needs to be influenced but also the strength of their feelings towards the change and where they stand in relation to it. A useful exercise for achieving this is force field analysis. This was developed by Lewin who borrowed the concept from Newtonian physics that for every force there will be an opposite and equal force. The analysis identifies the strength of the forces driving the change and those resisting it. Having done this, a strategy can then be designed to endeavour to reduce the restraining forces and harness the positive.

Figure 4.4 shows how this was used for a relocation project which required a movement of 350 posts from the South-East to the North-East of England. Driving forces behind the move were:

- the loss of considerable revenue to the Exchequer through an inability to attract and retain staff in the South-East

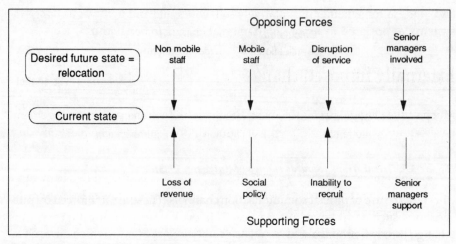

Figure 4.4. Forcefield for relocation.

- the social policy of the government at the time to create more opportunities in less developed areas
- support from senior management (apart from those whose work was moving).

Against these forces were:

- non-mobile staff who feared redundancy
- mobile staff who feared an enforced move
- disruption of the service
- senior managers whose work was due to move.

A strategy to reduce the strength of the opposition was then introduced. Three key elements were:

- a guarantee that there would be no redundancies and that staff would not be forced to move against their will
- parallel running and working alongside each other in the South-East allowed not just an effective handover but also a degree of camaraderie to build up between the old and new staff.
- the promise of assisted return transfers for senior staff for career moves helped to reduce their opposition.

The type of support needed and the way this can be influenced will inevitably depend to a large extent on the type of change that is being sought. Much will depend on whether it is being imposed from outside or generated internally, and, if the latter, whether it is relatively self- contained and involves a change in systems, as opposed to a more fundamental change in behaviour.

Externally imposed change

Much of the change associated most directly with the new public management has been imposed on departments or agencies from outside. The most obvious are:

- the Financial Management Initiative - which encouraged departments to define clearer objectives and start the movement towards greater delegation of resources
- the creation of Executive Agencies under Next Steps - which restructured departments between policy and execution
- the Citizen's Charter - aimed at improving service to customers; and
- Competing for Quality - which brought about a step change in the Market Testing programme.

❏ Drivers for change

Two very strong drivers for change in such cases are the power derived from legitimacy and resource control. Its imposition on the organisation from a legitimate authority means that it must be implemented. At the same time, if pump priming resources do not accompany the change, its level of priority is such that internal resources will have to be found.

❏ Resistance to the change

With the relative speed of these and other changes imposed from outside, there may be a feeling of initiative fatigue in departments. Senior managers can feel that they have hardly implemented one initiative before the next lands on their desk, while staff further down the hierarchy, on the other hand, may take the view that it is change for change's sake.

❏ Influencing strategy

The first emotion in the case of imposed change is often one of shock i.e. not another change from above. This is usually quickly followed by a denial that it will ever happen. Afterwards, as reality starts to seep through that it will, hostility and resentment are heightened, leading in turn to depression and a feeling of helplessness.

The most important strategy for the change agent to adopt in such circumstances is to endeavour to bring the change under control, since much of the hostility results from a feeling of powerlessness and anxiety about how the change will affect current working. This is especially heightened with initiatives such as Market Testing, where the threat of losing your job is a real one. The more influence that people feel they have over how the change is implemented, the less hostility and fear there will be.

Fortunately, while the initiatives are imposed on the organisation, generally they comprise broad principles and rationale for the change, as opposed to detailed prescription on how it should be implemented. Designing how this will be carried out, therefore, not only allows the change agent the opportunity to start to adapt the policy to suit departmental needs but also provides the chance to discuss it widely throughout the organisation.

The impact of such discussion will vary depending on how threatened by the initiative people feel. For example, in implementing the Financial Management Initiative it was important to include senior managers in areas such as the design of information systems for Ministers and decentralised budgetary control. In one case, personally experienced, a great deal was achieved by bringing together all those within a particular (vertical) command, to discuss how the change should be implemented within that command.

An initiative like Market Testing, on the other hand, needs to ensure that those whose jobs are being tested are fully involved from the start. A winning bid however, will depend as much on their attitude of mind as involvement in the design of the bid. In other words, if they are to take on the task in a positive frame of mind they need to understand the rationale behind the initiative.

A useful aid in allowing them to do this is the Six Thinking Hats problem solving exercise of De Bono (1990). Basically the exercise requires that a problem is viewed from six different and distinct viewpoints by metaphorically placing different coloured hats on the head whilst thinking. Wearing a white hat requires concentration on the facts of the situation. A move to the yellow hat requires us to look at what is good about the idea. This exercise in particular is useful for the public sector ethos which is often prone to spending too long looking at what is wrong with an idea. In other words, the 'yes, but' phenomenon, or, '... in principle I agree, but, in practice...'

Having forced us to concentrate on the positive, the negative is then given vent through the black hat. This is followed however by a further positive input, this time wearing a green hat, looking at the green shoots and opportunities that the idea has. Feelings and emotions are then allowed to be released through the red hat. Finally, the blue hat allows us to consider how things need to be controlled.

Using this exercise with staff about to face Market Testing has proved very successful in allowing them to break out of their mind set, which is concentrated primarily around the black and red hats. They see only the fear of redundancy and the anger of a feeling of betrayal. Making them concentrate solely on the yellow, green and white for a while starts to make them aware of the control they themselves can exercise over the change.

Imposed initiatives also provide a powerful lever for change in areas not directly related to the change. This is especially the case with regard to the customer focus of the Citizen's Charter which is allowing managers to introduce changes that they have long since nurtured under the broad banner that the initiative provides.

Internally generated change

Legitimate change imposed upon the organisation from outside may be relatively easy to implement and gain compliance to it. That should not be mistaken for commitment. In practice a change in behaviour is created by imposing the change whether or not the minds of those being changed are in agreement. Change generated from within the organisation can be handled in this way also. Alternatively, it can endeavour to change behaviour through commitment to a new set of values. This is examined now by looking separately at:

- 'hard issue projects' such as changes in systems, the implementation of an IT project for example
- 'soft areas' such as endeavouring to change culture.

Hard issue projects

Changes such as the implementation of new IT systems:

- are usually finite, in that they have an identifiable beginning and end
- can be easily measured in terms of how well they do what they are supposed to
- can be easily seen.

❏ Drivers for change

The main drivers for such changes are measurable improvements by way of positive investment appraisals. They are also seen as adding value to a particular part of the organisation, if not the organisation as a whole. They are therefore supported by those potentially benefiting from them.

❏ Resistance to change

Unlike change which is externally imposed on the organisation, change generated from within must compete with other users for resources. Not only is it probable that the benefits are factional, but also they may actually disadvantage another part of the organisation. The fight for resources often involves significant effort which in itself distracts managers from pursuing the main task of implementing the change. Uncertainty over resources also undermines expectations which can cause jealousy and insularity.

❏ Influencing strategy

To the manager of such a change, it is absolutely vital to obtain the resources necessary to deliver the project to time, quality and budget. So many people fail to appreciate one of the absolute laws of working life as shown in Figure 4.5.

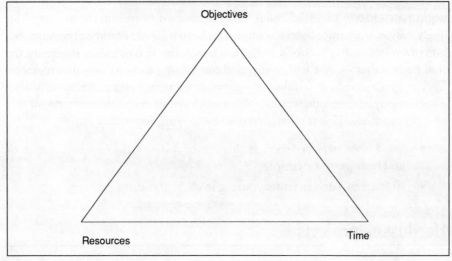

Figure 4.5. Triangle of feasibility

If you are provided with insufficient resources to do the job, assuming of course that the procedures are sound, either the objectives must be reduced or the time extended. If objectives are increased, either resources and/or time must be increased accordingly if the work is to be carried out on schedule. If, on the other hand, the job is required earlier, then either resources must be increased and/or objectives decreased. It is amazing how often this simple rule is ignored. What usually happens is that the change agent takes on the task with insufficient resources or time and is blamed when failing to deliver.

The manager should refuse to take on the task under those conditions in the first place. If it is taken on without complaint, this implies to the boss, through your silence, that the change can and will be delivered. It is better to draw his or her attention to the need to reorder priorities.

I was once given a time critical project with less than 40% of the resources I considered necessary to complete the job. Through persistence the issue was elevated to be debated by the Departmental Management Board. Gaining the necessary resources required not only taking them from elsewhere but also giving top priority to my project. Fortunately the Management Board gave me their backing and the necessary resources were found and priority given. Having escalated the decision, I of course had to deliver. To that end it was ensured that early successes were both achieved and publicised.

❏ Competing and accommodating

In this case, it was crucial for me to compete strongly for limited resources. The Management Board decided the priority of the project in terms of the corporate good. In practice, the balance is often a delicate one in terms of competing for your own area and accommodating the needs of others. As such it requires judgment and skill. Figure 4.6 (Thomas, in Pfeiffer 1991) shows this balance.

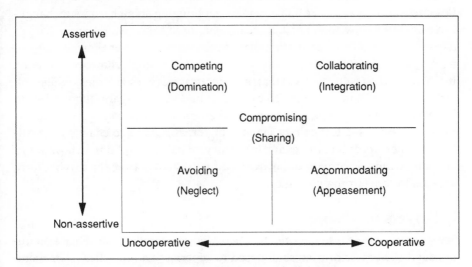

Figure 4.6. Competing/accommodating (Thomas in Pfeiffer, 1991).

The advantages of collaboration are obvious when everyone achieves what they want. In reality compromise is usually the case, particularly when dealing with your peers. In my case, the need to use such competitive behaviour in order to gain the necessary resources had to be matched by a significant effort in accommodating others for some time.

In reality, those who demand too much might achieve results in the short term but, having cried 'wolf' so often in the past, find themselves starved of support when it really matters. On the other hand, those who are too accommodating continually sacrifice their will for the good of others and, not only fail to deliver, but, worse still, pass the pressure, which they should be dealing with, down to their staff. In consequence they become diverted from carrying out their work by fighting their manager's battles without the power of authority that their position provides.

❏ Expertise

It is often in such changes that the power of expertise becomes crucial. To that end, it is important to recognise what expertise is required and when. In the project quoted above, there was only one person with the required expertise to teach the rest. At that point his power was absolute. Within three months when he had taught others, his power had declined. In other words, expertise often has a limited life and can be substituted in the longer term when the function is less critical, or when alternative sources have been found.

Soft areas

Resources and expertise are vital to a manager bringing about hard issue changes in a competitive environment. Like change imposed from outside, such changes depend on compliance in the first place in the hope that over time people will become committed to the new way of working. Increasingly, however, as noted in Chapter 1, it is being realised that, in order to achieve more for less whilst still satisfying the customer, the creative energy found within organisations needs to be released. This, along with changes in the psychological contract of employment and increased technology, is requiring organisations to change their culture. In other words, the values and taken for granted assumptions on how things are done within the organisation are needing to change. Here the driving force appears to come from two angles.

❏ Drivers for change

Senior managers realise the need to release the potential of staff. They also understand the power of peer, as opposed to superior, control. Many staff themselves on the other hand, are keen to have the opportunity to contribute more and have greater influence and involvement over what happens and why.

❏ Resistance to change

Resistance to cultural change, as with all change, comes from those with most to lose by changing the current system, where greater liberalisation and participation might threaten their power base. Sadly these are often the people who exercise position power i.e. senior managers and increasingly, as a result of delayering and empowerment, middle managers. Imagine a 57 year old Director of Finance who has spent his service in a highly centralised organisation where inputs have been the main source of control and finance the main vehicle for providing such control. For years little has been achieved in the organisation without his authority, or at least agreement. Ideas of decentralisation, let alone delegation, are diametrically opposite to all his understanding of the way that public finance should operate. Professionally therefore things are moving away from his understanding. Of even greater threat however will be the loss of prestige from his position. Instead of asking for his permission to vire expenditure, managers are responsible for their own budgets and waste little time in reminding the director of this fact. Little wonder therefore that the director is unable to offer the new culture his undivided support.

❏ Influencing strategy

Whereas actions drive changes in behaviour in many cases, for cultural change to be successfully encompassed appeal needs to be made to the attitudes and values of staff. This can only be done by allowing them considerable involvement in identifying the need for change and designing and implementing the changes.

In my experience this can best be achieved by:

* holding one to one interviews with senior managers
* focus group discussions with a variety of middle managers and a cross section of staff
* by carrying out a wider survey of staff opinion.

These should concentrate on defining where they are at present and where they wish to be in the future as shown in Chapter 2. Precisely how and when to involve staff often depends on the size of the operation and particular circumstances. In general, the greater the involvement, the greater the commitment.

Ideally changes in culture are led from the very top of the organisation. In practice this strength can also become its greatest weakness if behaviour does not match desire. To this end, the change manager needs to be aware of the concept of dynamic inertia. This is where the behaviour of senior managers gives the appearance of accepting change and pretending to move towards it, when in reality nothing actually happens. Sadly this has been the result of many endeavours over recent years. It is also an area which it is easy for public sector managers to develop to an art form. Expressions such as, 'let us make haste slowly,' need to be looked for. The change agent must therefore monitor the situation closely and never cease drawing attention to it. Failure to tackle such intransigence head-on will only serve to reinforce the delaying tactics. Often gaining support for cultural change requires long established practices and behaviour to be broken.

Frequently attitudes have built up over a considerable period, resulting in what is known as 'negative stereotyping.' This is where two groups start to blame the other for things that go wrong. Gradually their perception of reality makes them emphasise their strengths and downplay their weaknesses, while emphasising the other's weaknesses and downplaying their strengths. Such behaviour is especially common between support and operational units, both of whom exaggerate their usefulness to the business.

A way to break this vicious spiral is to have both sides record in private:

- how they view themselves
- how they view the other side
- how they think the other side views them.

The lists are then given to the other side and a meeting called subsequently to consider the perceptions. What is ironical about the exercise is the accuracy of their statements about how the others see them. Having brought the knowledge to the surface, an agreed strategy can then be arrived at to start to resolve the problems.

Gaining support from middle managers who are highly threatened by initiatives such as delayering and empowerment needs delicate handling. Training in coaching techniques is invaluable, along with a need to highlight their concerns and work jointly to reduce them.

Returning to the diagram on the orientation of staff towards change noted in Figure 4.3 earlier in this chapter, it is crucial to use those staff with a natural commitment to the change at an early stage. This can be reinforced by both recruiting supporters of the new culture and ensuring that the correct messages are sent to others by promoting those whose behaviour matches that which is desired in future. Throughout the process of gaining support it is crucial to understand the personalities, beliefs and attributes of the people with whom you are dealing together with an appreciation of your own power needs. Understanding people is therefore considered in Chapter 5.

References and suggested reading

Block, P. (1991) *The Empowered Manager* Oxford, Jossey-Bass

De Bono, E. (1990) *Six Thinking Hats* London, Penguin

Greiner, L. and Schein, V. (1988) *Power and Organisation Development* Reading, Mass.,Addison-Wesley

Handy, C. (1985) *Understanding Organisations* London, Penguin

Hunt, J. (1986) *Managing people at Work* Maidenhead, McGraw Hill

Kanter, R. (1983) *The Change Masters* London, Unwin

Kohn, A. (1986) *No contest* New York, Houghton Mifflin

Kohn, A. (1994) *Punishment by rewards* New York, Houghton Mifflin

Leigh, A. (1988) *Effective Change* London, Institute of Personnel Management

Lukes, S. (1974) *Power - A Radical View* London, MacMillan

Mintzberg, H. (1983) *Power in and around organisations* Englewood Cliffs NJ, Prentice-Hall

Morgan, G. (1985) *Images of organisation* London, Sage

Pfeiffer. J. (1991) *Theories and models in applied behavioural science.* Vol 3 San Diego, Pfeiffer & Co

Thompson, M. (1993) *Performance related pay* Brighton, Institute of Manpower Studies

Chapter 5

Understanding people

Roger Lovell

'Managers unable to command change in themselves cannot constructively change the conditions in which they command others.' *Revens (1982)*

In managing change we expect to spend considerable time looking at the future desired state, creating visions and missions, specifying the change, analysing the current reality, planning and monitoring progress. But how much time do we devote to thinking about the people and to analysing our own perspective and how that might affect others? How often do we take a uni-dimensional view of human nature, behaving as though everyone in the world thinks and acts like us, assuming that, if we tell them what is happening and why, they will understand and everything will be acceptable?

Importance of understanding people

One of the joys and benefits of using humans, rather than machines, at work is their rationality, free will and ability to think. Yet so often, probably without realising, we treat them as machines which can be turned on and off at will. This uni-dimensional view can also affect our images of our superiors, causing us to spend an inordinate amount of time pandering to our perception of their needs, at the expense of what they really need and of time which could be devoted to our staff.

❏ Personal baggage

The pull towards the desired future state may be shared and we are possibly keen to work towards it. We are however pulled back by the 'personal baggage' that we carry, by our value systems, by our socialisation and by our genes. In other words, we are all different and it is the richness of this diversity which has given us the ability to be creative and learn from each other. In managing change, rather than forcing people to change, or ignoring them if they do not, it is far better to take time in understanding why they are the way they are and endeavouring to release the potential within them in bringing about the change.

Few managers in the public sector have the opportunity to chose a project team. Instead they must make the best of the talent imposed upon them. In order to be able to do this it is important to know something about different types, their strengths and weaknesses and how they need to be treated if the best is to be brought out of them, or support for a change gained.

❑ Know thyself

Managing change is not like mathematics, where decisions and methods are correct or incorrect. It is not a science, where a check list approach will provide the same result time after time. It is not possible to award a BS 5750 certification in the management of change because each change is different. Even if the situation appears similar and the people are the same, one can never fully anticipate human behaviour.

As Barnard noted (Halal, 1984),

> ... the power of managers may appear to flow from higher authorities in the organisation, but true power is obtained by gaining the support of subordinates.

If managers are to be able to start to change the behaviour of others, they must start by knowing their own preferences, strengths and weaknesses. From this base they will then be able to begin to understand their interactions with others and why they and the respondents behave the way they do. Having achieved this, they will be able to consider how they can accommodate or change the relationship.

If everyone in the organisation starts by understanding why they are the way they are, this self awareness will in itself generate a higher level of tolerance towards each other by appreciating the strengths in others, which in turn will lead to improved relationships and, ultimately, better performance.

To start, let us look at the different ways people react to change.

Wild West view of change

In order to change, people need both an ability to do so and a willingness to go along. The clerk, for instance, who shows a reluctance to use a keyboard may be most conscientious in all other areas but fear of an inability to carry out the task may be making him or her reluctant. Figure 5.1 opposite looks at the skill/will phenomenon with reference to the opening up of the Wild West.

❑ Explorers

Just after the purchase of the Louisiana Territory, Lewis and Clark set out in

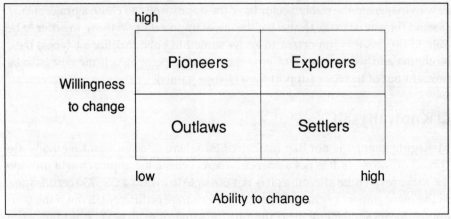

5.1. Wild West view of change.

1805 to survey the acquisition. They were 'explorers.' Organisations have such people, easily identified as those who cannot wait to see the future. They exist in the public sector, but, by tradition, have tended not to be encouraged. Howells (1981) comparing the culture of the Civil Service with Marks and Spencer, wrote

> There are many examples of successful and innovative management in departments, but they depend unduly on highly motivated individuals who behave in ways not normally associated with civil servants. The system does not produce individuals like this as a matter of course; nor does it ensure that people in the second rank, on whom so much depends, behave similarly. On the contrary, there is everything to be gained by keeping up with the paperwork and by avoiding risk. Greater incentives are needed for individual managers to counter-balance the forces of inertia and caution.

The dominance of a 'generalist' mentality, which implies that every person in a grade can do a job to an equal ability, can reinforce a tendency to place square pegs in round holes. An explorer may be placed in a job requiring initiative and the setting up of a new system. Having completed this within a tight nine month deadline, the person is then forced to remain to maintain the system for the next two years until it is deemed appropriate to move to a new post. Young bright talent cannot stand such frustration and may quickly depart the service. Those explorers who do not make the break may either become passive and withdraw into themselves or, if they continue to endeavour to be pro-active, are often marginalised and gain a reputation as being less than sound, which means they are ignored.

❏ Pioneers

Once Lewis and Clark had mapped the territory, they were gradually followed by 'pioneers.' The pioneers may have lacked ability but their willingness to change was paramount. Whilst explorers like nothing more than a clean sheet of paper in an organisation upon which to build their ideas, pioneers are their loyal lieutenants, willing to support the change in any way they can, usually without any desire for reward or incentive. They are crucial in starting to move what may be seen as an isolated idea into some form of reality. Their enthusiasm and support gradually gives the change impetus.

❑ Settlers

Once the pioneers proved that the opening up of the West was less dangerous than others had feared, they were followed by the 'settlers.' These people had more ability to succeed and survive in the wilderness, but were less than willing to make the first moves.

In organisational life, the settlers form the majority. Whilst explorers and pioneers are needed to initiate the change, it is not until the settlers become convinced, that the movement will gain pace and become the norm.

❑ Outlaws

As with the opening up of the West, some people have neither the will nor the skill to change. Whilst the outlaws of the West may have had ulterior motives, in organisations the 'outlaws' are often totally loyal employees. Unfortunately their support for existing systems is so strong that they find it not only difficult to change but also a betrayal of all that they hold dear. Their tolerance of ambiguity is usually low, or they have a large vested interest in keeping the system as it is, possibly through some fear of lost power. Ironically, these are the very people who, when the pendulum swings back towards the status quo ante in a few years time, may well defend the new as stoutly as they defended the old. The loyalty factor may indeed drive such people to leave the organisation. More often than not they are forced to practice the new and gradually acclimatise themselves to the situation, often at the cost of considerable inward suffering.

Whilst we can recognise the need to recruit the explorers and pioneers to the change team as quickly as possible, how can we identify who is most likely to be most at home in each role? One way is to look at personality types.

Jungian types

In 1923 Jung published his theory of personality. This has ultimately provided a model showing 16 different types. It is built up by looking at how we prefer to shape our reality and live in the world. We shape our reality by looking at how we perceive data i.e. through sensing (S) or intuition (N); and how we make judgements i.e. by thinking (T) or feeling (F).

❑ Perception

Perception includes the many ways of becoming aware of things, people, events and ideas. It includes information gathering and the seeking of sensation or of inspiration. It should be stressed that we will use both sensing and intuition but Jung believes that we will have a preference for one or the other. To that end, his approach is polar in that a preference towards one or the other is inherent.

Sensing

Such people tend to gather information from the bottom-up. They prefer this to be in a rational sequential form based on their five senses. They tend to prefer to work in the present and are more at home with facts and established skills in gradually building their view of reality. As such they tend to accept and work with what is 'given' in the here-and-now and tend to become realistic and pragmatic.

Intuition

The other way to discover is through intuition, which shows you the meanings, relationships and possibilities that go beyond the information from your senses. Intuitives therefore tend to look at the big picture and future possibilities. They tend to be interested in concepts and work in a top-down manner in trying to grasp the essential patterns. As such they tend to become expert at seeing new possibilities and new ways of doing things. They value imagination and inspiration.

Already, from a change viewpoint, it can be seen that people with a preference for gathering data from an intuitive viewpoint are more likely to be at home with a clean sheet of paper and feel comfortable in the explorer type of role. They are at home in the stratosphere seeing possibilities and grand designs. The intuitives' apparent lack of attention to detail at this stage infuriates more sensing types who, in building from the bottom-up, need to have most pieces in place before the larger picture emerges. The intuitive's apparent lack of concern for detail is of course either because they find it boring and less exciting than circling the earth, or, more likely, because they are unable to cope with too much detail. Whilst needing details to be filled in before feeling confident to travel, nonetheless the sensing type is invaluable for keeping the aspirations of the intuitive in touch with practicality.

An example of the two types in action might be a two year relocation project. With an intuitive in charge, the broad pattern would be quickly established and the project would start to move in the general direction. Details would be considered as they arose. With a sensing type in charge, little would move until the

detail was in place. While it is sensible to endeavour to have as much information as possible before moving too far and too fast, the need to know precisely
what is due to happen in week three of month 21 is not necessary in order to
begin the move.

❏ Judgement

Judgement defines ways of coming to conclusions about what has been perceived. It involves decision making, evaluation and choice.

Thinking

One way to decide is through 'thinking.' This predicts the logical consequences of
any particular choice or action. When you use thinking you decide objectively, on
the basis of cause and effect, and make decisions by analysing and weighing the
evidence, including even the unpleasant facts. People with a preference for making
decisions on the basis of thinking seek an objective standard of truth. They are also
frequently good at analysing what is wrong with something.

Feeling

People who make decisions on the basis of 'feeling' consider what is important
to themselves or to other people and decide on the basis of person-centred values. They tend to like dealing with people and are often sympathetic, apprecia-
tive and tactful.

Feeling types often see the respect of the people with whom they work as being
the most important reason for working. Thinking types, on the other hand, are
usually more concerned with material reward, seeing people as a means to an
end, rather than an end in themselves.

❏ Perception and judgement

Our shaping of reality varies therefore according to which of the four ways of dealing with the world are dominant. Mitroff (1983) draws distinctions as follows.

Sensing Thinking (ST)

ST individuals tend to be empiricists who sense and think their way through
life, making judgements on the basis of 'hard facts' and logical analysis. In that
sense they represent many of the values of the industrial world and have been
particularly at home in the day to day operations of corporate life.

Sensing Feeling (SF)

SF people also tend to pay a great deal of attention to data derived from the senses, but arrive at judgements in terms of 'what feels right,' rather than in terms of analysis. In change situations, it is possible for such people to identify with the 'outlaw' position in that they find it difficult to view the wider picture and may well have strong loyalty to the existing regime. Alternatively, if inspired by the values of the change, they may well work extremely enthusiastically on the details of how this might be achieved.

Intuitive Thinking (NT)

NT types tend to work their way through life by thinking about the possibilities inherent in a situation. Their actions tend to be shaped by ideas and insights rather than facts. At the same time, having produced ideas, they analyse their possible outcome in a relatively dispassionate manner. NT individuals tend to be at home in 'think tank' operations.

Intuitive Feeling (NF)

NF types tend to be guided by a combination of insight and feeling which pays much more attention to values than to facts. As such NF types tend not only to produce ideas but may feel that they have a moral dimension also. They can therefore turn into crusaders for their cause and may not be easily diverted from its course.

❏ Sources of energy

In arriving at his theory of personality, Jung also distinguished between how people prefer to focus their attention.

Extroverts (E)

Extroverts prefer to focus on the outer world of people and the external environment. They tend to be energised by what goes on in the outer world and this is where they tend to direct their own energy. Extroverts tend to prefer to communicate more by talking than by writing. In terms of change, they need to experience the world in order to understand it and thus tend to like action.

Introverts (I)

Introverts prefer to focus more on their own inner world. They tend to be more interested and comfortable when their work requires a good deal of their activity to take place quietly inside their heads. In terms of change, they prefer to understand the world before experiencing it, and often think about what they are doing before acting.

Myers–Briggs

In developing a means of measuring personality type, Myers and Briggs added a further dimension by looking at how people prefer to live their lives.

❑ Tolerance of ambiguity

This dimension particularly looks at how tolerant people are to change and uncertainty.

Judging (J)

People with a judging attitude tend to live in a planned, orderly way, wanting to regulate life and control it. In this respect, they like to complete things and make decisions, in other words, close them off before concentrating on something else. People with this preference like to be structured and organised and want things settled. From a change viewpoint therefore, they tend to have a low tolerance of ambiguity and need to know where they are, a situation which is rarely conducive to the chaos of the new.

Perceptive (P)

Those with a preference for perception like to live in a flexible, spontaneous way. When gathering information, they prefer to keep their options open, and tend to prefer to understand life, rather than control it. From a change viewpoint, they prefer to stay open to experience, enjoying and trusting their ability to adapt to the moment. They therefore have a high tolerance of ambiguity and will more easily come to terms with changing situations. Their problem however is making a decision and bringing things to a close.

From the four combinations of preference perception, judgement, sources of energy and tolerance of ambiguity, Myers and McCauley (1989), developed the sixteen-fold model of types shown in Figure 5.2a and 5.2b which note general preferences.

Use of type in team building

Any job will require a description of what needs to be done and the skill of the person to carry it out. The latter will either be brought by the person by way of natural talent or previous experience, or be taught through some form of training.

❑ Types of work

Margerison and McCann (1990) have identified eight types of work necessary in some degree or other in organising work tasks.

Advising

This work is associated with gathering information and disseminating it to others. People engaged in this type of work will typically gather data from reports or from contact with others and assemble it so that it can be used in decision making. Corporate planners, information officers and researchers often fall into this category.

Innovating

Once an organisation has gathered information about 'the state of the art', the work may then move into a different phase. Here people will think up ideas for improving the current state by creating and researching the fundamental idea.

Promoting

It is no good thinking up ideas unless they can be 'sold' to the organisation. Many good ideas are lost simply because they are poorly 'promoted' to others.

Developing

Once the idea has been 'sold' the work activity often moves into the developing phase. The idea must be made to work and therefore further development is often required. 'Developing' may involve prototype testing or the assessment of alternative versions of the idea to see which is going to be the best one to implement.

Organising

Now the idea is ready for implementation. Plans have been made, budgets approved and schedules established so that the product or service can be implemented. This requires organisation.

Producing

Once the plans and schedules are in place production can start on a regular basis to high standards of effectiveness and efficiency.

Inspecting

This is necessary to ensure that quality has been maintained and controls are established.

Maintaining

There is a need in all teams and organisations to provide the infrastructure that enables all of the above activities to proceed in the most efficient manner. This role is often provided corporately by the support activities of, for example, personnel.

Sensing Types

Introverts	**ISTJ** Serious, quiet, earn success by concentration and thoroughness. Practical, orderly, matter-of-fact, logical, realistic, and dependable. See to it that everything is well organised. Take responsibility. Make up their own minds as to what should be accomplished and work towards it steadily, regardless of protests or distractions.	**ISFJ** Quiet, friendly, responsible and conscientious. Work devotedly to meet their obligations. Lend stability to any project or group. Thorough, painstaking, accurate. Their interests are usually not technical. Can be patient with necessary details. Loyal, considerate, perceptive, concerned with how other people feel.
	ISTP Cool onlookers - quiet, reserved, observing and analysing life with detached curiosity and unexpected flashes of original humour. Usually interested in cause and effect, how and why mechanical things work, and in organizing facts using logical principles.	**ISFP** Retiring, quietly friendly, sensitive, kind, modest about their abilities. Shun disagreements, do not force their opinions or values on others. Usually do not care to lead but are often loyal followers. Often relaxed about getting things done, because they enjoy the present and do not want to spoil it by undue haste or exertion.
Extroverts	**ESTP** Good at on-the-spot problem solving. Do not worry, enjoy whatever comes along. Tend to like mechanical things and sports, with friends on the side. Are best with real things that can be worked, handled, taken apart, or put together.	**ESFP** Outgoing, easy-going, accepting, friendly, enjoy everything and make things more fun for others by their enjoyment. Like sports and making things happen. Know what's going on and join in eagerly. Find remembering facts easier then mastering theories. Are best in situations that need sound common sense and practical albeit with people as well as with things.
	ESTJ Practical, realistic. matter-of-fact, with a natural head for business or mechanics. Not interested in subjects they see no use for, but can apply themselves when necessary. Like to organize and run activities. May make good administrators, especially if they remember to consider others' feelings and points of view.	**ESFJ** Warm-hearted, talkative, popular, conscientious, born cooperators, active committee members. Need harmony and may be good at creating it. Always doing something nice for someone. Work best with encouragement and praise. Main interest is in things that directly and visibly affect people's lives.

Figure 5.2a   MBTI sixteen type classification – sensing types
(Myers and McCauley, 1989).

Intuitive Types

INFJ Succeed by perseverance. originality, and desire to do whatever is needed or wanted. Put their best efforts into their work. Quietly forceful, conscientious, concerned for others. Respected for their firm principles. Likely to be honoured and followed for their clear convictions as to how best to serve the common good.	**INTJ** Usually have original minds and great drive for their own ideas and purposes. In fields that appeal to them, they have a fine power to organize a job and carry it through with or without help. Sceptical. critical, independent, determined, sometimes stubborn. Must learn to yield less important points in order to win the most important.
INFP Full of enthusiasms and loyalties, but seldom talk of these until they know you well. Care about learning, ideas, language and independent projects of their own. Tend to undertake too much, then somehow get it done. Friendly, but often too absorbed in what they are doing to be sociable. Little concerned with possessions or physical surroundings.	**INTP** Quiet and reserved. Especially enjoy theoretical or scientific pursuits. Like solving problems with logic and analysis. Usually interested mainly in ideas, with little liking for parties or small talk. Tend to have sharply defined interests. Need careers where some strong interest can be used and useful.
ENFP Warmly enthusiastic, high-spirited, ingenious. imaginative. Able to do almost anything that interests them. Quick with a solution for any difficulty and ready to help anyone with a problem. Often rely on their ability to improvise instead of preparing in advance. Can usually find compelling reasons for whatever they want.	**ENTP** Quick, ingenious. good at many things. Stimulating company. alert and outspoken. May argue for fun on either side of a question. Resourceful in solving new and challenging problems, but may neglect routine assignments. Apt to turn to one new interest after another. Skilful in finding logical reasons for what they want
ENFJ Responsive and responsible. Generally feel real concern for what others think or want. and try to handle things with due regard for the other person's feelings. Can present a proposal or lead a group discussion with ease and tact. Sociable, popular. sympathetic. Responsive to praise and criticism.	**ENTJ** Hearty, frank, decisive, leaders in activities. Usually good in anything that requires reasoning and intelligent talk, such as public speaking. Are usually well informed and enjoy adding to their fund of knowledge. May sometimes appear more positive and confident than their experience in an area warrants.

Introverts

Extroverts

Figure 5.2b   MBTI sixteen type classification – intuitive types
(Myers and McCauley, 1989).

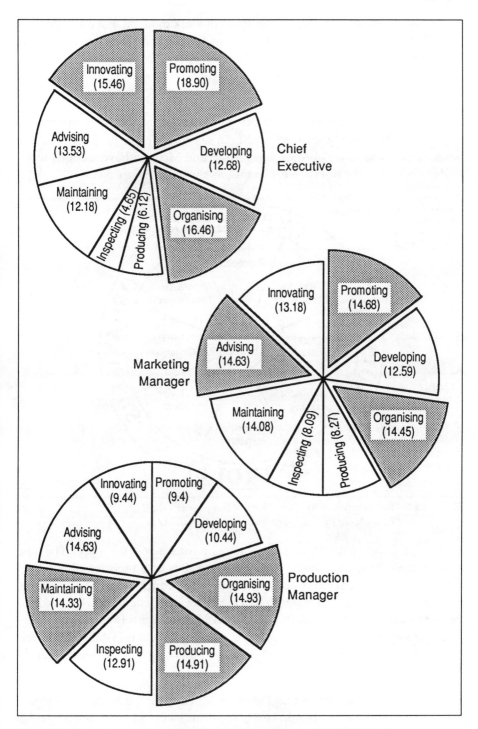

Figure 5.3. Type of work (Reproduced by kind permission of TMS(UK) Ltd).

A job can be described by the various types of work required. For example, Figure 5.3 shows the critical types of work for Chief Executives, marketing and production managers from research of carried out by TMS.

❏ Types of personality

Whilst job design and skills training may be important, all too often little regard has been given to the type of personality in selecting people for jobs. From the work of Jung and Myers-Briggs, Margerison and McCann have mapped work preferences on to the type of work model, as shown in Figure 5.4.

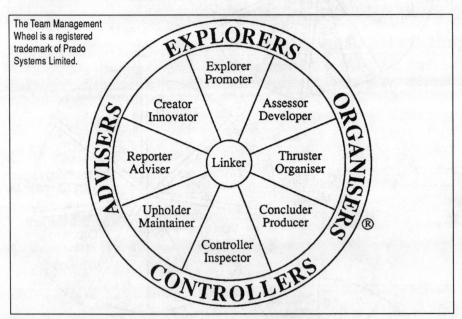

The Team Management Wheel is a registered trademark of Prado Systems Limited.

Figure 5.4 . The Margerison-McCann Team Management Wheel (Reproduced by kind permission of TMS (UK) Ltd).

Interestingly the result of this is to portray opposites across the wheel. The type of person likely to be at home with gathering data as a reporter adviser will enjoy researching data and taking time to reach conclusions. The opposite, thruster organiser, is more interested in receiving instructions on what needs to be done and driving the work through to conclusion as quickly as possible. Likewise, the explorer promoter will prefer to talk in generalities, while the controller inspector is more concerned with detail and checking that the finished article is correct.

To illustrate the implications, take the example of a creative innovator. Such people will be at home with a blank sheet of paper and will feel constrained by rules and procedures. Instead they need to be allowed to let their imagination roam if genuinely innovative solutions are to be identified. They have little eye for detail and see only grand designs. On the other hand, someone is also needed to put the idea into action and ensure that it is completed to specification. Placing a creative innovator in such a role does not mean to say that they would be unable to carry out the task. But it does mean, from their viewpoint, that they might be less than satisfied in doing the job and, from the organisation's point of view, that they are not being used to best advantage. Far better to use someone who is more comfortable in the role of concluder producer and release the creative energy where it can be used to more positive effect. The same principle applies throughout the wheel.

Right brain/left brain

The Herrmann brain dominance theory works on similar lines in drawing attention to different preferences in people. The model in the first instance divides the thought processes of the brain between the left (analytical) and right (creative) sides of the neocortex (or thinking cap), with the left (organisational) and right (emotional) sides of the limbic system (or doing part of the brain). This produces the metaphor in Figure 5.5.

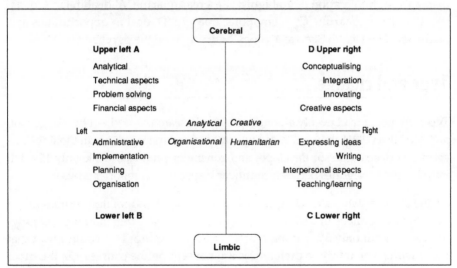

Figure 5.5 Herrmann model (Herrmann, 1986).

As with personality types, every individual will have some elements of every quartile but in different proportions.

Quartile A

People with a tendency towards quartile 'A' enjoy gathering facts, solving problems in a logical manner, measuring solutions precisely and understanding technical issues. They are particularly suited to finance and engineering, in other words, areas of precision. An example from the Health Service would be a surgeon.

Quartile B

People with a tendency towards quartile 'B' are practical, enjoy routine and like to know where they stand. They have a good eye for detail, particularly in dotting 'i's' and crossing 't's' and often find overlooked flaws. People in this quartile are good administrators who are comfortable with rules and procedures, referring more complex cases to those with more specialist knowledge. The Health Service analogy might extend to general practitioners.

Quartile C

Those with a tendency towards quartile 'C' have a high desire for harmony and intuitively understand how others feel. They give weight to values and are quick to pick up non-verbal cues of interpersonal stress. Nurses and social workers would tend to fall into this category.

Quartile D

People in quartile 'D' have a high degree of intuition, see the big picture and display a high toleration of ambiguity. Whereas quartile 'A' deal in facts, quartile 'B' in rules, quartile 'C' in emotions, quartile 'D' deal in opportunities and flexibility. The Health Service analogy here might be the psychiatrist.

Type and change

Types are not spread evenly amongst groups. Research carried out by Margerison and McCann (1994) shows 67% of English speaking managers are in the three categories between assessor developer and concluder producer, while only 15% fall into the three categories between controller inspector and reporter adviser.

Of the civil servants attending change management and related courses at the Civil Service College in 1993, a vast proportion were sensing, thinking and judging types, with only 3% having a preference for feeling. This could mean that those with more intuitive preferences are not sent on the courses. On the other hand, it could also mean that the type selected by Civil Service managers to manage change are driven by a bottom-up approach, at the expense of seeing the larger design and the effects of the decisions on people.

It might suggest that the dominant type within the civil service has an STJ orientation. Such a culture seeks to preserve rather than change and to act on instructions rather than think why things are being done. It is also highly task, as opposed to people, orientated. To this end, it is less than likely to consider fully the impact of change on people prior to acting. From the point of view of empowerment, the locus of control is likely to be external. In other words, people believe that control is in the hands of others than themselves. This is considered further in Chapter 11.

❏ Type and the change agent

So much depends on the situation of much change that it is difficult to speculate on what personality type makes the best change agent, added to which success depends on much more than personality. In general however it is reasonable to argue that intuition and the ability to see the broad picture is important. The need for the change agent to have a high tolerance of ambiguity would also point to a flexible or perceptive, rather than a structured or judging type.

The need to be able to sell the change and influence the internal political environment points to the use of an extrovert rather than an introvert. The ENP preferences therefore seem reasonable to assume. It is more difficult when considering thinking and feeling. The objectivity of the former may well be crucial on occasions when a realistic interpretation is needed. On the other hand, most change fails because of lack of consideration of its impact on people. While the ENTP might deliver compliance in the short term, it could be at the expense of support. The ENFP on the other hand, in taking account of the people and in possibly being more supportive of the change, might in the longer term deliver more commitment.

While it is not the case that no one other than an ENTP or ENFP can successfully manage change, the number of people selected to manage change with an ISTJ profile does not auger well for success.

❏ Type and team building

Research by McCauley (Hersch, 1992) notes:

> the more similarity between individual types on a team, the sooner the team members will come to understand each other; the more different the types, the slower the understanding;
>
> groups with very similar members will reach decisions more quickly but may make more errors because not all viewpoints are represented. Groups with many different types will reach decisions more slowly, and painfully, but may reach better decisions because more viewpoints are included;
>
> team members may often choose tasks that fit the gifts of their type;
>
> leadership roles may shift as the tasks to be done require the skills of different types on the team;

the person who is the only representative of a certain type e.g. the only introvert, may be seen as 'different' from the other team members;

team members who come to appreciate and work with different types may help to diffuse conflict;

successful teams with many different types promote the personal development of team members by encouraging learning from the gifts of other types;

teams that are 'one-sided' i.e. have too few types, will succeed if (a) team members use different types outside the team as resources, or (b) they make an effort to use their own less-preferred preferences as the tasks require;

extroverts may dominate discussions, and perhaps decision making, unless they make a special effort to involve introverts; introverts on the other hand may need to make a special effort to be heard;

good decisions will be made when the basic facts and realities have been taken into account (sensing), when useful possibilities have been opened up (intuition), when inconsistencies or consequences have been analysed (thinking), and when important values have been considered (feeling).

Hersch points out that in terms of change, IS types prefer to keep things as they are; IN types like to think about it; EN types like to change it; and ES types like to do it. In consequence, IS types are often threatened by EN types since one wishes to retain the status quo while the other wishes to change it. At the same time, ES types dislike IN types because the one wishes to do something about it while the other prefers to think about it.

While type can be useful in building teams, it is often more useful in analysing and solving conflict both within and between teams. Awareness of the concept is also useful in appraisal training. The consequences of sensing managers criticising intuitive staff for lack of depth and the counter of intuitive managers criticising for lack of breadth are too close to realism to be amusing.

❏ Handling the change

Finally in terms of managing change, it is important to recognise individual needs and concerns. Using the Herrmann metaphor, people with a preference for quartile 'A' are concerned with the facts. For example, in a relocation project they would want to know when the move is to take place and why. Quartile 'B' staff want to be given the instructions and plans of what to do and when. For people in quartile 'C', it is crucial to understand feelings and to empathise with them about the situation. And for quartile 'D', it is important to involve them, since they will design and lead the operation if given half a chance.

In contrast, applying blanket methods to all people on all occasions will not work. Providing facts to someone in shock in quartile 'C' will only serve to heighten their anxiety. Asking someone in quartile 'B' to initiate the whole exercise will equally end in disaster. Providing detailed rules and procedures to those in quartile 'D' will constrain them to frustration, and providing empathy to quartile 'A' people instead of facts will not help.

There are rarely more satisfying occasions in working life than fully functioning as a member of a team where your individual talents are being stretched to the full and everyone appreciates the efforts of the other, rather than operating as a collection of individuals. The achievement of change, as in most work activity, will be more likely to come about by managing the diversity and harnessing the richness of potential held within us all.

References and suggested reading

Halal, W. (1984) *The Legitimacy Cycle: Long-term Dynamics in the Use of Power* in Kakabadse, A. and Parker, C (Ed).*Power, Politics and Organisations*, Wiley

Herrmann, N. (1986) *Improving individual and organisational performance: the whole brain model* Lake Lure NC, Brain

Hersh, S. (1992) *MBTI Team Building Programme* Palo Alto CA, Consulting Psychologists Press

Howells, D. (1981) Marks and Spencer and the civil service: A comparison of culture and methods *Public Administration* Vol 59, No 3 (autumn)

Margerison, C. and McCann, D. (1990) *Team Management Systems* York, Prado

Margerison, C. and McCann, D. (1994) *TMS Research* York, Prado

Morgan, G. (1986) *Images of Organisation* London, Sage

Myers, I. and McCauley, M. (1989) *A Guide to the Development and Use of the Myers-Briggs Type Indicator - Fifth edition* Palo Alto CA, Consulting Psychologists Press

Revens, R. (1982) *The Origins and Growth of Action Learning* Bromley, Chartwell-Bratt

Senge. P. (1990) *The Fifth Discipline* London, Century

Chapter 6

Communications during change

Mike Dutfield and Chris Eling

Always remember you only know half the story, your own half. *Anon*

As you will have already gathered from this book, managing change is complex, usually more complex than managers expect. No matter how much effort an organisation invests in preparation there will be unforeseen difficulties. Many of the original writers on planned change saw it as a rational step-by-step process, although recent writers recognise that a whole range of different methods are likely to be more effective. For instance, Kilmann and Covin (1988) talk about change being a continuous process: Beer (1988) a reciprocal learning process. Despite this Kanter (1992) feels that many organisations are

> inclined to push faster, spend less and stop earlier than the process requires.

Certainly the survey results shown in Figure 6.1 (Alexander 1989) confirm her view that managers are often overly optimistic about what will happen when they start a change programme.

Of the problems listed in Figure 6.1. only item 7 is beyond the control of the organisation, although it may contribute to some of the other problems. Mabey (1992) suggested three general reasons for these problems:

- resistance to change (problems 1,2, perhaps 6)
- inadequate control or management of the change process (problems 3, 4, 5, 9, 10, and perhaps 6)
- the internal political system (while this could influence many of the problems, it is particularly relevant to 4, 8, and perhaps 1 and 2).

Most of the problems are to do with the way the organisation has managed and communicated about the change process. Given that change is frequently messy, chaotic, unpredictable and painful, it is vital that a communication process is established that will be able to cope with the stresses and strains that will have to be managed. The emphasis is on the word 'process'. All the writers see change

The top ten reasons why change strategies ran into problems during implementation were:	
Problem	**Percentage of Firms**
1 Implementation took more time than originally allocated	76
2 Major problems surfaced during implementation which had not been identified beforehand	74
3 Co–ordination of implementation activities not effective enough	66
4 Competing activities and crises distracted management from implementing this decision	64
5 Capabilities of employees involved were not sufficient	63
6 Training and instruction given to lower-level employees were inadequate	62
7 Uncontrollable factors in the external environment had an adverse impact on implementation	60
8 Leadership and direction provided by departmental managers were not adequate enough	59
9 Key implementation tasks and activities were not defined in enough detail	56
10 Information systems used to monitor implementation were not adequate.	56

Figure 6.1. Problems in implementing change strategies (Alexander, 1989).

as a process, not an episode, and as such communications need to be thought of in the same way.

Managers working hard at, for instance, producing only comprehensive announcements will not be effective. Each communication will be received in the context of the previous one and will influence the way the next one is received and understood. In this sense, the first communication in the change process will change the context of meaning for all subsequent communications. The process cannot be reversed, the organisation will not be the same again. People will interpret and reinterpret, not only the information they receive, but management's actions and their own feelings to it, in a new light. With these new interpretations will come an inevitable uncertainty about what people think, know and feel. It is in this area that a well thought out communication strategy can help:

- not to pass on management's information and thoughts, but to generate understanding
- understanding within the organisation about what the change means
- understanding about what problems it will create
- understanding about how different groups think about it and so on.

Of course, this does not mean that the problems of change will go away, but at least the organisation will be in a better position to find a way forward.

In this chapter we describe the work of the two researchers, Pugh and Kanter, who have each produced a set of rules for bringing about effective change.

Making the change process effective – Pugh

Pugh (1978) has identified six rules for managing change.

❏ Rule 1

Work hard at establishing the need for change

The change proposer or initiator will have spent many hours thinking through the need for the organisation to change. What for him or her may be obvious at the end of this process may not be readily understood or accepted by others. For instance, an improvement in a control system, which the finance group regard as necessary, may be seen as undesirable by managers in other functions, as it reduces their freedoms and autonomy.

Pugh found the reasons for change that were acceptable to most people and groups within an organisation tended to come from the environment, such as market changes, different customer needs or technological change. Change generated internally was liable to be interpreted in terms of the internal political system and therefore could generate resistance.

❏ Rule 2

Don't only think out the change, think through it

Pugh advocates that the changes should not just be thought out, in terms of costs and benefits from the point of view of the proposer. The change should be consciously and systematically analysed for all the people and groups involved. For instance, does the content of their jobs change, will they have to perform new tasks, what new skills and knowledge will they need, does it change the working relationships, will it affect their power and status and so on?

He maintains that a detailed analysis helps to identify potential resistances and builds for the change proposer a more complete understanding of what the change really means to all involved.

❏ Rule 3

Initiate change through informal discussion to get feedback and participation

It is unclear what Pugh means by informal discussion, but he sees the need for the manager to get feedback on the change proposals from all concerned. He maintains that it is virtually impossible for a person or a small group to foresee all the consequences of a change. Therefore, involving people tests out the change ideas and helps to identify any modifications that will improve it.

He supports the view that participation leads to effective change in organisations. He recommends early involvement in the process, which generates commitment to the changes and increased motivation to make it work.

❏ Rule 4

Positively encourage those concerned to give their objections

This is seen as important for two reasons.

First people do not necessarily resist change, but they do resist change that is thrust upon them. Raising objections is a way of involving people, which can lead to flexibility by encouraging them to see they can make a useful contribution.

Second it helps to identify the balance of forces in any situation. In Chapter 4 on 'Gaining support', the ideas of Lewin (1948) were discussed, particularly 'force field analysis'. Lewin maintained that any situation was a balance of forces, some driving for change and others against or resisting change. Altering this balance by increasing the driving forces can bring about change, but it does not get rid of the resisting forces. It tends to hide them, bringing about a potentially unstable situation, leading to unexpected consequences or surprises later. A better way is to deal with the resisting forces and to try to reduce them. This also changes the balance of forces, producing the desired change without creating excessive tensions within the organisational system.

❏ Rule 5

Be prepared to change yourself

Pugh thinks this is probably the most important rule. To quote

> modern managers cannot afford the luxury of believing that change is for other people, since a manager who proposes to initiate change joins in the process and must himself or herself be prepared to change.

He goes on to point out the dangers for the manager, who has invested considerable time and energy thinking through the change, that he or she can 'fall in love with their own idea'. In the process they become over-committed to certain courses of action, and can be defensive and resistant to other ideas, even if they improve the change or its implementation. Change is not always top down. It can be bottom up. Involvement processes and approaches such as Total Quality Management rely on the good ideas of subordinates to bring about change.

❏ Rule 6

Monitor the change and reinforce it

The manager needs to recognise that change is a process, not an event or episode. This is true even when the change that is being managed is the move of the organisation from one location to another. While the physical move may happen on one particular day, the process will have started before the move, with the planning and announcement, and will continue in the new location as people get used to the advantages and disadvantages of the new office. In many situations, for instance the introduction of a new computer system, the old and new may coexist together for a time. There is therefore a need to monitor the change process so that modifications can be made.

Change can be messy and uncomfortable for people. Given this it is important to demonstrate that the change is starting to work and delivering some benefits. If there is no reinforcement of progress, then people will remember the mess and the discomfort and the benefits will tend to go unnoticed.

Making the change process effective – Kanter

Drawing from her own work and the research of others, Kanter (1992) has produced her 'Ten Commandments for Executing Change'.

1 Analyse the organisation and its need for change

Any change process should start with a thorough understanding of how the organisation works, what are its strengths and weaknesses, what are its relationships with the environment and what are its needs to change. Only then can the full implications of a change be understood and effective implementation plans developed.

2 Create a shared vision and common direction

One of the key first steps is to unite the organisation around a vision of the future. This is more than a mission statement or well communicated strategies but is analogous to an 'organisational dream of what could be'. This in the words of Belgard, Fisher and Rayner (1988):

> stretches the imagination and motivates people to think what is possible.

3 Separate from the past

This is a similar idea to Lewin's (1947) unfreezing process. The organisation must identify what aspects of its operations are no longer relevant and be motivated to change them. Only then can the members of the organisation start to be committed to a new vision.

4 Create a sense of urgency

A sense of urgency seems to be important for the organisation to unfreeze and develop support for the changes. When organisations are in crisis, it is easy to create a sense of urgency. But ideally organisations should be more proactive in their change strategies and change before crises occur. It is a key function of leadership to generate this urgency, without creating false or unreal crises.

5 Support a strong leader

Several American studies such as Kanter (1983), and Nadler and Tushmann (1989), have found that a strong leader is critical to vision creation, motivating the organisation behind the vision and rewarding those who strive towards its realisation.

6 Line up political support

Leadership is not enough, successful change needs a broad base of support from all the stakeholders, including those who will lose, as well as those who gain from the change. In the UK Pettigrew (1992) has found little evidence of the 'transformational leader' being successful. In his long term studies of British companies he found that the successful management of change required similar leadership processes to occur. Although they were not identified with a single leader, it was important for the senior management, as a whole, to be seen to be involved and owning the initiatives.

7 Craft an implementation plan

While visions are necessary, the organisation also needs information about what will be done to achieve it. Beckhard and Harris (1987) see this change plan as a road map, giving clear direction and a route to take. Plans are a key communication tool, helping people to see the integration of the many diverse activities that will be necessary in a major change programme.

8 Develop enabling structures

The old structures and ways of working are unlikely to be adequate to support and sustain the change process on their own. Enabling structures are not the new or desired state, but systems and structures which support the transformation process during the transition from the old to the new state. They could include pilots, trials, parallel running, training and educational programmes and courses, consultative structures and new reward and career systems. At a symbolic level they could include new company names, new organisation logos and uniforms and office relocation and refurbishment.

9 Communicate, involve people and be honest

When possible there should be open communications and the involvement and trust of people in the organisation. Coch and French (1948) first identified the importance of involvement and participation in overcoming resistance to change. Their findings have since been replicated many times.

10 Reinforce and institutionalise the change

Managers need constantly to demonstrate their commitment to the change. They should reward the new desired behaviours and ensure they become part of normal day to day operations.

❏ Comparison with Pugh's rules

There are strong similarities between Pugh's rules and Kanter's commandments. Both stress the importance of establishing the need for change and of its being understood by the organisation. The need to understand the organisation and the implications of the change, in detail, is also stressed. Gaining support on a broad basis within the organisation is seen as necessary. Both identify the importance of involvement and participation. Pugh's encouragement of objections is liable to need enabling structures for it to happen, while both recognise the need constantly to reinforce the change.

Communication difficulties in change

Pugh's and Kanter's work clearly has implications for what needs to be communicated during the management of change. Their ideas also have an effect on how communication should be managed. In this section we are going to look at a number of difficulties which organisations and groups have in communicating effectively and how these can affect the management of change.

❏ Effect of hierarchy

The first set of problems relates to the existence of hierarchy, a central concept of organisation, particular in bureaucracies. Argyle (1983) found that communication up and down the hierarchy was particularly difficult. This manifests itself in a number of different ways. In an early study Burns (1954) found that instructions and decisions taken by a departmental manager were recorded by his deputies on only 50% of those occasions.

Interestingly some unpublished research of our own, in a pharmaceutical company, found the opposite. In this instance the Managing Director frequently sent information to his managers, but this information was perceived by those managers, in 60% of the cases, as instructions. However, both pieces of research identified how the hierarchical relationships had distorted the reasons for communicating.

Another unpublished study by Floyd and Mann (Handy 1982) showed a significant difference in the view between layers as to how well they understood each other's problems (as shown in Figure 6.2).

Managers tend to have a significant, influence on the reward and career structures. This can lead to subordinates distorting or omitting information in their communication to their bosses. An example of this comes from IBM. Peters and Waterman (1982), in their study of successful companies in the late 1970's, found IBM's open door policies and philosophy important to its phenomenal growth and success. However by the late 1980's and 1990's it had changed.

To quote Jim Cassell (Pontier 1993), an ex-IBM planning executive:

> the culture of IBM was such that you really didn't want to bring bad news forward to the top of the business.

The information went through six or seven layers of management before it was presented to the board. At each level the figures were massaged to make sure they were what the next level up wanted to see.

❏ Differing perceptions

Another major problem of communication comes because individuals, groups and departments have different perceptions, reflecting their own interests and knowledge. This is explained by Simon's (1957) concept of 'bounded rationality'. This concept is based on the assumption that in complex situations individuals cannot know everything and that they will operate with a view of the world or 'rationality' that is bounded by their knowledge, assumptions and interests. Schein (1985) comes to a similar conclusion from his studies of organisational culture. Instead of seeing communication breakdowns as a sign of defensiveness or lack of clarity, he main-

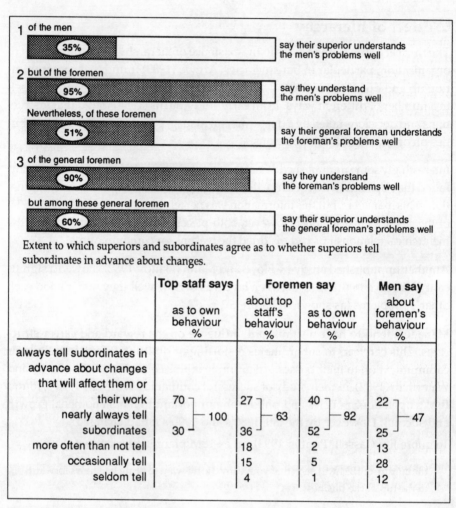

Extent to which superiors and subordinates agree as to whether superiors tell subordinates in advance about changes.

	Top staff says	Foremen say		Men say
	as to own behaviour %	about top staff's behaviour %	as to own behaviour %	about foremen's behaviour %
always tell subordinates in advance about changes that will affect them or their work	70 ⎤	27 ⎤	40 ⎤	22 ⎤
nearly always tell	⎬ 100	⎬ 63	⎬ 92	⎬ 47
subordinates	30 ⎦	36 ⎦	52 ⎦	25 ⎦
more often than not tell		18	2	13
occasionally tell		15	5	28
seldom tell		4	1	12

Figure 6.2 The communication gap.

Data from unpublished studies by Floyd Mann of power plants in a public utility. Adapted from Likert, (1961).

tains they should be seen as a result of real differences in how people perceive and understand things, because they belong to different cultural units.

In other words, as organisations are made up of different groups, with their own distinctive sub-cultures, we should expect misunderstandings. The following two examples from our work in managing change demonstrate how these concepts can affect communications.

In the first case an organisation was having to deal with changing customer requirements. This required the service it provided to be delivered in a completely new way. It embarked on an organisation-wide communication process to educate the staff in the reasons for the change and what would happen. It also stressed the importance of the changes for the long term health of the organisation. In this the organisation was very successful, but it was then that problems occurred. Certainly the changes were going to have a significant impact on parts of the organisation, bringing very different working methods, jobs and skills, a qualitative shift. However, in other parts it was going to require increased response times and flexibility, essentially changes that were currently being managed, but with increasing frequency. While this was going to create problems, it did not need new skills, but rather the skills were going to be used in different ways. In this sense it was a quantitative change. The communication, however, had concentrated on the needs to change customer service. This was essentially the view of the change innovators, in this case senior management's view. Although accurate it was a partial perspective, which parts of the organisation, while recognising its importance, could not relate to their day to day activities. The result was that some people did not feel empowered, but rather impotent to know how or what they could do to contribute to meeting the new challenges.

The second case involved the integration of two departments, which traditionally had worked closely together, although organisationally they had been separated on functional lines. There were clearly cultural differences between the two departments. These had led to frequent misunderstandings and the development of stereotypical views of each other. Conflict was not uncommon, with a heavy emphasis on blaming each other when something went wrong. A process of listing problems and comparing them, each department with the other, was used to help the integration. It was found that nearly half the listed problems stemmed from misunderstandings. Not only this, but they were frequently the most emotive and strongly felt problems, because the reactions of the other party seemed totally irrational from each other's cultural perspective.

❑ Overload

A common response by organisations and managers to the identification of a communications problem is to communicate more. This can lead to overload, where the recipient is faced with too much information and becomes confused or is selective in choosing which information to use or believe.

Festinger (1957) developed a concept he referred to as 'cognitive dissonance'. This states that people find it uncomfortable to accept or receive information, which conflicts with their beliefs. To avoid or overcome the discomfort, they have to change their beliefs or, much more likely, discount the information, hence expressions like, 'the exception that proves the rule'. In the situation where there is overload and people can be selective, cognitive dissonance means they will be more sensitive to the information that confirms their existing assumptions and ideas. In situations of change this process is, of course, liable to confirm their feelings about the change. This can lead to enhancing their view of the current state or reinforcing their fears of the future. Either would lead to increasing resistance to change.

❑ Partial or incomplete message

Individuals need stability and security to help them change. At work the people who are confident with their abilities tend to see change as a challenge and continue to strive hard for success. The less confident and secure become rigidly defensive in the face of change. Pugh (1978), Kanter (1992) and Peters and Waterman (1982) have found that the same processes operate at an organisational level. Paradoxically the most successful organisations embrace change willingly, while the least successful, with perhaps the greatest need to change, resist it. For these organisations, the need to change generates energy and commitment, but this is directed to current practices. The organisation's response is to work harder and better at what it currently does. Given that the need for changes often questions the appropriateness, rather than the efficiency, of existing methods of operation, such an approach is rarely successful. The energy and commitment then turns inward, identifying who has failed, who is not trying hard enough. This development or reinforcement of a blame culture naturally increases the defensiveness.

What is the implication for these processes and communication? During a change, most attention tends to be directed to those aspects of the organisation that has to be changed, for example, new skills, structures and methods. Most of the communication is directed towards generating an understanding of why the change is necessary and what needs to be changed. This is all essential and relates to Pugh's rules and Kanter's commandments. However, in the change process, not everything from the past will be thrown away or replaced. For instance, many of the skills and much of the knowledge which members possess will still be needed and may indeed be essential for future success. If the communication concentrates on the changes, with little emphasis on what will remain, then it risks exaggerating people's feelings of insecurity about the future, instead of building confidence in being able to cope and succeed. If this happens defensive resistance can follow.

Kanter and Pugh both discuss the importance of reinforcing the changes. Communication is vital in achieving this. Change is messy, new systems and structures are unlikely to work perfectly at first. Further change and modifications will be necessary as unforeseen problems occur. Without feedback on what has been achieved, it can feel as though the change has been unsuccessful and 'it is still all to do'. Again the communication must ensure that the balance between changes made and those still to be made is understood.

❏ Conflicting messages

As we have mentioned not everything is altered during the management of change. Also the changes do not all happen at once, implementation is often phased. For example the new structure may be in place, but new skills are being developed and new systems are still at the design stage. In this sense the old and the new co-exist. This allows for different messages to be received by organisational members, some from the new systems and ways of working and others from parts of the organisation that have not yet been changed. People are sensitive to conflicting signals or meanings in communications and management actions. As Kanter points out, members of the organisation are reading these signals to check out if management is committed to the change or simply paying lip service to it. For instance, consider a change to empower people at lower levels in the organisation and to allow them to have greater freedom in financial decision making. Financial systems could be introduced with delegated budgets. But if section managers still required the approval of their bosses to spend over £100, it would feel to the section managers as though little had changed, even though many new systems were in place, as is shown in Chapter 11.

Maintaining this sense of consistency is further complicated by the notion of immediacy. The more immediate communication drives out the less urgent. Imagine being in a queue to buy theatre tickets. A telephone call to the box office does not join the end of the queue, it tends to get answered immediately. This is an important notion in the early stages of change, as the day to day pressures will tend to take precedence over the longer term tasks. In the process the day to day activities, which are more likely to be rooted in the past, will have much greater impact. The manager must ensure consistency, by giving balanced and consistent communications about what should happen, but also balanced and consistent recognition of what has been achieved.

❏ Timing

When to communicate is never an easy decision. During change individuals will interpret what is happening in terms of its relevance and impact on them. Therefore if communication starts before all the decisions about the change have been taken, there will probably be a number of questions and concerns from staff that cannot be answered. Some managers find it hard to say they do not know and would rather wait to be more certain. On the other hand if the manager does wait until more is known, then he or she is liable to be criticised for not informing and involving the staff earlier.

Many of the questions asked will be to help individuals work out their reactions to the change, not just to gain information. In this sense the questions will not stop just because all the decisions have been taken. The manager will never know all the answers. However in bureaucracies, which traditionally have cultures of lower risk taking, there may be a tendency for managers to delay announcements until they feel more certain. In most situations this would be a mistake. Information leaks out and rumours can easily start. This could lead members of the organisation to feel powerless in the face of change and create defensiveness and resistance.

Another reason for not delaying refers to Pugh's rule 5. As management invests more energy and thought into the change process, it will inevitably become more committed to its own ideas and solutions. When these finally see the light of day and are challenged and questioned from different perspectives, the management can find itself defending its position. This will not help create a shared vision and common direction, which Kanter sees as necessary, nor will it gain the support of the stakeholders who have been excluded from the process.

While there are risks associated with involving people, they tend to be less than the risks of not involving them. As Kanter and Pugh have identified, the balance of risks favours involving the staff as soon as possible. Generally, communicate early is sound advice.

❏ Communications can be sent to many people, but individuals receive the message.

In many respects a number of change communications have the characteristics of the mass media. Memos, notices or carefully timed departmental or organisational briefings send the same words or intended message to many people. This is of course necessary. But as the recipients have different values and needs, and probably will be affected differently by the change, a different message may be received. However management can spend many hours polishing the communication, working out elaborate plans for timing of the communication and so on, as though this form of official organisational propaganda will generate the attitudes that management want. We exaggerate this point, but nevertheless feel more effort is spent on devising the message to be sent, rather than understanding what is heard.

Certainly the early ideas on mass communication would have supported this approach, but in 1960 the work of Klappers (1960) found that mass communication was only one influence 'working amid other influences in a total situation'. His ideas fit our own everyday experience. If you have attended an announcement or explanation of a change it is not uncommon to find, as the presenter finishes, that people turn to their neighbours in the audience and ask them what they think. Colleagues, family, members of professional groupings and subordinates are some of the people who affect our thinking. These, as well as the official communication, will influence the development of our attitudes to a proposed change and its method of implementation. Of course this is a dynamic process. We are constantly open to these various sources of influence and they will continue to reinforce or modify our views throughout the change process.

Guidelines for effective communication

The list of the types of communication problems that can exist during the management of change is not intended to be complete. However it is felt that they are the most typical and most important. Some of these problems suggest in themselves the way to avoid or overcome their negative effect on communication, for instance overload, or partial or incomplete messages. In addition there are some positive actions that can be taken, when developing a communication strategy.

❏ Purposeful communications

Be clear about the purpose of communicating. Giving information or keeping people up to date is rarely an adequate reason for communicating.

- Why do they need the information?
- What are they going to do with it?

Without answering these questions it is difficult for the communicator to be clear what information or how much information should be presented and hence there is the risk of overload.

Furthermore there is also the risk of lack of clarity. Being aware of why one is receiving information and what one is expected to do with it aids retention and understanding. Without this the recipient has to speculate on its relevance and importance, leading to potential misunderstandings and at worst the start of rumours.

Short clear messages will promote clarity, while complex communications are more likely to be misunderstood, so keep them as simple as possible. Of course short messages may well increase the frequency of communications and be seen by managers as an unnecessary effort, in comparison with less frequent, but more detailed, communications. However it is easier to check understanding in the case of simpler messages. In addition the increasing frequency will help to establish the notion of a communication process, rather than a series of separate presentations or briefings. This is vital to the creation of two way communications.

❏ Communication is a two way process, stimulate and hunt for feedback

Kanter (1992) maintains that:

> too often 'communication' translates into a unilateral directive.

Real communication requires both parties to be actively involved. This involvement can be thought of as covering a spectrum, from one extreme where the recipient is involved in simply feeding back what has been heard and understood, to the other extreme where a complete dialogue takes place with both parties' views being explored, listened to and understood.

The works of Simon (1957) and Schein (1985) discussed earlier indicate that different interpretations of communication are inevitable in organisations. These potential misunderstandings are not in themselves a reflection of poor communicating skill, but rather of the fact that individuals and groups experience organisational life differently, depending on their job, their knowledge, their status, their aspirations and so on. Poor communication stems from ignoring this, from blandly assuming that what is important and relevant to me will be the same for others. This leads to the belief that if I present, for instance, my ideas well and clearly, you will understand. Of course we do not intend to suggest that communications should not be well thought out and presented, but good communications require not only careful thought of what is sent but also checking out what is received.

This is a very simple idea that is taught on many management or supervisory programmes, so why do these mis-communications still happen? We believe this is frequently due to the belief that if people do not understand they will say so, that the responsibility for identifying misunderstanding lies with the recipient. In many situations this works adequately. Particularly in face to face communications where the sender picks up non-verbal signals of confusion. However the importance of the work of Simon and Schein is that neither party may be aware that there are any misunderstandings. In fact in this situation there is understanding, although each party will have a subtly different view of it. The responsibility for checking the effectiveness of the communication must rest with the sender or initiator, the manager and organisation must hunt for and stimulate feedback. Many of Pugh's rules and Kanter's commandments rely on this form of communication. In fact it is one of the advantages of involvement. Not only does it give people an ability to influence their own futures, but it needs and promotes open dialogue and communication.

This type of communication takes time and effort. However many experiments have shown that the extra effort has substantially increased comprehension and retention. In managing change, it can prevent the manager or change agent from making assumptions that later turn out to be incorrect. Nevertheless getting feedback may not be easy and it can be influenced by the problems of hierarchy mentioned earlier and this leads on to their next point.

❏ Use more than one communication structure

It has already been mentioned that people pick up information in a variety of different ways or from a variety of different structures, for instance from the hierarchy, expert groups, status or peer groups and social groups. Typically most formal communications use the first two structures. Some of the problems of communicating within the hierarchical structure have already been mentioned, so it will be important during change to use some of the informal structures (Pugh rule 3) and to create new communicating structures (Kanter's enabling structures). In this area multiple level or cross-functional teams or consultative structures can be useful. Training and educational programmes are also highly effective communicating devices, which provide an opportunity to stimulate feedback.

What is clear from the research is that management should not rely on one or two structures, but should utilise a number of different structures. This does not mean they should ignore the formal methods of communication, but they should not be over-reliant on them. In this way Kanter's ideas about a shared vision and a sense of urgency can be created.

Of course, it will be important for there to be consistency between the messages within the various structures. Pettigrew (1991) in his research on successful UK companies identified coherence and consistency within the organisation and its different functions, as a key factor leading to success. The identification and use of different communication structures is one way to build this consistency within the change process.

❏ Shorten the lines of communications

Try to keep the linkages in the communication as few as possible. The greater the number of people in the chain the greater the chance of distortion. This principle should also be used when designing enabling structures. A common way of short circuiting the formal channels is for the senior management to be more accessible. During its culture change programme, with its emphasis on customer care, senior executives of British Airways were present at all the customer care workshops, explaining the senior management's views and hearing first hand the reactions of staff at lower levels.

Kanter gives examples of senior executives 'walking the halls', going out of their way to see and meet staff at all levels. She stresses that management have found this approach useful, not because it helps them get their message across, but because it gives them access to information and opinions which they would not receive through the normal lines of communication. To quote Jack Welch of General Electric (from Kanter 1992):

> Real communication takes countless hours of eyeball to eyeball, back and forth
> .... It means more listening than talking... It is human beings coming to see and
> accept things through a constant interactive process aimed at consensus.

The importance of consistency and coherence within organisations and their communications has already been stated. Pettigew (1991) has found these qualities present in his successful companies. Another Pettigew finding was that successful organisations managed to link strategic and operational change. It is not uncommon to find that the top of an organisation is planning and implementing some form of change, while the lower levels carry on as though nothing has changed. Indeed many examples of this were found in the operation of the Financial Management Initiative within Government. There can be a number of reasons for this, but the distortions created by the hierarchy are certainly influential. Another stems from the notion that information equals power.

The face to face contact that Kanter discusses avoids these filters or blockages. It allows a better appreciation of strategic goals throughout the organisation, mobilising energy to change, with an identification with the vision. Just as importantly it provides the change indicators with a view of the organisation as seen by the staff who will be involved in the change, allowing this to be taken into account as the change strategy and process is being developed and designed.

About the authors

Mike Dutfield , BSc, FIPM, MIMgt, specialises in training and developing people management skills. After working as a Staff Development Manager in industry and as a Senior Lecturer in Organisation Development, he has been a consultant working in local government, the voluntary sector and a wide range of private sector companies. He is a senior partner in Wessex Organisation Consultants.

Chris Eling, B Tech, has worked in the area of organisation development and change for over 20 years, he has held positions in Staff Management Development in the electronics and leisure industries and for the past 7 years has been a senior partner in Wessex Organisation Consultants. He has experience of working internationally and has consulted in the public , private and voluntary sectors. He is a visiting lecturer at the Civil Service College and a tutor for the Open University Business School.

References and suggested reading

Alexander , L. (1989) Successfully implementing strategic decisions
in Asch and Bowman (eds) *Readings in Strategic Management*
Basingstoke,Macmillan

Argyle,M. (1983) *The Psychology of Interpersonal Behaviour* London, Penguin Books

Beckhard, R. and Harris, R. (1987) *Organisational Transitions* Reading, Addison Wesley

Beer, M. (1988) The critical path for change: Keys to success and failure in six companies
in Kilmann, R. and Covin, T. (eds) *Corporate Transformations* San Francisco, Jossey-Bass

Belgard, W. Fisher, K. and Rayner, S. (1988) Keys to success and failure in six companies
in Kilmann, R and Covin, T (eds) *Corporate Transformations* San Francisco, Jossey-Bass

Burns, J. (1954) The Directions of Activity and Communication in a Departmental
Executive Group *Human Relations* Vol 7

Coch, L. and French, W. (1948) Overcoming Resistance to Change *Human Relations* Vol 1

Festinger, L. (1957) *A Theory of Cognitive Dissonance.* Evanston, Row Petersen

Handy, C. (1982) *Understanding Organisations* London, Penguin Books

Kanter , R. (1983) *The Change Masters* New York, Simon and Schuster

Kanter, R. Stein, B. and Jick, T. (1992) *The Challenge of Organizational Change.*
New York, The Free Press

Kilmann, R. and Covin, T. (eds) (1988) *Corporate Transformations*
San Francisco, Josey Bass

Klappers, J. (1960) *The Effects of Mass Communication* New York, The Free Press

Lewin,K. (1947) Frontiers in group dynamics *Human Relations* Vol 1

Lewin, K. (1948) *Resolving Social Conflicts* New York, Harper

Likert, R. (1961) *New patterns of management* New York, Mcgraw Hill

Mabey, C. (1992) *Implementation* in Human Resource Strategies Course Materials
Milton Keynes, Open University

Nadler, D. and Tushman, M. (1990) Beyond the Charismatic Leader: Leadership and
Organisational Change *California Management Review*, Winter

Peters, T. and Waterman, R. (1982) *In Search of Excellence* New York, Harper Row

Pettigrew, A. and Whipp, R. (1991) *Managing Change for Competitive Success*
Oxford, Blackwell

Pettigrew, A. (1992) *Interview with Grahame Salaman* Milton Keynes, Open University

Pontier , M. (1993) *The rise and fall of IBM* Unpublished case study CITI Limited

Pugh, D. (1978) Understanding and managing organizational change
in Mayon-White (ed) (1986) *Planning and Managing Change*   London, Harper Row

Rayner, S. (1988) Vision, opportunity and tenacity: Three informal processes that influence
formal transformation in Kilmann, R. and Covin, T. (eds) *Corporate Transformations*
San Francisco, Jossey-Bass

Simon, H. (1957) *Models of Man* New York, Wiley

Schein, E. (1985) *Organizational Culture and Leadership* San Francisco, Jossey-Bass

Chapter 7

Managing the individual's resistance to change

Mike Dutfield and Chris Eling

Let me re-emphasise the point that resistance is by itself neither good nor bad. Resistance may be soundly based or not. It is always, however, an important signal calling for further inquiry by management. *Paul Lawrence (1970)*

One of the questions we are most frequently asked in our work is:

how do I get a person to change?

This normally means either getting them to stop doing something, or accepting new ideas and responsibilities, or changing the way they do an existing task.

In the last few years much emphasis has been placed on the management of change to cope with increasing competition, changing customer or client requirements, accelerating technological change and the information revolution. This has produced a whole series of books, some primarily academic, some based on personal experiences. There have been few books, however, on individual change. This is somewhat surprising, not because the books on organization change lack value, on the contrary many are excellent, but because they give only a partial view. In fact the majority of managers are not engaged in bringing about vast changes in organisations. They are more likely to have to concentrate on overcoming a subordinate's resistance to a new idea, improving his or her department's efficiency, introducing a new system or technology, increasing flexibility or developing his or her staff. It is true that many of these changes may be taking place within the context of a larger organisation change, but the focus is departmental or individual.

The manager's role has changed with the need to be more market, quality or customer aware. No longer is the bureaucratic virtue of adherence to rules valued, as the needs for responsiveness and flexibility are prized. The emphasis is not on compliance to procedures, but on development and freedom to act within clearly stated parameters. This means that many of a manager's actions and activities are to do with managing changes.

To give a simple example, say a manager and a supervisor are reviewing the differences between planned and actual performance for last month. In identifying what has happened and the reasons for this, the emphasis is not on apportioning blame for any problems that occurred, but on learning how to tackle similar problems in the future. In this way, by the positive reinforcement of what has worked and by identifying problems and possible solutions, the manager develops and changes the department and the supervisor. If the subordinate feels the manager is concentrating on the problems and on apportioning blame, the supervisor will tend to take few risks, become defensive and resistant to change.

If change is now a normal part of organisational life, not all of it can be resisted. What factors exist which encourage individuals to welcome and accept change?

Long ago, Hertzberg (1958) identified *achievement* as one of the key motivators of managers. Change provides managers with new *challenges* and the possibility for new *achievements*. In turn this can bring new *rewards, status* and *career* opportunities. We have worked in several high technology development environments, where the employees view new challenges as essential. For them the ability to keep abreast of new technologies and their implementation is essential to their career. Without this constant development of their capabilities, they see themselves being out of touch and their career adversely affected, both within their present organization and within the total labour market.

Always look for the positive motivations, which people bring into change situations. If someone is motivated by new achievements, it is much easier to build on this influence than to push to overcome any resistance they may have.

Resistance to change

If the manager's role is largely to do with managing change, then what sorts of resistances is he or she likely to encounter?

❏ Habit

Readers will know from their own experience that habits are hard to break, but the world of work is full of routines and habits. Sales representatives need to prepare their presentations when receiving new products but need to be careful that the new form of presentation does not simply become a habit. Who has met the sales representative who has only one way of presenting the product and who, despite all attempts to tell him or her that the listener is not interested, or has not got time, or has a different problem, still starts at the beginning of the presentation and goes through to the end without thinking?

❑ Primacy

The way that people first cope with a situation may well establish a persistent pattern. Research has shown that teachers, despite their original training and further in-service training, continue to teach much as they were taught. This pattern will often persist despite conflicting information. People can be very creative at producing self-fulfilling prophecies, remembering the instances when the preferred solution worked and conveniently forgetting the occasions when it did not.

❑ Self - interest

People will resist change if they feel that they could lose something of value or increase the chances of receiving something which is not wanted. Typically one of the losses which people fear is loss of status. Another example might be where a manager wants to increase the responsibility of a subordinate. In the manager's eyes this may be seen as a benefit, as extra responsibility which could further the subordinate's career, but to the subordinate it may feel like an increase in the risk of failure. The important point to note is that, where this occurs, people will concentrate on their own self-interests, irrespective of whether this coincides or conflicts with your or the organisation's best interest.

❑ Insecurity

Change will be resisted if a person feels that he or she cannot cope or work in a new way. The response may go as far as feeling the job to be at risk. This can and will happen when the individual rationally understands the need for the change, but emotionally cannot adjust to the new situation. Such subordinates will need support if they are going to cope with change.

❑ Lack of trust

Lack of trust may be particularly important when a manager is new, or relatively new, to a post. People will question the reasons for change and may lack the manager's understanding of the situation. Is the change for the manager's own ends or the organisation's? What commitment does the manager have to the subordinates? Do they believe him or her? In this position the manager will need to do things to demonstrate that he or she can be trusted. The right to trust will be earned by actions, not by words.

❑ Differing perceptions

Subordinates are unlikely to see the world in the way the manager does. For a start the manager may be privy to information and views not available to others, and they will have different responsibilities, which may mean that the same data means something different to them. For instance, in a production packaging department for consumer goods, the volatile nature of the market means that there is a requirement for frequent changes in packaging. The manager may want to bring in more flexible machines and ways of working to meet these changing demands. The supervisors, however may feel the frequent packaging changes are, in part, due to inadequate planning. The introduction of new machines will therefore feel like an acceptance by management of poor planning and that it could not be improved.

Henry Baker, a case study in managing change

This case illustrates the handling of change in a young subordinate. A situation and the subordinate's behaviour are described, two different character studies are given, both consistent with the behaviour and then ideas of how to manage the change are given.

❏ The manager's view

You are the manager of an Accounts Department in a large organisation. You are thinking about Henry Baker, one of your departmental managers. The organisation is changing, with an emphasis on more responsibility being pushed down the line.

Henry, aged 25, qualified as an accountant three years ago. His present job is his first managerial/supervisory position and he was promoted to this position 18 months ago. His department has about 15 clerks working through three supervisors to him. You have thought about his work and these are your conclusions.

Although he runs his department efficiently, his somewhat distant and dictatorial attitude to staff has created a great deal of underlying friction. He has a tendency to retain routine managerial tasks himself, instead of delegating them to his supervisors. For example, he insists that all leave applications must be dealt with by him personally. He frequently by-passes his supervisors, dealing with the staff directly. He personally controls absence and sanctions all overtime.

Through his work he has substantially improved the credibility and reputation of your department. On his own initiative, he re-designed the monthly statements issued to the manufacturing departments on outputs and cost against budgets and he ran seminars for the manufacturing managers on how to interpret and use these statements.

When he took over the department, absenteeism and timekeeping were bad. They have now improved and this has allowed additional tasks to be undertaken for management. Although the amount of work being done by the department has increased, the overtime has been reduced, because of new working methods that Henry has introduced.

His distant and at times arrogant manner has led to several disagreements with the union, which represents his clerks, and on one occasion only your intervention prevented a dispute from occurring.

Your general conclusion is that the increasing quantity and quality of work which his department has produced has exceeded your expectations. However, given the changes which the organisation is going to introduce, he must do something about his manner and way of handling people, especially where the union is involved. He must also start to delegate appropriate work to his supervisors.

Henry Baker Type 1

Henry is a very ambitious man. He has great confidence in his ability, too much in fact and he has justifiably been accused at times of being arrogant. However there is no doubting his potential or his ability. Because of his drive he wants to introduce new ideas and seek improvements, frequently at a faster rate than his staff or supervisors can cope with. Coupled with this he hates mistakes and has, therefore, tended not to delegate. In this way he ensures that the job is done correctly and quickly. He feels that the quantity and quality of work in his whole department reflects on him. Therefore any way that gets the best results will get him the recognition that will lead to promotion.

Henry Baker Type 2

Technically, Henry is a first class accountant and is always interested in keeping abreast of new developments in his field. He is a perfectionist and needs to feel totally certain before reaching an opinion. He is a shy man, who gives the impression that he would rather deal with his figures than with people. Figures are predictable and can be manipulated; people are unpredictable and this unnerves him. He is also very conscious that this is his first managerial position and that he is on trial. He feels that the quantity and quality of the work of his whole department reflects directly on him. He is aware of his perfectionism and his desire to be seen to be doing a good job. At times he has insisted on the work being done his way, and he feels his staff have seen this as being pedantic. This has reinforced his uncertainty about what his staff feel and how they will react, and he knows that he has coped with this by doing jobs himself rather than delegating as he should. It also avoids the situation where his subordinates might do the work in ways and at a standard that he would not accept, hence creating conflict. He dislikes conflict, always dealing with it by the rational approach, 'the figures show .....', but this does not seem to work too well with his staff. So this shy, uncertain man is seen by his staff as distant and unfeeling, and, as he is always technically correct, at times arrogant.

❑ How to get Henry to change

Let us assume first that in the coming year you want Henry to delegate the routine activities which he is doing to his supervisors. Taking Henry No 1 to start with, what are likely to be his possible resistances to change? Certainly self-interest will feature in that by doing the work himself he ensures effectiveness and therefore probably thinks it would in the end satisfy his career aspirations. Primacy may also be relevant. It works, it is no great effort, why change? Is there anything in the situation which is liable to make him change? Certainly his ambition and needs for high achievement and recognition could be used. If Henry could see a connection between satisfying his self-interest (ambition) and delegation, getting him to change should not be difficult. In other words, if Henry recognises that developing the skills of delegation would be a necessary requirement for higher level jobs, he will delegate. This would need to be monitored and reinforced as he may change quickly, which would probably confuse his staff. It is also possible that under pressure and in crises he would revert to doing it himself.

This approach is unlikely to work with Henry 2, in fact it may make him feel even more insecure. His major resistor would be insecurity. He already knows he should be delegating, but he is not sure how to, or whether he will cope. You will probably have to 'hold his hand'. Take a particular issue, such as overtime, work out with him how it should be controlled in future, how he should control his supervisor in this area and so on. The important point is that you would need to support him all through his change, taking it step by step, as this is the way Henry 2 will learn. He will not take risks knowingly, he will only go forward, when he is sure and feels safe to continue.

Now take a second area of change, Henry's relationship with the union, particularly the incident when the manager had to intervene to prevent a dispute. Assume that both Henrys were upset by your intervention. Henry 1 feels that you over-reacted and should have called the union's bluff. They would have backed off and there would not have been a dispute. Henry 2 feels that the disagreement was over an important matter of principle and that your intervention led to unsatisfactory compromise and your ideas will have to be implemented in the end.

In this situation Henry 1's resistance may again stem from self-interest or loss of status, but possibly from lack of trust. He will want to be clear about what his responsibilities are, so that a similar situation, of you having to intervene, does not occur again. Henry 2, on the other hand, sees the world differently and the resistance may come from differing perceptions. You will need to explore the different views you hold, so that he understands why you had to intervene.

Strategies for overcoming resistance

Given the resistances that managers introducing change are likely to encounter, what can be done to overcome them? What factors exist in the situation that may be used as a positive stimulus to change? There tends to be an appropriate strategy to overcome each of the different resistances to change.

❏ Negotiate

When the resistance stems from self interest the best approach is to negotiate. Of course you are not negotiating about whether the change will happen. The emphasis will be on negotiating or identifying possible advantages or incentives in the new situation, which will compensate for the perceived losses involved in the change.

❏ Educate

Misunderstandings, caused by habits or existing knowledge and practices or a lack of trust, can generate a range of worries and concerns about what things will be like after the changes. If this is the case the best strategy is to educate, developing an understanding of the reasons for the change and its benefits.

❏ Force and support

When people feel insecure or have worries about whether they will be able to cope, then force and support is an appropriate strategy. This seeks to break the chain: 'I can't cope - I must be inadequate and I am afraid, change must be resisted'. It works on the assumption that the imagined fears of the change are in fact greater than the actuality. The change is therefore implemented, the new behaviours supported and reinforced, generating feelings of 'this is not as bad as I imagined,' leading to increased confidence. This approach can also be used when the resistance stems from primacy or habit, as it breaks the established patterns of behaviour. However as people become to feel more secure or the habits are broken, it is possible for some of the other sorts of resistances to emerge.

❏ Participate

When differing perceptions exist, participation can involve the resistors and thereby help to overcome the problems of change. Participation not only helps to overcome resistance but, because it introduces different people into the change process, with differing perceptions, information and ideas, better solutions can be developed with a corresponding increase in commitment to them. Many people may be able to remember an instance when, given a new product to make or a new way of working, they encountered a problem which they could easily have predicted if only they had been asked.

Strategy style and role

Honey and Robinson in their work maintain that it is vital to choose an appropriate style for each change strategy. We feel that it is more than style that must be appropriate. The difference in the relationship, for instance, between a manager 'negotiating' with a subordinate and a manager 'educating' a member of his or her staff, during a change process is more than style. It also concerns the freedom and power of the individuals concerned, who has control and over what, who initiates and finishes the exchange, and so on. In other words the relationships are fundamentally different. However, Honey and Robinson's ideas are important and useful. They are summarised on Figure 7.1 (Robinson 1988).

Let us consider the case of Henry Baker, discussed earlier in this chapter, and apply the ideas about strategy and roles.

With Henry 1 his resistance to delegating was self-interest. Negotiation would appear to be the correct strategy. This would require a collaborative role or style to get Henry to recognise that it is a skill he needs to develop to further his career. It would be followed by further collaboration to identify new areas of work for Henry, which would mean he would have to delegate, in order to create the time to undertake new work.

The resistance of Henry 2 was insecurity and a force and support strategy would be appropriate. This would require a directive role to inform him that he will delegate in future, followed by a supportive role to tell him how to delegate and to help him work out how he is going to manage.

Constantly reinforce change

People do not change overnight or immediately. Change in organisations or people is not like turning on a light switch. It is not only that people change gradually, but that new ideas or ways of working have to be integrated with the old ways. Not everything is changed or substituted. In a change process it is as important to identify and articulate what is not changing as well as what is. In our experience this frequently does not happen and resistance is reinforced by man-

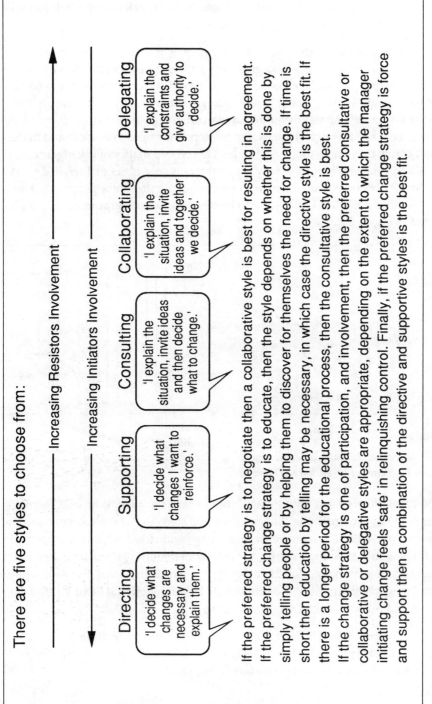

Figure 7.1. Styles for change strategies.

agers announcing a change and creating the feeling that everything is new and strange. In consequence, the change is seen to be threatening the relevance of the skills which people already possess.

Individuals need new ideas and new ways of working to be constantly reinforced to help them change and gradually adjust to new circumstances. In our experience, people can be classified into two basic types with regard to acceptance of change. There are people who change incrementally, and there are those who make an initial breakthrough and then often regress. We know people who have to be taken through changes step by step. They need to be clear and understand before they go on to the next stage. This is not a matter of intelligence, as is shown in Chapter 5, but the way they integrate new ideas or knowledge. We also know of people who return from a training course as 'new people', but who have forgotten it within two weeks! The two types are diagrammatically represented in Figure 7.2.

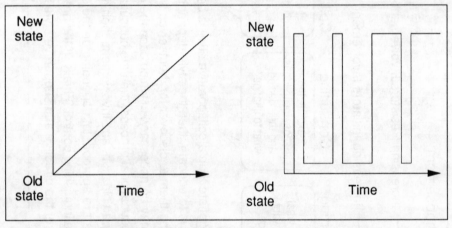

Figure 7.2. Types of acceptance of change.

Both types clearly need reinforcing if the change is to stick. With one, the manager may have to break the change down into steps that the person can assimilate and cope with. The manager would then provide feedback on progress made and this would give the security to take another step forward. This approach would seem patronising for the other type, who would need to be presented with the whole picture but then constantly be reminded that he or she had forgotten and reverted to old ways of working.

This chapter is edited from a chapter entitled 'Managing Change' in *The Communicating Manager,* Element Books 1990 by Michael Dutfield and Chris Eling and is reproduced by kind permission of the publishers.

References and suggested reading

Beer, M. (1979) *Organization Change and Development, A Systems View*
Santa Monica, Goodyear

Dalton, G. Lawrence, P. and Greiner , L.(1970) *Organizational Change and Development*
Homewood, Irwin-Dorsey

Dutfield, M. and Eling, C. (1990) *The Communicating Manager*
Shaftesbury, Element Books

Herzberg, F. Mausner, B. and Synderman, B. (1958) *The Motivation to Work.*
New York, Wiley

Kotter, P. and Schlesinger, L. (1979) Choosing Strategies For Change
in *Harvard Business Review* (March/April)

Robinson, G. (1988) Working Paper (Unpublished Course Notes)

Watson, G. (1966) Resistance to Change in Bennis, Benne and Chin (eds) (1974) *The Planning of Change* New York, Holt, Rinehart and Winston

Chapter 8

Helping individuals cope with change

Mike Dutfield and Chris Eling

The key to managing change is to create enough psychological safety to permit group members to bear the anxieties that come with re-examining and changing parts of their culture. *Schein (1985)*

There are many books designed to help managers think through the processes of organisational change, but the reality is, as we discussed in the last chapter, that most managers are concerned with helping individuals to change. In that chapter we looked at why people resist change and ways to overcome and manage their resistance. However this is not the end of the story. When the resistance has been managed it does not mean that individuals find adapting to the new situation easy. In fact people who welcome change may still find it difficult to adapt and cope with new working relationships, methods and tasks. This chapter considers these issues and offers a practical model of helping people cope with change.

Managers often have changes imposed upon them by new Government policies, by major shifts in resource allocation, by the introduction of another computer system, or by the latest fashion in management thinking. For those involved in the decisions to introduce these changes, the process may be intellectually challenging, but for those who have to implement them the key problem is how to persuade and help staff to work differently.

Reasons why people have difficulties coping with change

For a sense of well being, competence and identity, people need to perceive a balance between themselves and their 'psychological environments.' This sense of self will be put out of balance by the processes of change and, although this will affect people in different ways, certain key features of the psychological environment are particularly significant. An imbalance which creates uncertainty, a perception of loss or feelings of insecurity can make coping with the change difficult and the manager may need to take supportive actions with the individual affected in this way.

These features are reviewed here because, when using the model which follows, they can enable the manager to understand the attitudes and behaviour of staff and take appropriate action. The features of the psychological environment are:

- the use of skills
- loss of externally generated goals
- opportunities for personal control
- alteration to the variety of work
- loss of environmental clarity
- change of social contacts
- change in social position.

The list is illustrative rather than comprehensive, but it does make clear that these needs will vary in importance for different members of staff. It is these psychological characteristics which mean that some individuals will welcome changes, while others take an opposite view. For example, as shown in Chapter 11, empowerment of staff will enhance one person's feeling of independence, and at the same time provide another with insecurity because there is less direction and support provided by the externally imposed controls.

❏ Opportunities for the use of skills may be changed

A satisfaction in work comes from the familiar use of skills, enabling people to cope with both routine and new situations. Skills enable people to complete tasks, to obtain a sense of doing something useful and to be valued. Changes can mean that people feel undervalued and are only being asked to do things which are well within their routine capacity. The fear is that they will not be able to use their potential in the new situation, or that some other person will prove to be far more capable. The older someone gets, the more difficult it is to learn new skills and the greater may become this fear.

❏ Changes in externally generated goals

In formal organisations a person's role has with it certain requirements, obligations, or routine which have to be followed. For example, departments work on annual planning and budgeting cycles which often determine a significant pattern to the work of the staff. Meeting these requirements provides goals and certainty for people. We have often found managers who go on holding meetings long after the need for them has disappeared. Figures are still collected and returned to some central office even when they are no longer required. The purpose and objectives of these tasks are understood, so they contribute to security in a changing world.

The change from 'input' to 'outcome' measures in the public sector, as advocated in the new public management, means that familiar goals have been replaced. The increased emphasis on target setting and results can lead to uncertainties, lack of familiarity and consequent insecurity.

The need to have intrinsic goals is fundamental to human behaviour, and these are often provided by extrinsic goal setting systems. If the extrinsic goals change or are too difficult or complex, some people's reaction is to create goals which may or may not be consistent with the organisation's needs.

❑ Opportunities for personal control

In the world of work the opportunities for setting or deciding on objectives, scheduling tasks, determining methods, and evaluating outcomes vary considerably. Change will affect the opportunities for control over work, sometimes because, as the role changes, it will mean that others will take a more active part in these decisions, sometimes because the familiar cause-effect relationship will become less clear. For example, greater centralisation can mean that people have less ability to determine their own priorities. A change in policy or procedure may mean that it is some months before we are able to see what the results of our actions will be. Some staff will search for early opportunities to reassert personal control, while others will become anxious by the loss of security of knowing where they are, what to do and the precise boundaries of their responsibilities.

❑ Alteration of the variety provided by work

It is generally true that the more senior a job the more opportunities there are for variety in tasks and locations. Often the more junior jobs have very little variety, and this then has to be provided through social contacts, or through interests outside of work. A person undertaking a routine job will often find excuses for going out of their office to visit others when it would, in one sense, be more efficient to use the telephone. The visit may provide a very important element of variety. The introduction of personal computers and electronic mail systems has often reduced the need to move away from desks to exchange information. Changes which remove the variety of tasks may well be resisted.

❑ Change in environmental clarity

Sometimes people will feel that since certain changes were brought in they 'cannot see clearly' where they are going or what is expected of them. This can be brought about by a number of things. The change may mean that normal feedback is not available. It may take time for the changes to take effect, and for the consequences of the new ways of working to become clear. Changes will often mean that other people and systems will be working in different ways so that it is not possible to predict the effect of our own actions. Additionally it may not be clear what other people expect of our new role, what the acceptable standards are, and how judgements will be made about good or poor performance.

For staff with high needs for dependence this aspect of change will be threatening and they will feel lost. Typically these staff blame management for not providing the required direction.

❏ Opportunities for social contacts

One of the key motivators for people joining and remaining in organisations is the complex need for contact with other people. Most have a basic need to avoid loneliness, and to enjoy friendships, particularly those with more extroverted personalities as shown in Chapter 5. People spend more of their waking hours in work than anywhere else and it is often the place where social contacts are made.

Apart from this, social contacts provide support and help in the direct performance of work, in problem solving, and, less tangibly, emotional support when life both in work and outside becomes difficult. Many tasks in work can only be achieved through networks and groups of people, and these formal and informal structures are made effective through developed social relationships.

Festinger (1954) clarified for us that we are motivated to compare our performance and opinions with those of other people. This, of course, is part of the socialisation process that goes on in work, and can provide the continuous objective feedback that motivates some people. Sales people may need weekly or even daily comparison with others to keep up their high level of work. Contact with like minded people on courses often provides comparative information about work methods and standards.

Changes which are seen as depriving people of significant social contacts, especially if they have high needs for social support or lack contacts with other environments, can be very destructive and need to be managed with great care.

❏ Changes in social position

In the past public servants have been held in relatively high social esteem. The grading system has provided evidence of abilities and a ready comparison of status between departments and functions. Simply being a civil servant or local authority official carries esteem in the wider community. Title and role can give us a social position both within and outside of work. Market Testing, contracting out and other forms of 'privatisation,' mean that the 'valued social positions' are changing and in many cases being threatened. The loss of perceived social esteem can be demotivating and a key factor in personal resistance to change.

❑ Environmental changes can be welcomed

Generally the problems to be managed are created by the perceived loss from these environmental features. It is clear, however, that the changes can equally present perceived opportunities and then the changes will be welcomed. The change can mean an increase in the variety of tasks. Changes in social structures and processes of organisation may present opportunities for new social contacts.

People with high needs for independence and high self-esteem may see the breakdown of environmental clarity as presenting wonderful opportunities to develop a role, to set standards or negotiate new norms of behaviour. On the other hand, some people have less need for social esteem and are less concerned with perceived loss, in which case a new organisation may provide opportunities for different positions from which to gain social esteem.

Helping people cope with change

Just as the manager needs to understand the motivations of staff to find ways of improving performance, so it is necessary to understand these motivations to realise how changes are likely to affect, or are actually affecting, individual members of staff. There is little point in assuming that a change is exciting and stimulating if the staff see it as taking away the certainty of externally generated goals which have provided security. If individual members of staff are affected in ways which they see as threatening, they may need supportive counselling to understand the change and to find methods of coping with the change.

It will usually be clear when staff are not adapting to the new methods or roles. Performance will decline, people will behave in ways that are clearly resisting the changes, absence from work may increase, or there may be signs of disinterest and lack of commitment. Sometimes the worrying reactions are the opposite. Concern may arise because members of staff spend over-long hours at work, they may agree too readily, when previously they were willing to question, or they are pressing for answers when it is clear there is still uncertainty. These are all relative behaviour changes and may only be noticeable in the context of an on-going relationship, but for the experienced manager they will be the signals for help.

After many years working with and training managers we developed a model to enable managers to analyse, plan and work effectively with people in many situations. Here we apply that model to helping individuals adapt to changes. We usually refer to this as 'The Communicating Manager' model, (Dutfield and Eling, 1990). In much of the literature this helping process is labelled as 'counselling,' and there are certainly circumstances which demand a counselling approach, but there are others where the appropriate roles could be:

- information giving
- advising - coaching and mentoring
- straightforward instruction, to provide clarity and direction.

❑ The components of the communicating manager model

Adapting the model to helping individuals to cope with changes, the manager will need to do the following when communicating with individuals:

- clarify the purpose of the communications and identify the specific outcome to be achieved from particular meetings which make up the helping process
- identify and act in the appropriate role to create the relationship which will contribute to achieving the desired outcome
- recognise and manage the influences and pressures, particularly the perceived psychological effects of the changes, which are brought into the communication events
- understand how the values, attitudes, needs and expectations of both the manager and the person being helped will influence their communications
- use the appropriate skills to achieve the desired outcome of the meeting and contribute to the purpose of helping the person adapt to the change.

The model is shown graphically in Figure 8.1.

Each of the above elements is now considered in turn in more detail.

❑ Clarifying the purpose and desired outcome of the communication

During the process of managing a change programme the manager may be attempting to help all staff come to terms with their new roles, work with new systems, or provide a different service, so that the general purpose of many encounters or meetings with the staff will be helping them to cope with the changes. As we noted at the beginning of this chapter, each person will be affected by the changes in different ways, and the speed with which they are able to adapt will vary. It is therefore

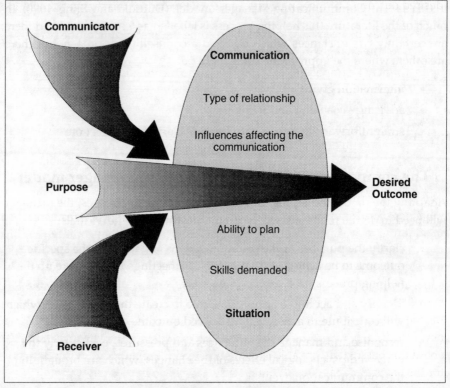

Figure 8.1. An integrated model of effective communication.

important that the manager is clear what specific outcomes he or she is trying to achieve from a particular meeting, and how that outcome will contribute to the overall, and probably longer term purpose of managing the change effectively.

This may be clarified by an example. Let us assume that the manager is responsible for implementing a change in reporting structure which has involved the removal of a layer of supervision. For some members of staff this has provided an opportunity for a little more autonomy. Responsibility for setting objectives and monitoring effectiveness will be given to staff because there will not be time for managers to monitor the work of all staff in detail, and this 'empowerment' is welcomed by some, even though the change may need some initial support. However, for some members of staff this will mean that there is no clear direction from management, that standards may slip because there will be less management monitoring of work, and there will be more work so that some important things may not get done.

In helping an individual person in this second category the general purpose of communications will be to help them cope with the changes. However, the specific desired outcomes from particular meetings will be very different from the desired outcomes of meetings with those who welcome the changes:

- it may be necessary to give them some understanding of the reasons for the changes
- it may be important that they leave the meeting knowing that their manager understands their concerns, and will provide support while they adjust to the new role
- it may be important for them to know that they will be provided with training in objective setting and project management so that they are able to monitor the work of their section.

The manager must be clear on what will constitute an appropriate outcome, given the member of staff's attitude to the change, and the stage already reached in adapting to the change. He or she must also recognise that communications must progress in a logical sequence. It may, for example, be necessary for the member of staff to express their fears and concerns about the changes, and gain some acceptance of them, and some reassurance that they will be given help, before they are able to listen to the logical explanations for the change and plan the required training into their schedules. If their fear is that they will not, in the new role, be able to use their well established skills, they may need reassurance about this before they are able to contemplate gaining new skills. The difficulty for the change manager is often that they have been part of the planning of the change, or they see the change as exciting, and will go straight to the action, in this case, perhaps, planning the training courses, before the member of staff has jumped what for him or her may be the first hurdle. Determining the sensible outcome for communications with staff during change will often be the most important decision in helping individuals.

❑ Being in the right role, creating the right relationship

We first approached this chapter thinking that it would be appropriate to help staff through the changes by being in a counselling role, and it is clear that this is sometimes right. The appropriate role is determined by the outcome the manager is trying to achieve with the particular member of staff. If the person is suffering from feelings of loss of position and this is affecting their approach to the changes, then a counselling role may be appropriate. If the concern is more related to changes in environmental clarity, then the role of instructor, or informer, about how the new systems will work, or how other people will be affecting them will be appropriate.

If changes have to be implemented quickly it may be necessary to be the boss and instruct staff to change, providing the support through counselling, coaching, or facilitation at a later stage. The important judgement is that the appropriate role is adopted and the relationship built which is consistent with the outcome that the manager is trying to achieve with the member of staff.

❏ Recognising and managing the pressures and influences brought into the communication events

Fortunately managers are usually involved with staff that they know well when helping them to cope with changes so that it is often possible to recognise the way that the change will create different pressures or have different influences on individuals. It will often be clear that one member of staff has a high need for personal control and if the change has altered their ability, for example, to determine their own priorities, or schedule their own tasks, then helping that person to recognise the areas of the job which have not changed may be the most helpful thing to do. If that person feels that all the usual controls are disappearing, stressing aspects which will remain unchanged may be essential to reassure them so that they are able to absorb the information about the changes. Another member of staff with high needs for competence recognition, may find it easier to accept the same changes if it is explained to them in terms of the opportunity to use particular skills. For yet another member of staff, the loss of controls which so worry the one can sell the changes to the person with a high need for independence.

Often the pressures or influences are more practical concerns which people bring to work. Some may be influenced by the effect that the change will have on their professional standards or the quality of their work. Some may be influenced by the opportunity, or lack of it, to demonstrate their competences and the way that this will affect their careers. Others may need help in selling or translating the changes for the staff who report to them, while some may need to know that they are not being affected unfairly in comparison to fellow members of staff. This could be particularly important in future as appraisal systems are more closely linked with performance pay and staff will be concerned at how a slowing down of performance due to the change might affect this. The effective manager of change will map out the pressures and influences that are significant for individual staff, consider how the change will affect them, and adopt a strategy that uses the pressures positively or supports the staff when they are experiencing the pressures as a particular burden.

It is also important that the manager recognises the pressures and influences that are affecting them as a result of the changes. It is not unusual for managers to be affected by change in the same way as any other member of staff. This is particularly so in some of the current initiatives being imposed upon departments. Environmental clarity may be lost, opportunities for control may alter and the manager may feel just as uncertain as his or her staff. Fashionable participation, without considering the effect, may mean that these pressures are passed to the staff and that uncertainty is increased. The fact that the changes provide challenges or variety for the manager may mean that he or she is blocked from recognising the difficulties being experienced by their staff. It is important to recognise the effect of the pressures and influences on the manager and to consider whether they are helping or hindering the management of change process. Figures 8.2 and 8.3 highlight some of these influences and pressures.

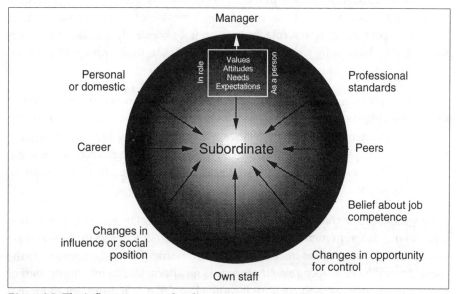

Figure 8.2. The influences on a subordinate.

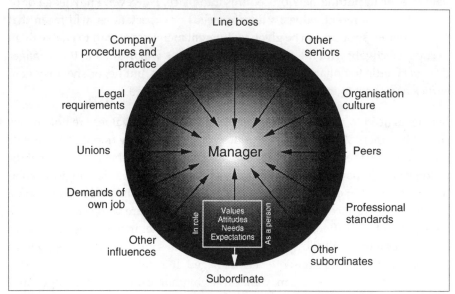

Figure 8.3. The influences on a manager.

115

❏ Values, attitudes, needs and expectations

Each of us brings to the world of work our unique blend of values, attitudes, needs and expectations. They will influence the relationships that we make in that compatibility and complementarity will often be the basis of friendships, or at least rewarding social relationships in work. On the other hand, we may share, or not, values and attitudes about roles, particularly the manager-managed roles. Consequently, we may find that our manager meets our expectations as a boss and we respect them in that role, but we do not necessarily like them as a person. We may have staff who do not have attitudes to their work which we respect, but we quite like them as people.

This tension between role and person is significant in many work relationships, and is often highlighted during periods of change. It is the attitudes to work, the needs which are met in work, the values and expectations which are brought to work which are disturbed by change. The effect of this disturbance can be negative or positive as outlined at the beginning of this chapter, but recognition of this is important.

The experienced manager will often recognise that the same change can be discussed with different members of staff in quite different ways so that it is acceptable to their value systems or chimes with their particular needs. Sometimes the manager will have to recognise that there is no alternative to informing staff of the required changes, and making it quite clear what is required of them in a new role, or in putting new procedures into place. However, knowledge of or sensitivity to different values, attitudes, needs or expectations, will mean that quite different support can be given to different members of staff to enable them to cope effectively with the change. Sometimes this will mean that the manager does very little to enhance the personal relationships, but he, or she, may gain sufficient respect to enable the change to be implemented.

Managers need to recognise, for example, that their own values are not always shared by others. A manager who values participation may find that some staff will appreciate the opportunity to share decisions whilst others see this as abdication or weak management. Another manager who values clear logical explanation as a way of explaining the need for changes may be perceived by some staff as cold and unconcerned with the difficulties that are being created. These value or attitude differences, if recognised, can sometimes be overcome with approaches which will allow for the differences, but sometimes they simply have to be accepted, and the consequences managed. It is important therefore to recognise that these differences may affect the communication of the changes, and intended messages will not always be heard by staff.

❏ Planning communications

When the manager is working with an individual member of staff to help them with aspects of change, it is often helpful to consider which aspects of the process should be planned and controlled by the manager.

Earlier in this chapter we stressed the importance of being clear about the outcome of the meeting or communication that the manager is having. Some parts of the change process enable the manager to be very certain about the outcome they want from a meeting. For example, if the desired outcome is that the member of staff knows that they will be losing two of their staff as a result of a budget cut, the outcome is quite clear, and the manager should be able to plan what he or she is going to say so that there is no confusion in the message. This is an interesting example because we have often found that when managers have to make what they perceive as an unwelcome announcement they are often very unclear, and in this case could open up a discussion about the alternatives when the decision has already been made.

If the changes mean that the manager needs to elicit some information from staff or a colleague before certain decisions can be made, it is important that the topics and questions are planned before the meeting. This may simply be good management since lack of preparation will mean time is not used effectively, but it may also enable the manager to plan the questions so that they elicit the information appropriately from that particular person.

The employment legislation which is significant in the personnel aspects of management may also influence the degree of planning which is required. If jobs are being changed it is possible that the manager can be seen as contributing to such things as constructive dismissal. Given the effects which changes can have on people, it is possible that managerial actions will be interpreted as victimisation, or some personal attack. If you know that this is a possibility you need to plan the discussion with great care.

On the other hand, if you want to obtain the collaboration of a member of staff, or you need their expertise to help you bring about the change, you may need to plan very little of the meeting. If a member of staff has come to you asking for help with a difficulty, you will have to let them have control of the discussion, at least in the early stages. The very nature of counselling or coaching through change means that the member of staff will need to take control and develop solutions which they can implement. Planning and controlling by the manager may mean that the solutions are not owned and consequently not implemented.

Helping a member of staff through a change will sometimes mean controlling and planning the structure of the meeting, even when it is not possible to control the content of the discussion. For example, the manager may clearly specify the purpose of the meeting, set an agenda of topics to be discussed, and clarify the outcome to be achieved. This will enable the manager to exclude discussion which is not helpful, and control the sequence of the discussion. The plan will often provide certainty and control for both the manager and the member of staff which may be very helpful as part of the change process. Figure 8.4 provides a checklist to assist you in planning the interview.

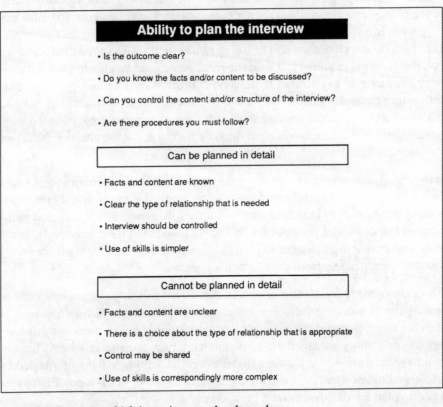

Figure 8.4. Extent to which interviews can be planned.

❏ Using skills appropriately

In our book, *The Communicating Manager*, we have discussed in detail the skills which managers use in inter-personal situations, and in this context it is important to recognise that the manager has at his or her disposal three basic sets of skill:

- the skills of eliciting information
- the skills of presenting information
- the skills of managing the emotional content.

All of these are relevant in the management of change. The active skill of eliciting and presenting information includes the skills used to check and ensure that understanding and meaning have been communicated. We call these feedback skills, and they are particularly important in working with staff to help them through changes. We have already identified many reasons why communications can be misunderstood, so these skills are vital.

Managing people through changes inevitably means feelings and emotions on the part of the manager and staff will affect understanding. The skilled manager will set an appropriate emotional climate, recognise that feelings will affect the situation and work to ensure that they do not prevent the achievement of the desired changes. Figure 8.5 provides a checklist of skills.

---

1. **Preparation**

   Mastering the information

   Being clear about the purpose of the meeting

   Planning the practical arrangements and the modes of communication (oral, written, visual)

---

2. **Giving information**

   Presenting the information in a sequenced and organised way

   Starting from where people are, what they already know

   Distinguishing between facts and opinions

   Distinguishing what is negotiable, what is not

   Repeating, summarising

---

3. **Eliciting responses**

   Checking understanding

   Choosing appropriate questions: open, closed, specific

   Listening, showing you are listening, playing back

   Distinguishing fact from opinion in what people say

---

4. **Managing the emotional content**

   Accepting and acknowledging feelings expressed

   Inviting expression of feeling , if suppressed

   Managing expression of own feelings

   Undertaking action or fact finding which is practicable

Figure 8.5. Checklist of skills.

At the end of the day, recognising the possible effects of change, who will see the change positively and who negatively, who will respond best to different approaches to communication, relies on the skills of the manager. The manager is more likely to use these skills effectively if he or she actively thinks through and plans the process thoroughly and sensitively.

References and suggested reading

Dutfield, M and Eling, C. (1990) *The Communicating Manager* Shaftesbury, Element Books

Festinger, L. (1954) A Theory of Social Comparison Processes *Human Relations* Vol 7

Greiner, L. and Schein, V. (1988) *Power and Organisation Development* Reading, Mass. Addison-Wesley

Schein, E. (1985) *Organisational Culture and Leadership* San Francisco, Jossey-Bass

Chapter 9

Stress management and the management of change

Tony Manning

Do you think you can take over the universe and improve it?
I do not believe it can be done.
The universe is sacred.
You cannot improve it.
If you try and change it, you will ruin it.
If you try to hold it, you will lose it.

So sometimes things are ahead and sometimes they are behind;
sometimes breathing is hard, sometimes it comes easily;
sometimes there is strength and sometimes weakness;
sometimes one is up and sometimes down.
Therefore the sage avoids extremes, excesses and complacency.
Lao Tsu, 6th century BC.

It is clear that organisational changes can have adverse consequences for the individuals within organisations and the organisations themselves. Individuals may experience a variety of problems with physical and mental health and illness, while organisations may experience an equally wide assortment of problems from poor performance to high levels of absenteeism and labour turnover.

It is, however, equally clear that the consequences of organisational change, for both individuals and the whole organisation, are not necessarily adverse. Individuals may remain healthy and organisations may prosper. What is important is the way in which individuals and organisations face up to and manage the changes.

This chapter is aimed at the change agent. It is concerned with the management of stress during periods of organisational change. A change agent may be defined as anyone responsible for managing and implementing change. Change agents may be managers or consultants, both internal and external, who have such responsibilities. In the process of managing change, they have to deal with stress in themselves as well as those they are managing.

The basic assumption behind this chapter is that in order to manage stress we need to understand it. We need to understand what it is and what it does to us, where it comes from and what affects it, and what to do about it.

What stress is

Stress and strain are engineering notions that have been applied to people. An individual may be said to experience stress when he or she perceives himself or herself to be under pressure. Similarly, an individual may be said to experience strain when he or she perceives that pressure to be unpleasant and uncontrollable. Perception is the key: we are not concerned with 'objective' pressures and their consequences but with people's perceptions of their situations.

❏ The stress responses

The body's responses to stress and strain can be usefully looked at as a complex two-stage process consisting of the primary and secondary stress responses (Livingston Booth, 1985).

The primary stress response

The primary stress response, or 'fight or flight' response, is an involuntary, all-or-nothing response designed to help us to deal with extreme threat or danger from our environment. The individual is prepared for immediate mental and physical action as a result of a cluster of bodily changes. These changes include such things as raised heartbeat, increased respiration to oxygenate the blood, the release of sugar into the blood by the liver, and the shift of blood from the digestive system to the muscles and brain.

This is a life-saving mechanism and is, therefore, fundamentally good. It may, however, eventually contribute to some health problems, if the response is often triggered without the individual actually engaging in some physical activity. This would be the case, for example, where an individual driving a car were involved in a 'near accident'. The body is prepared for 'fight or flight' but the individual remains inactive.

The secondary stress responses

The secondary stress responses are a complex pattern of nerve and chemical reactions initiated by the brain in response to what it senses we need. They involve the 'thinking' and 'feeling' parts of the brain as well as biochemical processes. Once again, the issue of perception is crucial. It is clear that the body's response varies according to whether our basic orientation to the person, problem or situation is positive or negative (Martin, 1987). The body responds one way when we 'want to' do something and another when we perceive that we 'have to' do something.

When we *'want to'* do something, the body calls into play the reticular system and releases adrenaline into the blood. This leads to an aroused state, in which we have energy and feel good. The effect is both pleasurable and motivating. It is a good form of stress, providing we do not keep up the pressure to the exclusion of our physical health. It helps us to deal with short term situations, for example, making rapid decisions, acting in emergencies and working to tight deadlines. It is a transient phase which is finished as soon as the deadline or activity is over. The basic signs that we are in this state are a general speeding up of activity, including walking, talking and eating faster, feeling under pressure of time and feeling driven.

In contrast, when we feel that we 'have to' do something, then we experience a continuous set of stress triggers. In these circumstances the body needs more energy and adrenaline is not enough. The body therefore calls on more powerful chemicals, called cortico steroids, which provide immediate high energy by breaking down fats and sugars into more usable forms.

In this state the fats, sugars and chemicals circulate in the blood unless they are burnt off during physical activity. However, if we are not sufficiently active, we may experience *adverse long-term health effects* as a result of:

- fats attaching to and damaging blood vessels
- fats, sugars and chemicals silting up the body and inhibiting normal, healthy functioning
- the effects of biochemicals, especially cortico steroids; these shut down bodily activities directed towards growth, reproduction and resistance to infection, in favour of immediate high energy provision; this makes the individual more susceptible to infection and illness.

The *final stage* of this process is the draining of energy reserves and increased susceptibility to illness and infection. This is a dangerous stage. It is also a stage that is frequently more easily recognised by others than by the individuals concerned. There are, however, warning signs that we can look for both in ourselves and in others. These are summarised below.

Recognising the warning signs in ourselves and others

It is important for change agents to be alert to the signs of excessive levels of strain in themselves and the people they are dealing with. Research into this area (e.g. Murrell, 1978) provides clear indications of the sorts of warning signs that are especially noteworthy.

❏ Recognising the warning signs in ourselves

We can recognise that we have been in the final stage too long by an increase in physical and mental health symptoms. The main signs to look for in ourselves are summarised below.

Physical health symptoms.

There is a variety of possible physical health symptoms associated with excess strain, including:

- recurrent headaches, migraines, etc.
- ringing in the ears, frequent head noises, etc.
- palpitations in the chest, chest pains, etc.
- heartburn, stomach cramps, diarrhoea, etc.
- trembling, twitching, leg cramps or pains
- skin rashes, dermatitis, eruptions, etc.
- getting any illness that's around
- disturbances of menstrual patterns in women.

Mental health symptoms

There is also a variety of possible mental health symptoms indicative of excess strain. These can be grouped under two broad headings, namely, impaired intellect and emotional disturbance. The signs of impaired intellect include:

- frequent thick cotton wool head
- being confused, unable to concentrate
- loss of memory
- difficulty in dismissing problems from mind
- reduced problem-solving, decision-making ability.

The signs of emotional disturbance, embracing both anxiety and depression states, include:

- feeling edgy, jittery, worried, tense, etc.
- uncontrollable emotional displays e.g. crying
- difficulties sleeping, nightmares, waking tired, etc.
- feeling tired, lethargic, low, dulled, etc.
- feeling of boredom, monotony, frustration, etc.
- being self-critical, poor self-evaluation, etc.

- joy, laughter and pleasure dried up
- feeling of anger, irritation, etc.
- reduced sexual desire, impotence, etc.
- pre-occupation with own problems
- lack of sympathy for others.

❏ Recognising the warning signs in others

It is also possible to recognise that other people are under excessive strain. This may manifest itself in terms of various personal, interpersonal and work behaviours. In the longer term, it may also manifest itself in terms of increased stress related illness.

Personal behaviour and habits

Excessive strain may manifest itself in changes in people's personal behaviour and habits. The change agent would be well advised to be on the lookout for people showing the following signs:

- shaking, trembling, etc.
- complaints of headaches and other aches and pains
- physical slowing, lack of energy, weakness, etc.
- mental slowing, failing memory and lower mental ability
- increased drinking, smoking or other drug use
- over-eating or, less commonly, loss of appetite
- less laughter, fun and joking
- more anger, irritation, rapid mood swings, etc.

Interpersonal behaviour and work manifestations

There are also a variety of interpersonal and work manifestations of excessive strain in others that the change agent should be alert to, including:

- deteriorating relationships, arguments, conflicts, etc.
- indecisiveness and unreasonable complaints
- lowered quantity and quality of work
- lowered problem-solving and decision-making
- increased absenteeism and lateness
- increased number and severity of accidents
- expressions of dissatisfaction, low morale, etc.
- acts of sabotage, restriction of output, etc.

Stress-related illness

The various symptoms described above may eventually develop into *stress-related illnesses*, that is to say illnesses that could be brought on by the long-term effects of stress, especially the effects of stress chemicals. There is some evidence to suggest that stress plays a part in a variety of illnesses, including allergic reactions, digestive difficulties, heart conditions, skin and joint conditions and mental illness. This is not to say that stress is the only, or even the major, contributor to such patterns of illness. It is well established that other factors, such as heredity, pre- and post-natal diet, exercise and exposure to neurotoxins, including tobacco and alcohol, are also likely to play a major part in the development of illness.

Change as a source of stress and strain

The number of potential sources of stress and strain is virtually infinite. Any state of affairs that an individual perceives as a source of pressure that is unpleasant and uncontrollable is a stressor for that individual. Stressors may arise from both changes and from ongoing pressures. They may occur in our domestic and personal lives as well as working lives. The effects of such stressors are additive, in the sense that they combine together to produce an overall level of stress and strain for each individual. The higher the level of stress and strain the more symptoms an individual is likely to have and the greater the long-term risk of stress-related illness.

Our concern here is with changes at work, their impact and management, especially in relation to stress management.

❑ The link between change and stress

There has been a great deal of research into the links between change and stress. Much of this (e.g. Rabkin and Struening, 1976) has explored links between major changes in peoples's lives, stress and illness. Some of it has focussed more on the way in which organisations respond to change (e.g. Lippitt, 1982). It is clear from such research that organisational changes may act as sources of stress in a variety of ways. They may, for example, create problems about:

- the quantity of work, including having too much or too little to do
- the quality of work, that is to say the fit between knowledge and skills and job requirements, including finding old abilities no longer required and new ones not yet developed
- roles, that is to say the demands and expectations on job holders; these include problems of role ambiguity, where people lack a clear and

unambiguous role, and role conflict, where people find various demands coming into conflict with one another (Kahn et al, 1964)

- interpersonal relationships, including interpersonal conflicts arising out of changes.

❏ Making things worse

These problems associated with organisational changes are likely to be exacerbated when people:

- lack awareness of and insight into their plight
- are not motivated to change, perhaps because they have a vested interest in the status quo
- do not possess the knowledge and skills needed to respond to the new circumstances
- lack the opportunity to acquire new knowledge and skills
- lack the resources needed to implement and manage the changes
- have inadequate opportunities to talk things through with someone in a supportive atmosphere.

Certain individuals may also be at particular risk because of their personal characteristics or habitual behaviour patterns. There is, for example, some evidence to suggest that individual differences do have a part to play in the management of stress (McCrae and Costa, 1986, Taylor and Cooper, 1988). It is, however, clear that the characteristics of the individual are not simply good or bad. They tend to be more of a mixed blessing, helping the individual in some situations and hindering them in others (Ivancevich and Matteson, 1984).

❏ Organisational stress, power, control and influence

It has been suggested that a major factor underpinning much organisational stress is the lack of power, control and influence possessed by those worst affected. Support for this notion comes from both theory and research. From a theoretical standpoint, it could be argued that strain was about the perceived inability to control pressures. Thus more control means less strain. However, this could be seen as mere tautology. What is particularly significant is the research that clearly indicates that, as we move down organisational (and social) hierarchies, the amount of stress symptoms and the incidence of stress-related illness increase (Cooper and Smith, 1985). At lower levels in organisations people experience more strain because of their relative lack of power, control and influence. It is hardly surprising, therefore, as we will see later, that one of the keys to successful stress management in organisations is the involvement and participation of staff in the process of change.

Managing stress in our own lives

The role of the change agent is intrinsically stressful. He or she has to cope with stress and strain in his or her own life, as well as having to help other affected individuals and the organisation itself. It is, therefore, important for the change agent to manage stress in his or her own life. In order to do this, it is important to adopt a healthy life style, as well as to manage both stressful incidents and major crises in a constructive manner.

❏ Adopting a healthy life style

Individuals who adopt a healthy life style are likely to cope more effectively with stress and strain (Taylor and Cooper, 1988). They tend to bounce back from peak periods of stress and are at reduced risk from stress-related illness. There appear to be three main sets of issues involved in maintaining a healthy life style, namely, physical health, mental health and social relationships.

Physical health

In order to achieve and retain physical health, it is important to pay attention to diet, exercise and drug use. In particular, the change agent would be well advised to:

- eat a diet that provides calories through whole grain cereals, and fresh fruit and vegetables
- eat a diet that provides most animal protein in fish and poultry.
- drink plenty of water
- limit the intake of saturated fats, dairy products, eggs, refined sugars and processed foods
- take regular, non-competitive aerobic exercise, for example, take a brisk half hour walk two or three times a week
- avoid smoking, excess alcohol and other drug use.

Mental health

The change agent would also be well-advised to attend to his or her mental health as well as physical health. More specifically, he or she should:

- allow plenty of time for rest, relaxation and sleep
- indulge in peaceful and relaxing activities, such as walks in the countryside
- do things at a leisurely pace
- find comfort in spiritual acts or acts of contemplation
- have fun, keep a sense of humour and avoid being over serious

- adopt a positive approach to life, including giving himself or herself rewards, looking on the bright side of things, and seeing changes as opportunities

  use techniques of relaxation, such as meditation, yoga, autogenics and progressive muscle relaxation (Keable, 1985).

Social relationships

The third element of a healthy life style involves developing and sustaining relationships (Ganster et al, 1986). The change agent would be well advised to:

- sustain and develop intimate, confiding relationships, in which there are opportunities to express personal feelings to others
- sustain and develop relationships that make him or her belong or feel a part of various social groupings, including the family, the work group and the wider community.

❏ Responding constructively to stressful incidents

In addition to maintaining a healthy life style, it is also important for the change agent to think about his or her responses to stressful incidents or situations. There are four major sets of issues for him or her to consider here, namely, the initial reaction, dealing with feelings, developing relationships and confronting the underlying issues.

The initial reaction

There is often a tendency to respond to a crisis by panicking, making over-hasty decisions or trying to do everything at once. This is, typically, a recipe for disaster. A more helpful strategy for the change agent, in the long run, is to stand back from the problem, stay calm, avoid panic or over-reaction and respond step-by-step.

Dealing with feelings

Once again, it is important to emphasise that it is healthy to be open, express our feelings and show our emotions. It is unhealthy to bottle them up, try to avoid them or deny them altogether. These principles are relevant when the change agent is responding to particular incidents or situations, as well as being one element in a healthy life style.

Developing relationships

From the earlier discussion, it is clear that sustaining and developing relationships is likely to have a positive impact on our health. It is also relevant to the change agent when he or she is responding to specific situations. In particular, it is likely to be helpful if he or she:

- explains and discusses his or her actions with anyone affected by them
- discusses matters with those in a position to help, such as line managers or team leaders
- seeks help or advice when he or she needs it.

Confronting the underlying issues

It is, at some point, likely to be necessary for the change agent actually to confront the issues underlying specific stressful incidents. Systematic approaches to problem-solving may provide him or her with a useful framework for doing this. These involve him or her in a sequential process typically consisting of information collection, problem diagnosis, the identification and evaluation of possible options, and the preparation, implementation and review of action plans. This tends to be most effective when the change agent carries it out with others, getting them to help him or her talk through the issues.

❑ Responding constructively to sustained strain

If the change agent finds himself or herself under strain for sustained periods and begins to show the sorts of symptoms described earlier, then he or she may need to take more drastic action. At this point, his or her energy reserves are low and he or she is susceptible to illness and infection. In these circumstances, the ideal things for the change agent to do are:

- take a two week break
- during this period, focus on rest, relaxation and recuperation; this is not a good time for particularly energetic activity
- at the end of the two week period take stock; think about what you want out of life; think about your situation and how you feel about it; think too about the particular problems you face and how you are coping with them
- if possible, talk things through with someone: it could be your partner, a friend or a colleague; you could also talk to a specialist; in the context of work, the welfare officer may be especially helpful, as he or she is specially trained and provides an independent, confidential service.

Helping others under strain

The role of the change agent, by its very nature, involves coming into contact with and helping people under strain. In order to be of assistance to such individuals, the change agent must recognise that they are under strain, provide practical help, provide counselling or advice as appropriate, make people aware of additional sources of help, and provide information, education and training.

❏ Recognising the need for help

Actually recognising that people need help is the essential first step to providing it. This involves being alert to the various personal, interpersonal and work manifestations of strain described earlier. The change agent will then need to approach individuals who display such manifestations and get their agreement about what, if anything, they would like to do about it. It is important actually to 'contract' with people about what is to be done, rather than simply assuming that they will accept what ever is offered. This involves having explicit agreements about aims, methods, timescales, responsibilities and the like.

❏ Providing practical help or assistance

It was noted earlier that the higher the level of stress and strain experienced by an individual, the more likely he or she is to display stress-related symptoms and develop stress-related illness. Thus, it is important for the change agent to provide practical help or assistance that will actually ease the burden on the individual. The sort of practical help given could be infinitely variable, although it may involve such things as temporarily moving people to lighter or easier jobs, providing staff to finish a particular task and allowing time off to deal with outside issues.

❏ Providing counselling or advice as appropriate

This is not the place to go into detailed discussion about the various strategies that may be used for helping individuals. Suffice it to say that the appropriate use of counselling and/or advice is likely to be useful to the change agent when dealing with people who are under strain.

Counselling involves helping people to help themselves. In order to counsel people effectively, the change agent should:

- give them time and listen to what they have to say
- try to understand things from their viewpoint
- show respect and avoid being judgemental
- be warm and friendly
- try to get them to face up to difficult issues
- encourage them to establish plans specifying the concrete steps they intend to take to deal with such issues
- agree review dates and follow things up.

Non-directive counselling need not, however, always be the most appropriate form of help. Much depends upon the individual concerned, the situation that they are in and the underlying problems with which they are faced. Sometimes people lack the necessary ideas and information to deal with their circumstances and welcome this from others. Under these conditions, a more directive approach may be appropriate. This is when the change agent may need to consider providing advice. Unfortunately, however, much advice is unwanted and insensitively delivered. If change agents are to give advice, they must ensure that:

- it is wanted
- they are competent to give it
- it is delivered with tact and sensitivity, allowing the individual to take it or leave it, as they wish.

❏ Additional sources of help

At some point, the change agent may come to the conclusion that he or she can no longer offer direct help himself or herself. They may, for example, feel that they are imposing strain upon themselves by helping, that they lack the relevant skills or knowledge to help, or that they lack the time necessary to provide the sort of help that they would like. In these sorts of circumstances the change agent may wish to encourage the individual under strain to seek additional sources of help.

An obvious first source of help at work is the welfare service. Many organisations provide a counselling, advisory and welfare service. This is typically an independent and confidential service, provided by carefully selected and trained staff and backed up by access to medical practitioners.

On the topic of medical practitioners, it is important to state that where the change agent comes into contact with individuals who report physical and/or mental symptoms, then those individuals should be encouraged to see their own General Practitioner. It is seldom the change agent's job to make medical diagnoses and prescribe treatment, although they can encourage people to get appropriate help.

❏ Providing information, education and training

In addition to providing practical help and offering counselling, the change agent may also help other people under stress and strain by providing information, education and training, related to their particular problems (Bruning and Frew, 1987). The actual problems may, of course, be infinitely varied. However, in the context of organisational change, they tend to revolve around four sets of issues, namely:

- stress management
- assertiveness

- career planning
- time management.

Individuals often want to know how to cope with stress and strain, how to confront difficult issues, what to do with their careers and how to organise their work and manage their time more effectively. The change agent may act as a provider himself or herself, although it is more common to put people in touch with other providers. These sorts of activities are usually referred to as individual-level stress management interventions and their aim is to help people to cope with stressful work environments.

It is clear that individuals who adopt the strategies outlined above do maintain a higher level of physical and mental health. Paradoxically, it is also clear that organisational interventions that focus solely on the individual seldom have a sustained and significant impact (Burke, 1993). There are probably two main reasons for this. Firstly, it is not easy to change these aspects of individual behaviour. Even if individuals are motivated to change, which they often are not, they tend to revert to previous patterns once they are back in their work routines. Secondly, the underlying sources of the problems remain largely untouched. This is not to say that individual level interventions are useless. They can work but only if there is adequate monitoring and support over the longer term. They are also more likely to work if they are accompanied by organisation-level interventions.

Managing stress in organisations

The concern here is with organisation-level stress management interventions (Quick and Quick, 1984). These are designed to tackle the organisational roots of stress and strain, rather than simply help people to cope. In the most general terms, such interventions seek to keep people informed, while providing a supportive climate in which individuals are encouraged to participate in purposeful activity. The basic rules are:

- let people know what is going on
- listen to them
- involve them in the change process
- encourage behaviour that is directed towards goals and tackles problems.

The sorts of organisation-level stress management interventions described and advocated most frequently in the literature include participative activities, team building, high levels of autonomy, job design techniques and the provision of high quality information.

❑ Participative activities

The change agent can promote participative activities oriented towards specific goals, tasks or problems. Ideally these activities involve systematic approaches to decision-making and problem-solving. Their value lies in the fact that not only do they systematically tackle some of the underlying causes of strain in organisations, they also involve people in the process.

❑ Team building

The change agent may initiate and encourage team building activities. These activities are designed to:

- provide a clear sense of overall direction, underpinned by a set of core values
- provide support to team members
- promote the adoption of team approaches to problem solving and decision making, as described above
- encourage the development of team working skills
- improve the overall effectiveness of the team.

❑ High levels of autonomy

The change agent may encourage steps towards the introduction of high levels of autonomy at work. In particular, he or she can promote the use of autonomous work groups, with delegated responsibility to choose work methods and determine work schedules. The value of such an approach lies in the increased levels of involvement and control given to staff and the subsequent reduction of stress and strain.

❑ Job design techniques

A further organisation-level option available to the change agent is the promotion and widespread use of job design techniques, such as job enrichment, flexible working hours and total quality management. These techniques typically provide individuals with:

- high levels of responsibility and autonomy
- meaningful tasks to carry out
- frequent feedback on performance
- a sense of achievement from their work.

Job design techniques are usually promoted to enhance organisational effectiveness through a satisfied and motivated work force. At the same time, it is also clear that they can help to reduce strain in organisations by increasing the involvement of staff in a supportive atmosphere.

❑ High quality information

Finally, the change agent may also provide, or encourage the provision of, high quality information on rules, roles and procedures, so that people know what is going on. This is crucial where the scope for participation is limited, for example, when organisational changes are imposed. In these circumstances, it is essential to tell people what is happening, tell them why it is happening and tell them as quickly as possible. It is also important to consult widely and listen to what people have to say, even if the scope for actual involvement is limited. In the absence of adequate information from official sources, the grapevine will usually fill the gap, even if what it fills it with does more harm than good. It is, therefore, important for the change agent to act quickly and decisively, getting information out before the grapevine gets going. The alternative is to waste time denying rumours and 'putting the record straight', while leaving others with the picture of the change agent as out of control.

About the author

Tony Manning trained as a behavioural scientist and lectured in this field before moving into management training and development. He is an independent consultant, specialising in human resource management.

References and suggested reading

Bruning, N.S. and Frew, D.R. (1987) Effects of Exercise, Relaxation and Management Skills Training on Physiological Stress Indicators: A Field Experiment
Journal of Applied Psychology Vol. 72, No. 4

Burke, R.J. (1993) Organisational-Level Interventions to Reduce Occupational Stressors
Work and Stress Vol. 7, No. 1

Cooper, C.L. and Smith M.J. (eds) (1985) *Job Stress and Blue Collar Work,*
Chichester, John Wiley & Sons

Ganster, D.C., Fusilier M.R. and Mayes, B.T. (1986) Role of Social Support in the Experience of Stress at Work *Journal of Applied Psychology* Vol. 71, No. 1

Ivancevich, J.M. and Matteson, M.T. (1984) A Type A-B Person-Work Environment Interaction Model for Examining Occupational Stress and Consequences
Human Relations Vol. 37, No. 7

Kahn, R.L. Wolfe, D.M. Quinn, R.P. Snoek,J.D. and Rosenthal, R.A. (1964)
Organisational Stress: Studies in Role Conflict and Ambiguity John Wiley & Sons

Keable, D. (April 1985 and July 1985) Relaxation Training Techniques - A Review
Part One: What is Relaxation, Part Two: How Effective is Relaxation Training
Occupational Therapy 1985

Livingston Booth, A. (1985) *Stressmanship* London, Severn House Publishers

Lao Tsu *The Tao Te Chung* translated by Gia-Fu Feng and June English (1972)
London, Wildwood House

Martin, P. (1987) Psychology and the Immune System *New Scientist* 9 April

McCrae, R.R. and Costa, P.T. (1986) Personality, Coping and Coping Effectiveness in an
Adult Sample *Journal of Personality* Vol. 54, No. 2

Murrell, H. (1978) *Work Stress and Mental Strain: A Review of Some of the Literature*
London, ACAS Work Research Unit, Occasional Paper No. 6

Quick, J.C. and Quick, J.D. (1984) Preventive Stress Management at the Organizational
Level *Personnel* September-October

Rabkin, J.G. and Struening, E.L. (1976) Life Events, Stress and Illness *Science*, Vol. 194

Taylor, H. and Cooper, C.L. (1988) Organisational Change - Threat or Challenge: The
Role of Individual Differences in the Management of Stress
Journal of Organisational Change Management Vol. 1, No. 1, MCB University Press

Part 2 — Instruments of Change

Introduction

The first part of the book has dealt with the identification of change and processes as to how this might be brought about. Chapter 1 also drew attention to the current environment within which change in the public sector is taking place and, in particular, highlighted trends towards the new public management. Two themes especially emerge. On the one hand, we see suggestions of certain management practices which might help achieve improved performance, and, on the other, initiatives driven, some might say imposed, by central departments with a similar aim.

Part 2 therefore examines some of these instruments of change by looking first at management techniques which should improve performance in making organisations more customer focused. Secondly we look at the two latest initiatives i.e. the Citizen's Charter and Competing for Quality.

In Chapter 10 Mahen Tampoe proposes a model for service excellence in the public sector. The model looks first at the needs of bureaucracy, recognising its usefulness for many of the routine tasks it is designed to carry out. Increased concentration on providing a service for the customer rather than to him or her means that reliance on the one-size-fits-all mentality of the past is no longer acceptable. To that end, the multi-customer focus of many public services means a need for greater awareness of the respective interests involved. The model therefore goes on to construct a blueprint for service excellence, taking account of these often competing pressures by considering the interrelationships between customers, Government, policy advisors and providers of the service. The chapter then goes on to consider the type of supportive management environment; systems, by way of processes that support people; and skills and competencies necessary for staff to 'delight the customer.'

Chapter 11 looks at the vital area of empowerment in some detail. Like the current fashion for learning organisations, empowerment is something which managers have been doing since time immemorial. It is highly dangerous therefore to consider such concepts as either new or panaceas. Used as an art form they will benefit organisations. Used in a scientific manner according to a manual, not only will little benefit accrue but they will also suffer the same fate as many other solutions which were seen as fads. Added to this, many people's view of empowerment has been influenced by a top down perspective primarily concerned with delegation and a fear of losing control. The approach suggested here takes a Hermeneutic view of the subject by endeavouring to look inside the mind of staff being empowered. Such a method allows managers to start by understanding what stops staff from carrying out their job and then demonstrates ways of how managers can meet these needs in a controlled environment.

The concept of Total Quality Management has been popular for some years in the private sector but has only reached the public sector within the past five years. As with empowerment, so often the topic has suffered from little understanding of its true nature allied, despite warnings of the long term investment before returns will flourish, to the belief that signing up to the concept and calling yourself a TQM site is sufficient. Needless to say such approaches quickly fail. Sadly the desire for a 'quick fix' is in danger of giving the topic a poor reputation which is totally unjustified. David Shaw provides a useful understanding of the history and concepts of the idea in Chapter 12.

Significant strides have been made during the past ten tears or so in improving the structure and systems of the public sector to make it more effective. Publication of the Citizen's Charter in July 1991 however unquestionably provided the focus of customer care towards which services are now pointing. In Chapter 13, Jenny Harrow looks at responses to the Charter to date and, in the light of this experience, offers managers advice on how to improve responses to the implementation of the Charter in future.

Shortly after the publication of the Charter, the Competing for Quality white paper of November 1991 not only reiterated the need for looking at all options in the provision of service but also increased the scale of the exercise significantly. Closely involved with the evolution of the policy during the past three years, lan Williams explains the policy and its results to date in some detail in Chapter 14.

The increase in contracting as a result of the Compulsory Competitive Tendering initiative in local government and Market Testing in the civil service, will require contract management skills on a scale hitherto unheard of in the sector. Much of the success of achieving good service through contracting depends on establishing the correct environment in the first place. Mahen Tampoe looks at the management of out-sourcing in Chapter 15, drawing the attention of managers to some of the pitfalls, and providing a model to consider when entering into a contractual relationship with external suppliers, which aims at optimising the relationship on both sides.

Chapter 10

Organising for customer service

Mahen Tampoe

Clarity of purpose, fairness in all its dealings and a consistency in the way it operates is particularly important for the public service. As the operational arm of Government the public service must always be even handed in the way it implements Government policy. To achieve this it has, through the years, honed a method of working which many of us would consider the epitome of bureaucracy.

When I complained about bureaucrats and bureaucracy a personnel manager reminded me that without them no big enterprise could function. It reminded me of Max Weber's views on the same subject in the early part of the century. It is true that large organisations with diverse interests and obligations must have order and must attempt to lead an ordered existence. This is also true for Imperial Powers. You cannot run an Empire unless you establish a well defined set of rules and procedures by which to administer it.

Bureaucracy depends on the fact that the people and systems within it will function in a consistent manner for at least 95% of the time. It is this certainty which enables managers to manage by exception. It is also bureaucracy that enables jobs to be de-skilled and decisions to be delegated to staff at all levels. Remove bureaucracy and the organisation will come to a standstill very quickly.

Bureaucracy is made up of rules and procedures which are then embedded in processes. An airline ticketing system is a bureaucratic process. The employees and passengers of the airline take comfort in its accuracy, accuracy which is derived from embedding a very rigid set of rules and routines into a suite of computer programmes which manage the whole ticketing process. Imagine air travel without a structured, well-ordered and immovable ticketing system! The payment of benefits to the unemployed needs to be done within a carefully structured and defined process so that the process, rather than the officer paying the benefits, ensures the fairness of the payments made.

Although, in the main, bureaucracy oils the wheels of organisations and enables significant benefits to be reaped, there is no denying that it may, sometimes, genuinely frustrate those who need to short-cut their way through the system or carve out a set of rules to suit the legitimate needs of the organisation they serve.

So why does bureaucracy have such a bad name? Probably because it is misused and also because in the wrong hands it can become encrusted with rigidity and callused with uncaring, the servant becomes the master. When that happens it becomes the refuge of the inefficient or indolent and a nightmare to those it is supposed to help, its customers.

Who is the customer ?

The customers of the public service are made up of Ministers and the Public. The public has three faces:

- the public as beneficiary is a member of the public who receives a service from the public service
- the public as paymaster is a member of the public whose direct or indirect taxes finance the working of Government
- the public as voter is the member of public who votes Governments in or out of office.

The public servant can be broadly classified as public servant advisors who provide policy advice to Ministers and the public servant provider who provides a service to the public. The Public Service has to serve both ministers and the public equally efficiently. To the first it owes obedience and loyalty and to the second it owes quality of delivered service. Figure 10. 1 illustrates the spread of the task that they face.

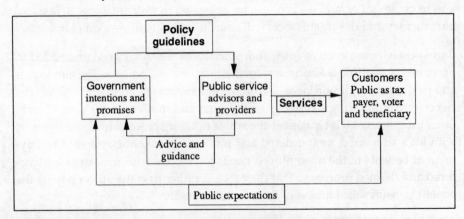

Figure 10.1. The links between policy makers, providers and customers.

The public service sits in the middle serving both groups. It assists the Minister with policy formulation and accepts policy guidelines for implementation. It serves the public by providing services. In the past the public have generally been fairly quiescent customers. They believed that public servants focused more on supporting Ministers than the public and reluctantly accepted the imposed extra burdens which bureaucracy placed on them. In such a uni-focused design customers saw themselves as intruders clogging up the well oiled wheels of Government and so did the public servants who were employed to serve the public. The contradiction of the distinction between the policy adviser and provider was recognised in the Next Steps initiative, which set out to change the structure of the civil service so that policy was generated by Departments, whilst provision was the responsibility of the Executive Agencies. The same organisational split can also be seen in the latest reforms in the National Health Service where the purchaser and provider have been clearly identified.

While such initiatives were focused on making the structure of the service more aware of the distinction between advice and provision, it was the Citizen's Charter (HM Treasury 1991) which articulated the need for the public service to become more customer focused by raising the expectations of the public by publishing the standards for service provision. Developments of the Charter are discussed in Chapters 13 and 23.

The effective organisation that provides services to meet these new customer expectations must be designed so that it can support the policy makers (the Ministers) and the customers (voters, beneficiaries, taxpayers) and enable the public servants to perform their duties without infringing their code of conduct or the requirements of the Citizens Charter. Figure 10.2 illustrates these inter-relationships.

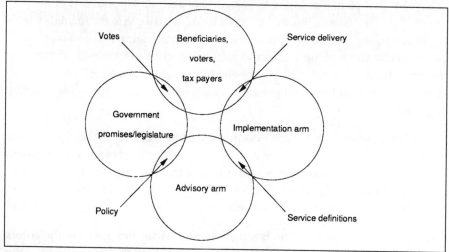

Figure 10.2. The components of an effective organisation.

Customers' interface with the policy maker is the ballot box (votes). The customer's interface with the service provider is through the delivery mechanism chosen i.e., tax assessments, social security claims, VAT returns etc. The interface between the advisory arm of the public service and the policy makers helps formulate policy and create the instruments of policy approval such as cabinet papers, green papers, white papers and statutory instruments. The interaction between the advisory arm of the public service and the implementation arm defines the services that need to be provided to satisfy the policy and the customer's expectations.

This suggests that the organisation structure that best suits the needs of the 'new' public service is one where the policy arm and the implementation arm can co-exist and support each other through an active interchange of ideas and an understanding of the actual impact of the policies on the implementation task. At the same time they should be able to specialise so that what they do is both cost effective and to the highest professional standards.

The effective organisation

The effective organisation for the customer focused public service as a provider organisation still needs to be built on the basis of Government policy and intentions, the duties and obligations of the public servant as embodied in the Citizen's Charter and the service's own code of ethics and behaviour, and the expectations of those it serves taxpayer, voter and beneficiary as illustrated in Figure 10.3. This model provides the guidelines for building an organisation which can discharge these new objectives. The policy guidelines and the requirements of the legislation (first box in Figure 10.3) influence both the behaviour of the public servant (left second row box in Figure 10.3) and the expectations of the customer (right second row box in Figure 10.3) and contribute to the formulation of a service strategy which in turn enables the systems, supportive management environment and staffing levels and staff skills to be determined. These relationships form a logical flow from policy to organisational performance. The spine is made up of three components; policy, service strategy and the effective organisation.

The policy dictates both the behaviour of the organisation and the entitlements of those it is designed to service and is expressed as a service strategy which helps define the nature and scope of a customer focused organisation, an understanding of which helps determine the staffing levels and skills, the supporting processes and the organisation structures necessary.

The success of the organisation is judged by the satisfaction given to the voters in general and those citizens who come into contact with the organisation. If the

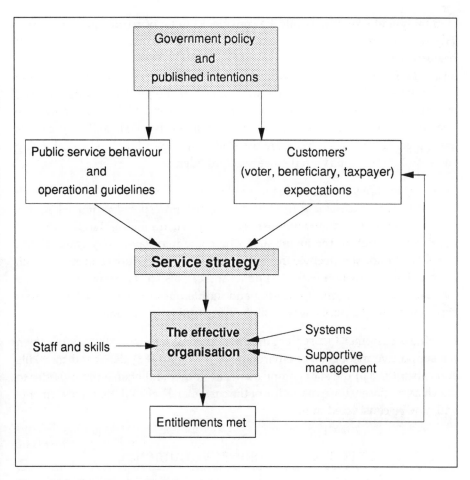

Figure 10.3. Organisation design model.

politicians have read the mood of their constituents and formulated the right policies, and if the public servants have put in place an effective customer focused organisation, then the customer (voter) would be happy and the Government returned to power. If not the voter uses his or her ultimate sanction. Policy formulation is therefore a very important aspect of voter satisfaction.

Therefore, the design of Government institutions must serve both objectives (citizen and ministerial) and do this within the framework of the performance criteria in the Citizen's Charter.

❑ The service strategy

Quality of service depends on many different characteristics. Among these reliability, responsiveness, competence, access, courtesy, communications, credibility and empathy would be considered to be of particular importance. The service concept within organisations demands flexibility in the use of resources, giving discretion and authority to the staff to deal with customers, and establishing processes which support the staff in meeting customer expectations within the meaning and context of the guidelines, statutes and operational rules. Customers are looking for service transactions where they are treated as worthwhile individuals, where their wants, needs and entitlements are respected and where they are assisted rather than hindered in achieving successful interactions with their service provider.

These expectations contrast with the public's perception of a public service which is bureaucratic, excessively rigid, uncaring and unresponsive and where the customer is not served but administered to. The frustrations of the customer are usually taken out on the junior staff who come into day-to-day contact with them. The junior staff feel victims of the processes, procedures and rules which govern their interaction with the public, and can also feel distanced from their managers who are seen as uncaring and indifferent to the day-to-day stresses experienced by the public who vent their frustrations on them.

Building a customer focused organisation requires a service strategy in which the supportive management environment, the support systems and the skills and capabilities of the staff complement each other and enable the provider to match more closely the expectation of the customer. Each of these three elements will now be considered in turn.

The supportive management environment

The supportive management environment is made up of three fundamental elements, people, processes and practices. The issues which refer to people involve structure, leadership style, their motivation, their careers, and their performance. The process related issues are to do with the systems, procedures and rules that facilitate people performance. Practices relates to the way people are managed and cover such aspects as style, culture and attitudes. In this section we review all of these aspects of a supportive organisation.

❏ The importance of organisation structure

Most organisations, whether in the public service or in the private sector are made up of a structured, measured, and sequenced set of activities, carried out by one or more individuals or systems, designed and focused to facilitate the efficient and effective execution of a service or the production of a product. It can generally be said to have the following components:

- structure - hierarchical or sequenced
- focus - designed to help staff, customers or both to meet the mutual obligations created by their interaction
- order - routine and flow such that variations stand out as exceptions
- appropriateness - in that it meets the objectives for which it was set up
- confers efficiency and effectiveness on those who use it
- knowledge transfer and help in decision making and skill to those who use it
- sponsorship.

The pyramid form of organisation meets all these criteria. It is hierarchically structured and divided into manageable units, each of which focuses on a specific activity or range of activities. Order is ensured through the different routines and procedures and the position and responsibilities each person has within it.

Its appropriateness is tested daily as it responds to the demands made upon it and it is modified to serve its customers better. Efficiency and effectiveness is derived from the clarity of the roles and goals of each unit and each person within it and knowledge usually flows across between peers and colleagues and from top to bottom between manager and staff member. Each departmental head is the sponsor of his or her unit and is responsible for ensuring that the unit is staffed and resourced to meet the obligations placed on it by the greater organisation.

It has its drawbacks too:

- it can be rigid
- the channels of communication can be constrained and be vertical rather than a network of criss-crossing lines
- the roles and goals of the different entities may have become fuzzy with time and areas of duplication set in
- the arterial sclerosis of office politics often clogs up the channels of co-operation and collaboration
- the organisation can grow fat with layers of fatty tissue which periodic diets of downsizing and rationalisation disperse.

Despite these short falls it is still the most effective form of management structure but perhaps the way it operates can be modified to meet the new customer orientation expected of the Public Services.

❏ Operating Principles

The way an organisation functions is often different to the way it is structured.

To help establish reporting lines and define roles an organisation structure may reflect a formal and rigid design, often expressed as a pyramid, with the different groups which make up the whole being clearly demarcated as illustrated in Figure 10.4a. However, to meet some of the aims of the 'new' public service it will need to behave much more like a team based organisation as illustrated in Figure 10.4b. Familiar examples of such teams are quality circles and project teams. In such a structure the hierarchical groupings focus on their specialism and can be made up of advisor groups and implementor groups. They would each operate independently of each other in carrying out their regular jobs, but when a policy decision is required and the full weight and skills of the organisation need to come together, those people who need to be involved will be brought together from different departments to form multi-disciplinary teams as represented in the circular shapes. The new public service will have to work more and more in the form illustrated in Figure 10.4b, although it may be structured as in Figure 10.4a.

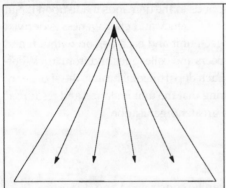 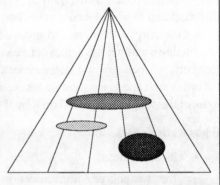

Figure 10.4a. Hierarchical structure with communications channels flowing up and down the organisation within groups. Inter–group communications achieved through meetings or leader interventions.

Figure 10.4b. Communication channels forged through combined teams formed from different structural groups and focused on solution building for customer or organisation.

❑ Key performance indicators

Among the performance indicators which the Citizen's Charter requires the public service to meet are:

- value for money
  independently validated financial and operational performance of services provided
- customer satisfaction
  monitoring and knowing customer perceptions of the services offered

- measurable improvements in service quality
  showing that the service is being continuously improved to meet newer (higher) expectations

- innovation
  introducing at least one innovation without additional cost to the taxpayer.

❏ The public service ethos

Staff in the public service work within the cultural and ethical values of the public service. They are summarised here from *A force for improvement in the UK Public Service* issued by the Cabinet Office(1991). It states that a public servant has the following duties:

- give undivided allegiance to the Crown when the Crown has a claim on their services

- put official duty before private interests and not use their official position to further their private interests

- be honest and avoid bringing discredit to the public service

- serve Ministers with integrity and ability

- keep the confidence to which they are party

- carry out decisions with energy and goodwill, whether or not they personally agree

- assist in the communication of government policies and decisions

- deal sympathetically, efficiently and promptly with the public.

This ethical and moral code of the public service, together with the requirements of the Citizen's Charter, forms the underlying or superordinate values to which every public servant is now expected to work and influences the way the operating principles are shaped. Care needs to be taken, however, that the ethos remains consistent with future decisions on accountability and responsibility.

❏ Leadership

Although it is difficult to argue that one form of leadership is better than another, it has become accepted that there is a difference between management and leadership. Management is often seen as the task of bringing together people, processes and resources and establishing their inter-relationship into an organisation (department, company, project team etc.) so that the organisation can meet predetermined goals. Leadership, on the other hand, is seen more as an inspirational activity which awakens dormant emotions and energies within people so that they deliver outcomes which exceed their own expectations. Bennis and Nanus (1985) say that:

> there is a profound difference between management and leadership, and both are important.

They suggest that:

> to manage means, to bring about, to accomplish, to have charge and responsibility for, to conduct.

On the other hand

> leading is influencing, guiding in direction, action and opinion.

Most organisations are very efficiently run by managers. Few are run by leaders. The anecdotal evidence and some empirical evidence suggests that there is a difference in the performance of an organisation that is managed rather than led. The evidence suggests that in a majority of cases dedicated leaders, through their drive, vision, and fixity of purpose can deliver results more consistently and dependably than managers, even dedicated and highly efficient managers.

Transformational leadership is perhaps the more recent expression of this style of leadership. Transformational leadership focuses attention on vision and draws on emotional and spiritual resources to energise and motivate the people in the organisation. It operates within the structures established by the leader but it achieves by getting people in the organisation to do the right things rather than do things right. Transformational leadership therefore requires greater self-discipline from the staff in exchange for greater trust from the leader. Bennis and Nanus (1985) suggest four key elements in staff attitude when they are being managed by a transformational leader. These are:

- significance
  strong feeling of being at the active centre of the organisation
- competence
  development and learning on the job
- community
  being strongly committed to the organisation and its purpose
- fun
  enjoying their work.

All managers and leaders have an obligation to order their organisations so that work is done productively and efficiently, on schedule and with a high level of quality. However, the difference between a competent manager, an excellent manager and an effective leader is how the staff feel about themselves, the organisation and their 'boss'. Those working for a competent manager will feel that they are 'earning a living', those working for the excellent manager will feel that they are well managed and those working for an effective leader will know pride and satisfaction in their work whilst being productive, efficient, on time and meeting quality standards.

Systems that support the public servant

The effectiveness and efficiency of any organisation depends on its people. But the people themselves need systems that facilitate their performance. These systems and processes range from those which can be very prescriptive i.e., payment approval to those which are enabling i.e., decision support systems. In this section we discuss these two key enabling mechanisms.

❑ Processes

The management structure is usually underpinned by management and operational processes which flow across the organisation and help knit each separate entity into a common unit to meet specific ends, i.e. payroll and accounting systems, Email and common shared databases, payment of expenses. Very few organisations can justify having more than a dozen or two dozen underlying processes. Some processes support single functions whilst others may support many different staff in different departments within an organisation. Some others may support staff in many different organisations, such as electronic data interchange to link supplier and customer. Effective processes enable organisations to make routine and to de-skill many tasks so that they can be carried out more cheaply and with a consistency and regularity consistent with the workflows that are placed on it. Effective and efficient processes enable the organisation to deliver and managers to control.

The interface with the public (as beneficiary or tax payer) will always occur through the public servant provider group when customer needs are assessed, specified and met through the streamlined administrative processes of the department. When working with the public the provider group will take the lead role. It will harness the skills of the organisation and provide a cost effective service to the public.

These organisations will be process dominant. A process is a structured, measured, and sequenced set of activities designed and focused to facilitate the efficient and effective execution of a service or the production of a product. A process dominant organisation is one which encapsulates its routine decision making processes in administrative or computer based systems, thus helping staff efficiently and effectively to carry out the routine work of the organisation.

Processes by their very nature are structured and tend to be hierarchical. They focus the activities of the staff, the customer and the organisation to achieve efficiencies. They introduce order and create routine. When well designed they confer efficiency and effectiveness to the staff and the organisation. They are effective means of transmitting knowledge and capability and then support operational, management and advisory functions.

Most organisations, even global giants such as IBM or GM have 12 to 18 main processes. Some support single functions and others the whole organisation. Most processes have an impact on organisational efficiency and effectiveness and can be used as competitive weapons and as means of achieving customer satisfaction. As the work carried out by the organisation changes and the demands on the staff change it becomes essential for the processes which support the functioning of the organisation to be reviewed and improved i.e. through business process redesign/reengineering (BPR). Any review must take into consideration the present and future direction of the organisation and the demands that will be placed upon it. For example, the review must determine whether the key deliverables, products and services which the organisation offers, will change. Based on this understanding the review should determine what organisational capabilities are needed to produce the desired outcomes and meet the business goals. Such a review will identify the depth of change that is needed and define the key processes and identify those that need changing either incrementally or radically.

Incremental changes tend to be less destabilising and disorientating and are usually carried out to make the processes more efficient and effective in that they help to do the same or a similar job more easily or accurately. Incremental improvements usually start from existing processes and use various organisational mechanisms, such as TQM, quality circles, suggestion schemes to identify and achieve the changes.

Radical changes tend to cause more upheaval as they often result in process innovations which radically restructure the way a given task is carried out, as with BPR. It is likely that the new design will use different, usually cheaper and more efficient ways to do the same things. Process innovation, in the context of today's emphasis on meeting customer needs, will start at the top or with customers and work inwards. It may require all those in the organisation to learn new skills and will usually cause upheaval and the re-drawing of old boundaries. Once the new processes are determined they need to be designed and implemented and evaluated and fine-tuned.

❏ Process dominant work

Examples of process dominant work are paying wages, paying pensions or benefits or preparing routine tax assessments. Figure 10.5 illustrates the interaction between an employee and the processes that support them.

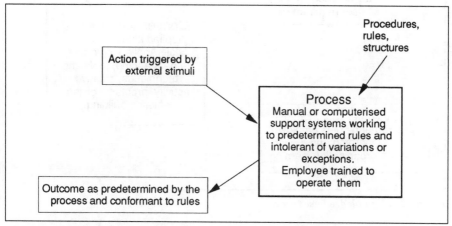

Figure 10.5. Process dominant work.

The routinisation of repetitive work enables managers to achieve high degrees of control as there is a consistency and uniformity in the way the work is carried out. Any exceptions are brought to the notice of management and dealt with either as an exception or are analysed and incorporated into the routine of the organisation.

❏ Non-process dominant work

Although all organisations depend on structure and process to carry out the routine tasks associated with their efficient running, processes in service organisations are usually a means to an end. Processes, even in the manufacturing organisation, are no longer the type epitomised by Charlie Chaplin in *Hard Times*. In these days of lean production, where every factory hand has the authority to stop the production line for a legitimate reason, processes support the worker and not the worker the processes. Non-process dominant workers such as technical specialists and professionals depend less on processes and more on applying their knowledge and skill to derive effective outcomes.

This change in attitude to factory, clerical, administrative and supervisory work and the flattening of organisation structures has tended to transfer power to staff at the lowest levels and make them more accountable for their actions. Work at all levels is tending to get more and more discretionary and rule based decisions are increasingly left to the person interfacing directly with the customer. The interaction between these knowledge workers and their work is illustrated in Figure 10.6.

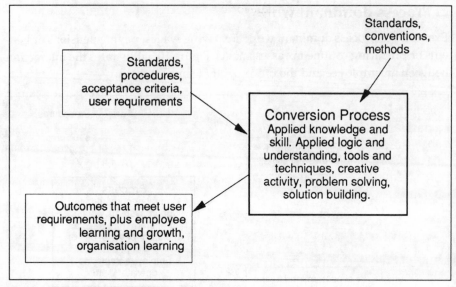

Figure 10.6. Knowledge based work.

❏ The climate of empowerment

Where workers have taken on this wider range of responsibilities and staff feel more empowered there is a corresponding need to tailor the working environment to fit better the employees of the 1990's. More and more of their work is based on knowledge and its application rather than on task competence, their decisions are based on applying the rules (discretionary) rather than confined by the rules (conformant) and their expectation of management is support rather than supervision.

In a research study carried out by the author into the type of working environment preferred by technologists, specialists and professional staff, eight key environmental characteristics were identified. These were an environment which:

- enabled them to understand the business and their impact on it
- rewarded them financially and offered satisfying work
- provided them with carefully defined norms, common values and rules
- enabled them to develop as individuals
- resourced and supported them to achieve the tasks assigned to them
- offered benefits which enabled them to share in the success of the organisation
- enabled them to show loyalty and commitment

- enabled them to exchange ideas and freely draw on the skills and capabilities of their colleagues by working across rather than vertically through the organisation.

Although these preferences were expressed by specialists, there is growing evidence that these knowledge workers are more widely spread in the organisation than first thought by the author and that the 'right-sizing' activity within organisations is forcing junior staff to be more self-managing and self-accountable. This actually means that their working environment must offer them greater flexibility of movement to operate effectively and the freedom to energise the organisation to help them achieve. Chapter 11 covers empowerment in greater detail.

❑ New rules for managers

In an organisation which affords staff the working environment discussed above, the manager has to become a transformational leader. The characteristics of such a leader can be summarised as someone who:

- participates with, co-operates with and involves staff; does less directing and second guessing
- releases operational control (let them decide the how) but takes firmer hold on the strategic issues (what)
- provides the resources, both the material and the operating environment, reviews and modifies the rules and procedures so that they are not hindered by them
- treats them as assets, invests in them
- releases, wherever possible, the inherent desire of staff to satisfy their achievement drive
- leads them by gaining their commitment to the organisation's vision and objectives
- empowers
- trains and develops staff so that they can use their empowered status
- regularly judges performance and re-instates performance criteria
- rewards with recognition as well as money when reward is deserved, recognition rather than flattery.

These ten principles of transformational management seem utopian. The reality is that with 'right-sizing' and the reduction in available people power to do the never ending stream of tasks that seem to assail managers and staff at all levels, the only way forward is to use the totality of the competences of junior staff, thus releasing senior staff for the strategic and to carry out tasks which experience and familiarity facilitate. Unless this utopian dream is realised, managers and staff will wilt and succumb under the unending load of work that passes for office life. Managers should not see empowerment as altruism but as a pragmatic solution to an ever increasing in-tray.

Staff, skills and competences

Staff competences are usually made up of a combination of knowledge, learning skills, personal attributes and the practical skills of applying this combination to achieving given outcomes. The learning skills refer to an employee's ability to absorb new knowledge and skills, understand their relevance and application. Knowledge is made up of two attributes, task relevant skills and domain relevant skills.

Task relevant skills are those skills which employees use to carry out their work effectively and efficiently. Being able to type at between 40 and 60 words per minute are task relevant skills for a typist. Being able to breakdown a large task into manageable sub-elements, assess what skills and resources are necessary to carry out each sub-element and then string them together in a way which enables a group of people to fulfil the whole task to time, cost and quality is the task skill of a project manager or unit manager.

Domain relevant skills are a combination of the wider ranging knowledge employees need to do their jobs and their ability to judge the relevance of their knowledge to the task they are carrying out. Knowing who to contact in another organisation or department so that an employee can successful complete a task is a domain relevant skill. Having the knowledge and effective recall of a wide range of case law so that the most pertinent precedent can be quoted in support of an argument is a domain relevant skill of a lawyer or advocate.

In addition to task and domain relevant skills employees must also have interpersonal skills, which they can use to manage their peers, to manage themselves, their immediate working environment, customers and managers.

These would be the main areas of staff competences which need to be nurtured. The personality of the individual and their intellectual abilities will have a significant bearing on how well they master and apply the competences discussed above. These aspects have been discussed more widely in Chapter 5.

❑ Motivation

Motivation is an inner drive which makes people expend effort to achieve a given objective. Although stimulated by external attractors such as the challenge of the task, the need to earn a living or the need to enjoy oneself or by fear, it is the strength of the inner drive rather than external pull that determines the quality of the outcome. According to motivation researchers and psychologists motivation has three key themes. The first is that there is an unsatisfied need which a person will strive to satisfy. Secondly, there is the belief that if the person expended energy and applied their competences they can fulfil the conditions which will enable them to satisfy the need and thirdly the belief that, when they have fulfilled their obligation, the need will indeed be met. The basic components of motivation according to many motivation researchers and psychologists are:

- a stimulus to act caused by the realisation of an unfulfilled need
- the arousal of the inner drive to assuage that need
- behaviour to satisfy the need
- an assessment of the outcome and re-stimulation if the cycle of events has produced the outcome aimed for.

This cycle of events is illustrated in Figure 10.7.

The crucial fact is that if, after the successful completion of the behaviour, individuals are not rewarded with the expected outcome, then it affects their self-

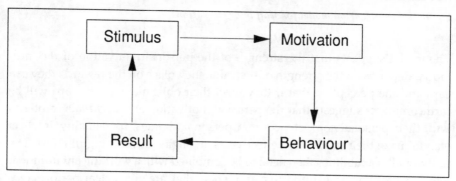

Figure 10.7. Basic components of motivation.

esteem and confidence and can reduce their willingness to try again. If on the other hand they succeed and are given the rewards they expected, it will increase their self-esteem and confidence and make them want to try again, perhaps an even harder task. Whether the individual fails or succeeds each expression of the motivation cycle will be a conscious or unconscious learning cycle and is part of the reinforcing process accompanied during any learning cycle. The role of the manager is to ensure that the employee has the competences, resources and the support to succeed as well as possible, so that employee confidence is increased and that in turn increases their learning and development. When these environmental factors are brought to bear a more comprehensive model of motivation can be developed as illustrated in Figure 10.8.

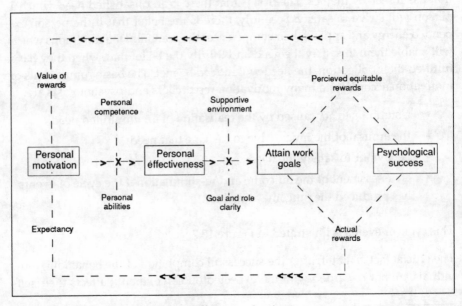

Figure 10.8. Motivation model for staff in organisations.

The model suggests that the strength of the personal motivation of the individual depends on the strength of the value they place on the rewards they can earn and the perception that if they meet their obligations the reward will be forthcoming. It suggests that the personal motivation of individuals combines with their personal competences and personal abilities, (personality, intellect etc.) to make their motivation effective as an engine of meaningful effort. The individual's capabilities then need to be combined with a working environment which is enabling and supportive and where they are given clear performance targets and role clarity. They will judge their actual rewards against the rewards they feel they should receive (which are computed on the basis of what they know or think they know others are getting) and if it meets their expectations it will please them and enhance their feeling of success.

Transformational leaders and excellent managers understand this cycle of cause and effect and draw on it to their advantage. Transformational leaders succeed in making the objectives and super-ordinate goals of the organisation or of their cause the stronger of the motivational stimuli. Managers are unable to do this as well, perhaps because they do not themselves believe as strongly in the objectives of the organisation they work for or because their personality prevents them from selling a vision which others will die for.

❑ Motivators

The rewards expected by staff take different forms. The research into motivators (those needs that drive people's behaviour) carried out by the author highlights four key motivators. These are:

- an enabling climate - a working environment which is conducive to high achievement. The components of such a working environment were discussed earlier but specifically comprised recognition, relationships, security, team spirit, management support and organisational loyalty. It did not include being required to show conformant behaviour

- personal autonomy - the ability of staff to determine how to carry out a given task but not strategic freedom, determining what task to perform

- task achievement - the sense of achievement that completing a task successfully gives staff

- financial rewards - earning a good salary and being offered the chance to earn a bonus for personal performance.

These findings are supported by the work of many other researchers in this field. Hunt (1986) identifies six motivators, comfortable lifestyle, structure (rationality and certainty), relationships, recognition, power (control over others) and autonomy (having control over their own lives). Hunt goes further and points out that professional staff and high flyers have a greater need for power and autonomy than clerical, administrative or process workers who had a stronger preference for comfort, structure and relationships.

❑ Performance – goal and role clarity

Staff performance is often a mixture of competence and motivation. If the employee has the motivation and inner drive to achieve and has the competence to carry out the work necessary to achieve the outcomes expected, it is often the lack of organisational support (discussed earlier) or a lack of clear goals and roles that impede them achieving. There is evidence that the mere fact of giving staff clear goals can increase their performance by up to 25%.

The manager needs to ensure that staff know exactly what is expected of them. The task must be clearly stated and performance criteria defined and quantified. Role clarity is how staff should behave when working to achieve their goals.

The benefits of providing staff with clear goals and role definitions is that it enables them to be more self-managing as they can judge for themselves how well they are performing against the standards set.

❏ Performance reviews

Once staff are given clear goals and their role is carefully defined and explained to them, the follow up action is to review their performance as a matter of course to ensure that they are meeting their goals and behaving as they are expected to. The review and feedback activity can be informal (brief acknowledgement of work well done or recognition of missed deadlines) or formal. Formal review and feedback needs time for preparation, for the formal interview, the documentation of the interview and the agreed actions and formal sign-off of the review document. It may also trigger follow-on actions to add to the busy schedules of both manager and staff member. This need for regular formal review and feedback is often avoided by both managers and their staff due to the sheer pressure of work or because of the administrative burden it imposes. Unfortunately, there is no substitute for the formal review and feedback process as without it staff cannot judge their performance, are unable to determine where they need to improve and the manager is unable to steer and re-direct the staff.

❏ Personal and professional development

In caring for staff it is important that their personal development is facilitated. As we have seen personal autonomy is a key motivator and personal effectiveness a facilitator of motivated effective behaviour (Figure 10. 6). Competence and self-management ability were also highlighted as being critical constituents in the whole set of attitudes, attributes and characteristics which make up the individual at work. The development of these different components of an individual's competence requires that they develop both personally and professionally. The manager's role is to enable this to happen. The employee's role is to put in the effort necessary to learn new skills and hone existing ones.

❏ Career progression

An important motivator for many, but not all staff, is the chance to move up the organisational ladder. Current trends reward capable staff by eventually promoting them to the ranks of management. Not all good staff members make good managers. Very few managers make good leaders. Employees must see a future for themselves which enables them to improve their quality of life. It is imperative therefore that the new public service offers staff who may not grow into managers other developmental opportunities. Horizontal staff movement can substitute for staff feeling 'boxed-in' to a particular department or specialist group with the accompanying stereotyping and typecasting that this brings.

Summary

This chapter has explored how an organisation which for centuries has been inwardly focused can respond to the pressures of the customer and turn itself around to be more customer driven. In attempting to do this the organisation must retain the best from the past and build in new approaches which blend both old and new into a 'new' culture and method of working. In this process old habits will have to be shed, old alliances broken and old values re-examined. What emerges from this heart searching and transformation is a 'new' management paradigm which enables new and old staff to benefit and grow in a new environment. The chapter suggests new approaches to reshaping the organisation to meet the new challenge of the Citizen's Charter and the customers. In this revised organisation there will be a greater correlation between the mind of the policy maker, the public servant as provider and the customer of the public services.

About the author

Dr. Mahen Tampoe is a management consultant and researcher. He has worked in industry as an accountant, and held senior posts within ICL's research laboratories including that of Managing Director of ICL's research laboratories in Ireland. His current research interests are in managing knowledge workers and managing knowledge based organisations.

References and suggested reading

Bennis, W. and Nanus, B. (1985) *Leaders: The Strategies for Taking Charge* New York, Harper and Row

Cabinet Office(1991) *A Force for Improvement in the UK Public Service.* London, Cabinet Office (OMCS)

Drucker, P. (1993) *Post Industrial Society* Oxford, Butterworth Heinemann.

Efficiency Unit (1988) *Improving Management in the Civil Service-The Next Steps.* London, HMSO

Filley, F.E. House, R.J. & Kerr, S. (1976) *Managerial Process and Organizational Behaviour.* Scott, Foresman and Company

Garden, Anna-Maria (1990) Career Orientations of Software Developers in a Sample of HighTech Companies *R & D Management* Volume 20, 4

HM Treasury (1991) *The Citizen's Charter: Raising the Standard.* London, HMSO, Cm 1599

Hunt, J.W. (1986) *Managing People at Work* Maidenhead, McGraw Hill

Steers, R.M. & Porter, L.W. (1987) *Motivation and Work Behaviour* Maidenhead, McGraw Hill International.

Tampoe, Mahen(1993) Motivating Knowledge Workers - The Challenge for the 1990' s *Long Range Planning* Volume 26 No3

Chapter 11

Empowerment

Roger Lovell

In his book on empowerment, Block (1991) wrote,

> ... control is an illusion, it is the people who work for us who decide what gets done.

This would never be appreciated simply by looking at the flows of power within most public or private organisations. How much energy is concentrated on 'impression management' i.e. trying to second guess what superiors want and managing operations to suit? This is one reason why bad news is suppressed, why ideas which are not in the main flow of current thinking are either never suggested at all or filtered out at an early stage. They appear to be less than system supportive.

During the past decade in particular, there has been a movement towards decentralisation and delegation through initiatives like the Financial Management Initiative in the civil service and the Resource Management Initiative in the National Health Service. The movement has taken place primarily through the delegation of budgetary control but has more recently been supported by further delegations from central departments like the Treasury and Cabinet Office.

The major thrust behind the argument for delegation is that decision making will improve the closer it gets to the customer, or end user. As such it has been popular in the private sector for some time. While issues such as equity of treatment, the need to execute legislation and the possible conflicts of customer requirements may make this more problematical in the public sector, the same general principles apply.

In recent times the word 'empowerment' appears to have replaced 'delegation.' Pushing responsibility further down the line can create 'physical' empowerment. It is a mistake, though, to believe that this act in itself actually gives greater power to the individual, or is productive in getting better service at less cost.

Unless the staff themselves feel that they genuinely have the power to satisfy a dissatisfied customer, the exercise will not only fail in its intentions but will also run the risk of making staff even more frustrated than before, since they are less sure of where they stand. In other words, as shown in Chapter 6, unless they feel 'psychologically' empowered, the experiment, as most attempts at cultural change, will fail to achieve its desired result. How therefore can true empowerment be achieved?

What is empowerment?

As Ripley and Ripley point out (1992), empowerment has been, and is being, used to cover a wide range of new management practice. At its most basic, it involves consultation with staff, at least asking them, even if not necessarily acting on their suggestions. This form can work for a limited period until the staff become aware that their suggestions are not being taken up, without adequate explanations as to why. The degree of cynicism created will then sully endeavours at co-operation in the future. Quality circles can flounder for this very reason.

A second level of empowerment allows the involvement of staff in job design so that they use a variety of skills and have a say in how the team works. Ultimately this can lead to the creation of autonomous work groups, who have the authority to implement their suggested improvements in terms of the way they work.

A third level of empowerment is observed when employees become involved not just in how they do their jobs but in the whole performance of the organisation, i.e. they look outside their own particular area and take part in establishing the goals and objectives of the complete organisation. In this form, every aspect of the organisation is different from that of a control-oriented one. Information is shared horizontally across the organisation, as well as up and down the hierarchy, which will probably have been flattened to allow easier communication, a wider span of control and provide greater opportunity for staff to fulfil their potential.

In defining empowerment, two fundamental points need to be made. Empowerment does not mean anarchy. Even the most highly empowered groups still need boundaries within which they operate. Secondly, empowerment means releasing the potential of the individual and in order to do this it must appeal to the psychological self. Empowerment, as far as this chapter is concerned is therefore (Ripley and Ripley, 1992):

> ... any management practice that increases a team or individual's sense of self determination, whereby their belief in their competence or effectiveness is enhanced, and/or, their belief in powerlessness (helplessness) is weakened.

Powerlessness

Power as a concept has been looked at in Chapter 4. Taking Kanter's (1983) fairly pragmatic definition of power as 'the ability to get things done,' it follows that 'powerlessness' is the inability to get things done. As Conger and Kanungo note (1988) the first place to start in examining empowerment must be to discover what causes staff to feel powerless or helpless. In other words, the starting point is to analyse the present situation, and what easier way is there of discovering what causes staff to feel powerless than by asking them what stops them getting their job done? This is far easier and more direct than carrying out a full blooded attitude survey and produces more specific responses. The results of this exercise generally fall into five categories.

❏ The Constraint of Legislation

The constraint of legislation and the equity of treatment surrounding the ethos of public management in this country are not to be denied. Nobody is suggesting that staff should be allowed to interpret legal requirements as they see fit and this will be considered later in the chapter when looking at establishing an empowerment zone. This does not mean however that legislation totally dominates how work is carried out in the public sector. On closer examination staff may often find that it is within their power to change at least some aspects of their procedures.

❏ Rules and regulations imposed from central departments

Considerable steps have been taken during the past five years, by the Treasury in particular, to transform rules into guidelines. Central departments are also willing to consider representations from departments and agencies on further delegations which they may require. Despite this, in the minds of many civil servants a deference towards the central departments still exists, which all too often provides the excuse not to act.

❏ Areas for discussion with superiors

Many of the other problems which emerge could often be eased, if not cured, through better dialogue with superiors in general and immediate bosses in particular. They include such things as:

- lack of clarity of goals
- badly planned reorganisation
- misunderstanding of what has been delegated
- insufficient authority

- boss too busy
- inadequate resources
- anxiety of the unknown.

Many of these issues arise not because they are inherently difficult to resolve but because of problems in existing relationships. The problem may simply be ignorance on the part of the boss that they are issues in the first place, or, on the part of the member of staff concerned, fear of raising them.

❏ Own power as a manager

Whether consciously or unconsciously, many of the issues raised are within the manager's direct sphere of influence. Typical issues are:

- staff attitudes
- apathy
- not invented here syndrome
- poorly trained staff
- lack of trust
- poor communication
- always done it this way syndrome
- lack of commitment.

❏ Own feeling of powerlessness

In practice, the deeper the examination of how it really is, the more managers begin to realise that much of their perceived powerlessness lies within themselves and their own attitudes. When I joined the civil service in 1962 it was customary to sign a letter to a superior officer, 'I am, Sir, Your Obedient Servant ...'

Despite a breakdown in certain areas of deference, the 'Obedient Servant' culture is still strongly inculcated in many places in the public sector, quite rightly in terms of the fair mindedness of the public sector ethos. It can however be so all embracing that it stops people, perhaps even subconsciously, from challenging outmoded practices and changing the way things are done. During training courses in recent years there have been many examples of course members citing 'central rules' as prohibiting them from achieving change when in fact the rules had been lifted some time before Colville et al (1993) record how, in work carried out in Customs and Excise, in over half of the issues where junior staff asked for more power, they already had the authority delegated to them.

The reality is that very few people can recall times when they have been stopped from using their own initiative. Indeed, they all tend to agree that their most valued staff are those who are pro-active and solve problems before they arise. Yet they are only too ready to use others or the system as the excuse for inaction, sadly to the detriment of the work, their staff and, most of all, themselves. What can be done about it?

How to achieve empowerment

Unlike most models of empowerment which concentrate on creating an empowered environment through strategy, structure, systems and culture, the model proposed in this chapter, as can be seen from the powerlessness exercise, starts from the basis of staff perception. It is therefore based upon a Hermeneutic concept of endeavouring to understand the other person's reality in order to be able to move forward. When this has been discovered, it is up to the manager to start to close the gap between what staff believe would help them perform their jobs better and the current situation. The manager's role in this is shown in Figure 11.1.

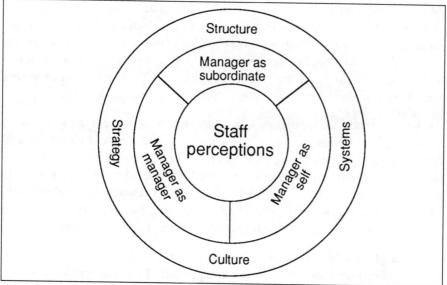

Figure 11.1. The bullseye model of empowerment.

❑ Manager as self

Before managers can manage effectively they must understand about themselves and, in respect of empowerment, where they stand in terms of their own feelings towards authority and control. Figure 11.2 looks at levels of control in comparison with the individual's desire for responsibility, introducing the concepts of 'rulers' and 'subjects'.

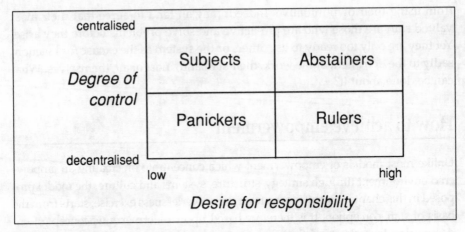

Figure 11.2. Subject/ruler diagram

For some managers, the move towards greater empowerment cannot come fast enough, since it is something that they have been waiting for for years. They are people with a high desire for responsibility and are quite comfortable with increased delegation. Indeed one might call them 'rulers' since they are happy to control. Such people may however be reluctant to delegate themselves and may become fairly autocratic once they have obtained power, since they may see power as a win/lose situation. In other words, if they release power, you gain it. It will be hard for them to create and feel comfortable in an environment with greater empowerment since they need to be in control of their own destinies.

At the other end, are managers with a low desire for responsibility and who prefer to be told what to do, to follow the rules and live in a controlled and centralised community. Such people have been invaluable to the public sector in the past, particularly in view of their reliability in doing as they were told. As such they might be deemed 'subjects.' The trend towards more delegated control over the past few years to such people however has made them 'panic.' A good example is the unimaginative way they control and spend their budgets.

There are also those who, despite having a very high desire for responsibility, which is often identified by the prestigious positions they hold outside work, do not believe that it is their place to take on more responsibility. They may be seen as abstaining from the new mood. In all these cases, much has to do with where people see their locus of control.

Locus of control

Locus of control describes the ways individuals attribute responsibility for events that occur in their lives to factors within themselves and their control, or to factors outside their control (Rao, 1985).

People who perceive an 'external' locus of control believe that the outcome of events is determined by factors extrinsic to themselves such as fate, luck and authority. People who believe that they have some control over their destinies i.e. that control resides within themselves, on the other hand, have an 'internal' locus of control. This can often be seen in practice in career development. People with an internal locus of control tend to be more pro-active in influencing the direction of their career than those with an external locus who are usually more willing to take a posting that is imposed upon them by a personnel department. Returning to the Myers-Briggs personality type described in Chapter 5, it is probable that someone with a sensing/judging (SJ) personality i.e. looking at things from a sequential viewpoint and preferring a structured existence, will have more of a tendency towards an external locus of control than an intuitive/perceptive (NP) type who looks at things from a more intuitive angle and has a higher tolerance of ambiguity due to their preference for a flexible existence.

Evidence at the Civil Service College suggests that the majority of civil servants are of an SJ orientation, which is both consistent with the 'Obedient Servant' mentality outlined above, and the type of people recruited as 'subjects.' How are such people who have been comfortable in a hierarchical bureaucratic climate throughout their working lives and were selected for their suitability to work in such a manner, to become more empowered? The answer is, gradually and within a relatively structured manner.

❏ Manager as subordinate

Virtually all of the issues identified above that refer to superiors stopping the job being done could be rectified by bringing them into the open and discussing them. Harvey (1988) talks about the Abilene paradox, where he describes a Sunday afternoon social visit to his nearby town of Abilene with his wife, children and in-laws. No one really wants to go on the visit but they all go along with the idea because they believe it is what the others want. It is only after the event, however, that this is discovered.

This type of relationship goes on all the time in organisations, especially in the boss/subordinate role, where, rather than clarify the situation, we second guess each other's behaviour, trying to please the other. The natural deference towards authority of the SJ types will also tend to prevent them from having the courage to lift the issues. A mechanism needs to be found, therefore, which allows this to be done at little risk to the member of staff. One way to do this is through the use of role set analysis, particularly if it is used by the member of staff on all of his or her relationships.

Role set analysis

Role set analysis requires the identification of the main people you work with.

Having done this, you write down what you expect from them in your working relationship. At the same time, they write down what they expect from you. Figure 11.3 demonstrates the type of relationships that a higher executive officer (HEO) in the civil service might have.

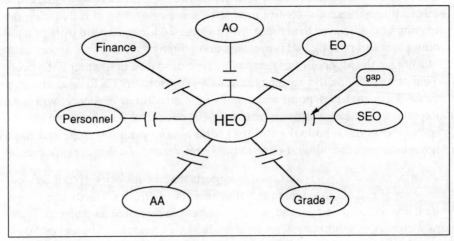

Figure 11.3.Role set analysis.

Having exchanged expectations, a gap is then identified between those expectations and the reality. Discussion can then take place as to how the gap might best be closed and a strategy agreed which will involve both parties changing their behaviour towards each other. Naturally, the more honest the endeavour, the more useful the exercise. This is largely in the hands of the subordinate. If he or she wishes to establish a meaningful relationship, then courage and persistence may be necessary. Raising the level of consciousness of the issues can only do good in the long run.

This is particularly so in the area of resources, as noted in some detail in Chapter 4. Increasingly managers are forgetting to prioritise tasks, leaving the staff to believe that they should all be done today. If greater consultation took place, objectives would be clear which, in turn, would reduce anxiety of the unknown. This was especially noticed during the first round of market testing, where, instead of taking effective action to discover what needed to be done, too many managers passively waited for instructions from above which, not only did not come, but also lost valuable time in preparing in-house bids. If your boss is continually too busy to see you, either book a regular slot of his or her time, and/or use your own initiative. If he or she does not like your actions, you will soon know and they will spend more time next time you ask for help. Remember how much we as managers appreciate staff who act responsibly rather than continually seek advice.

We ask students how often in their career they have been told off for taking an initiative. Rarely do they ever admit to its happening, and yet they hide behind the veil of restriction. If you feel tentative about taking an action, write down the worst that could happen if it went wrong. Then analyse the percentage chance that this would happen. Work out how you might reduce the risk as much as possible, then if the advantages still outweigh the possible consequences, 'do it' (Stewart, 1994).

❏ Manager as manager

This brings us to the area which you can influence most, your own staff. We have discovered that when role set analysis is used in the above manner, the expectations of superiors from staff are the same whatever the grade or position of the staff within the organisation. Likewise, the expectations of staff from their superiors are also similar. Added to this, the same things make staff feel powerless more or less whatever their position in the organisation. Unless these are released therefore and overtly dealt with, similar frustrations are being duplicated throughout the organisation to the extreme detriment of its operation.

The 'they' culture

Having realised that the issues which make them powerless are the same as those which make their boss and staff powerless, managers need to consider what they can do about it. This is where they are confronted by the 'they' culture. For some reason, managers rarely see themselves as 'management.' Instead they are frequently referring to management as though it were an alien force stopping them achieving their goals. When it is powerfully drawn to their attention that they are seen as 'they' by their staff, they start to look at the issues raised in a different light.

Keeper of the kingdom

Each manager is in charge of his or her own domain. Just because others insist on continuing to act in a Neanderthal manner, it does not mean that your staff have to suffer as a consequence. If the culture happens to be one where blame is easily administered and praise rarely given, we become frightened of making a mistake, do everything we can to avoid it, or at least cover it up, and spend our lives in a state of inertia, since the chances are that something will go wrong if we try to change a practice. Far better to leave it and avoid errors. That way, however, we never learn and never improve, merely go through the motions of survival. That survival however is no longer guaranteed, to say nothing of the decaying effect it has on our own self-hood and that of our staff. Just think for a moment of areas where you would enjoy more responsibility. This is exactly how your staff, however junior, will feel about their own situation.

Discretion and power

As noted above, much work in the public sector is determined by legislation and it is fully recognised that this cannot be overridden. Every level of job, however, has a discretionary component to it which is boosted by a source of power. These will vary depending on both role and position. Figure 11.4 demonstrates this.

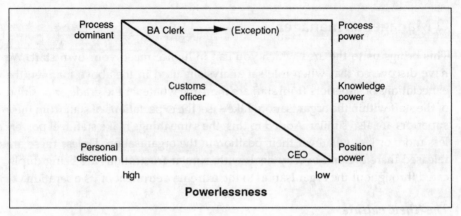

Figure11.4. Levels of discretion

Clerks in the Benefits Agency gain their power predominantly from the processes from which they work. While this provides their source of power, they are also constrained by the process, which can in itself make them feel powerless. At the other end of the scale, chief executive officers of Executive Agencies gain their power primarily from their position and have a fairly high degree of personal discretion over their work. In the middle are people, such as customs officers, who have a high degree of discretion in, for example, catching a smuggler, so long as their actions are carried out within the letter of the law. Knowledge workers are also in this category.

While processes define levels of discretion fairly closely, it is when exceptions occur that the level of empowerment felt by the person becomes a liberating, or constraining, force. Power increases or in the terms used in Figure 11.4, powerlessness decreases. This is particularly so in terms of satisfying a dissatisfied customer. Accepting that levels of discretion will vary depending on the person's power position, we need to look at a means of establishing an empowerment zone by identifying various areas of decision making and then considering how freedom to act may be increased.

Creating an Empowerment Zone

As we noted at the beginning of the chapter, empowerment is not anarchy. Boundaries of authority must be drawn. In the past some have seen those boundaries to be as narrow as a job description. They then wonder why people are unwilling or unable to use their initiative beyond this. To carry out the job to its optimum and capture all that a person has to offer, staff need to be able to expand their knowledge and authority and use their imagination to the full. Those boundaries are difficult to draw, since not only are we unaware of the full potential of the staff but they are also often unconscious of their own potential until faced with the opportunity to try.

We must first decide what really needs to be tightly controlled and what can be given greater freedom. The drawing up of an empowerment zone can best be done by using a decision making scale which runs from total control to complete delegation. The five point scale, below in Figure 11.5 (Scott and Jaffe, 1991), which is similar to that shown in Chapter 7, allows us to do this.

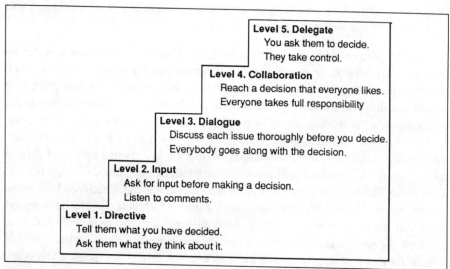

Level 5. Delegate
You ask them to decide.
They take control.

Level 4. Collaboration
Reach a decision that everyone likes.
Everyone takes full responsibility

Level 3. Dialogue
Discuss each issue thoroughly before you decide.
Everybody goes along with the decision.

Level 2. Input
Ask for input before making a decision.
Listen to comments.

Level 1. Directive
Tell them what you have decided.
Ask them what they think about it.

Figure 11.5. Five point decision diagram (Scott and Jaffe, 1991).

Having identified decisions against particular points on the scale, it is then important to decide what it would take to move each decision one, just one, step towards allowing greater freedom. In other words, start to reduce powerlessness or helplessness. This incremental approach has three main advantages:

- it provides a framework around which the many and varied decisions in managerial life can be examined, discussed and allowed

- in providing a flexible and gradual process it allows for an evolutionary approach

- it provides a basis for controlling the exercise, as opposed to seeing it in global and insurmountable terms.

By way of example, in carrying out this approach with students at the Civil Service College it has been interesting to note the various means of approval of annual leave and, in particular, ensuring cover between the Christmas and New Year holidays. The range of behaviour varies from point one to point five on the scale for what is essentially the same activity. The objective in all cases remains the same i.e. to ensure that adequate cover is available to serve the public, or internal users, during the period. Level one behaviour is where the manager decides who will be on duty without any consultation with the staff whatsoever. Believe it or not in this day and age, examples of this behaviour still appear. Some managers consult their staff by asking for preferences as to who wishes to be on or off duty, but do not enter into a dialogue with the staff, more than likely because, knowing the personalities of those involved, they are frightened of the personal involvement that this might give them. Other managers will enter into dialogue but still make the decision themselves, while others, at level four, will endeavour to ensure that it is a joint decision.

There are managers who have reached level five where they have been sufficiently mature to hand the decision over to the staff themselves. If you were a staff member, imagine the feelings that might be generated by this action. In the first place you would feel that you were being treated as an adult. After all you are allowed to act as one outside the work situation by owning a house, paying a mortgage, bringing up children etc. Surely it is easier to agree a roster amongst yourselves than under-take many of these more onerous tasks. Secondly, it gives you a feeling of control over your life, to say nothing of the greater camaraderie established through mutual agreement. Thirdly, you gain a feeling of self respect which is enhanced by a sense of importance. Most of all, you feel trusted, a trust which you will ensure is repaid since you realise that the decision to provide cover actually rests with you. The result on the surface is the same i.e. adequate cover etc. The reality is that the staff will be far more willing to go the extra mile when things get tough as the year progresses with level five behaviour than level one, since the latter will wait for instructions before reacting, rather than looking to be pro-active by ensuring that the 'crisis' does not occur in the first place.

Having established an empowerment zone, we need now to look at ways of reinforcing the correct environment.

Management Behaviour

Many organisations have endeavoured to change their culture or way of work-ing over the past decade to little or no avail. Quite apart from whether the organisation itself was ready for change, a principal reason for failure has been the inability, or unwillingness, of managers to alter their behaviour to match the new notion. Often the espoused values have been trumpeted by managers, many at the top of the organisation, only to fail because the theories in use have remained unchanged. The need is therefore to 'walk the talk.' In other words, behave in a way consistent with the new values. Examples of this abound in the case studies in this book. Failure, for example, to behave in a positive manner when mistakes arise, as they inevitably will when staff are changing their way of working, will undermine all efforts to change. Try all the time to place yourself in the 'shoes of the staff' and imagine how your behaviour must seem to them. For instance, it is no good making the grand gesture of going along to introduce a training day, confirming how strongly you support it, and then leaving immediately.

Collaboration and Participation

As Kanter says, (1983):

> ... change is always a threat when it is forced upon me, but it becomes an opportunity when I am involved.

Remember how you as a manager become frustrated when you feel excluded from decisions, how anxious you feel if rumour has it that a change is imminent which might affect you. Your staff feel just the same. Indeed, studies on stress reveal that the lower down the organisation you are, the more likely that stress becomes strain primarily because of a lack of control. This could be one reason why absence rates usually reduce once empowerment is introduced.

While, as shown in creating an empowerment zone, it is inappropriate on some occasions to consult with staff and allow participation, the chances are that there are far more times when it could be used and is not. Yes, it may take time, but the quality of decision making and, above all, the ownership of that decision, usually make it worth the effort, to say nothing of the enthusiasm which spins off to other areas of work and a general feeling of confidence. I recall being required to establish targets and service level agreements in personnel, office services and management services. I held meetings with every member of staff involved, giving them the chance to define their own targets. I was amazed both at the severity of the targets and how they not only lived up to them, but also improved upon them month on month.

As a project manager with very limited computing knowledge, I was given the task of managing a 150 man year project to convert a department's systems from one hardware manufacturer to another. No one wished to be associated with the time-limited task and my colleagues were forced to transfer staff to me. Needless to say, they were not their 'stars' as they saw them. Within three months we had achieved a major success and a queue of people wanted to join the team.

Over the three year period, the team proceeded to go from strength to strength and never failed to deliver to time, quality and budget. The whole enterprise succeeded on a site which had a very poor track record, because the staff were all allowed to work to their potential and as members of a team where everyone was valued for the contribution they could make. Bear in mind that these same staff had been considered of sufficiently poor quality to be released by my colleagues. I did no more than facilitate the enterprise by creating the conditions which released their latent abilities.

Such an approach is entirely consistent with the concept of managing by outcome. The main thrust behind the market testing initiative is to define the outcome of the task and allow the contractor to decide how it is to be achieved. Why therefore should the idea of defining what needs to be done and allowing staff to get on and do it be any different? Indeed there is nothing more satisfying and enjoyable about working life than working as a team in unison where you are all working to the same goal almost in a spiritual sense, without even the need to articulate things. That is the ideal state of an empowered workforce.

❑ Managerial interventions

In practice many managers have been used to managing in an authoritative manner. Heron (1990) sees this as being in three modes i.e. prescriptive, informative and confronting:

- prescriptive behaviour seeks to direct the staff by telling them what to do
- informative seeks to impart knowledge by giving them information on how to do the task
- confronting seeks to raise awareness of some limiting attitude or behaviour to which the staff are relatively unaware.

Compare this to the more facilitative behaviour of a manager in an empowered environment. Again Heron points to three types of behaviour i.e. cathartic, catalytic and supportive:

- cathartic behaviour seeks to enable the staff to discharge fear, pain, grief or anger
- catalytic behaviour seeks to elicit self-discovery, learning and problem solving on their own
- supportive behaviour seeks to affirm the worth and value of the staff's personal qualities, attitudes and actions.

Which of the sets of behaviour would you prefer from your boss? As noted in Chapter 1, technological change is forcing managers to move to a more facilitative role since they are no longer able to understand sufficient of the detail to manage in an authoritative manner. Far better therefore in moving to the facilitative mode to ensure productivity by establishing an empowered workforce. One way of starting to improve the climate is to establish a group vision.

Group Vision

Much effort has taken place during the past few years at devising corporate visioning statements. It would indeed be difficult to argue with many, if any, like motherhood and apple pie. One mistake in the visioning craze however has been to believe that everyone in the organisation is committed to it, even if they have been present at its inception.

As Senge says, (1990):

.. commitment cannot be legislated.

Sadly so many managers believe that it can and that, as Bate points out (1994), there is some unitary view out there which only needs to be identified for everyone to sign up to. In practice, the best that they can often hope for is genuine compliance. This is where the member of staff sees the benefits of the vision and does everything expected and more but follows the letter of the procedures. The committed person, on the other hand, makes a pro-active contribution to create the conditions necessary to make the vision happen.

Too much compliance will serve in the longer term to make the organisation moribund of fresh ideas. This is especially so in organisations who are sidelining anyone who is no longer seen as supporting the 'new regime.' True commitment is achieved when personal vision and group vision coincide. This can only be achieved by dialogue, patience and, above all, tolerance of the varying opinions which healthily exist in the plurality of organisational life. Allowing these to be freely expressed and endeavouring to take them on board can only help in building relationships. Even if eventually our ideas are overruled, we are much more likely to be supportive in enacting the decision when we feel that at least the ideas have been honestly considered.

Trust

Chapter 5 has looked at team building and balancing personality preferences and individual skills. Above all, however, an empowered organisation needs trust. If support of a vision cannot be legislated, it is absolutely certain that trust cannot be.

We know that the best bosses we have had are those who are willing to admit to making a mistake. The worst, on the other hand, have been those who become so adept at creating a 'blame culture' that their staff are frightened to admit a mistake and, in consequence, ensure that only good news is communicated up the line. Senior managers, realising that they are not getting the truth then go outside the line command and create wasteful resources to check up on staff and attempt to control the system from above. How can we be so hypocritical to believe that our boss should trust us, if we are not willing to trust our own staff?

Learning

Much more can be gained, as Honey (1991) suggests, by creating a learning organisation. To this end, managers should be seen as continuously learning themselves by openly discussing their learning with others, reviewing their successes and mistakes and the lessons learned from them, asking questions and soliciting feedback. Compare this to the many managers, especially senior managers, who see themselves as too busy to attend training courses, or, worse still, believe they do not need them.

In his latest book *The Empty Raincoat* (1994), Handy talks about empowerment metaphorically as being an inverted doughnut i.e. a round American doughnut, rather than its British counterpart, where the middle is filled in with the space on the outside. The core contains the things that must be done and may be shown in a job description. The space beyond is where the full potential of the job is achieved. As stated earlier, empowerment is not anarchy and even the space on the outside of the inverted doughnut must have a boundary. In reality, if the farthermost limits of the boundary are to be reached, i.e. where the member of staff is operating at the extreme limits of using his or her potential while still in limits acceptable to the organisation, these can only be achieved through operating within a learning environment.

Let us take another view of this. The concept of the Johari Window (Luft, 1961), points out that there will be four types of knowledge operating within our working environment. There will be things that we all know. There will be things that we know but others do not, this can be referred to as concealed knowledge. There will be things others know that we do not, and, finally, there will be things that neither of us knows. In other words, although the knowledge is there neither we nor our superiors or staff are aware of it.

Matching this concept to the idea of the inverted doughnut, we could liken the core to a description of the things about the task we all know about. Between the core and the boundary the other three types of knowledge will operate in varying degrees. In other words, there will be things that we know and do that others will be unaware of. There will be things that they expect of us but have not articulated them and in consequence we will be unaware of. There will, however, be things that neither of us are aware of until the boundary is broken, since it is not possible to foresee every eventuality.

As Wittgenstein (1980) said:

> If people did not do silly things, nothing intelligent would ever get done.

It is, therefore, when the boundary is broken that the tolerance of the learning environment is crucial otherwise the whole exercise will be undermined, possibly for good.

In creating a learning environment managers continuously provide learning opportunities for others by encouraging people to experiment themselves, by sharing knowledge, involving people in making decisions and in giving feedback. Such managers will also set aside time for learning during meetings and encourage a feeling of camaraderie to exist within the unit, particularly by ensuring that issues of morale are considered. They will also ensure that every problem presented by a member of staff contains a possible solution. Thus not only will the member of staff start to get used to thinking in wider terms but also, the more frequently it happens, the less need there will be for consultation in the first place. My colleague at the Civil Service College, Lionel Titman, has produced a useful list of 20 things which managers can do themselves to start creating the right atmosphere. They are reproduced in Figure 11.6.

A litmus test is given by Pedler et al (1991) as to how your environment stands in respect of being a learning organisation is to look at the way the last three errors, breakdowns or failures were dealt with:

- did people talk openly about them or did they hide away and avoid the subject
- what was learned from the mistakes
- did people get blamed, or did they feel empowered as a result of the post-mortem?

Undoubtedly organisations are more likely to succeed in creating empowered environments if:

- the strategic objectives are clear and reflect the views of the staff
- the structure is sufficiently flat to provide opportunities for control without stifling innovations
- systems are consistent with the outcomes of the business as opposed to promoting certain interests.

It will also be of enormous benefit in creating the right culture if there is genuine commitment from the top, as shown in Chapters 16 and 17.

It is a mistake however to believe that without these nothing can be done, just as it is a mistake to believe that with these empowerment will bloom. This chapter has endeavoured to demonstrate that empowerment starts and ends with the individual member of staff and their perception of their situation. The person most able to enhance this is not someone way up in the organisation but the immediate line

---

"What to do on Monday"
by
Lionel Titman

1. Decide what you want to do and how you will do it.

2. List what stands in your way:
   • about you,
   • staff and colleagues,
   • customers and suppliers,
   • superiors, systems and mandates.

3. Decide the easiest way to overcome every possible obstacle
   (especially those that arise because of you).

4. Start a folder. Prepare your plan for the future and put it in the folder.
   Put the folder in a safe place. Add notes as necessary.

5. Think of some recent examples where staff wanted to make a change or
   improvement and where you failed to help them get it done. Go back to them.
   See if you could make the change; discuss it with them. Find a way round any
   obstacles, together. If the change is really not possible, show your disappointment.
   Show how glad you are that the suggestion was made. [If no such suggestions
   have been made recently, think whether the fault could possibly be with yourself]

6. Did a member of staff do particularly well last week? Did they use their initiative
   in overcoming a difficulty? If so, did you praise them and thank them?. If not, do it
   today because it's not too late (it will be by next week). From now on - you will
   always respond to success, (and to innovation, going the extra mile, delighting
   customers and suppliers) in the same way. You will say thank-you and well done,
   and later praise them to their peers.

7. Look round the office. Is there something that drives everybody crazy? Such as
   a photocopier that is a pain to use, disputes over lunch breaks, problems about
   the flow of work. Can you put it right quickly? If so, do it at once. If not, set up a
   mini-project headed by a junior member of staff. When the project team
   responds, act on what they suggest. Do not worry if the subject matter seems
   less than earth shattering to you, personally. Firstly, we are looking at what the
   staff want to solve. Secondly, a small first step can be very advantageous.

8. Is there a major difficulty with a customer or supplier (internal or external)? Set up
   a project, or ask for suggestions or hold a discussion. Do not be too glib in your
   reaction - results are needed but not at the price of robustness. Action the
   solution.

Figure 11.6. What to do on Monday

9. Delegate at least two important responsibilities. If you have the authority, broaden spans of control, reduce the layers of supervision. Exploit the 'ink monitor syndrome' - e.g. give a junior the responsibility for working out the holiday/shift/duty rota. If there is a dispute, support the junior.

10. Keep on saying thank-you and well done, and praising change and innovation whenever it occurs. If Scrooge could improve dramatically, so can you.

11. Make it plain that you are encouraging openness and honesty. If you have been restricting information to a select few, make it available to everyone. Keep people informed. Next time somebody makes a mistake, try not to yell at them - quietly show how lessons can be learnt. If a procedure is at fault, change it.

12. Look in an unbiased way at your leadership style. Is it less than perfect? If so, decide what needs doing. Start the change. You will not achieve perfection this week but you can make a start.

13. Eliminate ruthlessly all unnecessary reports, especially those that you started yourself. This will show that you can change, that life can get better for everybody, and that anything can be challenged.

14. Are your staff super-skilled and super-knowledgeable? If not, initiate training. Ask people what they feel unsure about in their work.

15. Demonstrate to your staff some of the 'techniques' of creativity and innovation. Show how enjoyable and useful they are. Encourage their use. Use them yourself, as a normal part of everyday life.

16. Look at the systems, procedures, I.T., paperwork, filing, etc. Agree with your staff how they can be changed to make life more pleasant. Get action.

17. Tackle the meetings that take place. Get the staff to find ways of reducing the time spent on meetings. This means both reducing the number of meetings and cutting hard the time spent at each meeting.

18. By now there should have been a change in the internal climate of the office and in people's expectations of how they are treated. It is therefore possible for you to tackle those major items that you had recognised were areas of concern. It is time to take another look at the folder that you prepared earlier.

19. Take another look at the big things in the life of the office. Their nature will vary from office to office but may well include such items as:
    • staff attitudes, morale, culture, skills, knowledge,
    • relationships with customers, suppliers, stakeholders,
    • levels of service, quality, scheduling,
    • organisation structure, systems, I.T., performance levels, administration.

20. Change and innovate.

Figure 11.6. (cont.) What to do on Monday

manager. To achieve this they need to understand what stops their staff getting their job done, particularly the influence of their own behaviour and values. This will then assist them in tackling relationships with superiors in order to remove some of the barriers. Above all, however, they need to realise their potential for changing things within their own domain. In so doing they will recognise that the transfer of power is not a win/lose situation where they are losing and the staff are gaining. Rather, it is a game where everyone can win, since release of the hitherto untapped potential will far surpass previous performance, while at the same time allowing everyone to grow and develop from the experience. Yes it will take courage and cannot be done overnight. Chapters 19 and 20 however demonstrate clearly the power and ability of committed line managers in achieving it.

Finally, the following anonymous words on risk are worth consideration:

> To laugh, is to risk appearing the fool,
> To weep is to risk appearing sentimental,
> To reach out for another is to risk involvement,
> To express feelings is to risk exposing your true self,
> To place your ideas, your dreams before the crowd is to risk their loss,
> To love is to risk not being loved in return,
> To live is to risk dying,
> To hope is to risk despair,
> To try is to risk failure,
> But, risks must be taken, because the greatest hazard is to risk nothing,
> The person who risks nothing, has nothing, is nothing, does nothing... they may avoid suffering and sorrow, but simply cannot learn, feel, change, grow, love... live.
> Chained by attitudes, we become slaves, forfeit freedom, only the person who takes risks is free.

References and suggested reading

Bate, P. (1994) *Strategies for Cultural Change* Oxford, Butterworth-Heinemann

Block, P. (1991) *The Empowered Manager* Oxford, Jossey-Bass

Brooks, A. (1992) Building Learning Organisations: The Individual–CultureInteraction *Human Resource Development Quarterly*, Vol. 3 No. 4

Clegg, S. (1990) *Modern organisations* London, Sage

Colville, I. Dalton, K. and Thompkins, C. (1993) Developing and Understanding Cultural Change in Customs and Excise *Public Administration* Vol. 71 Winter

Conger, J. and Kanungo, R. (1988) The Empowerment Process: Integrating Theory and Practice *Academy of Management Review* Vol. 13 No 3

Handy, C. (1994) *The Empty Raincoat* London, Hutchinson

Harvey, J. (1988) *The Abilene Paradox* San Francisco, Pfeiffer and Co.

Heron, J. (1990) *Helping the Client* London, Sage

Honey, P. (1991) The Learning Organisation Simplified
Training and Development July

Kanter, R. (1983) *The Change Masters* London, Unwin

Ketchum, L. and Trist, E. (1992) *All Teams Are Not Created Equal* London, Sage

Luft, J. (1961) The Johari Window *Human Relations Training News*, 5

Lynch, D. and Kordis, P. (1988) *Strategy of the Dolphin* London, Hutchinson

Pareek, U. (1982) *Internal and External Control - Annual of Facilitators, Trainers and Consultants* University Associates

Pedler, M. Burgoyne, J. and Boydell, T. (1991) *The Learning Company*
Maidenhead, McGraw-Hill

Rao, T. (1985) *The Entrepreneurial Orientation Inventory: Measuring the Locus of Control* University Associates

Scott, C. and Jaffe, D. (1991) *Empowerment* London, Kogan Page

Senge, P. (1990) *The Fifth Discipline* London, Century

Stacey, R. (1993) *Strategic Management and Organisational Dynamics*
London, Pitman

Stewart, A. (1994) *Empowering People* London, Pitman

Ripley, R. and Ripley, M. (1992) Empowerment, the Cornerstone of Quality
Management Decision Vol. 30 No 4

Talbot, C. and Harrow, J. (1993) *Sharing or Withholding Organisational Knowledge? An Exploration of Changing Values in Managerial and Organisational Learning*
British Academy of Management Conference September

Wittgenstein, L. (1980) in *Culture and Value* ed von Wright, G. Oxford, Blackwell

Chapter 12

Quality and the transformation of the organisation

David Shaw

Historically, organisational change efforts have generally concentrated on structural and technological change. One view suggests that success has been limited over the long term by the failure to recognise that organisational structures and technological systems are systemically and dynamically linked to the human behaviours within the organisation.

Quality management has been developed to address this issue. Over the past decade it has been promoted in the United States and Western Europe across the spectrum of manufacturing, service, government, public and private sector organisations. Managers have lived through many new phases of organisational change and leadership techniques, so why should this new paradigm provide any true dawn?

Pursuing excellence

Total Quality Management, as it is frequently described (TQM is its acronym) is a strategic approach to producing the best products or services possible.

It must be TOTAL in that it applies to :

- all parts of the organisation
- its suppliers as much as its own departments /divisions
- intangible services as much as physical products
- everybody - clerks, operators, managers, policy makers, chief executive.

It must have the primary focus on QUALITY through:

- continuous, measured, improvement in the quality of the systems
- primacy of the customer as the judge of the organisation's success.

It must be MANAGED:

- as a structured, monitored programme of change

- by continuously improving the processes
- and implemented by all managers, but led by the top managers.

Standardisation of the methods of work to an accredited level of performance has been pursued by many organisations. They can acquire accreditation under the standards of ISO 9000 or BS5750, or can work hard at 'zero defect' products but their quality may still not be right. There are other functions and departments which let the organisation down. A research report conducted in 1984 found that 95% of companies deliver their goods late. This late delivery can have just as much impact on the future buying decisions as can increasing the price of the product by 5% (Atkinson 1990)!

This chapter initially examines the history of 'quality management' then discusses the fundamental concepts and concludes with a large scale 'routemap' for starting the transformation of the organisation.

The story of quality

Ancient history amply demonstrates that issues of quality have existed in societies as long as historical records have been made. Two millennia before Christ, Phoenician royal inspectors set harsh punishments for workers infringing quality standards. Egyptian inspectors checked the squareness of stone blocks with a string as the stone curer watched, and these ancient civilisations had complex rules to deal with equity of trade and complaint handling. In Western Europe apprenticeships and trade guilds developed in the 13th century. Craftsmen built quality into their goods and, being close to their customers, knew what those customers wanted.

❑ Industrial manufacturing influences

Modern industrial systems began to emerge during the Industrial Revolution and by the end of the 19th century in the United States Frederick Taylor had pioneered 'scientific management'. The workers and foremen had little part in the design and planning of the products, with virtually no contact with the purchasers and users of the items. Assembly line production enabled complex operations to be sub-divided into simple procedures, thereby producing low cost goods. Part of the procedures was inspection of the finished product, separating the non-conforming from the conforming products. Technical advancements in the early part of the 20th century enabled the mass populations to obtain products previously reserved for the wealthy.

Senior management began to realise that quality suffered because of these systems and during the 1920s Western Electric in the United States led the way in quality control. The company instituted an inspection engineering department to deal with the problems created by defects in their products and lack of co-ordination between their departments. In 1924 Walter Shewhart introduced statistical quality control. This provided a method for efficiently and economically controlling quality in mass production systems. Shewhart was also the first person to point out that quality has both subjective as well as objective aspects to it.

In 1935, E. S. Pearson developed British Standard 600 for acceptance sampling of incoming material to a factory and subsequent developments of national standards were seen throughout the next decade. World War II had quickened the growth of quality control technology and in 1946 the American Society for Quality Control was formed. Its first president, George Edwards, declared (Gitlow 1990):

> Quality is going to assume a more and more important place alongside competition in cost and sale price, and the company that fails to work out some arrangements for securing effective control is bound ultimately to find itself faced with a kind of competition it can no longer meet successfully

❑ The Japanese experience

At the same time in Japan the Union of Japanese Scientists and Engineers (JUSE) was established. Several of its members, among them Kaoro Ishekawa, developed and led Japanese quality control, including the birth of quality circles. In 1950, W. Edwards Deming was invited to speak to Japan's leading industrialists. Deming had worked closely with Shewhart at Western Electric in the United States. He had also succeeded in making a great impact on the efficiency of the US population census in the early forties and in other industries during the war. Members of JUSE were concerned with rebuilding Japan after the war, breaking into foreign markets and improving the quality of their products. Deming convinced them that following his methods, developed from the work of Shewhart, would lead Japanese quality to become the best in the world. The prestigious Deming Prize was subsequently founded in Japan to award achievements of improvements in quality theory or application. Companies with familiar names, such as Toyota, Nissan, Hitachi, Sony, have been recipients of the prize.

In 1954, Joseph Juran was invited to talk to middle and senior executives in Japan about their role in the pursuit of quality control activities. He and Deming led the way to an overall and holistic approach for quality in aspects of the organisation. In the 1950s and early 1960s, Armand V. Feigenbaum was developing basic principles of total quality control (TQC) at General Electric. A team of Japanese visited that company in 1958 and took away the name to develop their own brand of the fundamental concepts, also integrating the work done by Deming and Juran.

The holistic concepts of Deming and Juran expanded the TQC concept of quality, achieving conformance to customer requirements, to include quality of design and quality of performance. In addition to the traditional view of quality, TQC requires all in the organisation, from clerks and operatives to chairman of the Board, from suppliers to customers, and the community, to be highly conscious of and active in improving quality in the organisation.

❏ The West wakes up

During the 1970s and 1980s the quality of Japanese goods surpassed those of the majority of western organisations and were marked by a pursuit of quality in all facets of the organisation, finance, sales, personnel, maintenance, management, manufacturing and services. In the early 1980s western organisations began to wake up to the fact that the competition from the far east, and Japan in particular, needed to be addressed. An epic prime-time TV documentary programme in the United States in 1980, on the work and influence of W. Edward Deming on the success of Japanese industry and commerce, brought the full impact of the quiet revolution home to a wide audience. The telephone lines to Deming's home in Washington DC were jammed the following morning with senior managers wanting to know more about his approach to managing for quality. Momentum gathered apace and the new approaches began to be developed across the States and trickle to Europe through the subsidiaries of American organisations, as well as through seminars and consultancy work.

In the early development of quality management in the UK there was a tendency to perceive it as another system to bolt onto the organisation, or a set of systems to be applied to a standard which can be judged externally. This was the impression given to those first exposed to the British Standard on quality management, BS5750, that achieving set standards is what TQM is about. Many who have started at that point learn that there is much more to it than that. Accreditation has assisted a large number of organisations to improve their business performance but it is only one small step on a never ending journey of learning and improvement. Many organisations, in the public as well as the private sector, pursue quality through a variety of approaches but the majority of those who are making progress all have similar fundamental ideas at the heart of their programmes. The most important elements of the successful 'transformation' to a TQM organisation are the cultural, conceptual and behavioural changes. Setting standards, using the technologies and methodologies, are only elements in a complex set of changes which need to be achieved.

The heart of the matter

If asked to name a number of successful companies no doubt the following would feature in the lists generated - Sony, Toyota, Nissan, Hewlett Packard, Motorola, Phillips, ICI, Marks and Spencer, The Body Shop. Any discussion about the characteristics that make these companies top performers would end up with vague generalisations about their culture. People perceive them as having the ability to create, implement, and maintain leadership positions. So what is the culture that the TQM organisations are seeking to foster?

❏ Fundamental ideas of managing for quality

A survey of 20 companies (Linkow 1989) which are implementing total quality suggests seven core values and beliefs of total quality.

Customer focus

The definition of quality focuses on the customer's needs and requirements, though Deming stated that it is only in 'delighting the customer' that long term satisfaction is provided. The satisfaction of the external customer can only be met when all the internal customer requirements are also met.

Employee focus

The organisation's ability to serve its customers depends upon how well it serves its own employees. The organisation is committed to recruiting, developing, and supporting a highly motivated, world class work force.

Teamwork

Collective wisdom is virtually always superior to individual wisdom. The team and the individual are recognised and rewarded equally.

Safety

The organisation focuses on safety in everything it does, for all its employees, the communities in which it is located, and the people who use its products and services.

Candour

Each employee should feel able to speak the truth. Quality cannot be achieved when employees fear retribution for their candour.

Total involvement

Quality is the responsibility of everyone. All the members of the organisation must take a personal responsibility for quality.

Process focused

There is an emphasis on the continuous improvement of all the processes.

The adoption of these values requires a change to managers' traditional thinking and mind set. The new paradigms challenge many of the old concepts that have brought individuals success in the old culture of their organisation.

❑ What is quality

In his fascinating book, *Zen and the Art of Motorcycle Maintenance*, Persig (1974) demonstrates that 'quality' cannot be defined by reference to more basic ideas. It is itself a primitive idea. It is easier to approach it from the standpoint of saying what it is not.

The *features* of a product or service are those attributes of the product provided to meet the desires and wishes of the customer. For instance house builders will frequently advertise their houses as 'high quality' when, in fact, they mean they are adding features, such as double glazing, en-suite bathrooms, fully fitted kitchens. Experience frequently finds the opposite, the roof leaking, central heating breaking down, doors ill fitting. The impression trying to be created is that by adding features you will receive quality. When the car manufacturers offered different ranges of colour for their cars they introduced a *feature*. When the paints were developed so that they did not fade in the sunlight and had a smooth mirror like finish, they added *quality* (Tribus 1985).

Quality is frequently defined as 'conformance to specification'. Specification provides a definition of acceptability but in the market place to strive only to provide an acceptable level of service, or product, is to opt for mediocrity and ultimately last place. In the market place there is no law that guarantees survival. Quality organisations know that they must be constantly striving for improvements in the quality of everything they do.

❑ Quality and costs

Generally an increase in the features of a service or product is expected to cost more, for example a colour TV set with Nicam stereo compared to a black and white portable TV, or more information leaflets provided at the reception point of a Benefits Agency office. Costs, however, go down as the waste, rework, and complaints diminish due to more accurate and consistent service delivery. The need for inspection and checking procedures will also reduce, with consequent savings on costs. Feigenbaum (1983) referred to the 'hidden factory' where employees were busy fixing the mistakes and reworking whilst managers were meeting targets.The cost in terms of the good will of the customer cannot be fully calculated if they are faced with inaccurate tax demands or the wrong information given over the telephone about court procedures. It will waste time for the customer as well as the organisation in rectifying the situation at some future date.

❏ Quality and productivity

Myron Tribus, one time Secretary of State for Commerce in the US government and a senior executive at Rank-Xerox, and now an engineering and quality consultant, concludes in a paper to the United States government on *Improving Productivity in Government Services* (1983):

> The secrets of success of those who have obtained world records in productivity are very simple but almost universally misunderstood:
>
> The route to increased productivity is through increased quality:-
>
> * better quality of the design to meet customer needs,
> * better quality of incoming materials,
> * better quality of maintenance,
> * better quality of training,
> * better statistical quality control of every process.

These summarised points are based on important principles strongly emphasised by Deming. They need to be understood in order to improve the productivity of any system.

The system

If there is a desire to increase productivity of a system it is no good preaching about it. It is wasting management's time, and certainly the workers' efforts are likely to distort the system to deliver the measurable outputs, if there is a single minded emphasis on productivity. The productivity of the system will be improved by improving the quality of the performance of all the parts of the system. The inputs to the system from suppliers must be of high quality and every process in the system must be carried out with maximum effectiveness and efficiency.

The manager's job

Every manager should be involved in improving the system being managed. When a system is not working properly, 85-95% of the time it will be the fault of the system, not the employees. Unless managers therefore seek to improve the processes they manage, and that is a core function of their responsibilities, productivity will not increase.

Understand variation

Managers should make quality of performance their prime objective. This requires training in the tools and techniques of process improvement at all levels of the organisation. There needs to be a consistent endeavour to learn about the processes and systems in order to improve them. Everyone needs to be able to recognise good quality performance and how that is operationally defined and measured. This leads to an understanding of the variation inherent in any system and the statistical tools available to measure this are used to track down the things that prevent performance from being of a high quality. The workers should be involved in the pursuit of improvement (Deming 1985, 1993).

New view of the organisation

The majority of organisations are viewed as a hierarchy as in Figure 12.1 (Chandler 1977) displaying who is accountable to whom, the number of subordinates a senior person has under them, and the boundaries between areas of responsibility. The short-comings of this view are that it does not show the inter-dependence of the different functional divisions and that the flow of the work through the organisation is not apparent. There is also an absence of any focus on customers, internal as well as external.

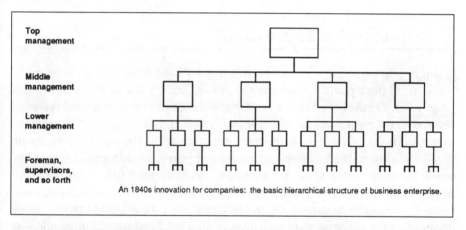

Figure 12.1 The old way to view an organisation (Chandler, 1977).

On the other hand, in order to develop a different way of thinking about the organisation, the systems diagram shown in Figure 12.2 (Deming 1985) can be developed. This model was first used by Deming in Japan in 1950.

The importance of senior managers working on this systems diagram of the organisation is that the inter-dependency of the different functional areas is quickly apparent and the suppliers as well as the customers can be clearly shown. Middle managers and their staff can also work from the same perspective and raise their awareness of the internal customer/supplier relationships. It aids managers' thinking of the organisation as one system and the need to have the different functions, within the flow of processes, working together as one team. The relationships can be developed with the aim of gain/gain being achieved. The quality organisation has no appetite for inter-divisional warfare.

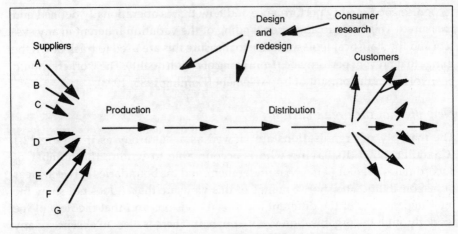

Figure 12.2 The new way to view an organisation (Deming, 1985).

Transforming the organisation

Changing the organisation is not a quick fix easy matter and authoritarian command from the top will not achieve the desired results. A well thought through programme for the initial stages needs to be developed with continual cycles of reviewing progress and learning from the work undertaken before moving on to fresh phases. In the very large organisations such as the Benefits Agency or the NHS, some of the following points may appear geared to a scale that is too small. However, while some different considerations need to be addressed, the points made can be integrated into strategies for larger networked organisations. These larger organisations are, in many respects, a multiplicity of small organisations and the fundamental principles of the development of people and processes in the organisation are the same. The organisation has therefore to be thinking of a steady, gradual growth, from the head office units to selected units in the field, to accomplish the transformation. This will take time, so an important ingredient of success is avoiding the temptation on the part of senior managers to seek 'instant pudding' (Deming, 1985).

The goals of the transformation should have consistency and method throughout the organisation. Clear communication is required to aid in the understanding of the people in the middle and lower levels of the organisation for the rationale for the change.The emphasis should be on the processes to be used to move the programme forward, rather than concentrating on the end results, e.g. 'these are the approaches we expect to be used in designing and implementing the change.'

The importance of the leaders themselves undergoing the change in order to demonstrate commitment, and the importance of the transformation, cannot be over emphasised. The informal behaviours of the managers give very strong messages to the staff and require to be considered as much as the formal support systems that are changed to assist the transformation.

❑ Top managers lead the transformation

It is to some extent inevitable that people think in linear structures because we experience time in a linear way. One hour follows the last hour, one day precedes the next. The reality of organisations, however, is different in that they are systems which are both social as well as structured, technical entities with simultaneous interactions between the sub-systems.

Linear models are inadequate to understand the complexities of the interactions of all the subsystems from suppliers to customers. Experience from many organisations which have introduced and worked to change to a quality organisation suggests a four phased model for change:

- education
- planning
- implementation
- continuous improvement.

This gives the impression of there being a linear approach, but in order to succeed effort needs to be made during each stage to direct thinking and action towards the next. Also no stage is ever considered finished. There is a continuous cycling through the phases in order that learning continues.

The education phase

The new ways of thinking initially require introduction to the top managers and subsequently to everyone else in the organisation. The fundamentals of quality management mentioned above are part of a system of inter-related thinking encompassing:

- a view of the organisation as a system which has inter-dependent parts, with a need to establish a long term aim to which all the members of the organisation can make a contribution

- an understanding of variation in the organisation's systems and processes, with a consequential need for training managers and staff in quality improvement techniques and a deeper understanding of data, to distinguish the changes in the routine outputs of the systems from those which have special causes requiring individual attention;

191

through these techniques, and a developing understanding of the performance of the systems, the organisation learns to do things better and deliver improved product or service to their customers

- the development of the people in the organisation, recognising they are individually different, they learn differently, that working in teams on process improvement provides extra dimensions to their work and greater involvement in decision making.

Top management support and involvement are critical ingredients to the transformation. Without this leadership in the learning and application of the concepts, tools and techniques, the transformation will not enable the organisation to achieve high quality services. There is no standardised approach to this phase, each organisation making its own programme suitable for its particular needs as the first step in establishing knowledge about quality, and gaining commitment to it. The Inland Revenue Accounts Office, at Shipley, ran a programme of one day workshops once a month for the senior management team over a number of months and some way into that programme had half day 'awareness sessions' for all the staff.

British Rail devised an education and awareness programme for its five hundred senior executives (Leadership 500). Leadership 500 was a one week residential course built around syndicates of senior executives related as far as possible by internal customer-supplier relationships. The main emphasis was upon effective leadership and sought to develop the key concepts of quality management.

Once the concepts of TQM are absorbed at the top of the organisation the desire for a programme of change becomes pressing. Precipitate action can lead to false trails and a serious dent to the credibility of management. So caution is needed for goals to be established and appropriate planning of tasks. It is only during the planning phase that resources, time, money, and people can be allocated.

Planning the implementation phase

A blue-print for a start-up period of eighteen months to two years is important so that it encourages strategic thinking and top management involvement in the planning process. Delegation of developing the plans is to be discouraged and the longer term thinking also discourages seeking 'quick fix' solutions. The main objective is the change of emphasis so that quality becomes a way of managing, not something extra to manage. Deming emphasised that in business an organisation's leadership must determine its aim to ensure that there is an organisational strategy. This means creating a vision or goal, laying the plans for reaching it, and executing the strategy.

❏ Thinking of the system

It is at this stage that the senior managers begin to consider their organisation as a system. This will include taking stock of the characteristics of the organisation and identifying the areas for change and improvement. There is a range of methods, from attitude surveys to discussion groups at various levels of the organisation, to provide feedback about how the organisation sees itself. It becomes a more powerful analysis if, at this stage, some understanding of the perceptions of the suppliers and the customers are sought to give a comprehensive picture. This information acts as a vital benchmark against which to measure achievement and to give some idea of the areas for improvement.

In order for there to be clarity of purpose and direction the top managers will need to work on producing an aim, goal or vision for the organisation. As Deming (1993) said:

> Without an aim there is no system.

This gives the direction and purpose for the whole organisation and can be a great energiser if other people, as well as top managers, contribute to its formulation. Alignment to the intention of the top team needs careful analysis for consistency. The statement of the aim is intended to influence others, so bland generalisations can lead to sub-optimization and disillusionment.

A clear strategy is required to guide the detailed plans in the implementation phase. Beware of the temptation to seek answers from other organisations and use them as simple models. Their starting point will have been different, their people different in skills and experience. This does not preclude comparing notes or finding from others what assisted their progress, but there is no easy role model to copy. The thinking needs to embody the understanding of where your own organisation stands, and what it wants to achieve, guided by insights into the concepts developed through the education phase.

❏ Organising for change

The programme cannot be progressed without organisation and leadership at the top. A structure for managing the plan is required and the overall direction and planning frequently rests with a quality council or steering group. Their primary responsibility is developing the overall aims of the programme and the main planning of the resources and reviewing progress (Finlay 1987). The multitude of administrative and logistical activities require planning and co-ordinating and can rest with a single individual or small team reporting to the steering group. The co-ordinator should be a capable leader who develops personal knowledge of the methods and tools of quality management ahead of others in the organisation. They usually act as a valuable resource to managers and steering groups, as well as developing and supporting team facilitators as outlined in Figure12.3 (PMI, 1990).

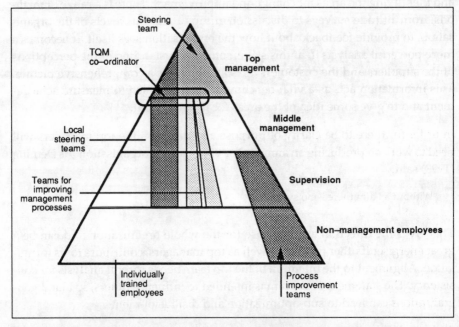

Figure 12.3 Populations for the quality transformation process (PMI, 1990).

Local steering groups are required, if the organisation is large, with the responsibility for enabling improvements in their local units. Their focus is on day to day actions to improve the work processes. There are normally as many local steering groups as there are divisions or business units. Care needs to be taken, however, to prevent this structure from developing into a 'quality empire', a bureaucracy intent on expanding for its own sake.

❑ Where to start?

Where do the senior managers look to start improvements? This is an extremely critical decision which needs to get the change growing from the existing culture. It also needs to build in the potential to grow into a comprehensive programme. One of the critical distinctions between the old and the new management cultures is the management of processes. A fundamental concept that Juran and Deming brought to the attention of the Japanese senior executives was that 85% and more of the problems faced by managers are the result of the processes and systems rather than the variation of the performance of individual people. The best way, therefore, of starting after the education into the concepts and principles, is to select processes for improvement. This means the top managers working themselves on the management processes. The type of processes might well be the communications system, the vocational and management training processes, the process of obtaining management information.

These will have been indicated by the information gained at the earlier preparatory stages in listening to the customers, suppliers, and the staff. This would lead to managers training in process improvement techniques and gaining insights from their application. The senior managers of the West Midlands Employment Service (see Chapter 18) worked on their management processes after the training programme had begun to roll-out, one year after the programme start.

❏ Developing expertise

The transformation will demand the involvement of teams of middle managers and more junior staff using the techniques of process improvement. Much of the earlier education and training will have been provided by external consultancy but the programme will require the development of in-house capability to continue the training, education and on-going support of the process improvement teams. This group of people will act as the internal process improvement consultants. They should be selected for their ability to learn the tools of process improvement, team and group development, and be willing to teach and coach others in their application. A further important attribute is the ability to gain the acceptance of their peers and superiors alike.

❏ Team working

The major element of the implementation phase will be process improvement teams or quality teams working on issues or processes for improvement. Great care must be put into the selection of the projects. They should have a high probability of success and the potential for high visibility with demonstrable savings or improvement for the customer. They should be clear tangible issues related to a clearly identified and limited process. The results of the project may involve the solving of a problem, the reduction of costs or waste, reduced error or re-work but the effort needs to be directed to an expectation of benefit to some identifiable customers.

Managers will have concerns about business performance which require attention, and will want the early efforts to pay attention to them. On the other hand, it is imperative to solicit suggestions from employees for project work. Managers will wish to learn from the different projects as to the way future projects are selected. It is essential to have a proportion of the projects linked to cross-functional processes so that internal customer-supplier issues can be explored and used for positive practical learning, as well as addressing the cultural issue of breaking down the barriers between functions or units of the organisation.

Implementation

Quality is something on which managers may focus only during TQM meetings. If managers commission a team to improve a process, but then tamper and attempt to prescribe results, lack of progress will become apparent. The implementation phase therefore needs to be addressing the cultural issues as well as the improvement processes.

❏ Changing the culture

The pace and success of the implementation phase will depend on the amount of time and effort that top management is able and willing to provide. It cannot be done haphazardly and needs to take account of the organisation's culture. The culture is the result of the common day-to-day experiences of the people who work in the organisation.

There are three important aspects of culture that should be promoted and specifically planned for improvement.

- There should be a programme for clarifying who the internal and external customers are and for identifying the customers' needs and requirements. Do the 'suppliers' see the 'customers' as real people who actually feel about the service they receive? Face to face discussion with a variety of customers to discuss ways of improving the service are more powerful ways of engaging in cultural change at this stage than sterile customer questionnaire surveys. These experiences can be used to develop a planned regular feedback from the customers.

- The scientific approach should be developed to reduce shooting from the hip and opinion offered as fact, though unsupported with data. Good data are used at all levels of the organisation.

- Constant improvement should become the order of the day and a major consideration of everyone. A clear recognition of the people who are constantly working to improve the processes should be the norm for managers. In all the improvement efforts the sequence of change which the Japanese call the 'Deming Wheel' (Deming,1985) should be employed.

  Plan
  Consider carefully and thoroughly how and what to do. Use data as far as possible to analyse the situation. Identify the key success factors and how they will be measured.

Do
Carry out the plan.

Study
As the plan is implemented, monitor and evaluate your efforts.

Act
Incorporate the improvements into the process as standard methods. Identify further areas for improvement.

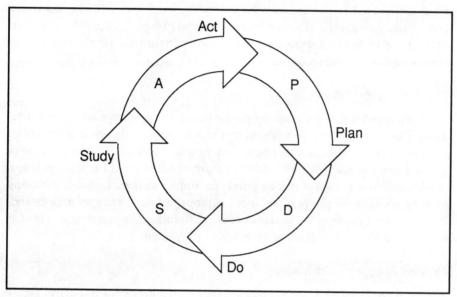

Figure 12.4 The PDSA cycle (Deming, 1985).

❏ Improvement teams

Attention needs to be given to the composition, organisation, working methods and mentoring of improvement teams.

Team members

The team leaders are appointed by the managers but the team members can be nominated by the employees. It can give confidence to their peers that managers are serious about involvement. The whole group should, however, work in the process under consideration because it is the actual manner in which the work is done that is under investigation. These people know exactly what happens and are fully aware of the difficulties in their work and will have many ideas about improvements. The membership can cut across divisional or unit boundaries and come from different levels in the hierarchy. It is advisable to have teams of between six and eight individuals.

Team progress

The teams meet regularly, initially weekly, to maintain a good momentum, but the intervals are likely to reduce to every other week or longer dependent on the stage of the project, the amount of data that they require to collect and the complexity of the issues. They will require developing as a group and be aware of the communication and inter-personal issues relating to their colleagues and managers who are not directly working with them. The managers will require progress reports from which they learn about the organisation's processes and what is involved in process improvement. The managers will also learn that lasting and worthwhile improvements cannot be rushed. Successful projects are meant to educate and inspire, and they require patience and persistence, as well as making improvements, so that the culture of the organisation begins to change.

The scientific method

The teams need training and development in the scientific approach to improvement. This is based on reason, sound methodologies, and the use of data. This is an important strand of process improvement which paradoxically requires to be applied hand in hand with the development of the team at the inter-personal level. It is also not suitable to look purely for implementing cherished solutions, or agree on some simple quick solution, without getting to a deeper understanding of the root cause of the issues in hand. Carefully collected data can lead to the main causes of problems or variation in the system.

Process improvement leaders

The teams will require support and guidance in addition to the initial training in the tools and techniques. This can be provided by both managers, who are knowledgeable of the approach due to their education and training in the concepts and application of the tools, and technical advisers. The technical advisers, frequently called Process Improvement Leaders, train and coach the team in the two areas of:

- organisational and team skills - conducting meetings, communication and other interpersonal skills
- an understanding of the tools of quality improvement - process flowcharts, cause and effect diagrams, data collection and analysis.

The advisers attend each meeting and provide training as it is required.

❑ Hazard warning

Project teams can be very successful and seduce management into believing they have achieved the transformation of the organisation if they mushroom across the organisation. But very much more is required, particularly the style of management from managers themselves. One person's traditional management behaviour can destroy the efforts of many to change the culture. Teams can be viewed positively but they are only one of the tools to transforming the organisation so that it is learning, developing and focusing on the customer in all that it does.

The continuous improvement phase

Earlier the point was emphasised that there are no 'quick fixes', no 'instant pudding'. The earlier phases will probably take between two and a half and three years from the start of the education phase. The new way of doing the business is now becoming the norm, moving away from the culture of fire fighting and 'if it ain't broke, don't fix it' syndrome. Steering group meetings originally designed to guide the transformation will have become a regular part of management's business meetings and one of the ways they lead the organisation.

Issues will be tackled pro-actively and plans developed integrating larger scale innovation of processes and systems. These plans sustain a more consistent effort and address the overall vision and aims of the organisation. There will have been a large training and development resource delivered in the previous phases. This will need to be sustained and become pervasive in all parts of the organisation in order to hold the gains and continue to move on to greater success.

Leadership by management will continue to grow, as will their understanding of variation in their processes. A different way of thinking will continue to develop. Individual departments, divisions or units of the organisation will be developing their own long–term quality plans. These plans will fit into the strategy plans defined at the earlier planning stage of the whole transformation. The organisation's senior manager must continue to make clear and strong expectations of continuing process improvement.

The concept of quality will need re–inforcing at every opportunity. Doubt and scepticism will need to be replaced by acceptance and participation in the new way of managing. Those who have not acquired the new skills will need continuing support and guidance. Education and training at all levels must become a part of the transformation effort and ways developed to expand it. It is only with continuous development of the people in the organisation that the potential to meet the future challenges is put in place.

About the author

Dr David Shaw is a psychologist who was a civil servant until becoming an independent consultant in 1990. Consulting assignments have included guidance, advice and training in the implementation of large IT systems and Total Quality programmes. He tutors at the Civil Service College, is an associate of Process Management International and is a member of the British Deming Association Alliance of Consultants.

References and suggested reading

Atkinson, P. E. (1990) *Creating Culture Change: The key to successful Total Quality Management* Bedford, IFS Publications.

Chandler, Alfred D. Jnr (1977) *The Visible Hand, The Managerial Revolution in American Business* Cambridge MA. Bolknap.

Deming, W. Edwards (1985) *Out of the Crisis*
Cambridge MA. MIT Centre for Advanced Engineering Study

Deming, W. Edwards (1993) *The New Economics*
Cambridge MA. MIT Centre for Advanced Engineering Study

Feigenbaun, A. V. (1983) *Total Quality Control* New York, McGraw Hill

Finlay, J. S. (1987) *Improving the Quality Management Process* Paper published by Process Management International October

Gitlow, H. S. (1990) *Planning for Quality, Productivity, and Competitive Position* Homewood, Ill. Richard D Irwin Inc

Linkow, P. (1989) Is your culture ready for Total Quality?
Quality Progress Vol XXI 1 No 11

Persig, R. M. *Zen and the Art of Motorcycle Maintenance.* New York, Morrow

PMI (1990) *Planning for Total Quality Management* Minneapolis, PMI

Tribus, M. & Tsuda, Y. (1985) *The Quality Imperative in the New Economic Era* Cambridge MA. MIT Centre for Advanced Engineering Study

Chapter 13

The Citizen's Charter:

some managerial considerations

Jenny Harrow

The growing familiarity of 'the Citizen's Charter' policy among public servants and the public emphasises the opportunities provided by 'ordinary' policy initiatives in inducing and sustaining change in the management and delivery of public services. This is a policy-into-practice programme where public organisations draw up, publish and then work to a set of operating standards - 'charters' - to establish the level and nature of the service which users may expect, responding appropriately and regularly to users' experiences and evaluations Introduced formally in a July 1991 White Paper, the policy, according to the Prime Minister (Cabinet Office 1991) is intended to be:

> ..one of the central themes of public life in the 1990s.

Prime Ministerially-led, the policy provides a centrally-inspired template for quality service delivery to citizens. By March 1994, it was presented as:

> a ten-year programme to raise the standard of public services and make them more responsive to the needs and wishes of their users.

A series of core operational principles underpin the policy and are expected to be reflected in its practical results. These have been variously expressed and interpreted since 1991. Consolidated in *The Citizen's Charter: Second Report* (Cabinet Office, 1994) as 'The Principles of Public Service', they are:

Standards - setting, monitoring and publication of explicit standards for the services that individual users can reasonably expect. Publication of actual performance against these standards.

Information and openness - full, accurate information readily available in plain language about how public services are run, what they cost, how well they perform and who is in charge.

Choice and consultation - the public sector should provide choice wherever practicable. There should be regular and systematic consultation with those who use services. Users' views about services, and their priorities for improving them, to be taken into account in final decisions on standards.

Courtesy and helpfulness - courteous and helpful service from public servants who will normally wear name badges. Services available equally to all who are entitled to them and run to suit their convenience.

Putting things right - if things go wrong , an apology, a full explanation and a swift and effective remedy. Well publicised and easy to use complaints procedures with independent review wherever possible.

Value for money - efficient and economical delivery of public services within the resources the nation can afford. Independent validation of performance against standards.

None of these core principles is individually especially remarkable, and herein lies an important policy strength, that what is being sought of public organisations and their staffs is what might be reasonably expected of them, in the provision of a 'good' if not 'quality' public service. Taken together, however, they present a potentially daunting set of organisational challenges.

The Citizen's Charter policy and its results to date have received a mixed press. The generalities of the language surrounding the policy have come in for criticism, and concern has been widespread that the 'well meaning' element in its nature may lead to its not being taken seriously, by service providers and/or users. Because the policy rests on a degree of organisational choice as to whether or not to participate, making charter documents 'compulsory' for all public bodies would in one sense help defeat the policy's purpose. Some public service practitioners and commentators express a 'take it or leave it' attitude towards the policy. Alternatively, the possibility of speedy disappointment with the results of the policy has been recognised, for example, by Kemp (1993), who argues that:

> ..unfortunately, the Citizen's Charter .... suffers from politicisation ...instant results
> of the kinds politicians want are not readily available.

Public service managers' responses to the Charter policy

How should public service managers be responding towards the policy and its range of outcomes? The government's view (Jackson, 1993) that:

> ..charters empower the consumers of public services, better enabling them to insist
> on good quality services and proper redress when things go wrong,

may be variously welcomed or rejected by managers already attempting to balance with equity the demands of the various stakeholders with an interest in their services. Even the use of the term 'empowerment' may be questioned. As Chapter 11 demonstrates, from employees' perspectives, the concept is not one to be used lightly.

It is particularly important that, from public service management perspectives, the policy is not dismissed as overly routine, lightweight and with minimal implications for organisational practice. It is complex, instructional, and demanding. It provides managers in public services with a range of goals to achieve, but leaves open to managerial decisions and choices the routes for achieving those goals. It requires continuity of managerial commitment to the Charter programme, once initially made, placing organisations on a continually upward moving 'improvement escalator'. It encourages a structured view of performance management in public services and, implicitly, the growth of internal competitive spirit as a range of organisations develop their own responses to the working implications of charter principles.

Kemp's description of the Citizen's Charter policy's development as positive and largely uncontentious may be variously interpreted, but may also be misleading, (Kemp 1993). An uncontentious policy is hardly the stuff of which public service revolutions are made. Nevertheless, it is possible that this policy area may turn out to be the tortoise to the policy hare of privatisation. Some policy critics have seen it as a manifestation of 'short termism', the 'quick fix', 'just get our Charter written and we can sit back', but as the policy ceases to be new and grows in familiarity and usage, this criticism is increasingly hard to make. Public service managers will vary in their assessment of when a policy initiative has taken root, but this policy initiative is now a fixed part of the public management scene, and may be judged as such. The Cabinet Minister with Charter responsibility has identified the extent of the claims for action generated by the charter policy (Waldegrave, 1993):

> ..what we are about is a long term, incremental, practical programme of quality improvement.

This chapter considers, primarily, therefore, the managerial challenges for public service managers which the Citizen's Charter policy provides. It examines overall charter growth and the central support given to the policy, and reviews a variety of managerial practice in charter contexts. It draws operational examples from a range of public services developing their interpretations of charter practice. The Charter policy , both as a means of helping achieving cultural change within public services, and as a programme 'reinforcing a range of techniques which control and improve quality' (Waldegrave, 1993) is reviewed. Finally, the chapter examines future possibilities for the policy's further development, as the basis for a harder-edged 'performance indicators' approach to service delivery, in the light of the contents of the 1994 'Second Report'.

Charter growth

By March 1994, 38 charters had been published (Cabinet Office 1994):

> covering the main public services, setting out standards of service and what people can do if those standards are not set.

Some early charters were 'macro' in application, for example the Patient's Charter and Tenant's Charter, setting outline national standards by which service users could gauge the quality of what they received locally, creating a template to which the operational levels of the services should (but might not) respond.

Many are necessarily more service-specific and linked to the growing number of Executive Agencies. The 'Citizen's Charter Second Report' shows that, of 51 Agencies serving the public directly, 40 had charters in place by March 1994, with all those remaining either intending to publish 'early in 1994', or having them 'under consideration' (Cabinet Office 1994). It may be tempting but too easy to dismiss this pattern as one of organisational 'me-tooism'. Evidence that charters, once set out, are capable of acting as dynamic documents, via which further organisational change may be effected (rather than being left well alone and 'set in stone') is to be found in the reports of those agencies which have already produced second or further charters in the light of their operational experience. These include the Benefits Agency, the Employment Service and the Contributions Agency.

The predominant style of the charters is one which sets out a series of 'deliverables', couched in a range of formal or less formal language, which provide users with the basis for making generalised rather than specific judgments about the services. Rather than representing contracts between provider and user, some managers may recognise the close parallels between some of these documents and organisational efforts to draw up appropriate mission statements and feasible and desirable objectives.

A few charters are prepared to state what is expected from the service user in turn. See, for example, the Taxpayer's Charter, which 'needs' the taxpayer to be honest, provide accurate information and pay their tax on time.

In parallel with this development has been the creation of innumerable 'micro charters', as individual hospital trusts, schools, particular departments of local authorities, and other public bodies operating in localities, publish their own versions, intendedly reflecting local needs and expressions of intent for local consumption. For example, at an individualised level of service provision (Cabinet Office 1994):

in England 30% of GP practices have produced or are producing their own charters. All GP practices are being encouraged to do so.

At a more intermediate organisational level, according to the same source, 29 of the 43 police services in England and Wales have published statements of their standards of service, with 12 more 'in hand'; with all police services in Scotland having published statements.

By choosing to design and deliver their 'home grown' charters, (in organisational behaviour terms, arguably, a valuable way of embedding the policy at operational levels) these organisations are setting themselves apart from others which are, as yet, 'non chartered'. By concentrating on the needs of their users, variations in public services and responses to demand may be expected, even encouraged. For example, among those fire brigades which have published 'local standards of performance' (numbers not available), the *Citizen's Charter Second Report* (Cabinet Office 1994) notes that:

..some local standards are more rigorous than the nationally agreed minimum standards ..... .

From this perspective, continual comparison across and between public services provision by their managers, and their users, is enabled. Such a development must raise questions about professional and managerial judgments, together resourcing issues. It also however counters the common criticism of any 'self-set' standards exercise, that it will necessarily reflect the lowest possible achievement levels, to provide the best possible picture. Perceptions of public service managers as mimimalist, rather than maximalist, providers are effectively challenged here.

Supporting the policy: the Charter Unit

The Charter Unit located in the Cabinet Office, has been charged from 1991 with overseeing and developing the Citizen's Charter policy. Its mission statement gives it the task of raising

..the standards of public service significantly and demonstrably year on year

and its work is promotional, advisory and exhortatory. Activities under the Unit's auspices include the conduct of a pilot 'Charterline' telephone advice service in the Midlands, an internal newsletter to encourage charter development, and six monthly seminars to maintain the impetus of the policy. It organises the 'Charter Mark' scheme, public recognition for the quality of charter-based work by specific services (considered below) and sources the yearly reports on Charter progress. In response to the concern, 'if things go wrong' the Unit supports the Citizen's Charter Complaints Task Force, set up in June 1993, and which plans (Cabinet Office 1994) to:

> carry out a programme of reviews during 1994 to see how public service complaints systems are really working.

With the Unit as a promotional rather than directional focus for the policy, the responsibility for developing, or not developing, charter statements or their equivalents continues to lie with individual Government departments. In turn, their varying structures mean that even if a simple 'top down/thou shalt' approach to charter-based activity were to be sought, uniformly, across departments, in practice this would be difficult to deliver. Thus, for example, the Home Office has responsibility for directly managed services (such as its Immigration and Nationality Department), for locally managed services (fire, police, probation), and for a number of Executive Agencies. Its range of charter-based initiatives must therefore reflect that internal diversification and variations in operating freedoms and managerial responsibilities are constraints. Simply 'telling managers to get on and write a charter' is a certain recipe for policy and programme failure, and a continual internal 'selling job' from managers in such departments, at a range of levels, is a necessity.

The 'Charter Mark' scheme involves public organisations' application (by self nomination rather than by their users) for the award of a 'seal of approval' on their chartered services. In 1992, 36 were awarded to a range of public services. In 1993 the Unit received 411 applications, over a 100 more than the previous year (Waldegrav, 1993). Judged by a panel of the 'great and good', the list of entrants for the awards is not published, nor are the details of the awarding criteria, although the *Second Report* (Cabinet Office 1994) emphasises that:

> many public service organisations use the self assessment guide to check how they measure up against Citizen's Charter principles, even if they choose not to apply for the Charter Mark that year.

Ninety three awards were made, as follows:

* health   9
* local government   49
* utilities   9
* agencies/central government   14 (including 7 Benefits Agency offices)
* other   5

The synopses of their services by the 1993 Charter Mark winners are a series of descriptions of activities, from which, it is implied, improved performance follows (Cabinet Office, 1993). These include surveys of users or the creation of 'user panels', increasing information availability to users, and developing flexibility of operating hours. Service users are most commonly described as customers, with the second most-used term in each synopsis that of 'partnership', between supplier and user. A small minority (ibid) refer to costs of services. For example , Bedfordshire County Record Office, where:

> striking results.. have been achieved on modest resources

and Park House Day Hospital, where:

> ..in addition to achieving greater customer satisfaction we were surprised to find that the service was significantly cheaper than the traditional alternative.

The emphasis is entirely upon output and result, describing the 'what' and 'when' but leaving open the critical managerial dimension of 'how' the results were achieved. It is this aspect of the charter mark winners' experiences that could most usefully be evaluated, or at least documented, perhaps under the Charter Unit's auspices, so increasing managerial as well as policy learning.

Redress under the charters

The concomitant of providing high quality services is to compensate for low quality provision. During 1993, parliamentary questions revealed the extent of financial compensation paid out by 'chartered' public bodies, as shown in Figure 13.1(Greenway 1993):

	Cost (rounded to the nearest £000)	Period	
		from	to
BR passengers charter	1,000.0	May 92	May 93
London Underground Ltd. customers charter	41.0	August 92	January 93
Benefits Agency customer charter	1,058.0	April 92	September 92
Jobseekers charter	89.0	April 92	March 93
Contributions Agency employers and contributors charters	63.0	April 92	March 93
Northern Ireland Railways passengers charter	0.4	November 92	April 93
Travellers charter	9.0	January 92	March 93
Total	**2,260.4**		
(Greenway, Hansard, 1993)			

Figure 13.1. Compensation for failures to meet service standards.

Further details of compensation payments for falling below set standards of services for the gas, electricity and water companies, for British Telecom, and for the Post Office, are given in the 'Second Report' (Cabinet Office 1994). Without corresponding figures for these organisations' operating costs, and , where appropriate, revenues, the effects of these payments on the organisations are however difficult to assess. There is an undoubted attraction to what may be described as the 'cashback' principle in public services, but its limited implementation and effects raise further problems, especially for those chartered services where such redress is not feasible. References to financial compensation are virtually absent from among the accounts of the services of the 1993 Charter Mark winners, and those concerning complaints systems are also few in number.

Managerial responses to Charter programmes

Against this background of policy content and development to date, how should public service managers be responding to opportunities to develop and build on service charters, and to the constraints on their freedom of decision making which some charter elements introduce? The following points are generalist in nature and will not be relevant in all service contexts. Nevertheless, they are offered to provide some potentially helpful aspects of managerial 'know how' and behaviour.

Managers at a range of organisational levels, (artificial divisions between 'strategic' and 'operational' managers may be seen as being unhelpful in many charter policy contexts) may find the following hints helpful where charters have or are about to be established.

Encourage staff involvement in the development of the charters

Where feasible staff involvement should cover a wide range of aspects of charter development, wording, content, style and standards. Assumptions that the experiences of those who deliver the services and of those who manage the deliverers should be separate in this process may lead to the development of charters which have little relationship with the practicalities of the service, and, critically, which may 'over' as well as 'under' promise what will be achieved. 'Who has been writing the charters' has never been a key concern of policy and programme analysts in this area, yet it remains important if an organisation's charter is to be seen as a managerial template for action rather than as a public relations exercise. From one perspective, this offers an empowerment opportunity for employees, which also involves an important degree of risk, as standards are made public against a background of continuing uncertainty about resource availability.

Be prepared to re-write

The temptation to sit back and let a set of standards 'speak for themselves' is understandable and this may be the more attractive if the pressure placed on managers was to produce 'a' document, rather than to sign on to the implications of the programme in full as shown in Chapter 23. Where re-writing has occurred, impressionistically, it has related to improving standards, or a greater willingness to specify service nature, a major criticism of charter content having focused on the problems of over-generalising.

Anticipate a range of internal reactions among staff

On the negative side, these may range from antipathy to apathy and indifference. Where the writers of service standards and deliverers of those standards are not the same people, difficulties may be inbuilt from the beginning. At some levels, a policy of diplomatic avoidance may develop; the attitude that work on charter creation and practice following charter-style models 'doesn't apply to us' can be influential in minimising the support for the programme 'further down'. At worst, the very ordinariness of the programme's core may suggest to some that this 'is not for them'. What may be described as the 'charter-free zones' of areas of public services may well be a testimony to this type of approach.

Negative reactions to such policy developments might of course be expected but so should positive support. Certainly some managers working regularly with the public have welcomed charter development and practice because it gives them an opportunity to make a definitive statement of what they do, how they do it, and how they may do it better. In turn, of course, these managers will expect those statements to be taken seriously by their senior managers who are removed from direct user contact. Where the latter have not been fully engaged in the policy, whilst nevertheless giving their formal support to what Pollitt has described as the 'veritable confetti of charters' that have arisen, problems may follow (Pollitt, 1993). If the 'throwaway' associations of Pollitt's imagery are drawn upon, it seems more likely that it will be the less senior managers who will be among the first to recognise that charters, once developed, cannot be set aside as a policy that has simply been accomplished. Anecdotally, it has been possible for a few of these managers to make use of the existence and content of charters to place pressure successfully on their senior managers in turn for increased support and resources to provide the services to the standards which they set themselves. In this sense, managers at a range of levels need to be aware that work on developing charters and delivering the standards set provides further opportunities for the empowerment of staff as shown in Chapter 11.

Look for the incremental 'small wins'

Once charters are in place, they give forms of internal leverage for bringing about quality shifts in public services. Their value may be less in the initial publicity gained and more to the extent that, over time, they encourage continual internal review of service procedures and ways of working the 'escalator' of improvement, mentioned earlier. Small scale changes - staff wearing name badges, a turnaround time for correspondence - may have a greater cumulative effect than moves to publicise service standards and create measures of performance written in global terms.

Conversely, do not look for immediate 'big wins' in organisational terms, and prepare for some immediate criticisms of the services, via an effective monitoring network

Kemp (1993) emphasises that:

..Politicians like the Charter to highlight horror stories about standards of service

but, importantly, emphasises that this is not its primary purpose. 'Chartered' services do not win themselves a trouble free life, as a reward for publicising what they do and what their users might expect, quite the reverse (although there is as yet no extensive data on whether complaints are rising or falling in 'chartered' as contrasted with 'non chartered' services).

First line managers will be familiar with the problems of responding to users who approach them, charter in hand, with the aggrieved tone, the wagging finger, and the key line ..'it says here...'. This again reinforces the importance of providing support for managers at those levels and of enabling them to engage with their own senior managers more directly in resources debates which affect their own performance. There can be no doubt that increasing organisational commitment to charter-based policies may also in some services have the capacity to place more junior staffs and managers at risk, and make them exposed. This alone emphasises the need for the implications of those policies to be understood fully at all managerial levels.

Find ways of praising staff and helping staff to reflect and 'stand back' from their organisational image and purpose

Some of the synopses of their work by the 1993 Charter Mark winners support this view, for example, the British Gas plc entry (Cabinet Office, 1993). Another, the Industrial Science Centre (Department of Economic Development, Northern Ireland), emphasises that:

..entering the Charter Mark Scheme meant that we had to stand back and 'see ourselves as others see us' and to consider how we as individuals contribute to the day to day running of the organisation.

The opportunities which the programme provides for staff empowerment find a particularly strong expression in the report from the award-winning Benefits Agency-South Devon District entry, which commences not with a description of 'what it does', but with a strong statement of its deliberately created work culture:

> ..underpinning all our District's achievements is the successful adoption of a strategy of developing team power. This was realised through creating an environment in which individual self-expression, passion and energy thrive within the work group.

Charter policy is thus valuable in terms of its processes as well as its outcomes.

Some current concerns for managers

The above ideas have indicated the extent to which managers drawing on charter policy and practice for developing, changing and improving delivery in public services, are working in both a complex and a long term policy area. Some of the more trite 'welcomes' for the policy warn that staffs themselves may misunderstand or misinterpret its intent. Thus, for example, Benton (1993) asserts that charters are:

> .. a new user-friendly way of disciplining the workforce -how else could you insist that staff smile all day...(it is) .. a management coup d'etat..

If the policy reputation of the Citizen's Charter 'outside' public service management remains like this, that fierce managers use the policy to create a superficial customer-compliant attitude among staffs, it is one which managers themselves will have to challenge. Whilst the case is made strongly that the experiences of change in public services delivery which are generated by the Charter, will percolate with good effect throughout the public service - that, for example Charter mark winners' ideas will 'rejuvenate other areas' (Fennell, 1993) - then much will depend on managers being willing to share not only 'what they did' but 'how they did it'. It may be a growing feature of management in public services that many will be less forthcoming, as increased competitiveness between services is sanctioned (Talbot and Harrow, 1993). Managerial learning from the implementation of charters, from the impact of standard-setting, and from the experiences of 'managing in' charters, all need to be both documented and open.

Nor can managers escape the resources debate which surrounds the Citizen's Charter policy. Some policy critics have argued that the value of designing and implementing charters in individual public services needs to be set against the contradictory pressures which are produced, as citizen expressions of demand coincide with 'top down' pressures to reduce costs.

Operational-level managers' keenness to set standards, and to be measured against their delivery, will thus be tempered; unless they themselves become part of the pressure for higher spending. Wilson is unequivocal:

> ..fundamentally, the problem with the Charter is one of funding. Improved services will almost certainly need increased resources.

Again, the issue here seems to be the need for more information to be available concerning the resource implications of introducing and sustaining of charter - based developments, in place of continuing assertions that the Charter programme is, or is not, cost-neutral.

Future developments and further managerial implications

It is possible that most long term analyses of the impact of the Charter policy will concentrate more on its general and cultural results than on the direct measurement of change in public services delivery as a result of charter creation. Butler (1993), for example, sees the policy as representing:

> the culmination of the movement towards output management

(requiring services to)

> ...shift their attentions towards the aspirations of the public and away from the interests of themselves as providers.

This reflects a unified view of public services' employee behaviour, and the service fragmentation currently occurring may make this view less appropriate.

At the same time, there is currently a lack of management research to report upon the extent, if any, of the 'performance gaps' occurring between charter statements and service quality. That limited amount which has been conducted, usefully, at micro levels, has reported significant mismatches between policy and programmes that leave managers either over concentrating on immediate operational concerns (as the most responsive course of action) or on wider strategic issues, couched in suitably global terms (because control over immediate operational questions is not fully in their hands) (Oliver, 1993; Butler, 1993). This is an area where the Cabinet Office's Charter Unit might be able to provide a lead.

If the Charter approach continues to reflect or require an element of competitive spirit among public services managers and staffs, then this must be set against the views of those commentators who regard co-operative alliances as the strategic direction for organisations during this decade (for example, Alter and Hage, 1993). In the meantime, we know that having to manage what are described as 'co-ordinated' services across organisational boundaries is a characteristic feature of the work of many public services managers. What happens if the respective charters of organisations are not coincidental in their offer? Or how is the cross-managerial work affected, if at all where organisations who are required to work together are chartered and 'non chartered'? Even the most fervent charter supporter would have difficulty in arguing that 'non chartered' services are, always by definition, of a lesser quality than those where charters are a familiar part of the organisational scene, but there remains a feeling that this ought to be the case. This suggests also that there are limits to 'charterism', given that not all public provision is in the form of direct services where customers can be identified easily, and as individuals.

In local government, where the Audit Commission is devising a nationally applicable set of performance indicators, in the words of Rodrigues (1993):

> drawing its legitimacy from the Local Government Act 1992 and the Citizen's Charter

the 'hardest' outcome from the charter policy may be looked for. By 1994/5, it will be mandatory for authorities to report and publish indicators (Cabinet Office, 1994) but this is to raise the wider problems of how indicator development makes for improvement and how the inevitably accompanying performance league tables will be judged. Rodrigues' case that a:

> purely competitive model (of indicator development) will build in incentives not to spread learning and will encourage local authorities to be defensive rather than open about the difficulties they face

applies also to the whole question of 'managing in' citizen's charters. (Rodrigues, op. cit).

Managers at a range of levels in public services appear to feel, at various times, both elated and defeated by aspects of the charter policy and programme. The experiences of drawing up standards and being prepared to be measured against their delivery is not, as hostile critics of public service might argue, being shied away from by managers. Performance standards, sensitively devised and implemented, give some performance benchmarks against which to demonstrate success as well as failure. (The case for the glossy charter literature is of course that it is seeking to celebrate success.) 'Defeat' may set in where line managers feel isolated by virtue of the demands placed on them which they are unable (not unwilling) to deliver, or where charter creation and 'implementation' has been of the Potemkin Village variety, to satisfy a range of stakeholders as 'having done that', without any understanding at strategic management levels of what charter principles and practice properly imply.

From a central perspective, the Citizen's Charter policy provides a unifying element for public services. The Treasury and Civil Service Committee (1993), for example, reported that:

> It can be argued that the Citizen's Charter effectively redefines the notion of public service, by pointing to the features which unite services used by the public, whether they are in the public or the private sector.

The policy-interlinking of the Citizen's Charter Programme, with those of the development of agencies and of 'market testing' public services provision makes for increased policy complexity and uncertainty (see Harrow and Talbot, 1994, and Cabinet Office, 1994). In fact, the Charter policy and programme is well able to stand alone. An increased focus on the 'how' and 'why' of charter management, the managerial journeys that have taken place to reach the situations somewhat descriptively conveyed in the Charter Second Report, on 'what we promised', 'what we have done' and 'future commitments', would surely help to demonstrate this.

About the author

Dr. Jenny Harrow is head of research for the management area at South Bank University's Business School and has published widely on developments in the new public services management. Her employment background is in the public and voluntary services, and her research interests include managerial and policy change in those sectors, managerial responses to risk, and managers' routes for self development.

References and suggested reading

Alter, C. and Hage, J. (1993) *Organisations Working Together* London, Sage Library of Social Research, Sage

Arnold-Foster, J. (1993) Is Citizen's Charter made to measure? in ed. Jones, G. *Local Government, the Management Agenda* ICSA Publishing in association with the Local Government Chronicle

Benton, S. (1993) The user-friendly way to win power *The Independent*, 5 August

Butler, R. (1993) The Evolution of the Civil Service Paper to the the PSA Conference, University of Leicester, 21 April 1993; revised paper published in *Public Administration* Vol 71, No. 3

Butler, S. (1993) *The Citizens' Charter and Patients' Charter: relevance and impact on the Mental Health Unit, Guys and St. Thomas' NHS Trust*
Unpublished MBA dissertation, South Bank University Business School

Cabinet Office (1993) *Charter Mark 1993, The Winners* London, HMSO

Cabinet Office (1991) *The Citizen's Charter: raising the standard* Cm 1599, HMSO

Cabinet Office (1994) *The Citizen's Charter, Second Report: 1994* Cm 2540, HMSO

Fennell, E. (1993) New Elite Makes Its Mark *The Times*, 27 October

Greenway , H. (1993) *Commons Hansard* 10 May column 308

Jackson, R. (1993) *Commons Hansard* 15 February column 14

Harrow, J. and Talbot, C. Central Government, the changing civil service
in Trinder, C. Jackson, P. and Lavender, N. (eds) *The Public Services Yearbook*
London, Chapman and Hall - CIPFA

Kemp, P (1993) *Beyond Next Steps, A Civil Service for the 21st Century*
Social Market Foundation, Paper 17

Oliver, A. (1993) *The Citizen's Charter and Performance Indicators: Overcoming Barriers of Resistance* Unpublished MBA dissertation, South Bank University Business School

Pollitt, C. (1993) *Managerialism and the Public Services, Cuts or Cultural Change in the 1990s* Oxford, Basil Blackwell Second edition

Rodrigues, J. (1993) Curtain up on Performance, in Chapter 6, Promoting Consumer Choice, in ed. Jones, G., *Local Government, The Management Agenda,*
Cambridge, ICSA Publishing in association with the *Local Government Chronicle*

Talbot, C, and Harrow, J. (1993) *Sharing or Witholding Organisational Knowledge, An exploration of changing values in managerial and organisational learning*
Working Paper, British Academy of Management Annual Conference, Milton Keynes, 20-22 September

Treasury and Civil Service Committee (1993) *The Role of the Civil Service*
House of Commons, HC 390-1   1993

Waldegrave, W. (1993) *The Reality of Reform and Accountability in Today's Public Service*
Inaugural Public Finance Foundation/BDO Consulting Public Service Lecture, Public Finance Foundation, 5 July

Waldegrave, W. (1993) *Commons Hansard*, 19 July column 13

Wilson, J. (1993) Political Environment and Public Service Activity
in eds. Wilson , J. and Hinton, P. *Public Services and the 1990s, Issues in Public Service Finance and Management* Wirral, Merseyside, Tudor Business Publishing,

Chapter 14

Competing for Quality: competition in the supply of central Government services

Ian Williams

Out-sourcing of services is certainly not a new idea in either the public or private sector. In earlier times, governments had to out-source service supply simply because of an unwillingness or an inability to increase their own resources, but this was not so in the twentieth century. In the private sector, management strategies have varied according to the external pressures being experienced at the time. In the 1960s and early 1970s diversification was often seen as the key to growth and profitability. The oil crisis of 1973/4 gave a jolt to the world economy, the reverberations of which are still being felt today. The reaction of some companies was to diversify further, the spreading of risk being a rational response.

A change in perception has taken place. Another oil price shock in the late 1970s, recession in the early 1980s, some deregulation and rapidly changing technology have led many companies to reappraise their approach to business. For these companies the 'synergies' which they had expected to emerge from diversification had not happened, and this together with more unpredictable economic conditions and more demanding investors, products of the liberalisation in Western markets in the 1980s, led companies to concentrate more on profitability than growth. This, in turn, made management question their business activities and to perceive that they might perform better if they maximised their resources on those activities that they were best at, and contracted out the others to an organisation that regarded itself as specialist in that area.

Background to the initiative

The similarities in the need for change in the public sector are apparent. Public services are under pressure to improve in quality to benefit the user but also not to increase the burden on taxpayers. If both of these parameters are to be met the only solution is to increase the efficiency of the conversion of taxpayers money into quality public services.

This is a not a problem unique to the UK. Governments throughout the developed world have been grappling with these two fundamental, conflicting pressures. The approach is therefore to try and create mechanisms which emphasise the need for, and the quality of public services, while at the same time clearly recognising the very heavy resource constraints under which they operate. That is the general approach being taken for example in New Zealand, with its radical structure of agencies and fundamental delegation of responsibility to Chief Executives, or in America through the Gore Commission and the many innovations at State or City levels described in Osborne and Gaebler's *Re-inventing Government* (1992).

This approach does not accept that Government is unable to match the productivity gains available in the best of the private sector, which allow a service to maintain its quality with less resource or improve it with the same resources. It sees Government as one provider of services among others, services which may have special duties and requirements laid upon them, but are nonetheless susceptible to many of the techniques for improvement developed in the private sector.

The present Government has, since 1979, been seeking to free up the latent ability and commitment in our public services through improvements in the way that they are managed. Initially this was done on what was essentially a pragmatic, individual basis, as each one, the civil service, local government, the nationalised industries and the NHS, seemed to require. Government withdrew altogether from many areas, especially the nationalised industries which, it was felt, could demonstrably be better run by the private sector, whose employees knew more about industrial management than the public sector could hope to do. As far as the rest of the public service was concerned, efficiency measures resulted in enormous savings. The delegation or scrapping of unnecessary budgetary controls gave local managers more power to run their operations effectively, and the incentive was provided to set and meet challenging targets in a wide range of areas.

Since 1991, the Government has been able to bring together all these initiatives in the different parts of the public service, under the Citizen's Charter. The Charter is a substantial milestone in demonstrating how the Government wants to move the emphasis towards public services with high quality outputs and with service to the citizen as an overriding concern. However better quality services do not happen by accident. They are being brought about by a series of policies each designed to serve a key objective in improving public service management.

❏ Prior Options

Analysis of the need for an activity to remain in government is normally carried out by testing the activity sequentially against a series of separate possible outcomes.

The *first* test is to ensure that those working in the public services do not waste their own time, and the taxpayer's money, on activities that do not need to exist on any basis. Abolition may be appropriate where, for instance, legislation has been amended.

The *second* step is to ensure that public services are engaged only in essential activities. This requires regular programmes to ensure that all activities need to remain in the public sector. Many do not, and privatisation has been a key approach throughout the last thirteen years.

Thirdly a productive partnership is encouraged, wherever possible, between the public sector and private industry. Some activities may still clearly need to be the ultimate responsibility of the public sector, but can nonetheless be run on the basis of a contract between the purchaser and the provider of the service. Some of these are being contracted out without further ado, for policy or management reasons. For others, it will be necessary to determine whether or not contracting out will be the most efficient way of carrying it out. This process of testing the viability of out-sourcing an activity is referred to as market testing.

The 'Competing for Quality' White Paper

In November 1991 the *Competing for Quality* White Paper was published which stated the Government's intent to expand its use of market testing and to:

> expose public sector spending to competition, increase the quality of public services, and give better value for taxpayers.

The main objective of market testing is to open up the supply of central government services to competition, thus raising the service supplier's awareness of the customer's demands which in turn will increase the efficiency of converting taxpayers' money into quality services. The competition for supply of services will ensure that either an external supplier will be awarded the work because their bid offers better value for money or, the in-house team will continue to do the work, in which case the process of opening up the activity to competition will in itself create opportunities for greater effectiveness. The market testing of activities will also continue to increase the commercial awareness of the public sector and change attitudes from the traditional view to one where the quality of the service delivered is foremost. Therefore, market testing will reduce the taxpayer's burden, and more importantly in many cases it will improve the quality of the services.

There are two points which it is important to note. First, there are no targets for the amount which is to be contracted out. Indeed, it would be meaningless to set such targets because, prior to market testing by competitive tendering, there is no way of knowing whether any particular function can be more cost effectively provided in-house or on a contracted-out basis. The result in each case will depend on the outcome of the competitive tendering process. This is first and foremost a management reform, and there is not some sort of hidden agenda, privatisation by the back door. Secondly, there are activities which by definition following the 'prior options' are considered to be essential as part of Government responsibility. They will still be carried out, and possibly to higher standards than before. The work, and the majority of jobs needed to do it, will continue to exist.

Where the market testing of an activity results in a contract being placed with the private sector, government employees may be redeployed, taken on by the new contractor, absorbed by normal retirements and reduced recruitment or in some cases made redundant, either voluntarily or compulsory. In many cases the Transfer of Undertakings, Protection of Employment Regulations (TUPE) will apply, so that staff will transfer automatically to the new contractor on the same terms and conditions of employment. In other cases the Regulations will not apply, notably where the contract is simply a contract for services in consideration of a fee.

Some elements of both the private sector management and public sector staff representatives suggested that the application of TUPE would, in some way, blow market testing off course. However, the response from most private sector companies, especially those supplying white collar professional services, suggests that TUPE provides a sensible framework within which to undertake a transfer. It may mean in some cases that the bid prices are slightly higher when TUPE applies, but this is not significant when compared with the savings that are being achieved. Departments and agencies, as well as potential contractors, should take legal advice about whether the specific circumstances outlined in a particular bid are likely to mean that the Regulations will apply. Where the Regulations do apply, the successful contractor will take over all the contracts of employment of those people currently doing the work which has been market tested. The employees will transfer to the new employer on the same terms and conditions they had as civil servants, except in relation to pensions. Each aspect of the terms and conditions of the employees who transfer will remain in force under the new employer until and unless it is specifically re-negotiated.

Procedures for competitive testing of activities.

A brief review of the procedures involved in competitively testing the supply of services highlights some of the main points of the initiative. Those readers who wish to obtain further information on the process should refer to *The Government's Guide to Market Testing* which was published by HMSO in August 1993. That document gives a fully detailed account of the procedures to be followed. Briefly, there are six distinct elements.

❏ Identification and scoping of the activity

The first element is the identification or scoping of the service required. Departments and agencies are identifying activities which are currently within Government, that have to remain a Government responsibility, but which could be performed for them by other suppliers. To do this they are looking at the whole of their operations to see which areas could most usefully by exposed to such competition. In the first year, many departments scoped activities for market testing on an existing *function* basis without sufficient consideration being given to the greater improvements in 'value for money' terms that can be achieved by looking at the *services* required. Having gained experience of the process some departments and agencies are now using more of a facilities management approach to a variety of services, grouping allied services to give greater potential savings and, incidentally, reducing the cost of market testing. Past experience has shown that activities which have been found to be particularly suitable have often been resource intensive, relatively discrete, specialist or support services, subject to fluctuating work patterns, subject to a quickly changing market or subject to rapidly changing technology, or new activities where the presumption is that these will be strategically contracted out.

In deciding which activities to market test, departments and agencies will need to address the following questions:

- is the function or activity essential
- what are the implications of *not* doing it? Or of doing it in a reduced or combined form elsewhere
- can the activity be performed more economically by other means (e.g. a press cutting service rather than provision of newspapers and journals)
- what is the full cost of the level of service presently provided and that which is deemed necessary, with costs including operating costs (staff, supervision and consumables), and overhead costs (accommodation, utilities and management)
- is the function or activity organisationally discrete
- what are the working methods, organisation and use of capital assets?

❏ Drawing up the specification

The second element is to specify the service. This specification will include the essential requirements for the delivery of the service, specifying output deliverables, performance measures, interfaces with other parts of the departmental business and, where applicable, existing equipment. However, departments and agencies will not be over prescriptive about the processes by which a service is to be delivered, the specification will be output based, allowing and encouraging bidders to offer innovative or novel proposals. Bidders will be required to state their proposed modus operandi and a statement will be included to the effect that:

> following discussions and mutually agreed modifications the successful bidder's modus operandi will form part of the contract document.

The specification will define in clear and precise terms:

- scope of work to be undertaken; output required, in amount and quantity; standards to be met; response times, and when and how the work will be measured
- responsibilities of the contractor and the department or agency and the interfaces between them
- identification of any key milestone events and approvals required before the next event commences
- commencement of contract; completion dates for work to be done
- contractors' continuing responsibilities on completion of the work.

The specification will also include quality standards and monitoring arrangements, e.g. random checks, regular inspection, 'customer' feedback. Information from the contractor may be sought as part of the contract to assist departmental monitoring, and to establish how a contractor will handle complaints of poor service.

❏ Competitive tendering

The third element is to instigate a competitive tender, which basically will follow existing departmental practice. The departmental or agency manager responsible for the competitive tendering process will develop:

- a contract strategy e.g. the type of contractual arrangement to be used
- outline contract documents (including the specification for the work, and the standards required)
- the process of identifying potential contractors and inviting them to tender
- a qualification process for potential contractors
- an evaluation process for bids.

The department or agency will wish to ensure that the market potential is fully explored and will normally use advertising to help identify suitable potential contractors. When the list of potential tenderers is too large, it may be reduced by 'screening'. The 'screening' process involves informing all potential tenderers of the outline of the work, the proposed form of contract, the location and the timing through to contract award. Information from potential tenderers will be sought to elucidate their capacity, competence and experience for doing the work, and may include:

financial status:

credit-worthiness (audited accounts, references etc); details of holding or guarantor companies backing the contractor;

quality of management and workforce:

experience; qualifications; proven competencies; technical status: evidence of design and production capability (where appropriate), record of achievement on similar work (by taking up references);

existing commitment:

evidence of the current and foreseen workload against current and planned resources.

The department or agency will select a final bid list. Successful and unsuccessful candidates will be informed of the initial selection decision. Those shortlisted will be required to reconfirm their intention to bid and comply with an (updated) bidding schedule which should incorporate timescales for:

- preparation of the specification of the work
- preparation of the standards of the work
- drafting of legal requirements
- any necessary management reviews
- release of the Invitation to Tender documents
- receipt of tenders
- completion of the bid analysis process
- approval of the recommended successful contractor and award of contract.

All responses to Invitations to Tender, including any in-house bid, will be conducted under 'sealed bid' conditions. Each bid must be submitted 'sealed' and kept secure by the department or agency until the bid opening time is reached. Bidders must sign a confidentiality agreement to confirm that there has been no collusion with other contractors in bidding for the work and there has been no canvassing or soliciting of departmental staff. Where necessary, copies of insurance certificates, certificates of membership of trade associations or professional institutions will also be provided.

The bids will also be required to specify:

- how the service will be carried out
- arrangements for staffing and supervision
- assets, equipment and material to be employed
- any plans for redeploying existing staff
- unless otherwise agreed beforehand, the terms of any leasing or hiring of assets belonging to the department or agency
- the extent of any sub-contracting and to whom
- details of experience in running similar contracts together with details of previous clients and contact names.

❑ Encouragement of an in-house bid

The fourth element is to encourage a bid from the in-house team presently supplying the service, so if in-house teams present a robust enough case their department or agency will give them additional support either internally or from the private sector. The cost of this support is a 'sunk cost' and therefore will not reduce the competitiveness of their bid. The in-house bid will be drawn up against the same specification and in the same timescale as all other bids. In-house teams may propose changes which could include, utilising external support services, different working practices and different terms and conditions of their employment. Remember, an in-house team could be very efficient but if they utilise an inefficient support service their bid price may not be competitive.

Management has the right to reject the use of alternative suppliers but should use the lower cost in evaluating bids and would have to absorb the additional cost of maintaining this inefficient service. This will probably ensure that the inefficient support service soon becomes a market test in its own right. Previously concern was expressed by some in-house teams that the private sector bidders could offer bids based on more advantageous working practices. To a certain extent this anomaly has now been removed. If an in-house team can identify better working practices or a remuneration package which may be more attractive to management than those which exist, they may include them in their proposal. It is important to note that, in the market testing context, changes in terms and conditions can only be proposed by the in-house team, management only having the right to accept or reject such proposals.

❑ Evaluation of Bids

The fifth element is the evaluation of bids. In-house bids will be sealed and delivered, and will be considered alongside bids received from other suppliers, all bids will be evaluated on the same basis, with no bias towards either private or public sector bids. Departments and agencies will be responsible for ensuring that there is clear separation between the in-house bid team and those responsible for the evaluation of the bids received. The department or agency will select the bid which offers the best long term value for money. Once a decision has been made all bidders, including the in-house bid team, will be informed of the outcome of the evaluation and the unsuccessful bidders will be able to request a de-brief on the reasons for the failure of their bid, although of course no commercially confidential information will be disclosed. Selection decisions will be recorded and the reasons for them, both to ensure accountability and to inform those responsible for monitoring and renewing the resulting contract or service level agreement.

The bid evaluation team will include members with expertise in assessing all aspects of the bids, including:

- capability assessment
- technical assessment
- commercial assessment
- financial assessment.

Capability assessment

This requires examination of the experience, capability and qualifications of the key personnel who will be managing the operation and the management and supervisory back up available to them. Where necessary, additional information will be sought from bidders. References provided by the bidder and, where applicable, their performance for other clients will be checked.

Technical assessment

Does the bid meet the requirements set out in the specification and does the contractor have sufficient capacity to fulfil them? Any modifications proposed will be checked to establish whether they are practicable, innovative and demonstrate a more effective approach.

Commercial assessment

The acceptability of any qualifications in the offers, for example variations to schedules of delivery or quality, needs to be checked.

Financial assessment

This involves examining the realism of the proposal, the quality of financial and operational analysis, the robustness of the bid, and the identification of any variables which might result in cost changes during the period of the contract.

During the evaluation process, it may be necessary to clarify details of the bids. The department or agency and the contractors will review and agree any areas requiring clarification in the specification or contract conditions before the contract is awarded. This will allow any adjustments to be made to the document and enable the contractor to operate more effectively while satisfying the needs of the department or agency. Care will be taken to ensure that any modifications made at this stage do not materially affect the earlier selection process, or discriminate against the other bidders.

❑ Monitoring of the service

So to the final element, which is the monitoring of the successful bidder to ensure that what was promised is delivered. This is considered further in Chapter 15. Following the market testing of every activity in government there will either be a contract where a private sector supplier is successful, or a service level agreement when the in-house team is successful. The terms of both a potential service level agreement and a potential contract will be identical, except of course that the service level agreement is not enforceable in law. The Government's intent, however, is to monitor all successful bidders in the same manner. This will ensure that whenever an in-house team has come up with a more effective and efficient way of working than the private sector, offering better value for money, they will be monitored to ensure they deliver the service within the constraints of their bid.

Initial results and implications for the future

The Citizen's Charter Second Annual Report (Cabinet Office 1994) stated that quantifiable savings achieved already were over £135 million, but that the final figure would be higher still. These are, of course, annual savings which will recur, year after year. Analysis of those tests where full information exists shows that the average percentage saving of individual tests is over 25% of the pre-test cost, irrespective of whether the outcome of the test resulted in the work being transferred to a private sector company or remaining in-house with the existing team. As an example of savings that have been achieved, Customs and Excise saved 20% on typing services in their London headquarters, while HMSO's stationery, storage and distribution function in Bristol saved 30% and the Hansard Press has been merged with the Parliament Press to produce long term savings of 35%. The interesting point is that in each of these cases the in-house team won. This in itself raises further questions. Why were departments and agencies unable to capture these savings using other efficiency studies and how much taxpayer's money was wasted in these areas in previous years prior to market testing?

Where the in-house teams have taken part, they have won about 68% of activities, but these wins represent only 17% by value of the total programme completed by the end of 1993. The 68% figure excludes those market tests which did not involve an in-house bid. These would include activities which were strategically contracted out or where the in-house team bid on the basis of a management buy-out.

It is important to note that the criteria for selecting the winning bid is best long term value for money. Therefore the basis for considering whether to accept an in-house bid or to award the work to an outside contractor must not only look at cash savings but at improvements in the quality of service available from innovative methods of service delivery. Results show that, of the tests completed by the end of 1993, 33% will result in a greater quality of service, in many cases also at lower cost, whilst virtually all the remainder will maintain the existing quality but at a reduced cost to the taxpayer.

The Government believes that work done so far represents a valuable start, but market testing, particularly in central Government, is still at an early stage. The Citizen's Charter First Report (Cabinet Office 1992,) made it clear that the targets agreed for market testing for central government activities in the period until the end of September 1993 were more ambitious than anything undertaken so far. The original target was for a fifty-fold increase in value of activities tested and that target has been achieved. Departments' and agencies' plans for the year to September 1994 are again ambitious. In addition to the work that is necessary to complete their 1992/93 programmes, they will be competitively testing work currently worth a total of £800 million, and covering 35,000 civil servants. In staff terms, this 12 month target will be more challenging than the previous 18 month programme. As for the future, the recent White Paper on the Civil Service (Cm 2627) shows how market testing will form part of the efficiency plan which departments and agencies will submit annually.

In order to achieve ambitious targets for future years it will be even more important to make the public sector/private sector partnership effective. As private sector suppliers get to know the public sector better and public sector suppliers review their own working practices, there will be new and innovative ways not just of performing present tasks better, but also approaching and securing the core objectives. This is the real goal. So the challenge is to bring about a major culture change within central Government. This is not a threat, but an enormous opportunity to move to more effective, but hands-off, management in the public sector. This will of course require proper access and audit to guarantee accountability. It will also require open and frank dialogue, between staff and management, and between public and private sector. There are some statutes which require certain activities to be carried out by a Minister, the principle that such activities can be carried out by civil servants on a Minister's behalf is well established (the Carltona Doctrine). The Government proposes an extension to this principle which will allow contractors as well as civil servants to carry out such work in appropriate cases. In consequence, legislation is being introduced to remove some of the statutory obstacles to market testing in both central and local government.

A key area is the quality of services, as value for money means maintaining and improving standards, as well as achieving savings. Much of the accent on quality is to do with the principles of the Citizen's Charter, principles which are all important to the customer, such as standards of service, information and openness, choice, courtesy, helpfulness and redress for mistakes. These are principles which are common to both successful private sector companies and proficient public sector organisations, who know that the customers needs are paramount.

References and suggested reading

Cabinet Office(1992) *The Citizen's Charter, First Report* Cm 2101 London, HMSO

Cabinet Office(1994) *The Citizen's Charter, Second Report* Cm 2540 London, HMSO

Cabinet Office(1994) *The Civil Service: Continuity and Change* Cm 2627 London, HMSO

Osborne, D. & Gaebler, E. (1992) *Reinventing Government* Reading MA. Addison-Wesley

Chapter 15

Managing out-sourced service providers

Mahen Tampoe

Market testing is being used by organisations in the private and public sectors to test the cost effectiveness and performance of many of their internally provided services. An important objective is to make public services more demonstrably cost effective. In recent years office cleaning, catering, waste management and similar non-core activities have been out-sourced. The 'Competing for Quality' initiative of the Efficiency Unit (Cmd 1730 HMSO Nov. 1991) has now brought this activity into sharp focus in the Civil Service and the trend is extending to services which are intimately intertwined with the strategic objectives of the organisation, such as IT services, personnel management, training and similar functions which support the core business or the deliverables of the business, as is shown in Chapter 21. This has meant that the services have to be out-sourced or implemented using a high propor- tion of bought out resources, primarily know-how. Managing these sources of sup- ply is proving difficult. In discussions with line managers entrusted with the unen- viable task of selecting and managing the suppliers, it is quite common to hear them say that

> most failures stem from before the supplier starts and can be traced to the original
> concept and procurement process.

They attribute their comment to the management environment in which the service is run, more often than not created by others, rather than the managers themselves.

Market testing - an overview

The aims of market testing, as expressed by the Efficiency Unit are set out in Chapter 14. These appear to be:

- to encourage competition
- to derive clearer standards and improved quality of service
- to encourage in-house and external bidders to be more innovative
- to ensure performance.

The same document highlights nine steps in the market testing process.

These are:

1. identifying the scope and nature of the activity
2. establishing levels of cost effective service
3. developing a specification and outline service level agreement
4. inviting tenders from potential bidders
5. selecting a suitable list of bidders
6. calling for bids
7. evaluating competing bids
8. awarding a contract or service level agreement
9. monitoring performance.

The aim of this chapter is to help practising managers by offering them a practical tool in the form of a management model to manage this process. These steps are embodied in Figure 15.1 and the relationships between these steps and the model are given in the table below. The logic of this model is explained later in this chapter in the section entitled 'the climate for success'.

Market testing steps	Fig 15.1 model component that relates
Identifying the scope and nature of the activity	Strategic business purpose
Establishing levels of cost effective service	Performance objectives and risk assessment
Developing a specification and outline service level agreement	Procurement and Contract Conditions (service blueprint)
Inviting tenders from potential bidders	Not discussed
Selecting a suitable list of bidders	Not discussed
Evaluating competing bids	Not discussed
Calling for bids	Not discussed
Awarding a contract or service level agreement	Supplier competence and supplier drive
Monitoring performance	Effective climate for success

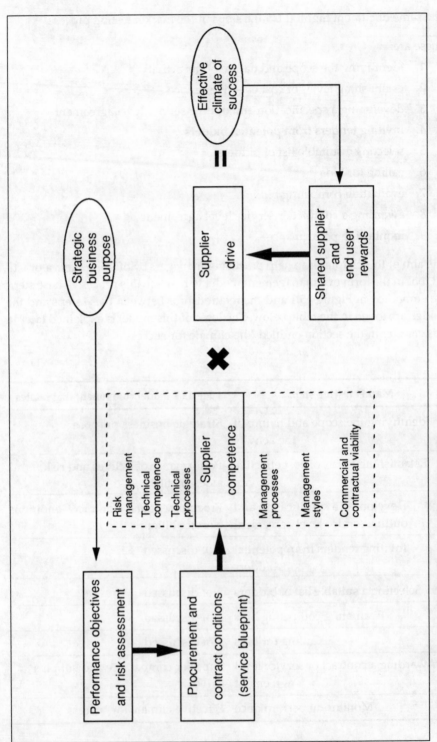

Figure 15.1 Model for managing out-sourced service providers.

The main participants

In discussing the issues related to managing out-sourced services it is important to identify the principal participants and to define and understand their role. There are usually three participants, the end user, the contract manager, and the supplier.

The *end user* is the beneficiary of the out-sourced service and is also accountable for its quality and delivery. The prime obligation of the end user is to provide a clear definition of the service expected. This definition should include service quality standards, financial parameters, management and reporting relationships and a clear statement of the strategic business purpose of the end user.

The *contract manager* could be from within the end user organisation or some one appointed to this task from another part of the organisation, perhaps the procurement department. The contract manager acts as agent for the end user and is responsible for:

- understanding end user needs and setting in motion those activities necessary to find and commission the out-sourced service
- guarding the end user's strategic business purpose in the context of this out-sourced service and expressing it in a way that is easily understood by future suppliers
- bringing discipline to bear on the procurement process by ensuring that the end users have carefully studied their needs and are certain that, if what is specified is delivered, those needs would be totally met
- ensuring that end user needs are conveyed to the supplier and to ensure that the supplier understands those needs and does not deviate from them during the tendering and setting-up phases without its being identified as a variation and the changes agreed by all parties.

The supplier is the organisation providing the out-sourced service, and the supplier team refers to the staff assigned by the supplier to satisfy the contract. Sometimes the supplier may have sub-contractors who supplement the supplier's skills and capabilities in providing the out-sourced service. A sub-contractor will not have any contractual relationships with the contract manager or the end user.

The climate for success

Figure 15.1 sets out a model by which out-sourced services can be managed. It shows the interrelationships between the strategic business purpose and the ultimate achievement of the out-sourced service, meeting the performance objectives of the end user. The performance objectives dictate the nature and scope of the key procurement and contract conditions. The procurement and contract conditions lead to the definition of key supplier competencies which combine with the drive and initiative of the supplier to fulfil the contract.

The six key supplier competencies which need special attention at the initial conceptual stage and need to be continuously monitored are:

- risk management abilities of the supplier
- technical competence of the supplier
- technical processes used by the supplier
- management processes used by the supplier
- management styles used by the supplier
- financial and commercial viability of the supplier.

In addition the contract manager must assess the drive and determination of the supplier as without this the eventual outcome will not match the initial expectations. The successful management of the out-sourced service satisfies the strategic business purpose and the expectation of shared rewards of the supplier. Some of the key issues that need attention are discussed in the rest of this chapter.

Strategic business purpose

Out-sourcing must be undertaken after a careful study of the impact of out-sourcing on the business as a whole. It must support the wider business objectives of the end user, the end user's strategic business purpose. It must specify the performance gains sought and quantify the consequences of failure in terms of the financial and other business factors, such as impact on customer satisfaction, loss of core skills etc. If the service is planned to deliver services which are integral to the organisation and which give it its distinctive capability this requirement is even more important. It does not, therefore, pay to shroud the procurement and bidding process with mystery in an attempt to be fair and even-handed. On the contrary, it is important to the final success of the service that the supplier and supplier team also understand these strategic and business reasons. Such an understanding will help the supplier gain a wider appreciation of the reason for the out-sourcing and will help the supplier to:

- offer alternative solutions based on their wider experience of providing similar services
- customise the service to fit these wider objectives more closely

- instruct the supplier's staff as to the sensitivities and importance of the service to the end user

- price the service and interpret the specification more accurately.

Alternative solutions are more likely to arise where constantly evolving technology and management methods influence the nature and scope of the out-sourced service. Box 15.1 illustrates this case.

Box 15.1 - Learning from potential suppliers

A recent personal experience of a potential supplier's being better informed than the end user, was where a client was seeking to out-source the development of a process management system. The initial preference of the client was that the existing systems should be replicated using more modern technology. A supplier suggested that the process should be re-engineered so that the processes being adopted delivered savings in cost and improved productivity without risking the reliability of the service. It was obvious to my client that if the supplier's suggestion was accepted it would place the supplier in a very favourable position to win the tender. However, using this information the end user redefined the terms of the tender to allow for a wider range of solutions and benefited from the experience of all the potential suppliers. It meant that the interaction with the suppliers was seen not purely as a tendering process but also as a learning process.

Shared performance objectives

The strategic business purpose is embodied in the shared performance targets for the out-sourced service. It is important that these performance targets are agreed and are jointly owned by the three parties to the out-sourced service. Examples of shared out-sourced service goals for out-sourcing software developments are given in Figure 15.2. It suggests that performance targets must be established not only for the system but also for intermediate goals and the management tasks surrounding the 'production' process. Clearly stated at the outset these, together with the strategic overview, provide:

- the contract manager with measures by which to monitor and control the performance of the supplier

- the supplier with performance targets

- the end user with early warning of deviation from course.

Success Factors	Suggested performance targets
Out-sourced service mission	Clear terms of reference with unambiguous statement of operational purpose and criteria of acceptability
Key results areas	Design validity, quality of staffing, management and technical processes, documentation, means of early identification of deviation from norm, plan integrity, motivation of staff, management style, out-sourced service team familiarity with out-sourced service mission.
Measures of success of product	Meets performance targets and has the in-built flexibility to change with changing needs without risk of overspend or loss of profits i.e. for an IT software product it could be portability, reliability, efficiency, human engineering, testability, understandability, modifiability.
Measures of success of end user management	Timeliness, budget and functionality, selection of out-sourced service manager and team, keeping fingers on the pulse.
Tools	Design reviews, progress reviews, trouble-shooting, payments, standards, testing, training, user surveys, random sampling and benchmarking.

Figure 15.2. Examples of shared objectives.

Out-sourced service risk assessment

Out-sourced service risk assessment covers a wide area. Some risks arise from managerial and staffing shortfalls whilst others can result from new technologies, processes and customer requirements. Where a new supplier is employed to provide a new service the risk is higher than where a familiar supplier is used to provide a familiar service. Partial knowledge can often create high risk out-sourced services because the contract manager and the end user may not be able to assess the true risk to the organisation of out-sourcing the service. Risk assessment must be carried out prior to determining performance and contractual conditions and value judgements made on the trade-off between performance standards and the cost and additional risks which these performance standards can impose on the supplier and end user. The final price paid for the services bought reflects the quality, functionality and uniqueness of the out-sourced service. For example, if the standards being applied to the service are those in common use by the chosen supplier it is likely that the price for the service could be negotiated to reflect this. If however, the supplier has to learn new standards and implement them for a specific customer the cost of learning will often be reflected in the tender price (Box 15.2). Some of the risk factors that need to be considered are discussed below:

Box 15.2 - Caveat emptor

A supplier undertook to develop bespoke software for a local authority. Part of the agreement was that the software, once finished and used by the client, would be sold to other local authorities with the supplier and the client benefiting from the sale of the software.

The supplier did not fully grasp the implications of this undertaking and found once the project began that the client's development methodology placed a very high administrative overhead on the project. The additional work increased costs with the result that the potential loss to the supplier would be almost equivalent to the contract price. Faced with an unyielding client the supplier had to bear the loss. However, it broke the partnership and mutuality of their relationship with the result that neither party eventually benefited from the commercial value of what had been created. Did this matter to the local authority who had received the software it needed? Perhaps not, but had it prevented a new opportunity to be exploited thus enabling it to reduce its IT cost? Perhaps yes. It seemed that neither party had judged the longer term viability of the contract they entered into or evaluated the mutual loss their behaviour caused.

❑ People related risks

The people related risks can be errors of commission and omission. They can lead to loss of the whole or part of completed work, requiring a re-start of some aspects of the out-sourced service or creating intense end user dissatisfaction. Staff movement within and in and out of the out-sourced service must be monitored and controlled so that it does not affect the productivity and effectiveness of the team or service. Many out-sourced services fail because sub-contractors and suppliers of minor deliverables fail to meet their targets. It is imperative that the same stringent management, technical and commercial processes are applied by the supplier to sub-contractors so that they do not cause out-sourced service delay.

❑ Transition management

The switch over from the internally provided service to the new out-sourced service needs to be seamless if end user confidence and ownership is to be achieved. Selection of the final supplier must be based as much on their ability to achieve this seamless transition as on the other aspects of the out-sourced service, particularly when the new providers are taking over from in-house staff who have also tendered for and lost to outsiders. Care should also be taken to make sure that a seamless transfer takes place if a different contractor takes over at the end of the first out-sourced contract. In this instance, two external commercially driven organisations may let their competitiveness over-ride the interests of their client. The dangers of being dependent on the supplier can be immense, especially if the organisation itself has lost the ability to be an 'intelligent user'.

Managing service quality

Service quality is made up of many different facets. It is the duty of the contract manager to ensure that appropriate measures which are acceptable to the supplier and the end user are put in place to ensure that throughout its life the out-sourced service meets its performance targets.

❏ Performance statistics and documentation

It is important that the progress of the out-sourced service is charted throughout its life. These statistics may relate to the work rate of the teams, the on-going agreements made at meetings and formal reviews to enable actions and decisions to be traced in the event of dispute or to record good practice for use in future out-sourced services. The end user should therefore determine what records are needed on the performance of the out-sourced service team members.

❏ Quality matrix

Quality must be measurable. To achieve this it is necessary for the end user to provide the supplier with a quality matrix. Such a matrix will identify the desirable features of the service and place a value on each feature.

These weightings can then be used by the supplier to assess the degree of attention to detail expected by the end user and to design for them. The end user in turn can use the matrix as a grading scale to assess the quality of the end product. For example, if you have a maintenance contract for the central heating boiler, what value would you place on 24 hour cover, regular maintenance, or immediate response between office hours. The viability of this approach is illustrated in Box 15.3 drawn from a recent consulting assignment geared to determining what measure could be used to judge customer expectation and satisfaction.

Box 15.3 - *Measuring quality*

The supplier was bidding to win a contract to maintain plant for a public organisation. In order to determine what service quality the potential customer expected the supplier drew up a list of seven key services that formed part of the total service package and asked the potential customer to prioritise the services and rate each one for service quality. When this was done the supplier used this information to tie its performance to these standards and offer the potential customer the choice of judging the supplier against these targets and apply a penalty if the actual performance fell short of the agreed targets.

❏ Quality process

Quality is endemic. It is not a mantle that a supplier can wear to win a contract. The end users must ensure that quality extends beyond the standard labels and accreditations common in today's quality fraternity. They must determine what the supplier's quality process is and how it is managed, whether it depends on adherence to rules and procedures or to the inherent craftsmanship of the team members and their enculturation to produce quality products. They must agree a quality process appropriate to the needs of this out-sourced service. Above all they must ensure that the quality plan and out-sourced service review process prevents the team from diverging into flights of fancy and chasing technology for technology's sake.

❏ Test procedures

To test the finished product and find it wanting is costly and counter productive. Testing procedures must identify faults and non-conformance almost as soon as the errors are committed. Testing therefore must start with each individual team member delivering and working to perfection. The quality assurance process must set out to facilitate this first. Fail safe procedures should then act as belt and braces to detect and return for rectification output that fails to meet the standards. In the case of services the service delivery system must be re-examined.

Commercial and contractual terms

The contract manager must ensure that the contract management and commercial processes governing the method of choosing the supplier, managing the supplier, paying for the supplier's services, protection of end user interests, retaining adequate control over the out-sourced service and its phased deliverables (giving the end user the optimum scope for manoeuvre in case of supplier distress or non-performance) are in place. By so doing the inherent risks of failure are moderated over the life of the out-sourced service. Understanding these risks alone is not enough. In addition the contract manager must create the legal and commercial framework for success. Some of the issues to address are given below.

❏ Control without stifling responsiveness and creativity

The need to be 'outcome' orientated in approach is recognised so as not to limit the freedom of the supplier in choosing *how* the service will be provided. Nevertheless, commercial and contractual terms must be carefully crafted to enable the end user to achieve considerable control over the supplier without reducing the supplier's freedom to act in the best interests of meeting the strategic business purpose and out-sourced service objectives.

❏ Enabling mechanisms

The commercial and contractual terms must be enabling mechanisms which strengthen the out-sourced service manager and his or her ability to control the supplier. It is not a question of abdication of responsibility once the contract is let.

❏ Rewards

Payment for services and bonuses for exceptional effort must be related to deliverables rather than to elapsed time.

❏ Penalties

The tendering process must hint at the likely commercial and contractual benefits and penalties so that suppliers can determine their bidding strategy. Naturally, the process must encourage as wide a range of viable and credible bidders, but the terms may put some potential suppliers off. They may find that the penalties and expectations are such that they would prefer not to bid. On the other hand, they may formulate a solution which enables them to bid and yet contain the risk by suggesting variations or using different methods or approaches. Once underway the service must be carefully monitored and shortfalls identified quickly and brought to the notice of the supplier for rectification. It is important that shortfalls are logged so that they can be used in evidence should a dispute arise. An example of a supplier making such a decision is given in Box 15.4.

❏ Safeguards

The tendency of some organisations, particularly start-up ventures, to fail commercially requires that the end users safeguard their interests by ensuring that

> **Box 15.4 - Choosing not to bid**
> End users can discourage potential suppliers from bidding by weighting the tender in favour of one supplier. Such a case came to my attention recently when many potential suppliers refused to bid for a contract because it specified proprietary products which gave one supplier a significant advantage. This was unintended. Fortunately, the end user responded positively to the refusal of the other suppliers and reassessed his approach and reissued the tender.

all out-sourced services and those involved in their provision can continue despite the commercial problems they may encounter, such as voluntary liquidation or being sold to another parent or a management buy-out. This is especially important in the IT area and once more cautions against letting contracts to suppliers who do not have a good track record.

Technical competence of the supplier's team

Technical competence of the supplier's team is often the result of their mix, staff quality and subsequent management. The role of the contract manager is to ensure that the end user specifies the levels of technical competence expected and that the supplier not only understands them but can deliver to them over the life of the out-sourced service. Some key issues are addressed below.

❏ Out-sourced service team mix, formation and management

The end user, through the contract manager, must satisfy him or herself, before the contract is awarded and during the running of the out-sourced service, that the methods used to select, form and manage out-sourced service teams will deliver teams that are capable, highly motivated and resourced. If necessary the contract should give the end user the right both to interview potential recruits and to refuse their employment where necessary. This is particularly important to ensure that, once the tender is let, the supplier does not use its 'second eleven' to implement the contract.

❏ Staff quality

The delivery of the final product must ultimately rest on the quality of the out–sourced service staff. Their experience and track record for delivering must be assessed. This can be done by talking to other organisations who have used the same supplier or it may pay to give the supplier a pilot project to manage.

For example, asking them to cater for a special occasion at very short notice, or to repair plant if the out-sourced service is for the maintenance of plant and equipment, or to clean up an area which has suddenly flooded. These opportunities to test the potential supplier do not present themselves naturally or often but it may pay to test them before placing the contract. Their ability to do the job (task relevant skills) and their wider understanding and knowledge of the service being provided (domain relevant skills) must be assessed and the volume of staff with these skills must be judged adequate for this out-sourced service. Out-sourced services which last long periods of time place special stresses on staff, and this means that, to sustain the level of commitment and freshness necessary to deliver a quality product, staff may have to be rotated. An example for the consultancy practice is detailed in Box 15.5.

Box 15.5- Benefits of supplier staff rotation

An employee of a prestigious consultancy company complained that she had not been moved from a particular client site for over an year. This was because the client liked her work and wanted her to remain. Her manager in the consulting firm was relatively happy with this arrangement as it was a guaranteed source of revenue and guaranteed customer satisfaction. The consultant was unhappy because she was not learning new skills, her prime reason for joining a large consultancy. Over time she had just become another employee of the client even though she was paid by the consultancy company, she felt she belonged neither to the consultancy company nor the client company. She resolved the deadlock by resigning and seeking a new career elsewhere. There was a significant risk that client dependency would eventually result in client resentment and dissatisfaction. She also found that many of her colleagues fearing the same fate (being stuck with the same customer for too long) avoided being assigned to this particular client, thus causing a climate within the consultancy where the best staff made themselves unavailable. The ultimate loser was the client who did not benefit from new ideas and fresh motivation that re-cycling supplier staff can give.

This implies a need for a second eleven of enough skilled staff to meet the manning levels required. If the supplier uses contract staff to supplement his own, the end user must ensure that the same stringent standards are applied in choosing subcontractors and that their track record stands up to scrutiny.

Capability of supplier technical processes

The technical methods adopted by the supplier to deliver the out-sourced service must be assessed for suitability and cost effectiveness. Often a careful study of the technical approach taken by the supplier reveals much more about the supplier's attitude to the quality and functionality of the service than detailed discussions and reviews can ever give. Similarly, the cost of the service will be reflected in the technical processes used and therefore an effective means of trading down costs is to evaluate the technical methods and processes and agree to different processes which provide the cost benefits sought by the end user. The following items might be of particular interest in this respect.

❏ Over-engineering

This means applying techniques and processes which exceed the perceived needs of the service but which may offer the supplier higher profits. Similarly, the technique may be the only one that the supplier can offer and this may point to the needs being twisted to meet the supplier capability rather than end user need.

❏ Inappropriateness of the technique

In this case the supplier uses a sledge-hammer to crack a nut.

❏ Untested techniques

Here the supplier is experimenting with new technologies and uses the out-sourcing contract to test them.

❏ Techniques used to build supplier dependency

In this instance the supplier uses techniques which will tie the end user in and reduce the future options of the end user (i.e. third party lock-in).

Management processes

Once the out-sourced service is in place the contract manager often hands over to the end user line management to carry on with the contract and supervise the contractor. Once the service is in operation the on-going management must ensure that the service meets the initial specification and contractual conditions. To do this certain critical success factors need to be monitored. The main factors are as follows.

❏ Change control

Variations to the original specification and 'creeping enhancements' are often the prime cause of out-sourced service delay and over-run. The end user must ensure and understand the change control process and how it is managed from both supplier and end user perspectives before the contract commences and must regularly employ the process once the contract is in operation. It is often claimed by managers that the quality of out-sourced services varies over the life of the contract, i.e. the quality of meals from external caterers is high at the beginning of the contract, becomes indifferent during the mid-point in the contract period and improves again just before its termination to ensure and enhance the caterer's ability to renew the contract for another term. If the change control process is used effectively this variation in standards can be prevented and possible staff dissatisfaction avoided.

❑ Out-sourced service structure and reporting lines

The success of out-sourced services depends on the quality of the suppliers staff and the quality of the supplier's management and management systems. However, the upward access of the out-sourced service to senior supplier management can help considerably when the 'going gets rough' and the supplier has to pull out all the stops. It is at these times that the positioning of the out-sourced service within the hierarchy of the organisation proves its worth. The procurement specification must suggest to the supplier what reporting lines the end user will find acceptable. At the same time it must be recognised that out-sourced service suppliers can gain access to senior client management with far greater ease than in-house staff and, unless the senior managers have a reliable internal communications channel to alert them of supplier shortfalls, their impartiality in judging in-house dissatisfaction can be affected.

❑ Management culture

The end user must judge if the management culture adopted by the supplier is consistent with the needs of the out-sourced service. Of particular importance to many well established private and public organisations are the ethics and morality of the employment practices of the supplier. Care must be taken to ensure that the terms and conditions of employment do not contravene statutory and legal requirements. Even more important, they should not diverge significantly from the code of conduct adopted by the end user. Failure to do this can result in public embarrassment, but more importantly it could undermine the viability of the service due to disaffection among the supplier's staff resulting in rapid staff turnover and a lack of continuity causing inefficiencies in the end user's own operations. Care also needs to be taken in this area if current staff are likely to transfer to the supplier on a permanent basis.

❑ Review mechanisms

Out-sourced services go wrong one day at a time. Therefore action to keep it on track must be taken daily. Adequate, formal and in depth reviews can detect and correct out-sourced services at risk of derailment. The end user must understand how out-sourced services are reviewed, what form these reviews take, their frequency, accuracy and who carries them out. It is also necessary to understand what authority the review process confers on the reviewer to require or instruct corrective action to be taken. It would also help if the processes enabled staff to highlight causes or events which may prevent them meeting their deadlines and targets.

Supplier drive

The inner drive, commitment and dedication of the supplier staff is the motive force of the out-sourced service. It is energised and sustained by a combination of shared rewards which are discussed in the next section. Whilst achieving the out-sourced service objectives would be a significant driver, other more subtle drivers also come into being. Among these are the self-esteem of the team, an understanding of the importance of the out-sourced service to the end user and the supplier and the team members' own careers and reputations. These strong drivers can be blunted by the vagaries of the out-sourced service life cycle. By starting off with the right attitude and managing the strength of the drive throughout the out-sourced service the likelihood of out-sourced service success is greatly enhanced. It is necessary for the contract manager to assess the drive of supplier management and staff. There are many ways to do this but practices which provide a clue to the real interest shown are discussed below.

❏ Reporting level of the contract

The contract manager must determine the importance placed on the contract by the supplier. A useful pointer to this is to determine how senior the supplier's contract manager is and to what level of management within the supplier's organisation the contract manager reports.

❏ Response to complaints

Is it quick or is it handled by 'passing-the-buck' down the chain of command.

❏ Supplier initiated improvements

Is supplier management taking an active interest in the contract and devoting time to it, even if that time is outside the strict contractual arrangements. Suggestions for savings or new services can be a clue as to whether this is happening.

Shared rewards

Each party to the out-sourced service will have their own objectives over and above the out-sourced service objective. The suppliers will have their own strategic business objectives, to gain profit and kudos from the out-sourced service, and the out-sourced service team will also welcome the kudos and enhanced experience of a successful out-sourced service. Within this context particular attention needs to be given to energising and sustaining the motivation of the supplier's out-sourced service team, sustaining the supplier's profitability and ensuring the end user's functionality.

Energising and sustaining staff motivation can prove difficult. It can become more difficult if the out-sourced service runs into trouble and the supplier sees profit margins erode. In this situation the out-sourced service staff may be pressurised to work without the usual payments for overtime or weekend working. It is, therefore, important that the end user should understand how staff will be motivated during the out-sourced service and what reward mechanisms are used to sustain motivation and commitment. The most likely time to obtain such a concession is before contracts are signed and therefore the right to offer direct inducements to supplier's staff may have to be embodied in the contract. Monitoring compliance can be difficult and may be seen as an intrusion of the supplier's privacy, but the right of audit by an independent third party offers an equitable way forward.

It is important that the end user does not place the supplier's profitability at risk. Placed in such a situation the supplier will seek to recoup the profit shortfalls by other means which could cause a reduction in the quality of the end user's out-sourced service. Payments to the contractor during the life of the out-sourced service must be used as both a carrot and a stick. Firstly, payment must be linked to discrete deliverables rather than to time. Secondly, the contract must enable the end user to withhold payment much more as an encouragement for corrective action rather than as a penalty for failure.

End user rewards take the form of an out-sourced service completed to time and budget, which meets and solves their problems. However, part of the sense of satisfaction derived by end users comes from their sense of ownership of the out-sourced service and its outcome. This is easier to achieve if end user involvement is initiated and sustained from the very beginning of the out-sourced service.

Conclusions

In this chapter the issues associated with managing out-sourced services have been addressed from the point of view of how the end user should convert the strategic business purpose into procurement and contractual conditions that will deliver the desired outcomes. The theme of the chapter is that success is more likely to follow if the pre-conditions for success are carefully studied and the essential elements embodied in the procurement and contractual conditions so that the end user management can monitor and control the supplier. The suggestions made require the end user to examine more critically the management competence of the supplier and the suitability of the staff and facilities the supplier offers. This is in contrast to taking a hands-off view of management when a service is out-sourced. At the end of the day the end user is still accountable to the organisation for the quality of the service and therefore has no choice but to examine the management and technical competence of the supplier as closely as if they were being made full time employees of the organisation.

Reference and suggested reading

Behan, P. (1994) *Purchasing in Government* Harlow, Longman.

Part 3 — Case Studies

Introduction

Parts 1 and 2 have considered the processes involved in managing change and some of the instruments for achieving change. We now look at a series of case studies. Most are written by people who have carried out significant change in the new public sector, others present the results of research into the implementation of change. Two studies consider change from the top of the organisation, one looks at a restructuring exercise, one describes the implementation of a Total Quality Management initiative, another considers the effect of a participative management style, two look at the increasing need for contract management and the final chapter provides the results of research into the implementation of the Patient's Charter.

Stephen Curtis is one of the few people to date who have been Chief Executive of two agencies, Companies House and, currently, the Driver Vehicle Licensing Agency. In Chapter 16 he gives a personal view of managing the current changes towards the new public management from the top of the office, taking full account of the need to stimulate staff to accompany him on his journey along the rocky road of change.

Many well respected commentators emphasise the difficulties in bringing about cultural change in an organisation, particularly in areas steeped in history and tradition like the civil service. The achievement of Michael Bichard, its Chief Executive, and colleagues at the Benefits Agency over the past three years in changing the culture and direction of the organisation has been significant both in terms of the size of the organisation and undertaking and, more particularly, the degree of supported change that has been achieved. Again with a view from the top of the office, Michael Bichard explains in Chapter 17 how this was achieved, along with some of the lessons learned.

Much discussion is currently taking place about the ideal structures for organisations providing service to the public and, in particular, the continued suitability of centralised pay and grading systems. One of the first organisations in the civil service to recognise the need to restructure its organisation if it was to deliver improved service to the customer in competition with its private sector competitors was HMSO. This required the implementation of a fundamental pay and grading review. Despite the fact that the exercise was completed some three years ago, the fact that much of the service is now embarking on a similar journey demonstrates how far sighted the initiative was. In Chapter 18 Michael Salt, who was head of personnel during the exercise, provides a detailed account of the process, including comments on the lessons learned, both at the time and subsequently, an appreciation of the place that the initiative had in making the organisation more dynamic and flexible for the further changes which lay ahead.

While support from the top of the office is tremendously helpful in achieving change, especially cultural change, the power and ability of managers themselves to bring about significant change should never be overlooked. Two such examples can be seen in Chapters 19 and 20.

The total quality initiative of the West Midlands Regional Office of the Employment Service, led by Martin Raff and Julie Beedon, is rapidly becoming a legend in the total quality field. In Chapter 19 they provide an excellent example of how incremental change has grown, from the seed of an idea five years ago to one of the most well known and successful initiatives in the public sector in the country.

Likewise, Keith Hodgson, Controller of the Stamp Office, demonstrates in Chapter 20 what improvements can be achieved in a small organisation of 150 people through trust, openness and a participative management style.

Examples of the operation of services in the civil service that have been successfully contracted out are at present still in their infancy. This is by no means the case in local government where the Compulsory Competitive Tendering initiative has had time to settle down. In order to learn some of the lessons from this style of management in central Government, we need for the time being to turn to the local government sector. In Chapter 21 Cheryl Coppell, who was in charge of the initiative for a county, Berkshire, regarded by many as the most successful County Council in adopting this style of operation, explains some of the experiences encountered over the past six years and some lessons for the future.

Meanwhile, the civil service is starting to appreciate the need to reorganise significantly its modus operandi to take account of the increase in contract management. In Chapter 22, Wilf Styles, John Cavanaugh and Bob Mandy explain how they are taking the opportunity at the Department of Employment, not simply to create a specific Contracts Branch but also in doing so to take account of many of the new managerial practices like total quality and benchmarking.

Finally, much has been published about the targets achieved as a result of the Citizen's Charter initiative. Less notice has been taken of whether those targets have been achieved within the ethos of the customer focus of the Charter. In other words, are organisations, as with many target setting approaches, superficially meeting the targets, or are they radically changing their whole approach by embedding the principles into all aspects of the organisation, not just in those few areas capable of measurement and publicity? Chapter 23 provides a brief description of some research carried out at the end of 1992 which looked at the implementation of the Patient's Charter in six hospitals within the same Regional Health Authority. The aim of the study was to look behind the results of the Charter rights and standards and into the management practices and cultures of the various units. From this it was possible to distinguish between the practices of the successful and less successful units.

The subject of change by its very nature is dynamic. Systems, practices and styles continue to move, and always will, to suit the ever evolving circumstances. A study of history serves to reduce the chances of our repeating mistakes, often learned at some cost, by our forefathers. Already the contents of this book will be dated. It is hoped however that its contents will serve to demonstrate how it is possible to hold reality for a moment and create a little stability in the ever changing chaos in which we live. Above all we must never forget that, while the speed of change increases, human nature remains the same. A high degree of gentleness and understanding is crucial therefore if people are to bring all the talents of human kind to contribute to the enterprise.

Chapter 16

Change: the rocky but rewarding road

Stephen Curtis

The management of change and its leadership are two distinct, although linked, processes. For the purposes of this chapter, I define the management of change as the ability to get from state A to state B efficiently, effectively and economically. Leadership is the process of deciding whether state B is the state you want to move to, and the process of persuasion that ensures that the organisation makes the change with understanding, commitment and belief in itself.

This gives rise to two initial points. Firstly, leadership is primarily about what are often called the 'soft' factors: vision, hearts and minds and so on. 'Soft' is a perjorative term. Nobody who has led change would confuse soft with its natural English synonym of easy. Secondly, a concomitant of leadership is followership. The long march will be unsuccessful if you are the only one on it. So taking others with you is vital. Yet the process of proselytising, communication and persuasion is understudied. It will feature in this chapter.

The vision thing

First, the view of where you are going.

❏ Where does the leader begin?

The first part of the process is an internal one. Faith may not be too strong a word for it. My experience suggests that the most successful change is not that which the accountants demonstrate has the biggest payback or which has the greatest panoply of committees controlling it. The most successful change is the one the participants believe in. There is an engineer's maxim:

> If it looks right, it probably is right.

The leader's maxim may be:

> If it's right, it will feel right.

❑ Judgement and intuition

Feeling right is an odd process. It requires a mixture of judgement and intuition. Judgement without intuition may work, but not in the wholehearted way that is the subject of this book. Intuition without judgement may also work, occasionally very well indeed, but the disasters will be equally spectacular. So, have a belief by all means but do not let it completely cloud your ability to listen to others or to rethink with a cooler head.

To take an example, in one organisation, to serve our customers well, we needed to dig out information for them. Clearly therefore (or so intuition said) we would do better if our targeting more accurately reflected the digging out process. New targets for retrieving files were introduced. Reports reaching my office showed that these targets were now being met. But service to the customer failed to improve. A quick look at the area amply demonstrated why. Files were being dug out at a great rate. They were not being put back again. The whole place was becoming a shambles. We had taken too quick a judgement of what was wrong and too simplistic a view of its solution. Service to the public was more holistic than we had given it credit for.

❑ Sources of vision

A vision is not something that sits ready-made on the library shelf. It is, as we have seen, an essentially personal acquisition. Where, then, do you acquire it? One source will undoubtedly be your own experiences and attitudes. This is the 'feeling right', referred to above. But ensure that you are a good, if enquiring, listener and viewer. Staff and managers in the organisation itself are likely to have ideas. The organisation's customers will soon let you know how they would like it to develop. Listen to what is said and test it out. Why are they saying that? Would it actually help me deliver better or cheaper services? Is their view broad enough and internally consistent? Most importantly perhaps, is it what I, as leader, want to do?

Besides these mechanisms, I have always found it immensely useful to look closely at other organisations and what they are doing. They are quite likely to be doing things you have never considered, such as using new technology in novel ways. Or they may be undertaking their work in ways you have rejected, yet can now see as successful. Such experiences, provided that they are approached in a learning frame of mind, can be challenging and broadening.

❑ The impact of a complex environment

Sometimes vision takes longer to develop than on other occasions. This may be because the procedures your organisation undertakes are particularly complex -

or more precisely that their effects are complex. Complex procedures may require some effort to understand. By themselves they do not make a vision more difficult to create. However, a complexity of effect can complicate the process of developing a vision. It is a characteristic of much of the public sector that the work it does impacts on a large number of stakeholders, many of whom would wish the efforts of the organisation to be tilted more firmly in their direction as shown in Chapter 10. In that case, where the job of the organisation involves balancing various interests, it may be less easy quickly to arrive at a vision for the business as a whole.

Owners

Similarly in the public sector, the leader of an organisation is rarely a free agent. He or she is likely to be required to operate within the ambit of other people's policies, such as those of central or local government. There may be intellectual effort required to ensure that those policies are consistent with the leader's own vision for his or her organisation, or it may be necessary to adapt the vision appropriately to take account of the wider scene. An additional complexity is of course that this scene may turn out to be deciduous rather than evergreen. Policies and emphases change, especially if the administration itself changes. It is important to accept these changes as features of life. They are not in themselves an argument for a lack of vision; a leader is required to cope with complexity. However, some circumstances are more straightforward than others. It may be an important part of the public sector leader's role to try to ensure that the messages that come from the owners of the business (to use a not entirely appropriate private sector analogy) are themselves clear, consistent and likely to endure.

Customers

So the 'owners' of the business are one group to which the leader must listen and which he or she may want to try and influence. Others are the organisation's customers and its staff. I will return to the staff dimension. The customer dimension is sometimes not straightforward. A very early question for a leader is not just 'what does my organisation do?' but 'why do we do it?' and 'for whom?'

As examples:

- driving licences are not issued only to benefit the holders of them: the information on the drivers databases helps the administration of law and order; the checks made before a licence is issued benefit road safety

- for somebody working on business statistics, the main day-to-day contact may be with the firms supplying information about their activities (whether those firms are or are not 'customers' is a generally sterile semantic point). However, the main purpose of the statistics may be for better, more informed, government

- in an historic setting, the most visible customers may well be the visitors. Any potential visitors who may be excluded for the benefit of future generations may be particularly vocal. Yet if conservation is an important part of the vision, the vocality of those who pay at the gate, or would want to, must not be over-whelming.

❑ Green field vision

A vision that understands the 'why' questions will be more robust than one that is formed solely from the 'what'. Is the vision strengthened or weakened by understanding the present? My own inclination is to try to form one vision that excludes where the organisation is now. This green field vision represents an optimum.

It is too easy, if you focus too early on the present state of the organisation, to look only at trimming round the edges of that. A green field vision, however, acts as a challenge. The process of judgement, already discussed, comes when it is necessary to fit the vision to reality. It is not possible to give any hard and fast advice about the end of the visionary/reality continuum at which you should settle but the presence of both poles is a constant reminder that it is always possible to try harder.

Just three additional points, that some readers may find helpful:

- the word 'poles' implies two dimensions. But, as already shown, the public sector leader will in many cases be playing with a multi-dimensional map
- for some leaders of some organisations, all this may hardly be an issue. Whether or not it is an issue will depend on how far the organisation currently is from where it should be
- when considering the multi-dimensional do not forget the dimension of time. How far you can move may depend considerably on how long you have to change attitudes, engage in staff training or undertake capital investment programmes.

Taking others with you

Having reached the point where the leader is clear in his or her own mind about where to head, it is necessary to turn towards the subject of followship, introduced at the beginning of this chapter.

❑ The imperative

Part of followship, and almost a sine qua non, is to give not just clear marching instructions but also reasons why you should march. Staff are not automata.

Those I have been fortunate enough to have worked with have been first class. It is that very ability and excellence which leads them to be questioning. Just as the leader has brought about self-conviction, so the followers need to be convinced. In my experience, the reasons for change are often more difficult to articulate in the public sector than in the private.

This is due both to the complexity of the organisation's relationships and may reflect what staff see as an inability to lose market share. In some cases, where the change reflects staff's own instincts, no imperative may be necessary. This is typically the case where the thrust is to improve customer service. It is the staff who are in the front line of service to the customer and they welcome measures and a direction that enables them to give a better service to those with whom they deal. Indeed, it may be something for which they have been asking their managers for ages.

However, some other potential directions are more difficult. Efficiency gains, major computer developments, a move to out-sourcing may all seem inimical to staff. Why are you proposing changes that may lead to disruption, fewer staff, less over the counter service to customers, untried means of service delivery or whatever? It is important to be ready for these questions. What is the imperative driving change? Why not stand still?

❏ Constancy

It is important to recognise from the outset that the process of change may be a long one (there is a section on pace elsewhere in this chapter). One strength that some private sector friends think they have over the public sector is being able to maintain a direction once set. They accept, for example, that a quality management programme may take up to five years to bring about tangible results but if it is fundamental to the success of their businesses they are prepared to embark on it. This is despite inevitable change in the external environment in the meantime. Some of these changes undoubtedly require adjustment, even on occasion tactical retreat, but it does not in the most successful organisations mean the goal is abandoned.

As new tasks, requirements, emphases, crowd in on the public sector manager, it is easy to get buried and lose sight of the goal. But if change is going to be successful, it must be applied with constancy. Tactically, you can be as adaptable as you like. Strategically, however, you need to be firm.

In the Driver Vehicle Licensing Agency (DVLA) we wished to do more to disseminate best practice, particularly among our 50 or so local offices. As part of that an 'Office of the Year' competition was introduced. It was met with some criticism on its introduction, being thought of as gimmicky and divisive. We have not abandoned the competition in the face of that but have now had the third round. Changes have been introduced to clarify the criteria, but the competition is intact. It is starting to be recognised for its strategic aims.

❏ Communication

This has many aspects. Primarily, I intend to deal with the issue of communicating to the organisation's staff, but naturally there are others to whom communication is vital. Foremost among them are your customers. They need to know what you are up to, (many of them may themselves have to adapt). Should they believe in the change, and you hope they will, they can be a very useful and powerful way of reinforcing the case for change with your staff and giving staff pride in the process. Of course where change seems inimical to a group of customers, for example when it is more regulatory, then they will equally let staff know of their distaste for it.

There are many ways of communicating. The traditional public sector way is by newsletter or other written medium. On its own, I have found this almost invariably a failure. For a start, written material is almost always too carefully written. Public servants use the written word to convey the intellectual not the heartfelt. Oral communication on the other hand enables staff to see the whites of your eyes and hear the timbre of your voice. It almost always leads to issues being conveyed in simpler, more accessible, language. Sincerity can shine through, so can insincerity! You are there to be questioned.

However, the initial communication is only a small part of the whole. People are receiving messages constantly, through a wide variety of senses. One of the most difficult tasks for any leader who has communicated a vision is to ensure that everything is consistent with it.

❏ Consistency

It is no use, for example, asking your staff to be more empowered and to become greater risk takers if the first time something goes wrong (as it will) you flail around with your criticism. It is no use, if you demand that your managers should be more active, then to complain that they are not available for meetings with you. It is no use, but it is terrifyingly easy to do. Yet one's actions send stronger signals than any words, whether written or spoken.

At DVLA I have stressed empowerment especially among managers of local offices. One of those has 300 staff and spends around half a million pounds a year. I congratulated him a while ago on a meeting he had held with the police (as a customer of ours) at their premises. I wondered why he had never been a host for such a meeting. His answer was that he had neither the authority nor financial clearance to buy a thermos flask so that he could offer them coffee! Apparently we allowed him only £10 a year in discretionary expenditure. Whatever the words about empowerment and trust, this was not much of a demonstration of it. Clearly the manager could not believe the words for he could not reconcile them with his own reality, a point made earlier in Chapter 11.

Here a warning is necessary. In my experience, consistency is perhaps the most difficult part of the whole exercise. There are two aspects to that. One is to repeat the inevitable fact that all sorts of phenomena will assault the organisation during a period of change and it is not easy for any human being to react tactically in every case in a way consistent with the strategy. The second is that it may not matter how you react or behave; what is likely to matter is how you are perceived to have reacted or behaved.

Let me take a common example. Your thrust is to improve the quality of service. Either because of the initiative itself or because of a rise in demand a backlog develops. You want it reduced, because requiring customers to queue, or taking overlong to process their requests for licences or whatever, is hardly good customer service. But is it good customer service to deal cursorily with those in the pipeline so that eventually (you hope) you can deal well with the others? What sort of messages about customer care does it send to your staff, and to the customers, if as soon as the going gets tough you apparently walk away from what you are supposed to stand for?

There is no easy answer to all this. It is, however, one of the reasons a leader needs not only to have a vision but to feel it. It is much more likely that a vision which is felt, a faith, can suffuse all you do than can a vision which is an intellectual construct.

❏ Coup de theatre

We have seen that belief by the organisation in change and that the change is going to happen is formed in a number of ways. Ensuring that the actions are consistent with the words is important but there is a negativity about it. Inconsistent actions and words are death to change but consistency may not of itself be enough.

There will be many important and fundamental aspects to change. Some of them will take some time to bring in or may come in gradually. For example, change may involve re-training. The first few people re-trained will have a negligible impact. It will be a while before it reaches a critical mass. These aspects must be given your full attention. They are basic to the success of the change. Yet, if change is in part a 'hearts and minds' operation, they may do little to capture them.

You should not be afraid of the occasional coup de theatre, the demonstration that things are different. It may not be a display of something that makes a great difference but it must be something that is symbolic that something new is happening. For example when Companies House became an agency, staff coming in on agency day found a television in every office. The launch ceremony was relayed to each set on closed-circuit TV; staff were asked to stop work to watch.

On the other hand, avoid the sort of coup de theatre that may be all too well remembered but which may give rise to unfulfilled expectations. The impression this gives of a failed leader is not a helpful piece of baggage to take through what may be turbulent waters ahead. When DVLA was being created as an agency, it was announced that one change would be staff bonuses for those who worked hard. It has still not been possible to deliver this, four years on, and although well-intentioned and said in a spirit of openness as to what was being discussed, it was with hindsight clearly a mistake.

It is very easy for us, particularly we in the public sector, to be rather snootily dismissive of mere fripperies. We should not be. Our role is to change our organisations, we need to be imaginative about how we do that. Pure glitz will be seen for what it is, and must be avoided, but opinion forming devices such as closed circuit TVs or hiring a local theatre for a conference can be enormously effective and economical ways of getting the message across.

One word of warning: do not let economy mean penny-pinching. A clearly portion-controlled event can cause resentment and disillusion. It can be worse, much worse, than doing nothing.

A change often made at a time of change is to re-organise the business. This is done to prepare it to deliver services in the new ways required, but little is talked about more or anticipated with more interest than a re-organisation. Do not ignore its psychological effect.

❏ The top team

If a re-organisation has an impact on the whole of the business, it clearly has an impact on the top team. It is worth thinking with especial care about your team. As has been said, you are not yourself going to be able to carry through change. You are going to need the help and support of others. The first line of help you will need will be from those who form the group that amounts to, even if it is not actually called, your board of directors. These need to be the right people in the right jobs, with an especially deep understanding of the change and organised in a way that is likely to be most conducive to success.

One thing worth considering is the size of the top team. How many people will you have on the organisation's top decision-making body (its 'board')? There are two schools of thought.

One would involve a quite large group of people on the basis that this gives as many managers as possible a stake at the top table and thus makes it more likely that they will buy-in to the change. The other suggests that the group should be small. We have recently shrunk our board from nine to five. In doing so, we have lost some good people from it. I know that some of them regret that they have lost the ability directly to participate in and influence this senior forum. Yet the smaller board is undoubtedly more effective, just as smaller scale meetings tend to be more effective than large ones.

❏ Pace

One feature of change that sometimes is not thought about sufficiently closely until people are well into it, is the question of the pace at which change should go. The manager of change will be up against competing pressures. There will be those who are likely to benefit from the change, either through lower costs or a higher quality of service, clamouring for introduction as soon as possible and those who may see a risk of suffering from it who want to slow up its introduction.

Among those who may feel that they risk disbenefit can be managers and staff in an area which believes it is functioning perfectly well now and that change, of whatever form and whatever eventual benefit, is only likely to bring short term disruption and degradation of their very good quality of service.

There are arguments for making change fast, there are arguments for going more slowly. My own natural inclination is for impatience. I suspect that, as well as having a critical mass, change also has a critical speed. Should it come to proceed at a crawl then it is likely to follow that with a stop rather than a canter. It may be possible to introduce change that is so gradual that its sneaks up on people without their truly realising what has happened but in many cases this would simply not be possible even if it were sensible to delay the benefits of change for such a long period. If difficulties are going to occur then it is best that they are addressed and addressed quickly. The quicker you are out the other side of them the more quickly the organisation can re-heal and look forward to a future in the new state. There is nothing more unsettling for staff than uncertainty. Rapidity keeps the period of uncertainty as short as possible.

Elsewhere in this chapter, though, I have talked about judgement. The change that is being introduced needs to be introduced well and it will need to endure. This may necessarily temper your pace. Over-hasty change may not embed itself fully within the organisation and it may not allow for all the necessary processes to have taken place. For example, I can remember introducing a new computer system that worked tremendously well and objectively seemed to give us both better quality data and lower cost. It was not, however, until its introduction that we wholly realised the effect of having missed out one of the stages and that was giving staff training in the typing skills that they would require to use the keyboards. We had thought of the computer system as something sophisticated and had given the staff training in this sophistication. We had missed out the basics.

My suggestion is to break down the change into its smaller parts. Set change milestones. They are a discipline and their achievement is a sign that something should happen. Provided you can get the commitment to deliver, the time taken to get to each of these milestones is likely to be a bit less than the organisation first suggests as necessary. The public sector, with its considerable powers of analysis, can be very good at seeing the various problems that may be encountered during a project. This can, though, lead to a certain over-caution. A re-direction, not to focus on the problems but on their resolution and on the project itself, can bring about a re-birth of activity.

❑ The fear of failure

One reason for occasional slowness in some parts of the public sector is a fear of failure. I remember asking an ex-colleague who had moved to the private sector how he thought it differed. Among the main differences, he suggested, were that the private sector focuses on and celebrates success, the public sector focuses on and emphasises failure.

A fear of failure can be wish-fulfilling. It is of course necessary, as made clear at the beginning of this chapter, not to lose all judgement. But concentrating on everything that could possibly go wrong is not the way to drive a project or to inculcate the right attitudes in those most involved in it. Stay alert to the possibility of failure, but promote success. How's the change going?

❑ The role of management information

Undoubtedly the leader of change is going to want to keep in touch with it in some formal, systematic, way. Management information has a considerable part to play. If the management information system is to be a good one, it needs to avoid some pitfalls:

- the information must reflect, or be a good proxy for, what you want to achieve
- the system must not distort the organisation's effort into satisfying what the statistics seem to be asking of it, rather than what is actually required

- the production of the information must not itself consume undue effort or be a distraction from getting the job done.

The first two of these objectives are closely linked. You might for example measure the success of a customer care programme by the extent to which it reduced queuing times in your offices. But the Machiavellian manager can achieve short queuing times by being brusque or by allowing each customer only one transaction after which they return to the back of the queue. Just as in the example given earlier about getting out files at Companies House, service to the customer would be failing to improve and staff's efforts would become unbalanced despite your chosen indicators' seeming rosy.

Similarly in a change project, you need to ensure that the reported milestones are the important ones rather than the most noticeable. Otherwise too little emphasis may be put on the project's underpinnings, a failing not realised until too late. It does require some effort to think about what you want to measure. There is a tendency to fly too fast to measuring the readily measurable. This is understandable but, as shown above, may not be helpful. It may not even be neutral in its effect, it could be positively harmful.

Sometimes it is necessary to accept that what you want to achieve is the sort of change for which process measurement (numbers of forms shifted, hours spent in the lecture theatre and so on) cannot be a primary measure. Customer satisfaction surveys or staff attitude surveys may be alternatives or valuable supplements to what you can generate internally.

However, one lesson from this part of the chapter is that the passive leader, he or she who waits for the management information to roll in as his or her source of intelligence, is unlikely to learn everything they need to know. The most powerful form of management information, in my view, is obtained by 'walking the course'. The course is both keeping in touch with your staff and talking to your customers. The process may be an anecdotal one, and thus disputed by some, but it provides a means to test what the figures are showing and to explore issues with those who matter. It can suggest not only success or failure but also the areas in which success or failure is happening. It is not therefore just a backward looking process of assessing progress to date but provides a means for testing out ideas for future work.

Summary

Leadership of change is not something that can be done in the odd intervals between other work. It needs to suffuse and be the driver for all you do. It is both an intellectual and an emotional exercise. As this chapter has shown, among the clubs needed in the bag are:

- a clarity of objective and a belief in what you are doing
- an ability to analyse your organisation, what it stands for, and how others see it
- a preparedness to articulate the reasons why change is important, in ways that will disseminate your belief to others
- a willingness and ability to communicate during a period that may be unsettling for everyone, in a simple form that will be widely understood
- a constancy of strategic objective even if it is necessary to be flexible over tactics
- a recognition that everything you do or say will be set against your espoused intentions and an awareness of the importance of being seen as consistent
- a willingness where necessary to stimulate the organisation with the unusual or unexpected
- a top team that will join with you in what you are trying to do
- a chosen pace of change
- a focus on success rather than failure, coupled though with a sensible assessment of risk
- a variety of sources for keeping in touch with the change process, including not only management information systems but also management by walking around.

About the author

Stephen Curtis is the Chief Executive of the Driver and Vehicle Licensing Agency, having previously been Chief Executive of Companies House.

Chapter 17

Change and managing it in the Benefits Agency

Michael Bichard

The Benefits Agency is an Executive Agency of the Department of Social Security. It was established under the Next Steps programme in April 1991 to manage the delivery of most social security benefits in Great Britain. Because it is the largest Agency within the Department of Social Security it also provides some corporate services to the Department and its other agencies.

The Agency is led by a Chief Executive, Michael Bichard and a management team of six Directors. It delivers service to customers principally through 472 local benefit offices and from two national processing centres in the Blackpool and Newcastle areas. The directors and most of the Central Services functions are based in Leeds. The Agency has (mid 1993) around 65,000 staff.

Establishing the Agency and its core values

The formation of the Benefits Agency and the Contributions Agency at the same time represented two major changes in the structure and operation of the DSS.

First, as far as responsibility and accountability to the Secretary of State were concerned, it represented and required a separation of policy formulation from policy delivery. Previously various operational arms had policy formulation responsibilities accountable through different management chains, yet there was no single mechanism for ensuring that there was clear advice to Ministers on policy delivery issues.

Second, the change represented a restructuring of the Department's organisation into one in which the major operational management commands, the agencies, corresponded to the major distinct lines of business namely:

- benefit delivery
- contributions collection and recording
- information technology services
- resettlement units.

Not only were the types of business distinct but so in many cases were the customers. Thus the formation of agencies also laid the foundations for a clearer customer focus in our work.This structure has since been developed on the same basis with the formation of a Child Support Agency and of a War Pensions Agency.

So the formation of the Agency itself involved substantial change in the responsibilities of middle managers and organisational structures, even at relatively junior levels in the Agency. At the same time we were at the peak of the implementation of the Operational Strategy, the computerisation of the main parts of the benefits system, in what has been described as the largest integrated civil IT project in the world. Although this change had been in planning and development since 1982 the first pilot systems did not go live until 1988 and implementation, conversion and the consequent resourcing adjustments were still in full swing as the Agency was being established.

Nonetheless it was clear that other changes would be required if the Agency were to be successful:

- at all levels people wanted to do a good job but felt that the 'system' did not allow them to do it
- management attention was on reacting rather than planning
- the organisation's self-image, bolstered by the media and even by popular TV comedy, was poor.

So two key changes needed to be put in place quickly to provide a basis for the Agency's development:

- the establishment of a basic organisation which would allow responsibility to be effectively carried out at the right level and that could provide a stable foundation for further change
- the establishment of a clear identity and a culture of core values which would allow people at all levels to articulate their shared beliefs about how the Agency should relate to them and to its customers.

❏ Organisation

The previous structure and chain of command, dictated by the mixture of lines of business within even relatively small units, was simply too top heavy to take proper advantage of the management freedoms which agency status offered. It was also unlikely to achieve the step change in performance which was expected by Ministers. Too much operational decision making was at the centre, some because it had always been held there and some because local managers did not feel empowered to take decisions themselves at their level. Conversely the concentration on day-to-day operational matters left senior managers little time or energy to devote to their proper function of formulating strategy and communicating it clearly to those who would deliver it.

Reorganisation often creates the illusion of change rather than the reality. The key to building the foundations for a more effective agency was to ensure that there was a clear differentiation of the roles of different levels in the organisation. The model established for the Agency had three basic tiers:

- Districts
- Areas
- Board.

This compressed the previous five-tier model into at most three, and for crucial **operational** decisions into just one.

The District

The foundation was the District. Although social security operations had long been run on the basis of around 500 local offices it was clear that, as a management unit, the local office was too small to allow managers the flexibilities to develop their service to the public and to achieve internal efficiencies. Grouping local offices together in a single management command created opportunities and flexibilities within existing resources which were not visible before.

Two features were most evident

First, the District structure **allowed managers a better basis on which to plan their service to the public.** The District focused management attention on the geographical area to be covered and the population within it. The structure also made more apparent how the service should be linked with that of other public agencies, including local authorities.

Second, the District structure allowed managers flexibility to locate work in an efficient and effective way within their command. Instead of every office being expected to contain a full range of both customer-facing and internal services, the District Manager was given discretion to change the location of functions provided that service to the customer was at least maintained and, if at all possible, improved. Furthermore all managers had to make their own decisions with their staff on how the service was to be delivered. Those decisions could properly take into account the location of customers, routes of communication, geographical spread and the constraints of premises, (at least in the short term). Overall however the result has been a shift towards rather more outlets accessible to our customers and, at the same time, a concentration of back office and overhead functions with consequent economy in resources.

The Area

The second tier was the Area. Despite the temptation to have no level between the local, accountable, manager and the Board it was felt that this would have meant that functions proper to line management would need to be carried out by central staff and equally that strategic decisions about the longer term delivery of services would have had to be taken centrally. There were also the practical problems of geography and of ensuring a management span that would allow time for senior management to help develop and coach and monitor the performance of their people. Finally there were some specialist functions, such as fraud investigations, which needed to be linked to local operations but whose effectiveness would be enhanced by being managed as a series of larger distinct units.

Two features of the Area structure were designed to prevent any temptation to refer upwards matters more properly decided at District level. **First**, strict limits were set for the resources for the Area staff themselves. This meant that the Area Director and staff could only carry out someone else's responsibility at the expense of not carrying out their own. **Second**, the role of Area Directors in determining strategy was buttressed by ensuring that they were closely involved in the development of strategy for the Agency as a whole.

The Board

The top tier was the **Benefits Agency management team**, the Board of the Benefits Agency. It was decided to keep it small:

- less than half the size of the equivalent level in the Agency's predecessors
- focused on strategic or corporate issues, and on monitoring the performance of the Agency as a whole.

❑ Culture and identity

Organisation provides the context in which people can do good jobs. But achievement requires:

- a matching of the goals of the organisation with the goals of individuals working within it
- the establishment of a group identity with which individuals want to be associated
- the self-confidence that goals can be achieved.

In the Benefits Agency none of this could ever be done by command. It required instead consultation with those affected to identify what they believed and what they wanted and the achievement of some consensus on the way forward.

For some organisations a simple mission statement can provide that focus: a clear, concise and practical vision of the organisation's goal to which people at all levels can relate. That was not sufficient for the Benefits Agency because of the wide spread of our work, the need to balance the needs of our customers and of our other stakeholders and the wide variety of functions and specialisms. A single mission statement would have been either too abstract or too indigestible for individuals within the organisation. However, consultation showed that there was widespread support for a statement of core values which not only described the aspirations of the new Agency but also provided a framework and to some extent a pattern for the subsequent innovation and change.

The four core values were:

- service to the customer
- value for money
- caring for staff
- bias for action

Service to the customer

The Benefits Agency has 22 million customers, people who claim and receive the benefits which we deliver. Most staff in the Benefits Agency deal with individual citizens on a one-on-one basis day by day, and there was a belief at all levels that we should serve those customers better by providing services which responded better to their needs. Often staff were frustrated by the inability of the organisation as a whole to deliver the standard of service that they personally wanted to give. At the corporate level the establishment of the Agency, and the early work at that time which was later articulated in the Citizen's Charter, gave a clear expectation that the Benefits Agency would improve customer service. We had to change the focus of the organisation away from itself and towards its customers.

Value for money

As a public sector organisation our income is set not by what the market will bear but by what Ministers and Parliament will grant and, ultimately, by what taxpayers are prepared to give. Efficiency, economy and effectiveness are therefore at the heart of the Benefits Agency's management of resources. At an individual level staff who are motivated towards achievement in the organisation want to see resources used towards that achievement and not wasted in any way, whether that waste is obvious or whether it is more pernicious (for instance in an unnecessary procedure). However value for money does not necessarily mean cheapness. Indeed there was a strong feeling among managers and staff that by under-investing in physical or human resources the organisation had a history of doing things cheaply rather than right, and that this had been a false economy.

Caring for Staff

Many staff felt that:

- some aspects of the way in which we worked unnecessarily cut across the personal needs of people within the organisation
- insufficient attention was paid to the development of skills and knowledge
- equal opportunities were not embedded in the way in which we worked
- generally their contributions were not valued.

There was a need to change from a culture of command and prescription to a culture of involvement and consent where contributions were valued.

Bias for Action

In any organisation people doing the work, especially those dealing directly with customers, usually have a clear vision of what needs to be done. But somehow there is a delay, and often a disconnection, between idea and action. In a public sector organisation there are inevitably additional layers of control, often the surviving remnants of previous phases in the organisation. The key transformation which this core value embodied was that people at every level should ask not 'why?' but 'why not?' and, with a clear understanding of the framework of essential controls, be free to act within it.

The change programme

Organisation and values provided the Agency's identity. However it was clear that change in key aspects of the Agency's identity would need to be carried through systematically and corporately. In particular the support which people dealing with customers needed from the organisation as a whole, procedures, IT, management, training, resourcing, information, needed to be redesigned to focus on the actual needs of those who depended on it. Eight areas for key improvement were identified.

Empower local management

The aim was to focus the Benefits Agency management team on its strategic role and to provide local management with a clear framework within which to manage, with the maximum devolution of responsibility and with the skills and confidence to accept it.

Reshaping middle management and service delivery

The aim was to devise a middle management and service delivery job structure for Districts and the Benefits Directorates which reflected the tasks to be done, and an implementation plan to match the people to the posts.

Create a more flexible and motivated workforce

The aim was to devise pay and personnel systems which developed, managed and motivated the workforce in such a way as to meet the business needs of the Agency.

Serve the customer better

The aim was to raise measurably the standard of service as perceived by the public, by changing both behaviours and delivery systems.

Develop the relationship between the centre and the field

The aim was to develop a clear and constructive relationship between the field and the Central Services of the Agency.

Build a better basis for resourcing

The aim was to provide more effective resourcing mechanisms which lead to better value for money.

Simplify benefits processing and information handling procedures

The aim was to simplify and standardise systems and processes to improve efficiency and services.

Improve communications

The aim was to make more effective the communications between all parts of the Agency and release the potential of service delivery staff through enabling them to contribute more effectively to the Agency's business.

❑ Deciding the change programme

To ensure that the management team as a whole owned this process of change it was decided to ask each Director to take responsibility for one of the areas of change on a personal basis with the links between them provided by a Change Programme

Director working to the Directors individually and collectively. Although the precise arrangements for the management of each 'strand' were the responsibility of the Director concerned, some fundamental features, project groups, networks, local projects, consultation papers and quick wins were common to all.

Project Groups

A project group of about 10-15 was formed, led by the Director, comprising people chosen for their ability to make a personal contribution and not just to ensure that all the relevant functions were represented. The groups also consisted of people from different levels in the Agency and from both operational units and the central services that supported them. In some cases the groups also included people from our major stakeholders or our internal IT supplier, but again people chosen for their ability to make a personal contribution as well as for their position in the Department as a whole.

Networks

The groups established networks for the formal and informal consultation with a much larger cross-section of Benefits Agency staff. By enabling people to put forward ideas outside the normal management chain and in a way which was clearly risk free the groups were able to collect a host of practical ideas for change.

Local projects

Many of the groups sponsored local change projects which had been planned by local managers and which had been offered to the group as examples. In this way local managers gained corporate backing for changes which they had hoped to introduce and the change groups gained first-hand experience of how some of the ideas would work in practice.

Consultation papers

Each group produced a formal consultation paper on its emerging findings. These were used in a number of ways to gain support for change and to identify further work which needed to be done to address staff concerns and to ensure the ideas would work in practice. Each consultation document stimulated a significant number of responses from individual members of staff, often of very high quality and demonstrating a surprisingly wide view of the Agency and its role. Each consultation document also formed the basis for local managers to discuss the ideas with their staff and work through the implications for their particular unit. Many Districts produced their own collective responses to the consultation documents reflecting the spectrum of views at local level. In addition, for the customer facing change groups, customer service and service delivery, there was a period of public consultation on the emerging findings and options for change.

This provided a wealth of comment and contribution from outside the Agency, including national organisations representing our customers.

Quick wins

Since the objective of the programme was change not paper, each change group was empowered to see through wherever possible changes which could be made quickly and which would give early benefit, 'quick wins'. These were seen as essential to the credibility of the change programme with staff and other stakeholders. They also, of course, reflected the Agency's core value of 'bias for action' and gave powerful signals down the organisation about top management's will to start changing the way business was done.

❑ The business vision

The design phase of the change programme concluded with a two day residential board meeting at the beginning of March 1993. The outputs from the change programme had been consolidated in a 'business vision' of how the Agency should look to its customers and operate internally. Crucially it set out not only those areas in which there was to be a corporate standard but also those areas in which there was **not** to be a corporate standard. In many cases the distinction was between 'what was to be done', which could and should be specified corporately, and 'how it was to be done', which was best left to the discretion and initiative of local managers operating within a clear framework of accountabilities.

The key driver

The change programme had also identified a key driver for all the changes which needed to be made. The service delivery and customer service strands, supported by an efficiency scrutiny carried out for the Agency, had proposed a goal of a One Stop service, in which an individual customer could contact just one place, have their transaction dealt with by just one person, and do so just one time. The comments from both staff within the Agency and from the national organisations representing our customers were unanimous in supporting such a concept if it could be achieved.

Moreover the concept fitted closely with the goals set out in the Citizen's Charter and Ministers indicated that they would support strongly the Agency's proposals in this area. It was also clear from the work which had been done by the change groups that operating in this way would significantly improve efficiency, reduce errors which arose from double-handling and cut down on fraud and abuse. Finally the One Stop form of service delivery would require a strong sense of 'ownership' of their work by individual members of staff. This would enhance job satisfaction, produce a real driver for quality and encourage further innovation.

The importance of One Stop was not just its effect on our customers. It also provided the stimulus for carrying through the other proposals from other parts of the change process. It was apparent that full achievement of the One Stop vision would require very much the types of change in management, staff, resource allocation and communication which were being proposed by the other groups. Conversely those other changes needed a strong customer-facing business driver in order to stimulate action and to underline their own necessity. One Stop provided the agenda and the timetable for business change into which other initiatives could be fitted.

Management team structure

The decisions in March 1993 included one to restructure the management team itself to ensure that most individual directors had responsibility for a share of field operations, some staff functions *and* some corporate initiatives. This helped spread some of the workload more evenly and ensured that each director was well placed to take an Agency-wide view closely tied into the day-to-day operational delivery of service to our customers. It tackled head on the chasm which had existed between the centre and the field.

❏ Implementation

With the decisions taken in March 1993 the change programme moved into an implementation phase. The first step was to communicate quickly the decisions which had been taken and the direction in which the management team now wished to lead the Agency. It was particularly important to ensure that managers shared the whole picture and had a context into which to fit the specific change initiatives which would be presented to them.

Next there was urgent work to turn the proposals into specific action plans which were owned by the organisation as a whole. This involved work with managers and staff at all levels, often in a workshop format, to draw up specific milestones and to identify the products which would be needed to achieve them. It also gave the opportunity for second-order issues and points of detail left over from the change groups to be debated and resolved. Not only would these have been impractical to deal with in the change groups themselves because of time and of skills, but also they were much easier to address and resolve within the overall framework of the vision which had been articulated. The implementation design process also gave opportunities to communicate the business vision as a whole and audit that the communication processes had been effective.

Lessons learnt

The process of change within the Benefits Agency is still continuing. Many of the changes which have started will not give their full fruits until the second half of the decade. But already some lessons about the management of change stand out from what has been done.

❏ Importance of communication

First, communication is, as in all management, essential. Openness about what is going on, what the goals are, and how people can contribute, creates a positive climate of expectation and prepares people for change.

As noted in Chapter 6, it is also essential to use the full range of channels available and not just rely on a single, specific channel, particularly if that channel is seen as the mouthpiece of top management. Existing staff magazines edited by staff (the Benefits Agency has one for all staff and another specifically targeted at middle managers) provided opportunities to keep managers and staff in touch with developments and achievements. Newsletters and other channels aimed at particular specialisms within the organisation also gave the opportunity for more targeted messages. The consultation papers made widely available to staff gave specific information about particular areas of change, including options for the future.

The most important channel of communication in a change process is, however, along the management line. It was essential that the managers were seen to be participating in the change process and communicating it to their staff. This signalled to the staff that their managers were knowledgeable about the change proposals. By presenting information within the context of the individual management unit change was given an internal as well as an external aspect. Moreover it also compelled the managers to understand the change proposals and to take part in the change process. By communicating change proposals themselves they could not distance themselves from them.

Communication of change cannot be a one-way process. Staff must be given the opportunity to feed back their comments and their ideas, and be shown that those comments and ideas are being taken into account. At the same time the change managers need a constant feedback to gauge the operational feasibility of their proposals and the acceptability of them by the staff who will actually have to operate them.

❏ Involvement of service deliverers

Second, it is important to ensure that the people who actually deliver the service of the Agency are directly involved in the change process. The lessons of the 'inverted' organisation, in which the centre supports those directly delivering service to customers, are of special importance in the change process. To be fully carried through the change must be owned by those in the field, not imposed upon them. At the same time the change manager can, by involving front-line people, draw upon a wealth of new ideas as well as gain a friendly sounding-board for change proposals coming from elsewhere.

Operational managers and staff have another unique value to add. It is inevitable that all the quantitative data needed to analyse proposals for radical change will not be available from the organisation's existing management information systems. This is because those systems usually embody the existing procedural structure and management concerns, and do so in a different hierarchy of data from that which is relevant to the change manager. Managers and staff motivated to help the change process can obtain more relevant data more quickly than the existing management information systems can be modified. Indeed for the testing of new ideas a major investment in information systems is hard to justify. In addition any time delay in the provision of information means that infeasible ideas cannot be killed off as quickly as they deserve and so distract the energies of the change managers.

The point that information systems embody the existing structure of organisation and procedures cannot be made too strongly. Like many other organisations the Benefits Agency has a legacy of major information systems which reflect previous business models and organisation. Over the next few years we will have to re-build its main business IT systems so that they can support the customer focus which is at the heart of our business vision.

❑ A simple goal

Third, there is a need to find a simple and fundamental goal on which to focus the entire change programme. It needs to be one to which staff at all levels can relate their own work and, where possible, which the vast majority can personally sign up to. Moreover the concept needs to be a practical one relevant to the core business of the organisation and not just its internal operation. Initially the four core values provided that focus and they remain a very important reference point for all we do. More recently the One Stop strategy has become an even more potent force for change. Its achievement will touch directly upon the day-to-day work of the vast majority of staff within the Agency and the establishment of a goal with backing from all levels in the organisation makes it that much easier to accomplish other changes which, if presented in isolation, would be obstructed.

❑ Implementation by line management

Fourth there comes a point at which the responsibility for the implementation of change needs to be taken up by the line management structure of the organisation.

The achievement of change needs to be managed through the normal line, albeit with special monitoring and specific milestones. Ownership by the line managers leads to commitment and thence to achievement, and line managers are the only people who can balance the needs of the change against the needs of other tasks of their unit. This transfer of ownership needs to be carefully handled and it has been beneficial in the case of the Benefits Agency to allow managers to 'pull' that responsibility from the centre rather than 'push' it onto them.

❑ Timely support

Fifth the requirements of managers to be able to carry through the change, information, communications material, training products, IT systems and resources, need to be identified with them early, and then provided to them in good time and to high quality. This is not only a managerial necessity. It is also a practical commitment which top management and the central services need to be able to demonstrate. In addition the same principles of participation must apply to the development of these products. Nothing will do more to undermine confidence in the achievement of change than unsuitable, inadequate or faulty products coming from the centre. Both the requirement and the quality assurance need to involve those who will actually use them.

❑ Monitoring

Finally change needs to be monitored, and the monitoring system needs to track actual achievement rather than reported intentions. This points to embedding the monitoring mechanisms in the standard performance monitoring systems, both numbers and milestones, so that they can be tracked through the line of management as well as providing a corporate picture. It also provides data to show the extent (if any) to which the achievement of change is impacting the achievement of other targets and for any conflict for scarce resources to be resolved at the lowest level possible.

The future

The external environment of a public sector agency is no less susceptible to change than one in the private sector. In the Benefits Agency's business the introduction of new benefits and the amendment of existing ones creates a constant stream of change. Moreover the continual requirement to improve service to our customers and the effectiveness with which it is delivered, together with the increasing use of the private sector to provide services, will lead to further major change in the way which we operate. Indeed the successful achievement of the current change programme will itself suggest other changes which can further enhance our performance. All this will be seen initially as threatening to people, just as the current change programme was at the start. However the great strength of the culture and the organisation which the change programme has put in place is our ability to work collectively to change ourselves.

We now have a management structure in which the pivotal management level, the District, can both participate in the formulation of change and in its delivery, and we have a set of cultures in which people can participate as individuals in devising and implementing change. Moreover our record shows that we have been able not only to achieve substantial change but do so at the same time as significantly improving our day-to-day performance against the targets set by Ministers. By integrating the implementation of change into the mainstream of management processes in the Agency we hope to be able to continue to change and develop to meet future business demands.

About the author

Michael Bichard was appointed Chief Executive of the Benefits Agency in 1990. He was previously Chief Executive of Gloucestershire County Council and the London Borough of Brent.

Chapter 18

HMSO: restructuring pay and grading in an Executive Agency

Michael Salt

Between 1988 and 1991 HMSO embarked upon a radical restructuring of its pay, grading and personnel systems in response to a rapidly developing competitive environment, using the flexibilities devolved from central government as part of the wider programme of civil service restructuring. This chapter describes that experience and its aftermath.

Since 1 April 1980, HMSO had been operating as a Trading Fund under the provisions of the Government Trading Funds Act 1973 and, with the exception of minor votes, been self-financing. Trading fund status prompted the introduction of commercial approaches with clear financial targets, rigorous management disciplines and a much sharper approach to all activities, particularly after April 1982 when government departments which previously had no choice were free to choose whether or not to use HMSO's services. The trading fund environment and the growing competition guaranteed that HMSO's efficiency and effectiveness were under constant scrutiny as a result of the pressure of market forces. Throughout the 1980s HMSO succeeded in meeting its financial targets every year, dramatically reducing its resource costs whilst increasing its sales and improving value for money to the taxpayer. This was achieved by a major programme of modernisation, rationalisation, internal economies and some broadening of the customer base.

Despite these successes it became apparent that corporate performance was in danger of levelling off and that the way forward was likely to be through the increased productivity and motivation of staff. So HMSO took advantage of the Next Steps initiative and, with Treasury agreement, commissioned a feasibility study into a pay and grading structure more relevant to HMSO's business.

The aims of the restructuring study were defined as being:
- to improve HMSO's efficiency and effectiveness
- to reduce its overheads, thereby enhancing price competitiveness

- to improve the performance of its people by releasing potential and investing in their development
- to produce greater personal accountability
- to relate remuneration more closely to an individual's contribution.

The strategy was to restructure the hierarchy with fewer levels of management, increased delegation of responsibility, fewer but more motivated people and reward for individual performance. As HMSO's Deputy Chief Executive, Mike Lynn, put it at the time:

> Other organisations do not go about their grading arrangements in the way that we do in the Civil Service. We have grown up with a grading structure that does three entirely separate things within the same system: it determines pay, it determines organisational position and it determines career progression. All three things are linked to grade. In outside organisations, it isn't always done that way. What we are proposing is a system under which those things are separated.
>
> For pay purposes we actually want more flexibility, and more pay ranges, because the differences between AO, EO and HEO are in fact too crude for the variety of jobs that we have to do in HMSO.
>
> In the case of organisational hierarchy, we want to go in the opposite direction and have fewer levels, not more, because the more you have the more unproductive work you are creating, the more you are stifling personal initiative, the more you are reducing personal accountability. People who are given extra accountability do rise to the occasion, do get more job satisfaction, do get more productive output, without physically working harder.

There was a wide consensus in support of the broad thrust of this initiative in HMSO, including support from the non-industrial trade unions. All were aware that the process of giving departments greater freedom to buy wherever they could find better value for money, which had begun in 1982, was gathering pace, and that any resistance to change in buying habits among major departments was subject to challenge by the efforts of the Central Unit on Purchasing (CUP) and by the continuing pressures to increase value for money.

The following extracts from a trade union letter written in March 1988 show the extent to which union thinking ran in parallel with that of management:

> ...the civil service chain of command is too long
>
> ...responsibilities too limited
>
> ...structures are inflexible and unresponsive

... consensus decisions eat up time and do not engender a professional organisation in the minds of customers who increasingly expect a rapid and definitive decision.

Levels must

... reflect the responsibility

... be attractive in market terms

... and value officers, for their contribution to the organisation and pay them accordingly.

The momentum for change following the publication of the Next Steps report in February 1988 provided a sympathetic policy environment for HMSO to take charge of its future by seeking to match its employment and reward structures more closely to the tasks it had been given. The Next Steps report had included HMSO on the list of potential agencies. A 'restructuring project' was a natural response to that move, and the proposed extension of managerial freedom into the fields of pay and grading agreed with HM Treasury:

... to secure the same level of delegated authority in personnel matters that HMSO had achieved in financial matters

was more in keeping with HMSO's commercial orientation.

Planning the change

A project team of senior managers was quickly assembled with support from consultants with expertise in the design of pay systems and it produced a detailed report by the summer of 1988. The report confirmed that the traditional civil service pay and grading structure inhibited flexibility in matching remuneration to responsibility and performance and restricted the ability to achieve further efficiency gains. It contrasted unfavourably the narrow spans of management control and separation of performance from pay with the situation in commercial analogues. The confirmation of HMSO in December 1988 as the third Government Executive Agency set the scene for turning theory into practice and the study moved without a break into consideration of the means by which it would be implemented.

❑ Putting the package together

A Restructuring Project Consultative Committee with representatives of management and of all the staff unions was already in place. Its purpose was to keep the unions informed of the progress of the study and to provide a forum through which the commitment to achieve agreement on change with them could be managed. Consultations on the restructuring report started in October 1988. A key undertaking from the start was that there would be no compulsory redundancies as a result of restructuring (although no individual would be guaranteed a particular job). This provided a platform of confidence on which constructive dialogue could be built.

Discussions on the study group's report were inevitably demanding and drawn out. Despite the earlier agreement on broad principles, conflicting requirements now surfaced. The aims of HMSO management had to be reconciled with those of the Treasury and HMSO's trade unions and staff. It nearly always followed that where one of the parties liked something, another did not. As one participant later put it, the challenge was to knit agreements between consenting stakeholders faster than dissenting stakeholders could unravel them. Negotiations on the new performance pay arrangements focused the disagreements.

HMSO faced conflicting pressures from the Treasury who wanted performance related pay at minimum cost, and the unions who did not want any form of merit pay arrangement. The resolution of those pressures was based on the concept that cascaded business plan targets tied every individual to achievement of the organisation's business plan. This plan in turn provided for the cost of that performance pay by reducing employee numbers as part of the required efficiency improvements. Since HMSO expected to meet its business plans it followed that most employees who were able to contribute effectively to the business would thereby earn their performance pay. This elegant, but sharp, concept was predicated upon a unitary organisation with ever increasing efficiency which the later commitment to 'federalism' with greater autonomy for the constituent businesses, their differing contributions and less clear role for corporate services, including personnel, clouded.

Quite apart from the reconciliation of stakeholder interests, there were difficult technical questions. It was accepted that the new pay and grading system ought to be based upon a system of job evaluation and it was necessary to design and test one that met HMSO's particular needs. Job evaluation is a means by which the size of a job and its relative position to other jobs can be established so that it can be placed in a pay structure. It also provides a means for formalising the purpose and requirements of a job and helps to avoid equal pay disputes.

The conclusion was to design a pay spine with 18 overlapping pay bands into which all non-industrial jobs would be placed by a job evaluation process.

❏ Selling the concept

While management, according to both the letter and the spirit of HMSO's Executive Agency Framework Document, involved HMSO's unions fully in the design of the new pay and grading systems and sought and eventually achieved agreement with them, it was also clear that the nature of the implied cultural change required more than reliance on union channels of communication with staff. A series of Restructuring Newsletters gave comprehensive information on progress and explained in detail the new aspects of the system. However, effective communication required more than the printed word. Each division appointed Restructuring Liaison Officers who, after training, made face to face presentations to all divisional employees and undertook to answer their questions. This also proved valuable in feeding back to the project team the main concerns and areas of misunderstanding which could then be addressed by revised briefing or made the subject of future circulars.

The extensive exposure to restructuring aims, theories, explanations and promises from early 1988 onwards, against the wider background of Next Steps developments and publicity, gave ample opportunity for people to explore and come to terms with the prospect of change to the point where reluctance became anticipation and threatened to become frustration. This played a significant part not just in the result of the eventual vote but also in generating tolerance of some of the tougher practices necessary for implementation which just a couple of years earlier would have produced an uproar.

❑ Anticipation

In a survey undertaken during the first half of 1989, when the restructuring aims had been published and consultations were in progress with trade unions, middle managers were invited to review the changes that had taken place since HMSO had become a trading fund back in 1980. They identified greater accountability, responsibility for preparing and keeping to budgets, the need to manage staff time and the importance of delivering services to customers, whether external or internal.

Although their jobs had changed significantly since HMSO became a trading fund in 1980, managers did not report that there had been any significant implications for careers. Like the rest of the civil service, career progression was still dependent on the decision of a promotion board as to the individual's suitability for a higher grade. Career progression was often described as a case of 'send for the next fit person'.

It was difficult for those interviewed to comment on agency restructuring as it was in its early stages. However, the most common views expressed about the likely effects of restructuring were:

- there would be fewer middle management jobs
- there would be even more responsibility and accountability than in the past

- there would be more emphasis on performance as it would be related to pay
- there would be less job movement because people would cling to their existing expertise in order to ensure career progression.

Asked to look forward to the possible advantages of restructuring for them they identified:

- a new pay ladder which would recognise the reality of varying levels of responsibilities within grades
- a greater say in promotion decisions.

Their concerns centred on a loss of status for grades whose jobs were banded at the lower end of the pay range, and that specialists and people in revenue generating posts would enjoy favourable bandings. There was a pervasive concern too that agency status might mean a further move away from their being public servants working in a public service environment and that agency status with a move away from civil service grades might be the first stage of privatisation. One manager argued,

> if we see a loosening of constraints and a higher profile for responsibility and reward for effort, then we shall have a good organisation on our hands to such an extent that in five years time we could be privatised.

The majority of managers interviewed saw the prior change to a trading fund as creating a more challenging environment in which to work. Many said they enjoyed their work far more because they were accountable, the aims of the job were clearer and they could ensure better value for money.

Most managers hoped that restructuring would constitute a real reorganisation and not a cosmetic exercise, though there was scepticism about whether the restructuring would be as radical and beneficial to them as they had been told. They looked to the unions to safeguard their interests, status, jobs and careers.

❑ The restructuring package

All jobs were to be restructured from 1 April 1991. The position of a particular job on the pay ladder was determined through the application of the job evaluation scheme. A job analysis questionnaire (JAQ) was completed for each job and the job was evaluated against each of the factors, giving a score under each factor and consequently a total evaluation score for each job. HMSO opted for a job evaluation scheme based on a points rating system using 13 factors:

Literacy	Numerical Analysis	Innovation
Interpersonal Skills	Equipment Skills	Decision Level and Freedom
Control of Staff	Control of Resources	Information Systems
Impact on Business Performance		Experience
Job Related Knowledge		Pressure and Environment.

The JAQ was completed initially by the manager responsible for the job. The completed questionnaire was passed to a job analyst who sought clarification of any points from the manager as necessary and then evaluated the job. The proposed evaluations were subject to confirmation by a review committee on which trade unions were represented.

Considerable work went into the preparation of the scheme to get something that would be acceptable to all. Management and trade unions agreed a list of about 75 jobs that were broadly representative of all the main grades. After the JAQs had been analysed independently by a team of evaluators the 75 jobs were compared twice, one with another, giving a total of 5,550 comparisons. These were distributed, by a computer produced questionnaire, equally amongst 17 panel members, requiring each to respond to 326 comparisons. Each panel member compared whole jobs using the JAQs as the basis for reaching a decision. A consensus rank order of jobs in descending order of perceived worth was produced. This provided the basis for weighting the factors.

HMSO's performance pay scheme made progression within pay bands dependent on achieving key targets (KTs). KTs applied to the financial (calendar) year and were to be agreed at the beginning of the year between job holders and their reporting officers. KTs typically covered business results, budgets/costs, service levels, quality improvement projects and management of staff. Mandatory quarterly reviews would help to highlight difficulties, take account of change and thus ensure that job holders achieved their KTs. A final review at the end of the year would determine performance pay, which would be paid with effect from the following April. Those meeting their KTs would get a 5% increase, and near misses 2.5%. The scheme was defined in a new Performance Assessment System (PAS) in which all staff would be given formal training.

Conditions of Service were related to pay bands instead of grades though most remained unchanged. After the initial appointments were made, new and open procedures would apply to the filling of vacancies. Apart from jobs filled by external recruitment, all jobs would be advertised internally and all staff who considered themselves suitable would be eligible to apply.

The pay arrangements were designed not only to provide the motivation for greater efficiency, but also to encourage staff to obtain job related qualifications and to provide a more professional service. Anybody gaining a specified qualification was promised a reward of a lump sum of £700 or £350 depending on the level of the qualification.

Every member was guaranteed personal pay protection on movement to the pay bands, eighteen bands altogether, overlapping on a single pay spine replacing more than 40 civil grades all with their own pay scales.

Those who had received an annual pay increase the previous April would get at least 5.5% in October on moving to transitional assimilation scales, and would then receive another 2.5% the following April if they agreed to move on to pay bands. Unions were also attracted by the management assurance that it expected the overwhelming majority of its staff to gain performance pay the following year, 1991 i.e. no quotas.

Other vital aspects of the agreement from the union point of view were the openness of the new reporting and appraisal systems. The Performance Assessment System (PAS), which determined whether performance pay was payable, would be completely open and reviewed quarterly with staff by their reporting officers. The Personal Development System (PDS), which provided for an annual assessment of an individual's training and development needs, gave each individual the right to an interview with their personnel officer, designed to ensure that staff received not just sufficient training to carry out their current jobs but also encouragement to develop skills required for movement to other areas of work.

The complete restructuring package was put to staff and unions held consultation meetings during September 1990. The unions recommended support for the proposals. While they acknowledged that it met the management criteria of 'breaking away from Civil Service Pay and Conditions' they believed that it also introduced a number of safeguards and benefits for their members which were absent from the original proposals.

With the union endorsement, which they frankly argued on the grounds that rejection of restructuring could well lead to privatisation, staff voted overwhelmingly in favour of accepting the package. Union representatives therefore signed the restructuring agreement on their behalf after final negotiations early in October 1990.

Managing implementation

The key elements in the implementation were setting an organisational structure, filling the new jobs and then fixing procedures for filling jobs in the future.

❑ Redesigning the organisational structure

The delayering, which was a key part of the restructuring concept, was implemented through a complete redesign of the organisational structure. Each of HMSO's divisions re-assessed its needs in the light of the new philosophy and drew up new organisation charts known as DRPs, Divisional Restructuring Plans. The aim was to cut out unnecessary management and supervisory levels. Job descriptions were then drawn up for each post in the new structure by divisional restructuring representatives and the resulting jobs evaluated under HMSO's new job evaluation system. These defined the pay band into which each job fell. Though these pay bandings were seen as secondary from the senior management perspective, which placed more weight upon the function and role of the job, almost inevitably staff viewed these pay bands as grades and evaluated them by what they paid rather than by the purpose of the jobs placed within them. This subsequently proved to be the most difficult corner in the whole change exercise.

The scope of this organisational redesign was limited by more than the width of the paper. It was simply not possible against the background of many business changes, not least those flowing from the change to agency status, to redesign transaction and decision support systems as well as formal organisations. New organisation design and delayering had therefore to assume the continuance of corporate systems, essentially unmodified, with all the constraints to which those gave rise. This strategic gap was filled by the parallel introduction of a Total Quality Management (TQM) programme. The restructuring timetable prevented the application of TQM methodologies and its benefits being achieved as part of restructuring, though many were achieved later. TQM remains the essential strand in HMSO's corporate strategy, though now supplemented by a major programme of business re-engineering.

❑ Applying for new jobs

During September 1990 staff were briefed about jobs in their new divisional structure. They later had the opportunity to see other divisions' organisation plans and get details of any jobs of interest to them. In October an option form was sent to all members of staff in order to obtain their preferences for restructured jobs at their existing grade level. There was also the option of seeking a transfer to another Government department or the expression of an interest in early retirement (on the most favourable terms). The promise of no compulsory redundancy provided an ultimate assurance if they were in the event unsuccessful in getting the job(s) for which they had applied.

Despite all the communication and briefing it is doubtful whether all staff really understood how best to exercise their options and to make best use of the opportunity they were given. Many simply looked through the DRPs and opted for what appeared to be the nearest analogue to 'their' job. Those who couldn't find such an analogue sometimes became confused. Others took the philosophy that anyone could apply for any job literally and nominated higher posts for which they had neither the qualifications nor any relevant experience. But the majority dutifully complied with what they took to be rules of the game.

❑ The selection procedure

With the issuing of the option forms, the work of implementing restructuring passed from the project team to the personnel structure and divisional management. It was difficult to make much advance preparation since many important decisions were made during the last hectic phase of negotiation, and naturally enough the mechanics came low down the agenda when the parties were wrestling with major and novel issues of principle.

To Personnel Services, its personnel officers and their support staff fell the responsibility for managing the programme which would enable the target implementation date of 1 April 1991 to be met. The administration of the selections was formidable. There were some 2,200 staff applying for a rather smaller number of jobs, and each employee was entitled to make up to three options, which included the right to request consideration for early retirement or transfer to another civil service department. In addition, staff were able to choose whether to take their appointments on existing terms or accept new contracts of employment. No process for handling these options existed. Radical steps were necessary.

Decentralisation of personnel staff

Firstly, all personnel officers who had previously been grade managers and based in the personnel 'ivory tower' were decentralised. Each was allocated to a division and made responsible for all staff up to pay band 9 (roughly Higher Executive Officer level). Management of senior staff was retained in the centre. Apart from the smaller corporate service divisions where the responsible personnel officer remained in Personnel Services, the personnel officers were physically relocated to become a part of their divisions. This was important in ensuring that staffing redeployment decisions had support from the managers concerned.

It was also vital that personnel officers were no longer seen as bureaucratic paper shufflers. All personnel officers were encouraged to become professionally qualified and a personnel specialism was established with younger personnel staff being sponsored to take the Institute of Personnel Management diploma. Personnel officer appointments remained under the control of the Director of Personnel to ensure that both the people and their actions met professional standards.

Computerisation

In April 1990 a small personnel computer system had been installed. It had not been designed to support restructuring, no one knew what would be required when it was specified, but it was clear that such a tool was essential if the administrative burden of restructuring appointments was to be carried through to meet the very tight timetable. The Restructuring Agreement was signed in October 1990 and all staff were to take up their restructured appointments on 1 April 1991. It could not be done without computer assistance. With the co-operation of the supplier, the personnel team quickly adapted its facilities to enable all option forms to be entered into the system and reports to be produced showing who had applied for which jobs and, when appointment decisions had been made, to produce offers of appointment and new contracts of employment.

Paper boards

On 1 October 1990 staff were transferred to assimilation scales for pay purposes. All staff stayed in their existing jobs at this stage. Appointments to restructured jobs were made 'top down', by grade. In October HMSO's Controller re-appointed the Directors. Below this level there were appointment panels chaired by senior managers from personnel with line management representation. Panels matched staff to jobs within occupational groups. They first considered staff whose grades read across to the pay bands of the jobs being considered. Jobs which remained unfilled were then advertised and applications were invited from staff in grades immediately below the pay bands of the advertised jobs. Because of the numbers, time constraints and general complexity it was impracticable to carry out interviews for these posts. All appointments were therefore made on the basis of paper records mediated by personnel officer and management knowledge and judgement.

Strict timetabling

Timetabling had to be strict. At any grade level there were eight divisions to which appointments had to be made. The larger trading divisions could occupy a whole day while the smaller divisions could be dealt with in half an hour. The potential for 'body wrangling' between divisions for the better staff was potentially severe but fortunately ameliorated because most staff 'played safe' in making their option nominations and those seeking a move were in the minority. It remained, though, a stressful aspect that 'X' could be declared essential for a particular post by Division 'B' in the afternoon after having been appointed to Division 'A' in the morning. Close advance contact between personnel officers headed off most such potential difficulties.

As soon as the sessions were complete, the schedules recording the appointment decisions were handed over to the support staff for entry into the computer and production of the offer of appointment letters. The dates on which the results of each grade would be announced were published in advance and a new weekly circular, *Job Opportunities,* was developed for the purpose.

Training for setting key targets

In addition to the administration of the appointments, newly appointed staff had to come to grips immediately with the need to set 'key targets' from 1 April to 31 December 1991 as an essential part of the performance pay system. It was the achievement of those targets which would generate the funds necessary to underpin the payments. The system was well heralded and every member of staff underwent formal training to ensure their understanding and commitment to this vital system.

❑ Continuing appointments process

Job Opportunities was necessary not only to announce restructuring appointments but also because the appointments situation was not static and the transition had to be managed on top of normal day to day business and personnel developments, with new requirements and people moves continuing to take place. The agreed new appointments process had therefore to be introduced well before 1 April 1991. It was an inherent part of the restructuring philosophy that the old civil service panel promotion system would be replaced by a new system that advertised each job individually and allowed any member of staff who considered that they could undertake it to apply. The procedures for this had to be developed in parallel with the re-appointment process and operated to meet business needs. This meant of course that there were overlaps with the staged restructuring appointments, 'holes' developed unexpectedly, and completed stages required revisiting to fill.

1 April 1991 did not see the end of restructuring. The extent to which restructuring invalidated, changed or at least brought into question every cultural understanding, expectation and procedure had not been fully foreseen. While many staff were revitalised by restructuring there remained significant numbers who were disoriented by the extent and ultimate rapidity of the changes and were unable to empathise with the new directions. This was amplified because some staff had to be designated as 'project officers' until proper restructured jobs could be found for them in line with the no compulsory redundancy guarantee. These surplus staff were mostly placed within six months thanks to the continuing generous voluntary early retirement scheme.

Assessment

Research into the effects of restructuring was carried out by Templeton College in three phases:

- between January and March 1989 after HMSO had become an Executive Agency and while restructuring was still in the early stages of negotiation
- between June and September 1991 immediately after the implementation of restructuring
- and finally between April and June 1992 when the effects of the changes had a chance to crystallise.

In each case the interviews were carried out with predominantly the same group of about 20 experienced middle managers. On balance managers were positive about the changes, seeing them as increasing commitment to HMSO and improving the service to its customers.

❏ Freedom and responsibility

The jobs of most interviewees had changed in the sense that some were in new jobs and had lost certain responsibilities and gained others. Those managers who had 'lost a layer above' felt they had gained more access to senior management. However on balance most interviewees reported relatively little change in their responsibilities. Indeed some argued that responsibility and freedom in the job had decreased, either because they had a manager in between them and the director to whom they used to report, or because they were drawn into clerical duties because of losing junior staff. Most cited an increase in pressure on them to reduce costs.

❏ Status and career choice

The majority of the interviewees spoke of their jobs being more specialised in the sense that they no longer expected to be able to move across divisions. Many were sceptical about claims that restructuring had increased career choice since most jobs were going to those with previous experience in the area. Some interviewees believed that they had lost status following restructuring. Although the number of levels had decreased on paper, in practice pay bands were seen as the new hierarchy.

❏ Key targets and incentives

The major performance change spoken about by interviewees was the new performance appraisal system. Key targets (KTs) had been set for all managers. Some managers saw key targets as clarifying their priorities, however there were many more who raised concerns about the process itself:

- what if people cannot achieve their KTs because other people fail to deliver
- how can comparability of KTs be assured across the whole organisation
- how could they be assured that all KTs would be equally judged?

It was clear that not all managers had fully understood the benefits that open discussion of the issues could bring about. There was also concern about what happened to incentives when people reached the top of their pay scales and could not earn additional performance pay under the scheme. The latter point has generated increasing concern over time as more have exhausted their headroom.

Yet despite their concern on this point, managers were also hurt that the restructuring seemed to be based on the premise that they were only motivated by money. Distaste for this assumption was expressed by several managers who gave examples of their pursuit of initiatives which they felt would contribute to HMSO yet jeopardised the achievement of their personal key targets.

❑ Management style

Several managers were concerned that the final stages of the restructuring were rushed. One manager argued:

....because it was rushed through, people see the changes as something they have got to do, rather than a real chance to change the way we do things.

Some managers argued they voted for restructuring because of union advice that failure to do so would result in privatisation. Most managers felt union power had been reduced because of restructuring and some expressed concern that management would become more macho in future.

❑ Security and comfort

The more negative comments made by managers were not so much a reaction against the concept of agency and restructuring since, for most managers in HMSO, it was a logical extension of changes begun by trading fund which were generally viewed as positive. It was rather that expectations had been high and the extent of cultural change was under-estimated. It was also seen as being something of a final hurdle with smooth water on the other side. The turbulence they found instead tested managers to the full, and some found it beyond them.

Above all, the emphasis on performance in the new restructured HMSO undermined the previous security attached to grade and was deeply discomforting to many. A disproportionate attachment to pay band as a substitute for grade and certificate of status was a reaction. The open appointments system led to rapid advances by the more able and the more skilled, leaving 'middle of the roaders' with an uncertainty about prospects and doubts about self-worth. At the same time as traditional managers were undermined from below, the thrust towards empowerment and team working associated with the quality programme removed another comfort factor from the managerial chair. Restructuring had been a catalyst but it was only the most elaborately signalled of a cataract of changes all flowing from fundamental redefinitions of the role of the public sector in the UK.

❏ A new beginning

The certainty and finality which many, particularly the trade unions, tried to attach to the written agreement on restructuring signed in October 1990 was overborne by the pressure of events. From the perspective of 1994 it broke a dam rather than set a seal. A decisive shift took place in perceptions of the agency's capacity for change, the role of its managers, and the forces acting upon HMSO, with a corresponding rebalancing of the internal power structures.

Conclusions

It may be helpful to finish the chapter by bringing together the main conclusions which emerge with the benefit of hindsight.

❏ Wider interests in change

The negotiations leading to the agreement were long, many detailed provisions seeking to safeguard existing rights and expectations were written in, and earlier feverish expectations of rapid change were cooled by the length of process. Some three years had elapsed between the first proposal and its implementation. Despite the recognition right from the start that it was the increasing freedom of the public sector market place that dictated the need, this was undoubtedly due in part to the dominance of the immediate interests of the three stakeholders, HM Treasury, HMSO management, and HMSO staff and their trade unions. Attention to the needs of customers received little formal attention during the process itself.

The concentration on these relationships overshadowed the changes taking place in the wider environment and these, in particular the increasingly sharp expectations of customers for commercial standards of performance and care, together with the slowing, if not freezing, of the normal processes of change during the long drawn out negotiations, meant that 1 April 1991 saw a sudden acceleration in the rate of change rather than the satisfaction of a major achievement.

Pay and grading, appraisal and development, cannot be divorced from the purposes of the organisation which they must serve. Consideration in isolation risks conflict with harsher realities. Proceeding by agreement with its trade unions and staff as HMSO did, and was obliged to do under its Framework agreement, was important in gaining acceptance of the necessity of change and helping to change mindsets, but it also resulted in procedures and expectations that could not always be sustained.

❑ Implementation pragmatism

The establishment of a separate project team to develop and negotiate the restructuring package, although inevitable for workload reasons if no other, left implementation to be carried through by those who had the line responsibilities. There had been little opportunity to consider implementation aspects at other than a high level and inevitably line managers were faced with an almost endless series of questions for which there were no obvious answers, and finding solutions sometimes involved interpretations of the agreement which surprised the parties to it. In retrospect there would have been benefit from a greater line management input earlier.

It was inevitable that the time spent in negotiation would run up to the wire and leave only the minimum for implementation, although there could be no certainty how much time would actually be required. If it had been calculated in detail it would certainly have been more than six months. In practice the arbitrary and 'unreasonable' timetable proved an advantage. There were no competitors to take Personnel's responsibility for implementation, it was obvious that there was no time for further debate and nobody wished to be seen to be accountable for failure. The responsibility for a unique and vital change proved highly motivational to the personnel staff who had to carry it through.

❑ Culture runs deep

The extent to which all existing personnel procedures, and more importantly staff understanding of them which ran deep in the corporate culture, were invalidated and had to be redesigned was insufficiently appreciated. The first year after restructuring took place had to be devoted to creating ad hoc solutions to problems that had no precedent and to the development of new procedures to replace those which had been rendered obsolete by the process of restructuring.

This was exacerbated by two other phenomena which were the direct, and indeed in part intended, outcomes from restructuring. Managers who had been encouraged to believe that they would be able to deploy more personal authority and discretion sometimes sought to exercise it more widely and radically than even residual central personnel policy and procedure could accept. On the other hand there were many staff, often supported by managers too, who found great difficulty in recognising and coming to terms with some of the changes that were inherent in the restructuring process. The loss of old familiar landmarks, such as grades and invariable interviews for each appointment, and the new managerial culture proved disorienting.

❏ Change goes on

These narrow reactions to pay and grading restructuring are rapidly being overtaken by the wider changes which HMSO is driving through to meet its business obligations:

- the commitment to quality which, both personally for many and corporately for all, has come to play a much larger part in the daily agenda
- the emphasis on serving customers rather than rule driven abstractions
- the encouragement to teamwork through empowerment and the setting aside of hierarchy in the striving for achievement
- the recruitment of employees from the commercial sector with skills which HMSO cannot develop internally, particularly marketing and selling
- an extensive voluntary early retirement programme for those unable or unwilling to adapt
- above all the widespread recognition that in a competitive and commercial world the business need must predominate if jobs are to be secured.

The need to come to terms with a changing environment which was the initial impetus for restructuring remains the challenge today. That challenge is not now seen as being to move away from a single inadequate civil service model of personnel management. There are proliferating numbers of models with ever widening boundaries of flexibility. HMSO's primary focus today is on the customer. Its future depends upon the extent to which it can identify its markets, profitably satisfy their needs and sensitively care for its customers and their concerns.

❏ Remodelling the roles

The last two years have seen significant changes in HMSO's human resourcing structures, policies and procedures. In July 1992 the previously operationally separate Personnel Services Division responsible for white-collar staff and the Industrial Personnel Division which managed industrial relations for blue-collar employees merged into Human Resources Division. A steady harmonisation of policies and procedures has begun and is gathering pace. The training and development of personnel officers and industrial relations advisers is being unified and already 'dual competence' personnel officers are in place with much wider remits than before and a redefined role to serve their 'customers', the managers of the businesses.

This process has been accelerated by increased autonomy given to HMSO's primary business operations; Office Supplies, Office Equipment, Print and Publishing. Each business now has its own personnel officers whose line responsibility is to the business management. Human Resources Division retains control of appointments to the professional structure and practitioners are responsible to the Director of Human Resources for their professional conduct, and the maintenance of HMSO's personnel policies and procedures. This 'arms length' relationship is sustained by regular meetings of personnel officers chaired by senior Human Resource managers which discuss operational problems and ensure a consistency of approach and a sharing of experience.

The creation of largely independent and customer driven businesses within HMSO has changed the power structures in the Agency and forced a re-assessment of the personnel role. This has been particularly difficult in a civil service environment where explicit controls from 'Whitehall', and consequently HMSO's own policies and procedures, have not always been relaxed at the same pace as that required by the divisional businesses. This has led from time to time both to strains of conscience and systems, with perceived 'ad hocery' as the result of an attempt to meet the needs of both internal customers and individual members of staff. The former see an inability to help them meet business pressures. The latter (sometimes the same people who in their managerial role demand one thing but as individuals challenge the effect that is the consequence) feel the vulnerability that flows from not having a personnel 'umpire' to see fair play. The change of mindset from a prescribed dependency on 'the rules' to that of self confident and responsible interpretation of policy has been difficult for many.

❏ The road straightens

Over the more than three years since restructuring there has emerged an understanding and acceptance of the dynamic that is driving the organisation and its components towards a common aim, putting the customer first. The dissolution of the vague but deeply held values of 'public service' in favour of the realisation that a trading organisation stands or falls upon its ability to attain, retain and satisfy its customers has required an extensive corporate culture change programme. All customer facing staff have been trained in customer care and a more fundamental re-orientation is underway. HMSO is re-assessing its culture and the extent to which it is changing, and needs to change further to meet the commercial challenges ahead. Studies are being conducted into customer care strategies which will impact on the whole organisation and its processes. This is being supported by a radical programme of business process redesign which is taking out whole swathes of resource, cost and complexity which do not add value to the product or service delivered to the customer.

As part of the regular review process for Executive Agencies, a review of the options for HMSO's future development which will best accord with its business orientation is underway.

Once again shoulders are being braced for further changes affecting the relationships between HMSO and its employees, but for HMSO change is inherent in its history and living experience. The accelerating changes of the last fifteen years through trading fund, executive agency, restructuring, market testing and ever greater commercialisation have left a professional, resilient and determined management team that welcomes change as a necessary ally in its commitment to quality and service to the customer.

About the author

Michael Salt was Head of Personnel at HMSO during most of the events described in this chapter.

Chapter 19

Total quality management in the West Midlands Employment Service

Martin Raff and Julie Beedon

Running a Total Quality Programme can be a frustrating and exhausting experience. There are periods of great optimism and excitement when there is evidence of progress made, alternating with ones of equally great depression at the realisation of how far there still is to go. The emotional effort that is needed to take forward a culture change programme is infinitely greater than that needed for running a business within an existing set of organisational values and beliefs. Most managers think that their professional lives are very demanding already as a result of continually increasing pressures on them, so why should they start a quality programme and make their lives even more tiring? This chapter will try to show from our experience why they should and why a quality initiative can be the most rewarding experience of one's professional life.

The Employment Service (Figure 19.1) in the West Midlands has been running a Total Quality programme for the last five years. The programme involves all 5000 ES employees in the Region, including management at all levels and front line staff who deal with our customers, unemployed people and employers. When we started in 1989, we felt we were taking a big risk. We were not aware of any public sector quality programme which aimed to include everyone in the organisation from the start, although there were some initiatives in specialised parts of a few public sector organisations. There was also no literature we could find about quality in service industries, all the work that had been written until then was about manufacturing processes.

o So why did we start?

There were two main reasons. Firstly, the West Midlands was consistently failing to meet the requirements of its Annual Performance Agreement (APA), its contribution to the annual performance agreed for the Employment Service nationally with Ministers. The Region had always been one of the worst performers. People in the Region had low expectations of themselves. Martin Raff, as Regional Director, had tried various conventional ways of changing this culture and improving performance, exhortation, setting demanding objectives,

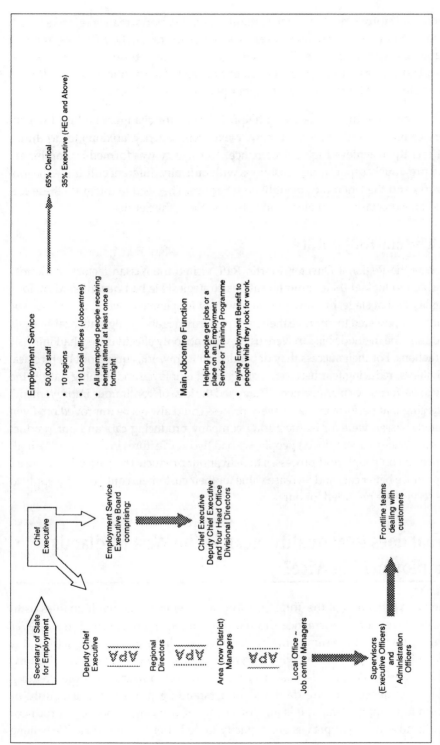

Figure 19.1. The Employment Service.

agreeing improvement strategies, regular detailed performance reviews which involved crawling over quantities of laboriously researched figures, moving managers who failed to deliver – all with no impact on our Regional results. Desperation was settling in! Secondly, like the rest of the public sector, the Region was being asked to achieve ever higher performance targets with less staff.

But at the same time there was a helpful climate for change. The Employment Service had recently become a new 'Next Steps' agency, anxious to do things differently to achieve high performance. The agency was formed by combining two previously separate organisations with radically different cultures – the Job-centres and the Unemployment Benefit Service. The need to integrate these created an expectation of major change by people in the Service.

o The starting point

In 1989 the Regional Director, Martin Raff, visited the Nissan factory in County Durham to look at their communications strategies. He had never heard of Total Quality at that stage, but saw there a new way for people to work, in enthusiastic teams, empowered to improve their own performance and using statistical analysis to do so. The methods Nissan were using were not only effective, they had intrinsic attractions. For their success they depended on teamwork, cutting out hierarchical privileges, reducing fear between manager and employee and valuing data as the key to performance management. They used the idea of 'continuous improvement', believing that performance and every process could always be improved on. Even though Nissan were a manufacturing company producing cars and our product was a service to unemployed people, we had two key features in common. We both depended on people and processes to deliver our product. The methods they used to produce better cars and increase value for their customers could equally apply to the service we provided for ours.

What does total quality mean in the West Midlands Employment Service?

The main attraction of the Total Quality way of working is that it enables us to deliver levels of performance dramatically higher than the Region has ever achieved while at the same time developing people's skills and capacities. It is 'win:win'. The organisation wins, and the people in it win. It embodies the aims of 'Investors in People'. Because it works through empowering people, creating interdependence, valuing data and understanding processes in a culture of continuous improvement, it is an ethical way of working. It not only produces results now, it also improves our capacity to do better in the future. We believe in it. So do an increasing number of our people in the Region. We believe that Total Quality offers the public sector a constructive way of dealing with the pressures created by the combined effects of cuts in public expenditure and our customers' higher expectations of the public service.

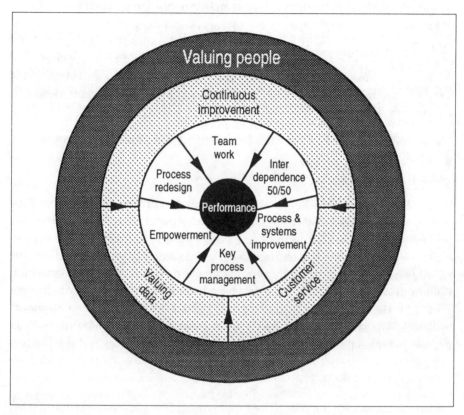

Figure 19.2. The main features of the West Midlands Employment Service.

○ Valuing people

The first circle in Figure 19.2 shows the basic value of the programme – valuing people. Our people produce our 'product' (service) at the point of sale. Our performance is produced by the face to face contact that our front line staff make with unemployed people and employers. If we are to get more productivity, ie a higher standard of service with a diminishing resource, we need to get more of our people's 'discretionary effort'. Most people are capable of giving (and will enjoy giving) more effort to the job than conventional ways of managing work allow. By creating a culture that values people and allows them to have control over their own jobs, and by giving them responsibility for improving their own performance, they are able to perform better and feel proud of it.

We have tried to create a sense of 'all one Regional team', reducing internal competition. We have abolished league tables and aim to use performance information as data for analysis instead of as a means of punishment and reward. In this way we encourage local office teams to learn from each other instead of competing. We have redefined the manager's role as one of team leadership and reduced the trappings of hierarchy. For example none of our managers, including the Regional Director, now have offices. We all work in open plan. We have also aimed to reduce the amount of internal politics by encouraging open and honest debate. People are now more ready to accept feedback, even if it is critical, as long as it is an honest expression of view. Increasingly people are ready to give this sort of feedback to their managers, who in turn, are more ready to seek it.

The next circle in Figure 19.2 contains the three other core values of our programme.

o Valuing data

We teach everyone in the Region the basic Statistical Process Control tools, flow charts, run charts, brainstorming, Pareto charts, cause and effect diagrams. We encourage front line staff to use these tools to improve their own work processes. We empower them to feel free to make data based changes. In addition we require any views expressed by people in meetings, in work related conversations or in written argument to be data based. Personal opinions have to be supported by data, including 'soft' (impressionistic) data when this is all that is available. The challenge of 'where's your data' dogs people who continue to express personal pet theories or prejudices.

o Valuing customers

We, in common with the rest of the Employment Service, have taken down the counters and screens that traditionally separated customers from our people. The standard of offices and our people's attitude to customer service is one which any service organisation, including the private sector, would be proud. We are now setting up panels of customers in offices to ask their advice on how to improve our service to them.

o Continuous improvement

Process and system improvement is a continuing business. Performance through customer service has no upper limits. In the early days people used to say to their managers:

... we have improved all our processes – what shall we do next....?

This question is not asked as frequently now.

o **Key routes to quality**

The segments in the inner circle in Figure 19.2 mention the key strategies we are currently using to take forward quality in the Region. Some of these, like 'teamwork', have been there from the start. Others, like 'key process management' and 'interdependence' we introduced last year. Some of these will change in the future. They are discussed later in this chapter.

o **Performance**

All the arrows in Figure 19.2 lead to 'performance'. Our aim is to improve the performance of the Region in terms of the contribution it makes to the targets set for the Employment Service nationally in its Annual Performance Agreement with the Secretary of State for Employment. Other major benefits have resulted from our quality programme:

- morale is improved
- the pace of people's personal development has speeded up dramatically
- job satisfaction and commitment to the Service have increased.

Visitors are always astonished by the evidence of these when talking to our people. But a programme which had a sole aim such as improving morale or people's development would be sub–optimal. The Employment Service needs our performance to survive and prosper. The other benefits are fundamental to the programme, but their primary significance is in the contribution they make to the organisation's performance, now and in the future.

o **Personal change**

Changing organisational culture involves all individuals in the organisation in personal change. Perhaps the greatest change that needs to take place is in leadership behaviour. Martin Raff writes

> I have had to change. I was very much a 'command and control' leader, with a preference for personal involvement at many levels in the business. People liked the detailed interest I took in the subject matter of their work and referred as many decisions to me as possible. I liked taking decisions and I felt valued and in touch as a result. This is where my job satisfaction came from. But people were dependent on me, and afraid of me because of my demanding style. I divided people into the able (my model) and the rest and valued only the former. People told me what they thought I wanted to hear rather than what they really thought.

It has been difficult to change to a style which allowed people to develop, contribute more and become less dependent. Now I have to get my satisfactions in the longer term by seeing the Region's performance and its people develop. I am encouraging people to be responsible for their own jobs and trying to develop my role in a strategic way.

I have also had to learn to value criticism of my actions. People do not tell leaders they are afraid that they have made a mess of things or, even that they disagree with them. To be told that you handled a meeting really badly is difficult to take at first although you can value the honesty of the feedback! But leaders really need feedback, negative as well as positive. Not only does feedback about your own performance help you to improve but as the trust of an open and honest relationship with the people who work for you develops, they tell you more about everything that is going on. As a result I am vastly better informed about what is really happening in the Region.

I have also learned to value diversity. I frequently wrote people off because I thought they were less able. But in teamwork one needs to use all the team members' talents. Encouraging rather than judging people enables them to contribute more. We now use personality profiles such as Myers-Briggs and Margerison McCann (see Chapter 5) to understand people's work preferences and how best to use them in a team. It is amazing how much more talent I have found in my colleagues working in this way. Before I thought talent was thinly spread in the Region, now I feel almost embarrassed by the richness of it. They are the same people, only led differently.

How we went about it

Telling people the story of 4 to 5 years of work on a radical change programme means that one is always working with the benefit of hindsight. What was a series of actions, reactions, and reviews can be presented as a grand master plan with a logical progression and identifiable phases. Those 5 years' worth of learning and investment can seem like a huge agenda that has to be tackled all at once. Before telling some of the highlights of how we reached where we are now we offer some words of caution and, we hope, encouragement....

- we started slowly and knew little at the beginning
- we tackled things in parts
- we only really managed to plan one year at a time
- we sometimes left people behind

- we often made mistakes and felt quite incompetent

but

- we stuck with it (so the purpose, or vision stayed the same)
- we were prepared to experiment and stay open to all ideas
- we reviewed actions and sought to understand if and why things did and did not work
- we learnt from our mistakes
- our understanding grew over time and as a result our strategies got better
- we still feel we have a lot to learn and a long way to go.

In this section of the chapter, we have tried to address questions that are usually brought up by visitors to the West Midlands, firstly, by plotting the historical progression, then drawing out some of the issues and explaining how we have tackled them, threading quotations from people throughout to give a feel for what the front line experience has been.

o **The historical sequence**

Looking back this can be seen as five almost distinct phases, each lasting about a year and probably matching our annual round of planning. Each year has some key aspects and activities so that the whole can be represented by Figure 19.3.

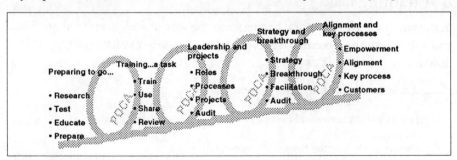

Figure 19.3. The PDCA cycle.

The PDCA or Plan, Do, Check, Act cycle of continuous improvement can be seen to be overlying and cycling through the whole, enabling an iterative process of improvement to take place in the planning and implementation activities. We now look briefly at the activities and lessons of each phase.

o **Preparing to go**

We conducted our research by looking for books and examples in the service or public sector and found little. We looked at the work of the 'quality gurus' and we found the work of Deming to be of most relevance to our situation. His philosophy of management has remained the cornerstone of our approach throughout, although we have also incorporated many compatible ideas of other management theorists. We chose to test out some of the techniques and approaches in 2 or 3 offices. We found this work to be invaluable and from these test locations we learnt:

- that flowcharts and analysis were very effective for our clerical processes
- more about our culture and how it affected the people who worked in it
- what the benefits of change might be on a wider scale
- what sort of materials might support the next stages
- that we needed consultancy help to move forward
- we had a lot to learn.

The final stages of this year involved the senior managers in the organisation looking at what we had learnt from the research and testing and deciding how to proceed.

By the end of the year we had decided to launch all 110 local offices in a rolling programme over 18 months. We had appointed and trained a number of facilitators and developed a training plan.

o A training task

In the past, one of our cultural barriers was the way in which our well qualified and enthusiastic new recruits were trained to operate our systems strictly as laid down ...

... that is the way we have always done it

... just follow the codes and don't question

... we have to follow the rules – it's legislation

... you don't need to know why.. just how to do it.

Over time their ability to contribute proactively was stifled. We hoped through wholesale training in the 'tools of quality' to equip them to participate in decision making. We taught everyone brainstorming, flowcharting, fishbone diagrams, data gathering, run charts, pareto analysis, bar charts, control charts and a basic model for process improvement.

There really has been a sea change in our organisational culture and our approach to data. Staff at every level of our organisation have been given the skills to collect and analyze meaningful data. This included data on their own contributions to ES performance, teamwork and improved customer service. Before long our staff were only too eager to measure everything and everyone that moved.

John Lee Local Office Manager

Whilst the training was being 'rolled out', senior managers worked to use the techniques themselves. They started by flowcharting the planning system and discovered they knew less about it than they thought! Further work explored their own added value and gave insights into where their requests for information were an unnecessary burden. This initiated our work on management processes as part of the system looking at such things as meetings, performance reviews and information systems.

Up to this point we had seen the whole thing as largely a training task, sometimes missing the subtleties of cultural change. On top of this we had only started to tackle the 'leadership issues'.

o Leadership and projects

As feedback from offices filtered through it became clearer that the system and the culture was affected strongly and often adversely by the management processes we used. The roles and activities of leaders were going to have to change. Many activities in this year engaged with the leadership issue:

- we designed a workshop called 'facilitative management' to look at how managers could operate in a facilitative way
- we changed the purpose of one level of management to allow them to focus on cultural change and performance improvement. They worked, with facilitators, on developing the new role, removing barriers and supporting its introduction
- we worked out a means of communicating what quality was all about called 'Features Of a Quality Service', involving staff in the design of it
- we learned the further quality tools for management and planning
- we changed our senior management meetings by working on teamwork in the group.

In the field, work on quality had moved away from training but was often project focused with many projects unconnected with performance.

It was sometimes difficult at this stage to say how far we had got and what gains we had made with quality. We then discovered the idea of doing a 'stocktake' of where we were. By the end of 1991 we had designed a questionnaire to use for a full census of all staff, to gain information which could inform our planning. Questions covered the penetration of training, views about the quality philosophy and the extent to which the culture in offices had changed. It was encouraging to see how well the aims of our approach were understood but not too much of a surprise to see how little progress on involving staff had been made.

o Strategy and breakthrough

The next identifiable stage was when we really started to understand 'strategy'. What has worked for us (see Figure 19.4) is:

- to work out the overall purpose and keep to it
- to develop supporting strategic objectives
- to agree strategies to progress these
- to modify the strategies if the situation changes (or if reviews show they are not working)
- to allow people to develop their own detailed tactics and plans.

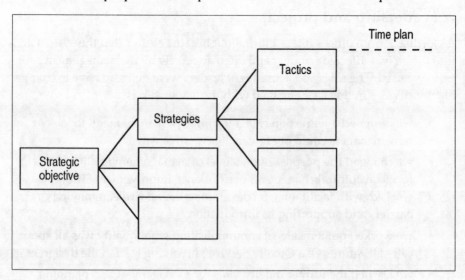

Figure 19.4. The strategy.

In practice this has meant that the Regional leadership worked together :

- to produce a set of strategic objectives they were all signed up to
- to translate these objectives into area strategies
- to use these to focus local improvement plans and tactics
- to communicate the links between the quality process, customers and performance.

One of the major strategies started with work on concepts of innovation as opposed to incremental improvement. By creating belief that radical improvement is possible, innovation can occur. The Region has used two 'campaigns' to catch the imagination and to focus and catalyse all quality improvement efforts around key customer related performance indicators. The first in May 1992 called 'Breakthrough' focused on unemployed placings as they are key performance indicators, and the second in May 1993 called 'Grey Matters' focused on a wider set of objectives.

> Breakthrough was an act of faith. We questioned our ability to radically alter our traditional processes and bring about a quantum leap in performance improvement, but we did it: and that visible achievement was a major confidence booster.
>
> Phil Davis Coventry Area Manager

The power of harnessing all our collective, creative and improvement energies on one major process was soon tangible in the form of radical sustained performance improvements.

o **Alignment and key process management**

Our work on strategic management in the next stage has developed into alignment through the use of processes which provide for:

- identification of a range of stakeholder data
- recognition of the validity of 'soft' data
- interaction between groups of stakeholders
- involvement of all levels in the development of the key strategic objectives
- collective agreement and shared responsibility
- alignment around a common purpose and strategy
- development of ownership and commitment.

Our local office work to develop process improvement skills has moved on to introduce the concept of Key Process Management. Offices are using this to study the systems and processes in their offices to determine the key processes that are central to the health of the whole system. These processes need ongoing data collection and monitoring.

> KPM addresses issues of concern with a common sense approach. Used on a day to day basis it improves systems and performance. It soon becomes part of your

daily routine and makes continual improvement a reality. I've been involved in two projects recently and both are already showing improvements. We are moving on to design a rolling programme, so that as one project finishes we can smoothly go on to the next.

Jenny Bennett, Executive Officer, Wellington Employment Service Jobcentre

Our current work has moved on to:

- review key process management and ensure it generates continuous improvement rather than problem solving
- work with teams including Local Offices and Head Office to redesign some of our key business processes
- look at the relationships between levels and build ways in which these can operate 'interdependently' so that each understands the other's needs and that plans take account of all needs.

Some of the issues we have tackled

It is always interesting to note that the questions visitors ask are generally related to the issues we have been wrestling with. The next part of this section moves away from the historical sequence and discusses some of those questions and issues and how we have tackled them.

o How do you do it as part of a large organisation?

We are fortunate in that the move to Agency signalled a new era of management in the Civil Service. Whilst the whole organisation has not been using our approach, the commitment to quality, people, and new ways of working, has allowed us the freedom to experiment, develop our thinking and apply it.

It may be useful if this is explained through an analogy. Imagine the quality philosophy we are using as a computer operating system such as Windows. Packages which are designed for other operating systems need some programming work to make them operate. They are probably never as effective as they might have been had they been designed for that operating system but they can still work and add value.

So strategies designed to work within the wider Employment Service system can be transformed and made to work in ways which are compatible with our approach. One example of this is performance pay where we have worked to develop an objective setting and appraisal process which supports teamwork, valuing people and the use of all types of data.

I was asked to be part of an Objective Setting Design Team to come up with a strategy for colleagues to use when setting objectives. The team's members ranged from Grade 7's to myself, an AO. For me a session we did on finding common themes was very important. It made me realise that people in higher grades had had the same experiences as me at some time. This brought the group together and made sharing views easier. Different techniques were used throughout our meetings, always steering us toward group decisions that we were all happy with.

Craig Pavey Administration Officer

o What do you mean when you talk of the Employment Service as a system?

The early work we did was to focus on trying to understand the West Midlands Employment Service as a system:

- with the aim of placing customers into jobs and paying them benefit whilst they are seeking work
- with supporting internal processes which interlink to find and display vacancies, set up and refer customers to programmes
- with inputs in the form of policy, guidance, resources etc. from Head Office
- with the service produced largely by Local Office staff at the point of delivery.

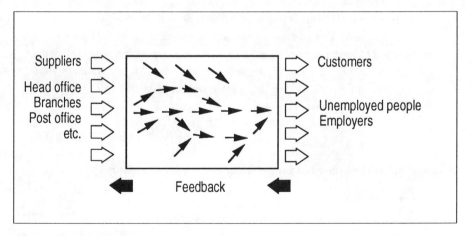

Figure 19.5. The working environment.

We then started to realise the complexity of our internal relationships and the need to improve our services to one another (Figure 19.5). Every job began to be seen as part of a system with suppliers and customers interlinking chains, each link of which could be improved through obtaining and responding to feedback. Even management came to be seen as a process whereby managers were the suppliers of a service for staff.

o Do you really have customers and do they have any choice?

This was one of the early questions we wrestled with and essentially we have had to turn the whole organisation to face in the other direction. The idea of the recipients of Unemployment Benefit as valued customers was not our traditional approach, particularly since we have a role in ensuring that those who receive the benefits are 'entitled', as is emphasised in Chapter 10. Yet this concept could be related to the retail sector where all people are regarded as valued customers but systems are in place to protect against shoplifters, who are treated differently. Naturally those who would behave in this way are in the minority in any system and our behaviour to our customers should reflect this, treating the minority of those who get unemployment benefit without being entitled as 'shop lifters'.

We are developing new skills in listening to customers through surveys, questionnaires and data gathering on specific processes. This has been supported by our work on the Jobseeker's (Citizen's) Charter Standards where many offices have worked to meet and exceed the standards and have used them as an incentive to work on their aspects of customer service.

> Jobseeker's Charter was seen as another opportunity to count the time it took to deliver a quality service to our customers. The Government's targets specified that we should see every client who sought our services within 10 minutes of their arrival even if they do not have an appointment. In due course our data showed that we took an average of 83 seconds to attend to them – BUT we wanted to do better! More data was analyzed by a working group who surveyed all of the office team and recommendations were implemented. More customers were coming through our doors each day yet we were now taking an average of 42 seconds to attend to them, cutting waiting time in half.
>
> John Lee, Local Office Manager

Some of our offices now hold regular customer panel sessions:

- to work with customers
- to obtain information about customer service
- to find out customers' needs and concerns
- to explain new developments and obtain advice
- to try out and test ideas
- to agree development actions and priorities.

All involved [in Customer Panels] felt they were keen to seize the opportunity of being able to take empowerment a stage further – to the customer. The concept of actually asking our customers for their views is excellent but to be meaningful there has to be an open and trusting environment created and maintained. The need to involve the customer proactively is vital to conducting a meaningful review of the level of our service.

Rob Walters, Marketing Manager, Worcester Employment Service Jobcentre.

o How do you overcome resistance?

In the early days we often met widespread or total resistance. It would have been normal in these circumstances to back off and say this is not going to work. We have found that any resistance can be overcome by working through a process which responds to how people are feeling and moves them one step at a time. An example of this is the move we made, before the main quality programme started (although inspired by Nissan), to move managers out of their offices. The first reaction to this was universal refusal and a catalogue of fears and concerns. A few people were persuaded to experiment, the Regional Director himself made the move. Very soon they were enthusing and persuading their colleagues of the benefits. Now there is almost universal adoption of, and genuine support for, the practice.

We have learnt to expect and anticipate resistance at every level. Our 'understanding change' theory has taught us:

- to seek to identify the sources of dissatisfaction
- if necessary to draw out the resistance
- to use those who are most critical/resistant to plan the way forward
- to engage in a constant process of sharing the leadership vision
- to encourage people at all levels to have their own vision and to articulate it
- to use interaction to develop ownership and commitment
- to value the things people are doing
- to help people to see the constant nature of change
- to provide everyone with as much information as possible so they can make the right decisions for themselves
- to encourage people to seize opportunities and to look for them in every situation
- to create a belief it can be done and it will last
- to value people and let them know they are valued by using their expertise, interests and experience.

The change process has had to mobilise everyone and to build an expectation that personal change is something we must all commit to if we share a vision of a change that is worthwhile.

o **What does SPC (Statistical Process Control) mean and how do you apply it to non–manufacturing work?**

We recently asked a group of staff from local offices what SPC meant to them:

... more than control charts

... all analysis of data

... mechanisms for flagging up systems that need attention

... moving away from knee jerk reactions

... what visitors in particular feel is the enthusiasm of staff

... working out soft measures for behaviour

... understanding and using data

... all the techniques for looking at things and planning.

We have found that SPC, or the use of data, impacts on the culture and affects teamwork, customers and communications. SPC is used throughout the organisation on a range of projects large and small and by many people in their daily work.

The use of data and SPC can be seen as a virtuous cycle which starts with the need to improve and the recognition that there is a performance gap. This is then moved by the desire to involve people into the need to use data and SPC to do so. Then there is a delay factor. During this delay people are equipped with the necessary techniques, they need to overcome their traditional mistrust of management and lack of confidence in themselves. As insights are gained and changes made, pride and job satisfaction grow.

By this stage you are coming to the end of the delay and some cultural change has been achieved. It is only then that the whole cycle (Figure 16.6) starts to see real improvements and we return to consciousness of another performance gap.

Once the first cycle is completed, then each future cycle will see an ongoing interaction between the use of data and the development of the culture. We have found that you cannot start by changing the culture but by asking people to contribute and equipping them to do so. As processes are changed, based on their data and analysis, the change in culture starts. As people become eager to be involved, performance gaps are recognised and techniques are learned and valued, the virtuous cycle of continuous improvement is in place.

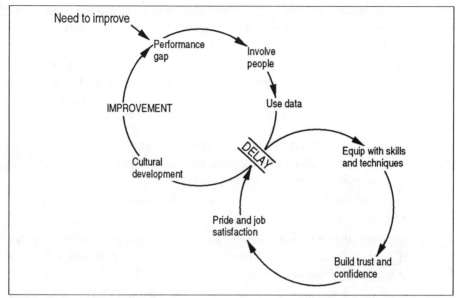

Figure 19.6. The SPC cycle.

This cycle is also impacted by the discernible changes in the way the Region is managed. People observe the way in which data have become friendly or at worst neutral rather than a punishment. Decisions are not made without data:

- hard data about performance trends
- analysis of relationships and causal factors
- soft data about people's perceptions and feelings
- soft data in the form of opinions of those who actually do the job.

People value the way in which Senior Managers seek data and feedback, and use it. This impacts positively on the cultural changes we are seeking to progress.

o What do leaders need to do?

One thing which has been a major factor for us has been the role that the Regional Director or unit head has played. He started with and has always retained three key things:

- a belief that it is all possible (this was probably born out of his visit to Nissan where he saw it being done and realised that our people were at least as good as those at Nissan in Washington Co. Durham)
- desire to make it work in the sense of wanting what it can do, not only for himself but also for others; the staff, the customers and the stakeholders.

- vision of something truly great for the organisation. He has been heard to say 'I am sure that the worst enemy of change is low aspirations'. His own aspirations have always been huge.

Senior managers started the journey as a networked group of unit heads. They have had to work throughout the change process to become a leadership team with a common purpose. They have done this through various means:

- specific work on understanding the diversity and contribution each individual makes to the team using such tools as the Team Management System (TMS) and Myers Briggs
- development of their meetings as a process, investing in planning, defining their purpose and goals
- work on other processes such as resource management and allocation of performance objectives to ensure that the needs of the whole Region override any individual requirements
- working with a model that they are not competing to be the 'best' Area but ensuring that they 'contribute' as much as possible to the Regional performance.

To a large extent they have acted as very effective project managers who have been convinced that they want the change. They have thus worked successfully to implement quality, working mainly as catalysts in the change process.

We have a number of levels of middle management. A key group of these are our local office managers, who are generally responsible for all the staff in one location, often up to 80 people. They probably have the most difficult job in the organisation:

- the local office delivery unit is the place where all the policies, strategies, plans and instructions impact and come together
- any change, whatever its source, will impact on their area of responsibility
- they have the key responsibility for performance as their commands are the ones that deliver it
- they are in the middle in that pressure for change and resisting change is coming from 'above and below'
- in the past they have been trained to manage and administer and have been given a range of duties to carry out checks etc.
- the size of the group has meant that they have not been able to have as many first hand opportunities to learn and develop their understanding of quality.

We have not yet fully worked out the role of a local office manager in a quality context. Whilst many of them are actively engaged in working this out, some are finding it difficult to make the change from what they were trained to do and what has always been valued by the organisation. Normally new roles and responsibilities would be laid down for us in guides and codes and we are beginning to appreciate that if the transition is to be effective then people will have to participate in developing the new role and for some this is uncomfortable.

These local office managers report directly to Field Operations Managers (FOMs), who report in turn to Area Managers. The FOMs are the group which has had the greatest success in changing their role. Their operational responsibility for a number of locations gave them a traditional role which involved them in a range of activities relating to every aspect of the operation. We worked with them to forge a new role focusing on performance improvement and cultural change. This new role has become a model for a complete restructuring within the Employment Service to remove the Area layer of management and create smaller Districts with hands-on managers of this type.

> We worked together to develop a new FOM role using a mixture of new tools, concepts and a lot of hard work. My personal learning increased and I became greatly aware of how my behaviours could influence or affect others. This time of personal learning has been most challenging but extremely enlightening and rewarding.

> Dave Arnold, Field Operations Manager.

Results

One of the key indicators of performance which can be recognised by customers and stakeholders alike is the number of people we place into jobs. If we look first at West Midlands unemployed placings figures from the beginning of the financial year in which our quality programme was launched, we can see that performance was reasonably stable (Figure 19.7). This was during the roll out training period.

When performance improvement activity was focused on placings, through our Breakthrough and Grey Matters campaigns, significant shifts in performance resulted (13.9% shift in mean for Breakthrough, 26% shift in mean for Grey Matters).

One of the difficulties in looking at the impact of a quality programme is in determining the extent to which improvements are due to external factors such as a general recovery in the economy. A look at the national trends (Figure 19.8)

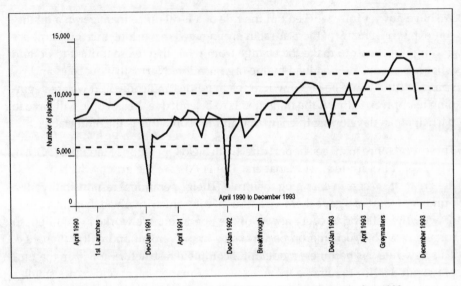

Figure 19.7. West Midlands unemployed placings April 1990 to December 1993.

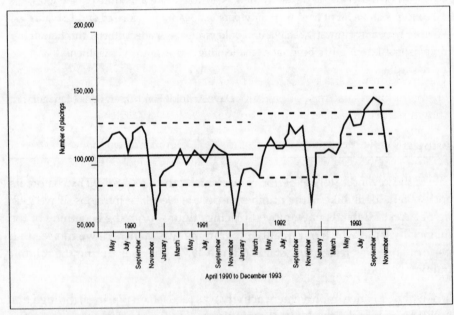

Figure 19.8. National unemployed placings April 1990 to December 1993.

shows that whilst there were improvements at the same time, they were not as significant (3.3% shift in mean at the same time as Breakthrough and 20% shift in mean at the same time as Grey Matters).

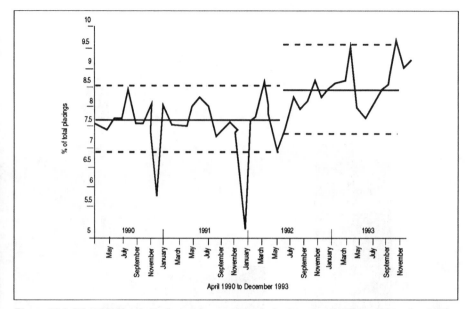

Figure 19.9. West Midlands % share of unemployed placings April 1990 to December 1993.

Further investigation of West Midlands percentage share of the national placings reveals the extent of the impact of our quality programme (Figure 19.9).

The Breakthrough strategy saw a 10.1% shift in the mean of our percentage share of unemployed placings. Significantly, prior to Breakthrough, December had shown particularly disappointing results for the West Midlands.

Why should our percentage share decrease in December down to levels as low as 5.5%? December of the Breakthrough period saw offices looking at this month as a common rather than special cause of variation as it happened every year and the resulting percentage share was over 8.5%. This December it has risen again to 9.1%.

We are justly proud of achieving this degree of impact on a performance indicator which means that so many additional unemployed people are now at work. We also have evidence of the way in which we have impacted on our organisational culture. Our annual stocktake showed us last year that 34% felt that their opportunities to use their initiative and be involved in decision making had improved over the year. An encouraging 70% of our staff say that these opportunities are good. Over 80% of our staff say they are involved in discussions about performance and 62% use data regularly.

We have also seen what can only be described as a development explosion. From a position where books/articles and input on quality were regarded with suspicion we have moved to the stage whereby any book/course or learning material

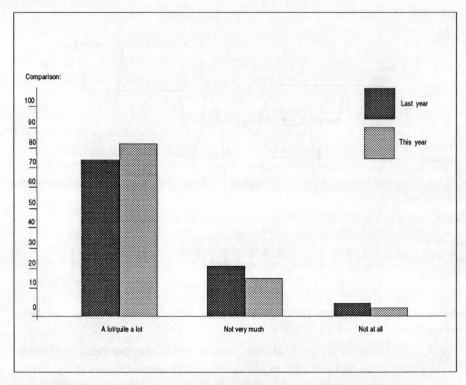

Figure 19.10. How much are you involved in discussion about office performance?

is vastly over-subscribed and we are being asked to develop new supporting materials constantly. Where people would have complained that they were obliged to fill places, the most common complaint now is that people are being deprived of first hand learning opportunities.

The consequence of all of this has been that people throughout the organisation have developed new skills and a fresh outlook. Involvement in improvement projects has meant that they have the data, analysis and confidence to present their story effectively. Visitors to our offices are always keen to describe the 'buzz' which they experience in talking to the teams.

We also feel that we have been catalysts in many ways for developments within the Employment Service nationally.

> By capturing the imagination and energy of its people, our West Midlands Region has achieved high levels of commitment and performance. They have proved that by valuing people you get added value in return. This certainly shows in the improved results they have achieved

> Mike Fogden, Chief Executive of the Employment Service.

Sir Geoffrey Holland KCB said, on leaving the Employment Department Group:

> No Region has been more in the vanguard of all the remarkable achievements of the Group than the West Midlands Employment Service. You and yours have, between you, transformed the Service out of all recognition. You are setting the pace for the future. And on the way you have helped hundreds of thousands of people to a job and a much brighter future.

The business as a whole in the West Midlands has benefited from our involvement in quality. As we have been speakers and contributors to various events and articles, we have drawn a number of visitors. The reputation we have thus developed has helped us to forge new business relationships, for example we have been working on a business partnership with Rover Group who are one of the main employers in the West Midlands.

Our Total Quality programme has begun a major transformation in the Region's culture. We still have further to go, but already people feel more valued, they are able to contribute more of their talents, and they now have high expectations of themselves and the Region. When we started five years ago our stated ambition was to be the best performing Region. At the time that ambition seemed unrealistic, in fact slightly megalomaniac, now we are the best performing Region on many indicators and everyone believes our aim of top performance on every front is achievable in the next year or so. The most satisfying thing about the programme has been achieving high performance by a process which has developed people and made them feel valued. None of these results would have been worthwhile unless we had, as Deming would say, 'delighted our customers'!

Customers who use our services recently said:

> Quite simply, I wish to thank your employees for the sensitive and seemingly caring way that they have conducted themselves with me and from what I have seen, with other clients. It is no easy task dealing with people who are upset, maybe feeling that the world is against them and then having to differentiate between those genuine cases and those who will make every effort to defraud. I hope not to have to darken your doors again but should that happen at least I know that I will be treated like a human being.

> Have you noticed how easy it is to write a letter of complaint and how hard it is to write a letter of commendation. This letter is written to compliment one of your staff on the way she did an excellent job. I am not much good at this 'signing on'. So when I went to 'sign on' I didn't do everything correctly. The young lady who looked after me handled the situation with firmness, tact and great skill. She should be complimented on her professionalism, which reflected well on her and on the training you give your staff.

About the authors

Martin Raff CBE is the Employment Service Regional Director for the West Midlands. He has had a wide range of experience in Civil Service policy and management jobs including a spell as labour attache in the British Embassy in Washington. Martin will be leaving the Civil Service at the end of the year to start his own consultancy.

Julie Beedon, a mathematics and statistics graduate, is Regional Quality Co-ordinator for the West Midlands Employment Service. She has served in the Women's Royal Naval Service (WRENS) as an MOD procurement executive, and worked for Marconi Space and Defence systems as a contracts manager. For the last five years she has worked with Martin in developing the Region's quality approach.

Special thanks go to Sarah Warner and Peter Bates for their help in compiling this chapter and to the entire staff of the West Midlands Employment Service for making it possible.

Chapter 20

Customer service in

The Stamp Office

Keith Hodgson

Stamp duty is the oldest tax administered by the Board of Inland Revenue. Although the existence of a form of stamp duty can be traced back to Roman times, most historians agree that in its current form it originated in the Netherlands in 1624 as a result of a competition to find a new form of tax. There is no record of the inventor's name but the winning idea required that certain legal documents be written on stamped paper. Stamp duty was introduced into this country in 1694 during the reign of William and Mary as:

> An act for granting Their Majesties several duties on Vellum, Parchment and Paper for 4 years, towards carrying on the war against France.

In those days the duty ranged from one old penny to 40 shillings on a wide variety of documents. These included:

- grants of honour, promotion, pardon and land
- copies of wills
- certificates of admission to Inns of Court
- certain affidavits, leases, writs, deeds and summonses.

The earliest stamp duty yields were about £50,000 a year. The duties proved so successful that they were continued.

Today stamp duty is a tax on a variety of legal and commercial documents which give effect to the sale and transfer of certain types of interest in property. The administration of stamp duty does not require any special system of enforcement. The main sanction against non-payment of the duty is that, except in criminal proceedings, a document is neither admissible in evidence nor is it available for any purpose whatsoever unless it is properly stamped. It is, therefore, in the interest of at least one of the parties to the transaction to ensure their documents are properly stamped in order to be fully effective. Stamping more than a short period after execution is subject to interest and penalties. From this it will be seen that stamp duty is largely self-collecting. Payment of the duty is indicated by stamps of appropriate value impressed on the documents at the time the duty is paid. The two main types of document which give rise to a charge to stamp duty are those relating to land and buildings, and shares and securities.

The Stamp Office

Stamp duties are administered by The Stamp Office. The Stamp Office is an Executive Office of the Board of Inland Revenue, having acquired this status on 1 April 1992. A total of just over 200 people are employed in 12 offices throughout the United Kingdom and Northern Ireland. The Office handles around 6 million documents and transactions each year from which around £1.7 billion of duty is collected. Over 3,500 customers are served every day, of which around 80% are members of the legal profession. Our highest denomination of stamp is £1,000,000.

The work of The Stamp Office can be divided into three business functions:

- the Stock Market
- Mainstream
- Adjudication.

❏ The Stock Market

The Stock Market is, for all practical purposes, a self-contained part of our business. It accounts for around half of the duty we collect but only employs a handful of people. The Stock Exchange collects the duty on our behalf through its computerised settlement system known as TALISMAN. Our job in this area is related mainly to the liability of non-standard transactions.

❏ Mainstream

In terms of staff and customers Mainstream is by far the largest of our business functions, incorporating all of our offices open to the public. It is a largely informal process in which customers either send their documents to us through the post, or bring them in person to our public counters. In both cases the documents are, with very few exceptions indeed, accompanied by the duty estimated by the customer to be payable. Our job involves confirming the duty payable, stamping and returning the documents. Around 97% of the documents we receive are handled by our Mainstream business.

❏ Adjudication

The remaining 3% of documents are handled by our Adjudication business. Adjudication is a process in which we make a formal determination as to the amount of stamp duty payable on a document. This often occurs because the customer and the Mainstream office are unable to reach agreement about the amount of duty payable. In addition there are certain types of document for which adjudication is a statutory requirement. Adjudication work is handled centrally.

The changes required

Our oldest recorded customer complaint dates back to 1765 when the attempted imposition of stamp duties upon the American colonies met with opposition. Protest meetings were held and the outcry of 'no taxation without representation' was raised.

The arrival of ships bearing consignments of stamped paper was attended by major rioting, the most well known being the Boston Tea Party. Even in those days not getting it right first time was an expensive business! We are told that the Treasury had hoped to raise £93,000 (a lot of money in those days) in this way. Instead they were out of pocket to the tune of £3,000!

❏ The turning point

Some 220 years later, or thereabouts, we were still receiving customer complaints, although not, we should hasten to add, of a nature expected to cause such international repercussions! The complaints concerned the length of time being taken in a number of our offices to stamp and return documents, in some cases eight weeks or more. Our customers were also concerned that, in response to a staff inspection report, consideration was being given to closing the network of local stamp offices, a facility greatly valued by them. At the same time the Board of Inland Revenue had issued a Consultative Document entitled *The Scope for Reforming Stamp Duties* focusing upon the scope for modernising, harmonising and possibly removing the duty in particular cases. The outcome of this was destined to have an impact upon the work of The Stamp Office.

Furthermore various management reforms were taking place across the Inland Revenue. For us the most significant and welcome was the delegation of financial authority accompanying line management budgeting and the creation of cost centre structures. It is possible that all of these changes could have been accommodated in the traditional manner, although there must have been question marks about just how well equipped we were to cope in this way. However the opportunity to make more radical and wholesale changes proved irresistible. After all we had as near a blank sheet of paper as one could wish for. The key driver was the desire to run The Stamp Office along business lines delivering a quality service at a value for money price. A three part strategy was adopted:

- the development of a fully integrated financial management information system helpful to managers at all levels
- a reorganisation of The Stamp Office with the emphasis being given more to customer needs than self interest
- a greater emphasis on the management requirement of those officers in charge of local offices and sections.

❑ The Management Information System

The Management Information System was designed to inform us for each business, and every office in those businesses:

- the volumes of work received, work processed and work on hand
- the amounts of duty collected
- staffing resources used
- running costs incurred.

From this we would be able to derive the basic management information needed to underpin managing The Stamp Office in a business-like manner:

- unit costs
- collection costs
- productivity levels
- backlog costs.

One of the more important features of the Management Information System concerned the delivery of customer service. The collection of stamp duty is not a process in its own right but is generally part of a much wider process. When handling conveyances, for example, we are part of the house purchase process. Our customers and their clients are potentially put to some inconvenience if we do not stamp and return their documents speedily. From experience we had learned that backlogs of work could build up and get out of control all too quickly and all too easily. Failure to take appropriate remedial action at the right time was potentially costly and time consuming.

The new system was designed, therefore, to include the facility to identify the cause and consequences of backlogs as they arose, thereby enabling the right decisions to be taken in managing them and keeping them under control. For example, the system identified whether a backlog occurring was of a short-term nature caused by something such as an unexpected and temporary absence, or whether it was more deep rooted such as the work growing to the point at which it was outstripping the resources assigned to it. The weekly dissemination of this information to key managers has, it is believed, helped to keep firmly under control any backlogs that have arisen since the system was introduced.

Targets

Shortly after introducing the new Management Information System we set ourselves the target of turning round all documents in our Mainstream business within five working days. At a time when it was not unusual for some offices to be taking eight weeks or more to return documents to our customers, this was viewed with scepticism. However, simply having something concrete to aim at, the information to manage it effectively, and the means to measure progress, in this case the length of time taken to turn round documents and the cost of not turning them round timeously, enabled us to make rapid progress. By the end of 1986/87 we were meeting this target for 97% of documents. Since then, with very rare exceptions, we have turned round all documents in our Mainstream business within the target time.

Staff involvement in design

The Management Information System was designed with the help of a local office manager specifically chosen for the job. This was important in order to ensure the new system was comprehensive, meaningful and helpful to all concerned, especially local managers and their immediate line manager. Equally important was the need to create credibility and joint 'ownership' between local and senior managers of a system radically different from what had gone before.

Dissemination of information

The Management Information System is compiled on the last working day of each week in local offices and sections and sent to the headquarters of The Stamp Office for aggregation. Aggregated information is then disseminated monthly to all managers up and down the line. This enables everyone to see how they are progressing and the contribution they are making to the organisation as a whole.

At the top end of the Management Information System is the information provided to the Board of Inland Revenue on a regular basis enabling them to see the progress of The Stamp Office (see Figure 20.1). At the start of the year the key business indicators are agreed. For each indicator a target is agreed or forecast

KEY INDICATORS	TARGETS & FORECASTS				Q1–Q4 (monthly progress, Apr–Mar)	Year To Date	Estimated Outturn
	At March 93	⊘	/	●			
1. OUTPUTS							
1.1 Documents/Transactions processed	5.764 million	>100%	95–100%	<95%		109%	6.1 million
1.2 Duty collected	£1,683 million	>100%	95–100%	<95%		104%	£1,700m
2. INPUTS							
2.1 Number of people employed	220 manyears	<100%	100–102%	>102%		93%	205
2.2 Direct running costs	£5.090 million	<100%	100–102%	>102%		93%	£5.420m
3. CUSTOMER SERVICE							
3.1 Documents/Corres processed in 8 working days	97.5%	>100%	97–100%	<97%		101%	98.5%
3.2 Documents/Corres processed in 15 working days	98.5%	>100%	97–100%	<97%		101%	99.6%
3.3 Customer satisfaction survey	1993>1989	93=89	93>89	93<89	survey conducted		
4. COST EFFICIENCY							
4.1 Documents processed per employee	26,200	>100%	97–100%	<97%		116%	29,750
4.2 Cost of processing 1 document/transaction	99 pence	<100%	100–103%	>103%		85%	89p
4.3 Cost of collecting £100	34 pence	<100%	100–103%	>103%		89%	32p
5. COMPLIANCE							
5.1 Documents/transactions attracting additional duty	57,300	>100%	95–100%	<95%		81%	43,000
5.2 Additional duty collected	£6.45 million	>100%	95–100%	<95%		85%	£5.4m
5.3 Documents/transactions received with too much duty	2,700	<100%	100–105%	>105%		75%	2,000
5.4 Excess duty repaid	£0.4 million	<100%	100–105%	>105%		87%	£0.25m
6. CARING FOR STAFF							
6.1 Employee satisfaction survey	1993>1991	93>91	93=91	93<91	survey results awaited / n/a	n/a	n/a
6.2 Amount of Training/Coaching provided per employee	50 hours	>100%	95–100%	<95%		60%	30 hours

Prepared by Keith Hodgson
14 February 1994

Figure 20.1 The Stamp Office –Annual Management Plan 1993/94 Business fundamentals progress table.

determined. By means of simple illustrative graphics progress can be monitored at a glance. This reporting medium is an example of something I have seen used to great effect in the private sector on more than one occasion. The report constitutes a significant part of the writer's own annual performance agreement.

❏ Reorganisation

Reorganising The Stamp Office was effected on a gradual basis rather than with a 'big bang'. The objective of improving customer service while keeping costs within our existing budgets and Public Expenditure Survey baselines underpinned our actions.

The local offices were already starting to respond well to their greater management responsibilities (of which more is said in the next section) and it was becoming apparent that their small size was a real asset in delivering our Mainstream business. They had:

- a good rapport with customers
- good team spirit
- a flexibility (which hitherto had lain dormant) to cope with fluctuating workloads
- a considerable potential for what is now referred to as 'ownership' of their work.

The Management Information System also indicated that local offices provided the best value for money in our Mainstream business.

Consequently, instead of closing them and centralising the work (the preferred option of the staff inspectors which had caused concern for our customers) we decided to entrust as much Mainstream business as practical to the local office network. Even so, because of the reforms to stamp duty, some of the local offices were still too small to be viable and two of them were closed.

There were also two mainstream offices in London, one located in the City, the other less than two miles away attached to our head office in Bush House. The lease on the office in the City expired and the annual charges on new accommodation in the area were going to be between one-quarter and half a million pounds. Considering that only 15 people were employed in the City office, an annual accommodation charge overhead of £20,000 to £30,000 per person did not represent good value for money and was more than could be afforded. By decentralising some mainstream work from London to local offices and making better use of our accommodation in Bush House, it was possible to close the office in the City altogether. It was recognised that closing this office was removing a facility from customers, consequently some of the savings from the merger were used to improve and enhance the service in Bush House, especially for those who were previously customers in the City.

One other significant aspect of the reorganisation was to build a cost centre structure which mirrored The Stamp Office both functionally and geographically (see Figure 20.2).

LOCATION / FUNCTION	London	Provincial Network	Worthing	Edinburgh
Mainstream	Bush House:— Public counter Postal section Stamping section	Belfast mainstream Birmingham Bristol Cardiff etc		Mainstream
Adjudication		Belfast adjudication	Adjudication	Adjudication
Stock Market			Centre Office Stamp Duty Reserve Tax Unit	
Management and Support	Management Personnel Engineers		Management	Management

Figure 20.2. The Stamp Office organisation (in part) by cost centre structure.

The purpose of this was to enable us to identify the cost of any of our businesses in any of our offices, thereby aiding decision making and squaring the circle between the Management Information System and the organisation. In some of the larger offices there is more than one cost centre for a particular business function, but never the reverse. This is to facilitate the delegation of management to its appropriate level.

❏ The role of managers

A starting point is a belief in empowering people. People are capable of a lot more than we think, but all too often we do not give them the opportunity to develop their capabilities. At the start of our change process the main duties of officers in charge of local offices and sections were dealing with the more complex documents and queries from customers, and supervising their staff. Most of them had been given their jobs on the strength of their technical skills, with management ability being incidental. It is doubtful whether more than one or two regarded themselves as managers in the true meaning of the word. Management, including workstate problems, was perceived to be for the more senior people at The Stamp Office headquarters. This situation had to change in order to realise the potential benefits offered by the Management Information System and organisational changes.

We started by changing priorities and making management the first responsibility of officers in charge of local offices and sections. Whenever vacancies arose for officers in charge, particularly in local offices, the main pre-requisite for selection was changed to management ability. In one particular office dogged by persistent arrears of work, changing the manager and putting a square peg into a square hole produced an improvement in productivity of over 40% in less than a month.

Shortly thereafter the advent of Line Management Budgeting provided a tremendous opportunity for empowering local managers. We had no hesitation whatsoever in delegating authority and responsibility for budgets to local office and section level. Within the overall limits of their budgets, managers were empowered to resolve their own problems. The area where this had immediate impact was in managing workloads and backlogs. Previously a small group of relief staff controlled and organised by head office was responsible for providing help to local offices. Using the Management Information System, local knowledge and taking relative costs into account, local managers, in consultation with their immediate line manager if necessary, decided how to solve these problems for themselves. When they deemed it appropriate, managers continued to 'buy' relief, although increasingly this came from other local offices rather than head office. Other methods utilised included overtime and employing casuals. There have even been occasions when local offices have transferred work between themselves. Within a short time the pool of relief staff at head office was surplus to requirements. Customers were getting a better service. Costs were going down.

The success of delegating Line Management Budgeting to local office and section level very soon persuaded us to do the same with Public Expenditure Survey (PES) forecasting. A system was developed whereby once a year, in the autumn, budget holders have to complete a spreadsheet on which they estimate their current year's outturn, bid for the following year's budget, and forecast their PES requirements (manpower and money) for the three years after that. This too has proved successful. Our record to 1993/94 shows that we have never sought to increase our PES baselines other than for permitted price increases. Occasionally we have offered to reduce our baseline. Our budget bids have been equal to or less than the PES baseline and we have always lived within our budget.

One other important aspect of converting officers in charge into managers was the introduction of an annual Stamp Office Managers Conference. The main purpose of the conference was fourfold:

- to share strategic management information with all managers, particularly that relating to the year ahead
- to review progress
- to provide a forum for the exchange of experience, ideas and best practice

- to acknowledge publicly the contributions of our managers to the success of the business.

At the same time as putting our management house in order we ensured our technical standards did not suffer.

❑ The results

All of the foregoing had the objective of focusing people's attention on bringing a more business-like approach to the work of the office in order to deliver a quality customer service. We adopted a simple analogy from the outset, and we are still using it. Customers need our stamps. If they have got the money, we have got the goods. Basically the transaction is no different from going into Marks and Spencer to buy a shirt. For the right amount of money they will sell you a shirt. For the right amount of money we will sell you a stamp.

During this period customer service was generally gaining a higher profile within the Inland Revenue. The Board of Inland Revenue, jointly with the Board of Customs and Excise, issued a Taxpayers Charter emphasising in particular that all taxpayers were entitled, inter alia, to expect courtesy and consideration, fairness and impartiality, help and information.

❑ Our first customer survey

In 1989 we decided to conduct our first customer survey to ascertain whether:

- the organisational and management changes we had made had led to an improvement in the service provided
- we were meeting our obligations under the Taxpayers Charter
- we were providing enough information to customers about stamp duty.

The survey was confined to our Mainstream business and conducted with the help of the Operational Research division of the Inland Revenue. The survey concentrated on three main areas: Personal service, Office Environments and Communications. Nearly 3,500 questionnaires were issued of which 58% were completed and returned. We discovered that over 80% of our customers use our service at least once a week and 96% at least once a month.

Personal service

Personal Service was measured in terms of speed, competence, fairness, efficiency and courtesy. Overall we were pleased with the results. In all aspects nine out of every ten customers rated our service as good or excellent, one out of every three said we had improved, and, with the exception of one office, only one customer out of every 95 said we were poor. At that one office one customer in ten said the speed of service was poor. It was a measure of the progress we were making that the staff of that office needed no encouragement whatsoever to set about improving matters. They revised the office layout, revised procedures and by means of their own newsletter kept their customers informed of how they were responding to the need for a speedier service.

The offices

The public areas of our offices were measured in terms of layout, cleanliness, and tidiness. The results were encouraging in as much as one out of every three customers said we had improved. The results were otherwise very mixed. Some offices were rated highly while others were rated poorly. In response we improved facilities at the two worst offices straightaway. This was followed by the introduction of a five year rolling programme of office refurbishments with the order of priority being set by the customer.

Subject only to budgetary constraints, local managers were given complete freedom over refurbishing and redecorating their offices. This was in keeping with the philosophy of giving them greater 'ownership' of their offices in the belief that in turn this would lead, inter alia, to better delivery of the end product to our customers.

Communications

Communications were measured in terms of the clarity and legibility of correspondence and the availability of information on stamp duty. We also asked customers whether they wanted more information and if so in which aspects of stamp duty they were interested.

Although nearly two-thirds of our customers rated our correspondence good or excellent, one in fifteen rated it poor. It was clear that we had let ourselves down on the presentational quality of our forms and letters. As a consequence we standardised all of our stationery into a consistent style and layout (we had previously had a diverse variety of letter headed paper lacking in consistency). 80% of our customers said they had not seen our stamp duty leaflets and those who had gave them mixed ratings. The overwhelming majority of customers said they wanted more information on various aspects of stamp duty. On the basis of responses from the survey and monitoring telephone enquiries, we identified the aspects of stamp duty of most interest to our customers and introduced a new series of distinctive stamp duty leaflets accordingly.

❑ Importance of the survey

The customer survey was a very helpful and valuable experience for The Stamp

Office. It increased our level of awareness of the need to focus attention upon serving the customer. Furthermore, our staff took deserved satisfaction from learning how well the level of personal service they were providing was regarded by their customers. This in turn raised morale. The survey established the baseline from which we could measure progress and identified areas for improvement, thereby setting the agenda for the future.

Keeping it going

By 1991 we had delivered the strategy outlined in the early part of this chapter. A customer survey of our mainstream business had been conducted, a baseline established, and an action plan initiated. The problem was knowing how to keep the momentum going. We turned to consultants experienced in the delivery of customer service and quality.

❏ Staff survey

The consultants started by conducting a comprehensive Stamp Office employee survey to establish attitudes and perceptions towards such issues as quality, customer service, management style, organisation and communications. The results contained some good news and some uncomfortable news, the latter not unexpected. On the good news front we learned that the commitment to customer service of people in The Stamp Office was higher than in any other organisation with which the consultants had been associated, including a high street retailer well known for the quality of customer service. At the other end of the spectrum we found people had major concerns over their long-term future and career prospects. In between these extremes we found that:

- generally the aims and objectives of The Stamp Office were fully understood
- there was an above average loyalty to people's immediate superiors
- communications had improved and were above average.

❏ Management workshop

The consultants followed this up by conducting a two-day workshop for the senior management team, the aims of which included:

- a greater understanding of the ideas and concepts associated with quality and excellence
- an introduction to the customer/supplier chain

- focusing upon service delivery to our own customers, internal as well as external.

Perhaps the most significant and far reaching piece of work to emerge from this was a Stamp Office mission statement:

COMMITTED TO PROVIDING THE BEST QUALITY SERVICE
IN THE BUSINESS OF GOVERNMENT

❏ Mission statement

The mission statement has helped to clarify and focus our attention on what we are trying to achieve and has stimulated ideas and actions. We have conducted customer surveys in our specialist businesses of Adjudication and the Stock Exchange and of our telephone enquiry section. All of these surveys:

- have produced satisfying results
- have established baselines
- have led to actions designed to improve the service further
- will be repeated at two yearly intervals.

One outcome of the telephone enquiry section survey concerned investing in telephone queuing equipment. We were prepared to install this equipment until our customers said they preferred to get an engaged tone rather than hang on until a line was free. It left them free to get on with other work. Without this customer input we would have spent money in the belief that we were providing a welcome improvement in the service when in fact we were doing nothing of the sort.

❏ Customer promise

Our public offices prominently display The Stamp Office Customer Promise. This is a full size poster containing our mission statement, the level of service customers can expect, and what to do and who to turn to in the event of being dissatisfied with the service. The poster features the name and photograph of the local manager. Satisfaction sheets are also displayed and made available at every public counter.

❏ Training

Training plays an important part in delivering customer service. Everyone in The Stamp Office has received customer service training using the medium of inter–active video. Customer service also features in our new entrant introductory training course. An important part of the Controller of Stamps' job is to put in an appearance at this introductory course, not only to meet people new to The Stamp Office, but also to emphasise our mission statement and the priority we give to customer service and quality. Everyone in The Stamp Office also receives training in telephone techniques and more recently we have developed our own Quality Awareness training course based upon the Sunday Times business video series. All of our senior and middle managers have received this training and we are now extending it to everyone else within The Stamp Office. Again it is regarded as essential for the Controller of Stamps to put in an appearance so that no one can be in any doubt about the commitment to quality and customer service.

❏ Latest results

The latest customer survey of our Mainstream business has just been completed and the results show that we have continued to make significant improvements in all areas. 95% of our customers now rate our level of personal service good or excellent, of which nearly half rate us excellent. Furthermore, in several aspects there is not one customer who rates the service below average. Customers find the public areas of our offices more agreeable and the quality of our correspondence improved. The new series of information leaflets is being seen by more customers (although still not as many as we would like) with the quality of the leaflets rated very highly. A new action programme is being drawn up by reference to the survey results.

Conclusion

It has been a long journey to get where we are today. We have followed our instincts as much as the textbooks. We have made our fair share of mistakes along the way and with the benefit of hindsight we could probably have made progress more quickly. However we have achieved much of what we set out to do. A huge slice of the credit for this is down to the people in The Stamp Office, especially those dealing directly with the customers. They have responded well to the new challenges and worked with a pride, dedication and determination which all too often is taken for granted. We are now much more like a business in the way we operate, with customer service firmly embedded as our top priority.

The pursuit of customer service can produce some gratifying surprises. Most recently, at one local office, a group of around 30 customers, on learning of the impending retirement of one of our people, organised a collection amongst themselves. Representatives of the group came to the office, made an appropriate farewell speech and presented our retiring officer with a bottle of perfume and a cheque for £140. We still have a long way to go, but having discovered the absolute satisfaction of a customer saying a genuine 'thank you', we remain more than ever

COMMITTED TO PROVIDING THE BEST QUALITY SERVICE

IN THE BUSINESS OF GOVERNMENT

About the author

Keith Hodgson joined the civil service in 1965. After serving in the Ministry of Transport, the Civil Service Pay Research Unit and various parts of the Inland Revenue, he joined The Stamp Office as its Deputy Controller in 1982 and was appointed Controller of Stamps in 1990.

Chapter 21

A positive approach to contracting-out in Berkshire County Council

Cheryl Coppell

Berkshire County Council has gained a national reputation for its externalisation policies. Externalisation is a word coined by Berkshire, and now in wide use, which loosely means transferring functions previously undertaken directly by local government into the private or voluntary sectors. This policy has led to some dramatic organisational changes at Berkshire. Twenty major contracts have been placed covering a broad range of activities from grounds maintenance to financial services. The policy has significantly reduced the directly employed staff and changed the nature and shape of the organisation. This chapter deals with the thinking behind the policy of externalisation at Berkshire and provides some insight into the experiences Berkshire has gained over the last five years.

The remainder of the chapter is divided into the following main sections:

- a brief background to Berkshire County Council
- the local government scene
- local government and competitive tendering
- externalisation in Berkshire - the early stages
- broadening the strategy to white collar CCT
- general lessons from Berkshire's contracting experience
- implications of contracting for the organisation as a whole.

Reference is made to three case studies, covering school meals, highways and planning services and financial services.

Brief background to Berkshire County Council

Berkshire is a mid sized county. It is long and thin, straddling either side of the M4 from Slough in the east to Hungerford in the west. It is a very varied county both geographically and socially. The centre is dominated by the county town of

Reading. The edges of the county are extremes. Slough is a busy industrial town bordering London, while Newbury District is rural and sparsely populated, spreading outwards through areas of outstanding natural beauty to the edges of the Wiltshire Downs.

Berkshire has experienced a prolonged and sustained population growth over the last thirty years. The new town of Bracknell is within its borders. Most areas of the county have benefited from the growth of new hi-tech industry moving into the Thames Valley Area. This growth has made Berkshire a relatively affluent area.

However, this has not resulted in Berkshire County Council's budget situation being an easy one. The County has, over the last few decades, had to upgrade the local infrastructure substantially and continues to service a large loan debt as a result of this activity. This means that the County is in the position of having to find savings and force out efficiencies at every budget cycle. It consequently struggles to provide the sort of capital investment in services that is required by many of the legislative pressures emerging both from central government and from Europe. The County has been traditionally Conservative controlled, although the towns of Slough and Reading deliver a substantial number of Labour councillors. In recent years support for the Liberal Democrat party in areas such as Windsor and Maidenhead and Newbury has grown substantially. After the local government elections in 1989, the Conservatives still held control of the County but only by the casting vote of the Chairman of the Council. A by-election in late 1991 was lost to the Democrats and control of the Council was formally taken by a Labour-Liberal Democrat Alliance in May 1992. In the 1993 local government elections the Labour-Liberal Democrat Alliance gained clear overall control of the County and has held it ever since.

Since 1988 the Council has changed significantly under both the Conservatives and the Liberal-Democrat/Labour Alliance. In 1988 the County was a very traditional County Council, a large organisation, typified by large scale operations, by professionalism, departmentalism and central budget controls. The appointment of a new Chief Executive took the County through a period of rapid change as he sought to bring the organisation down to manageable proportions. He introduced devolved management, empowered small business units to manage and control their own budgets and introduced new attitudes and new skills into the organisation. Within this framework, the externalisation policy grew and came to form a major part of the organisational strategy of the County. This strategy succeeded in straddling the political divide and surviving a change of political control.

Figures 21.1. and 21.2. illustrate graphically how much the organisation has changed since 1988. Its current organisational structure does not lend itself to traditional hierarchical management charts and new ways have had to be found of depicting the way it is organised.

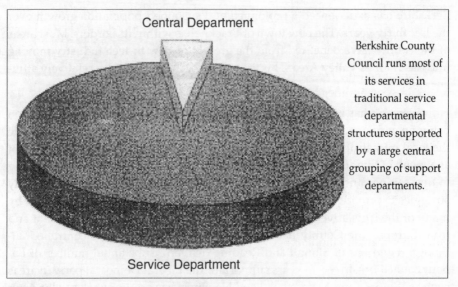

Figure 21.1. Berkshire County Council 1988.

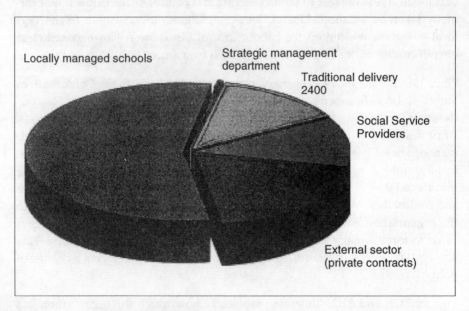

Figure 21.2. Berkshire County Council 1993/94

The Local Government scene

The last ten years have seen local government under siege. Immense legislative change coupled with stringent financial constraints imposed by central Government have dominated local authority thinking and action. The Government has:

- introduced legislation to force councils to tender competitively for some of their traditional services
- changed the face of education through delegation of management responsibilities to schools
- removed further education and careers services from local government control
- enforced changes in social services provision through care in the community
- increased pressure for performance through the Citizen's Charter initiative.

But, rather than sinking, local government has risen to these challenges and has undertaken a radical overhaul of itself, introducing many new and innovative methods of delivering services and getting closer to their customers and communities.

Given the scale of change, it is perhaps not surprising that no single political or organisational strategy has emerged. Rather, a whole series of strategies has been developed across the face of local government. The Local Government Management Board, in their publication *Fitness for Purpose*, have recently categorised the kinds of organisational responses developed by local government into four broad categories :

- those with an emphasis on direct service provision
- those with a commercial approach
- those focusing on community governance
- those with an emphasis on a neighbourhood approach.

❑ How Berkshire's strategies fit in

Berkshire County Council typifies the commercial approach, indeed it has probably moved further and faster down the commercial route than any other local authority. In 1988 Berkshire was a very traditional local authority. Now it typifies many of the features to be found in local authorities that have attempted to introduce a more business-like approach to delivering services:

- Berkshire has considerably slimmed down both its committee system (the process whereby elected Members take decisions) and its departmental structure (its executive arm)

- the organisation has been broken down into manageable cost centres or business units. They operate on a semi-autonomous basis, taking responsibility for delivery of services and managing their budgets. The business planning process is well developed
- the cost centres delivering direct services act on a contractual or quasi-contractual basis in purchasing services from other parts of the organisation (for example they have a direct relationship with the contractors providing payroll and IT services to them)
- Berkshire has moved down the route of introducing purchaser/provider splits within its organisation
- it has devolved more responsibility than is statutorily required to its schools
- the delivery of Social Services has been separated from the purchasing side of Social Services
- performance indicators and performance information are considered an important way of judging achievement.

Berkshire has not adopted this organisational emphasis to the exclusion of other organisational strategies, although it has probably been the dominant strategy. Berkshire is also interested in empowering neighbourhoods and communities and there has always been a strong drive towards community governance. The County also has a strong service bias. Support functions are clearly seen to exist to further the better delivery of responsive services to users. But Berkshire has always seen itself as something much more than just the sum of the services it provides. It retains a determination to influence the environment as a whole for the benefit of its residents.

❏ Local government and competitive tendering

Those authorities that have adopted a commercial approach tend to be the ones most comfortable with the implications of the Government's Compulsory Competitive Tendering legislation. In 1988 the Government introduced legislation to force local authorities to tender for certain services previously carried out by local government itself. The thinking was that the introduction of competition to services such as refuse collection, grounds maintenance, cleaning and catering would introduce new efficiencies into local government. This legislation has now been extended and over the next three to four years local government will be forced to tender at least partially for services such as finance, legal, personnel, general administrative and construction related activities.

Along with the primary legislation, the Government introduced a fairly prescriptive set of guidelines and procedures that local authorities have to follow when they tender to place contracts. These regulations have been systematically tightened and, together with European Community Directives, Standing Orders and financial regulations, provide a formidable panoply of 'red-tape' through which a local authority must now find its way prior to letting a contract.

The stated aim of the Government rules and regulations has been to provide a level playing field for private contractors and thus create a market for the services which the Government believe should be exposed to competition. Local authorities are still allowed to bid as 'direct service organisations' (DSOs), but the Government's regulations seek to ensure that internal DSO bids do not have an unfair advantage over private contractors.

The local government response to Compulsory Competitive Tendering (CCT) has been as varied as the organisational strategies outlined above suggest. Some local authorities have fought hard within the legal framework to retain as many DSOs as possible. Others have adopted a more agnostic approach. Yet others, typified by Berkshire, have sought to place their contracts directly into the private sector and discouraged DSOs.

Although there is a broad split along political lines between authorities that have sought to retain DSOs and those that have sought to place services with private contractors, the split is by no means a political one alone. Indeed, many of the arguments used to justify Berkshire's externalisation policy have stood the test of Berkshire changing political control from Conservative to a Liberal-Democrat/Labour Alliance. The reasons for this stem from the belief that the Government's legislation and procedures are flawed and do not result in the best deal for either the service or the staff involved. Thus, even if DSOs win contracts, in the long run many believe this may not be the best solution for either the staff or the services.

Berkshire, along with some other authorities, believe that DSOs are an inherently unstable or temporary form of contractual arrangement. This is because, so long as a DSO is involved, prescriptive Government guidelines continue to govern the way the contract is run. For example, legislation forces local authorities to place contracts of a certain length, and forces authorities to re-tender at certain times if the contract is won by an internal DSO. External limits on trading profit and loss are also imposed. The Government also retains the right to force Councils to retender part way through a contract if they believe that significant losses are being incurred by the contractor. On top of this, the trading activities of DSOs are strictly limited. They are set up to operate a particular contract with a particular local authority and may only trade with other organisations under strict guidelines. Trading is limited to other public sector bodies and, even then, it must be only 'at the margin'. In other words, a DSO cannot form itself into a larger business on the back of the contract that has brought it into being.

These regulations have led many, including Berkshire, to believe that DSOs have a constant up hill struggle to survive.

- They must initially compete openly with the private sector. As the market grows and big business becomes involved, it is increasingly likely that the bids will become more competitive or worse, a large private company may choose to 'buy' a contract by bidding as a 'loss leader' in order to gain a foot-hold in the market or in order to improve their market share.

- If a DSO wins a contract, there is little opportunity to expand the business base. On re-tendering they face similar hurdles to those encountered initially, but in the meantime the external market has grown stronger, and external companies will have had the opportunity to gain experience and a skill base by managing other contracts.

- Some believe that the Government's intention may be to eliminate DSOs from the market altogether. The regulations so far have made it increasingly difficult for DSOs. It is only a small additional step for the next legislative or procedural change to forbid DSOs from bidding in the next round of tendering.

- DSOs are not backed by private companies that may be prepared to provide substantial investment to improve productivity or service quality. Local authorities simply do not have access to that sort of capital, quite apart from the regulations which control investment in internal contracts.

This is a rather pessimistic scenario for DSOs. Those that support the Direct Service Provision model would acknowledge many of the above difficulties but continue to fight for the survival of DSOs in the belief that the role of local government as a local employer is a vital one and that the public sector ethic will be lost if all contracts move into the private sector. Many also fear private sector manipulation of the market once sufficient market share has been gained. Nevertheless, given all of the above, it is clear that under the current legislative framework an argument can be constructed that contracting directly to the private sector has many advantages:

- in the private sector contracts can be placed for a contract period considered appropriate by the local authority

- the activity ceases to be affected by the Government's rules and regulations which govern the compulsory tendering route while DSOs are still bidding (although European contracting guidelines do still have to be followed)

- the staff can be placed with a contract in the private sector with an agreement that their terms and conditions are protected; this right is now being enshrined in law via the Transfer of Undertakings Regulations (TUPE) as noted in Chapter 14, although the exact level of protection is still the subject of some debate

- the private firm can develop its business base, providing a better chance of its winning the contract the next time round and better opportunities for staff development and growth as it wins contracts and expands into other areas

- a contract negotiated with a private firm, particularly a large firm, can be hard negotiated. There may be more opportunities for insisting on high quality performance measures, quality systems and a good price than when negotiating with a hard pressed DSO battling to keep its margins down

- private firms can bring with them the potential for growing and investing in the business in a way that in-house DSOs cannot, given the hard pressed financial position of most local authorities.

It is against this background that many local authorities, including Berkshire, have chosen to embrace the external market as the best opportunity to protect their staff and service levels in the face of the Government's Compulsory Competitive Tendering legislation.

Once the attitude towards contracting-out becomes a positive rather than a negative one some of the benefits of competition can be openly discussed. In Berkshire, with its history of embracing the market, a more even handed approach is often taken to competition than would be the case elsewhere. The following analysis of the opportunities as well as the dangers is typical of the thinking at Berkshire. If used carefully competition is an opportunity to improve quality because it means :

for the client side

- specifying the service (what is really required rather than what history dictates)

- a chance to get new ideas and approaches from the market

- a test of value for money against all comers

- in the case of central support functions it provides an opportunity to re-orientate specifications towards the front-line customer rather than the more traditional centralist approach

- the introduction of contract management techniques which focus on quality of outputs not processes.

for the staff group

- a stimulus towards real blank page examination of the service
- rapid cultural change towards a customer orientation
- if they swing behind the move into the market then it can produce a real rejuvenation in commitment
- for some support services, market testing/externalisation will be the only way to retain valued staff because a declining internal market will mean redundancy unless they can widen their customer base
- staff can be offered a relatively secure long term future.

Dangers

Berkshire has chosen to follow the contracting route as a strategy for making the best out of the prescriptive Government regulations surrounding the compulsory competitive tendering legislation. However, it is always realised that there are inherent dangers in following this route:

- if you specify the service badly and/or do not build sufficient flexibility into the contract you can get tied into the wrong service, the worst of all worlds
- the collapse of your supplier if the market is not strong
- unless special measures are taken the period of transition from in-house to external provider always marks a temporary drop in quality
- client side expertise is essential as a real contractual relationship is in place from day one
- in the long term there is no guarantee that the market will not be taken over by a small group of suppliers who can control price and quality.

Externalisation in Berkshire – the early stages

The Government's first phase of compulsory competitive tendering legislation was focused on the 'blue collar' local government workforce. It targeted services such as refuse collection, school meals, grounds maintenance and highway maintenance. This first phase of blue collar CCT caused problems for Berkshire County Council as it did for many other local authorities. Many of the services designated for CCT were already in difficulties. For example, the school meals service was struggling and overspending, and the Council was unable to contemplate how it could find the capital required to upgrade kitchens to meet all of the new health and safety and hygiene legislation.

A number of contracts had been let to DSOs, but the DSOs had already begun to lose money. The exact reasons varied between contracts, but the overriding theme was the lack of expertise of the management within the contracts, inherited problems of weak management from the past and an underlying lack of capital investment to improve plant and equipment.

Given the overall drain on resources, the difficulties of some of the DSOs and in the face of the rolling CCT programme, the Chief Executive and members decided to call in some expert help. They appointed a Director of Commercial Services. He was from the private sector and had experience of contracting. This proved the turning point for contracting policies in Berkshire.

It is still the case that many local authorities are somewhat frightened by the idea of the private sector. The private sector certainly used to regard local authorities with some disdain. Bringing both together into open discussion is often the obstacle that many authorities fail to get over. The new Director of Commercial Services quickly appraised the contracting possibilities within Berkshire and then set about explaining to the private sector that there were good business deals to be struck that would be mutually beneficial. Several successful externalisations were accomplished over the next few years.

❑ Case study 1 – the school meals service

The school meals service employed 1100 staff, managed by five area managers. It was traditionally overspending by £110,000 per annum. When faced with Compulsory Competitive Tendering the 350 schools were divided into eight contract districts, all of which were won by the Direct Service operation. This was no surprise as there was very little competition from the private sector at this time. But there were severe question marks over the long term viability of the DSO. The overspend had not been turned round, the same management was still in charge and there was no money to fund the improvements in equipment required in the kitchens to meet the requirements of the 1990 Food Act.

The Director of Commercial Services set out to explain to the private sector that the school meals contract was a multi-million pound business in which they should be interested. After some negotiations a partner was found, B.E.T. The business was transferred with a package to ensure each school could gain part of the returns, that the contractor would provide funding towards new equipment costs and that the staff were transferred on their existing terms and conditions. Within a short period of time the contract had been turned round. Private sector experience of management in the catering trade and new equipment, together with the dedicated school kitchen staff, have combined to provide a high quality service to Berkshire's schools ever since.

The contract was extended in 1993 at the request of the schools themselves. Since the original contract was signed, new legislation governing the local management of schools has meant that schools, not the local authority, now have responsibility for arranging their own contracts for services such as catering. Nevertheless, when the contracts came up for renewal, the schools unanimously asked for the County to re-let a corporate contract.

Contract monitoring has been shared between the schools, who have responsibility for the day to day administration of the contract, and the Central Contract Services Management Unit, which has responsibility for in depth hygiene and health and safety checks. This arrangement seems to have won the confidence and support of schools and has proved a cost effective method of providing contract management.

The same pattern began to emerge for other blue collar CCT services. Externalisation policies developed and soon Berkshire had moved to the position of having no internal DSOs.

❏ General lessons from the first phase

The policy could not have been so successful if it had been based on savings alone. One of the key factors in its success has been that it had been able to win the confidence of the workforce through the negotiation of deals that transferred across the existing staff in their existing terms and conditions. In other words, Berkshire had commenced a 'Transfer of Undertaking' policy long before it became a talking point in placing local government contracts. It was this aspect of the policy which gave it sufficient all party support to enable it to survive the change in political control in 1992. The Labour and Liberal Democrat Alliance supported the concept that support services, which were not direct service provision, should continue to be externalised if it resulted in protecting staff, while delivering savings which could be re-directed towards direct service provision.

Broadening the strategy to white collar CCT

By 1991 the policy of externalisation was well established and the County was seeking to come to terms with the changes that had taken place over the last few years. A review of support service provision commenced which aimed to set a direction for the services likely to be subject to white collar CCT. This extract from a June 1991 committee report spells out the changes that had happened and were still expected and it epitomises the sort of changing organisational thinking that the early externalisation policies had generated.

> Over the past four years the Council has made substantial strides in focusing management effort towards improving services to its clients; Berkshire has moved from a monolithic, hierarchical, bureaucratic organisation to an increasingly more

efficient and effective one, based on modern business methods using devolved cost centre management, a clear split between client and contractor functions and an enabling style which has seen a number of services pass to new management in the private sector, or the Council's own Commercial Services Department.

❏ More change is planned

The pace of externalisation was likely to quicken under the impact of capping and the continuing drive for efficiency. The challenge for support services both within service departments and within central departments was to be responsive to these changes and to reduce costs, keeping overheads to a minimum whilst ensuring that 'the enabling authority' had the right level of central direction and monitoring capability to give the Council corporate control of the organisation and its full range of responsibilities.

Since 1988 about 2500 staff had been transferred out of the Council's direct control through externalisation programmes, taking with them contracts for the provision of about £28m worth of direct services. The programme had been in response to the explicit objective of government policy that local authorities should withdraw from the direct provision of service. The pace of change in direct services was still not slackening; delegation to schools was due to pick up in 1991 and 1992, further education was to be removed from local authority control, Social Services was splitting its direct provision of services away from its core role of assessing needs. These changes in service provision needed and ought to bring with them substantial reductions in central overheads.

The numbers of central support staff in total had declined over the last three years. However, within the overall total some had shrunk considerably, particularly through externalisation policies while others had grown. Given the numbers of service providers moving outside direct Council control it might have been expected that a more significant drop in central support staff could have been achieved. It was therefore a high priority to review and plan a new structure for support services which delivered substantially reduced central overheads.

Against this background Berkshire decided that for all support services, many of which were soon to face white collar CCT, it would be more advantageous for the authority and its staff to plan well in advance and to arrange contracts which suited Berkshire rather than the Government. Each service identified the functions it covered and 'services' offered to other parts of the organisation (for example, payroll and IT maintenance) and separated these from corporate functions which are necessary to the running of any large democratic organisation (for example, corporate budget and IT strategy). The 'service' elements were then moved into business units where they were given two years to prepare business plans and organise themselves for the future.

In the face of planning for a future in which they faced white collar CCT and increasing downward pressure on their budgets, several staff and management groups opted to plan positively for the externalisation of their services. The main reason for this was the success of past externalisation policies where staff had been protected and contracts and businesses had thrived in the private sector. In contrast, were they to be forced down a compulsory competitive tendering route, even if they were contracted as a DSO, they feared they would not be able to grow their business and that their future would be uncertain.

The first management and staff group to begin actively courting externalisation was the Highways and Planning Department. They began to canvass political views on their plans as early as 1990. Following the review of support services the County Treasurer and his staff also requested members to externalise the finance function, as did the Estates and Valuation Division of the old Property Department.

❏ Case study 2 – Highways and Planning externalisation on the 1 April 1993

Berkshire County Council externalised its entire Highways and Planning Department. Over 300 staff, including the senior management, transferred to the private sector as part of the largest contract for professional services awarded at that time by any UK authority. The contract was worth over £9m per annum in fees. The contract produced direct savings to the Council in excess of £1.3m per annum and it still dwarfs the Government's proposals for a limited amount of compulsory competitive tendering in construction related services.

As has been said, the initial move towards externalisation was made by the management of the Highways and Planning Department themselves. The Department was made up of a merged County Planning and Surveyor's Department providing high quality integrated services to the County. However, despite its reputation as a well run and innovative department, the management recognised that there were powerful external influences, competition, local government review and uncertain financial regimes, which would mean it would be increasingly difficult to sustain the current range of services and avoid irreversible reduction in existing capability and capacity.

The Government's compulsory competitive tendering legislation was seen as a particular threat. The legislation seemed likely to pick out various parts of the service and force those parts to compete for contracts. The department could not see the sense in this and feared the proscriptive nature of the Government's tendering route if they waited to be forced into action.

The financial position in Berkshire was unlikely to improve. Budget rounds were going to get tougher and some changes were inevitable. The management of the department reasoned that it would be better to take the opportunity of completely re-specifying what Berkshire wanted from the integrated service and then re-align the department to deliver those services contractually. Staff would then be in a better position to pick up additional work as the Council's own requirements (or funding) for work declined.

The local government review was also a strong consideration. Clearly, whatever the outcome of the Government's review of the structure of local government, there was going to be a need to provide strategic planning and highways functions. The management of Berkshire's Highways and Planning Department reasoned that they would provide these services to smaller unitary authorities via contract.

All of these pressures came together to lead the management team within the Highways and Planning Department to propose that the Council consider a possible external future. They canvassed the staff who were prepared to support the initiative.

The Council set up a small policy panel to begin the long investigation of the advantages and disadvantages of the external route proposed by the management. A significant amount of time was spent by this small group of members considering all of the issues that had to be satisfactorily resolved before a recommendation to proceed could be given. High on the list were the following issues.

- How would 'sensitive' planning issues be handled? If the new company were to prepare and defend the County's structure plan those same contractors could not be allowed to sell their services to other clients who sought to find ways around that same plan.

- Was it sensible to contract for an integrated service, or should Highways and Planning be separated out into its constituent parts? Would this give better value for money?

- How would the areas where the Council itself was legally obliged to undertake specific duties be tackled?

After lengthy and due consideration the Panel recommended that it would be in the interest of the Council to proceed to test the market on the basis of contracting for a fully integrated Highways and Planning consultancy and there would be strong competition for the contract.

The management of the Highways and Planning Department then took a brave decision. They would not put forward a management buy-out proposal, they would wait to see who bid from the market and join the winning team.

After a pre-qualification and full tender process, it emerged that the analysis had been correct. There was strong competition for the contract. 148 organisations expressed an interest and over 50 subsequently provided detailed submissions. Sixty percent of the submissions were from specialist firms while the remainder were interested in providing an integrated service. A vigorous sieving exercise produced a shortlist of five consultancies. All five submitted formal tenders. Management and staff all played a part in the assessment process which was led by a team of central managers supported by external consultants.

The result was a good one for the Council and the staff. There were some redundancies as a result of the specified level of services being lower than that which the Council had previously supported. However, these reductions in service levels were budget driven and not as a result of the contract itself. They were the result of the Council clarifying its long term likely service requirements.

A small client side of around twenty people was retained by the Council to provide advice directly to elected Members and to manage the contract. The contract was let with internal quality control mechanisms to minimise duplication between client and contractor.

❏ Case study 3 – financial services

In June 1992, the County Treasurer proposed an employee buy out (EBO). His initial proposal was to negotiate a contract which left only one or two financial staff inside the organisation with the contractor delivering the vast majority of services from outside the Council. The Council responded by setting up a small panel of members to investigate the whole question of contracting for its financial services and in particular to investigate the sense of proceeding down the employee buy out route. The requirements for financial services had changed dramatically since 1988 and were still changing. The group no longer controlled the budget centrally but facilitated a process of devolved financial management. In addition, the overall quantity of service required was falling.

Previous externalisation policies had removed staff from the payroll, further contracting out was planned, the direct grant maintained schools could potentially remove a further large chunk of staff from direct employment by the authority, and the Government's plans for care in the community was putting pressure on social services providers to reorganise and possibly move to the independent or private sector.

The thinking of the EBO team was that, in this uncertain business position, it would need to build up new business elsewhere as business from Berkshire declined. As a DSO they would be unable to do this as they would be limited in their ability to trade externally. They also believed that by going early with a contract which offered an integrated range of services they would place themselves in a key position in the market.

The panel of members met to consider the whole issue. Was it sensible to externalise a service such as finance? If so, how much? Were there some services that were so critical to the running of the organisation that they should be kept in house? Should internal audit be let as part of the same contract or would this lead to conflicts of interests? Would the EBO give the Council best value for money?

The panel decided they needed expert advice and called in consultants Ernst and Young. The Ernst and Young report confirmed that they saw no reason against the contracting of financial services. However, they set down some ground rules to be followed:

- the Council should retain sufficient internal strategic advice to ensure it did not 'lose its sovereignty' over financial matters
- there was a developing market for financial services and the EBO should be tested against this market to ensure value for money
- a pre-qualification and full tender exercise should proceed
- the Council should consider carefully the advantages and disadvantages of including internal audit as part of a single contract for financial services.

The Council decided to take Ernst and Young's advice and a full market testing exercise proceeded. At the pre-qualification stage, Touche Ross joined the EBO, adding to the pool of expertise available to the authority and providing financial credibility to the proposed new company. Tough specifications were prepared, altering the original proposals from the EBO to ensure benefits for the Council and to ensure that sufficient flexibility was built in to accommodate future requirements of the County. In order to ensure value for money across all elements of financial services a group of pre-selected companies were asked to bid for individual elements of the service (payroll, audit, income collection, etc.). In addition a smaller group of four companies, including the EBO/Touche Ross partnership were asked to bid for individual elements of the service and the whole suite of financial services.

In the event, the four companies bidding for the whole package of financial services offered the best deal. Their bids were influenced by the belief that gaining the whole package of services would place them in a strong position in the market and allow flexibility to grow the business. When the tenders were fully analysed (with the help of independent consultants, Arthur Andersen) the EBO/Touche Ross bid won by a very narrow margin. The Council moved forward to sign a contract which offered a broader range of financial services to a single contract than had previously been placed by local government.

The Council retained a strong strategic team to carry out the Council's legal responsibilities and to set financial and budget strategy. It also retained some specialist contract management staff. The contract delivered some strategic advice, organisation of the budget process, payroll, income, payments and internal audit services.

The debate as to whether or not to include internal audit into an integrated contract had been a long one. If the contractor was delivering the organisation of the budget and all of the exchequer services, then arguably it would not be able to audit itself for matters of probity or system audit. In the end a compromise was reached. In Berkshire, the very high level of financial devolution means that most of the systems and procedures for approving and paying out Council funds are undertaken by cost centre managers, not by the central finance function. The contract could therefore take the responsibility for systems and probity audit in respect of cost centre managers and could undertake specific value for money or other special investigations. A small team of auditors was kept in house with the client side to undertake audit checks of the corporate finance systems managed by the contractor.

The contract was successful in that:

- staff transferred to the new contract under Transfer of Undertaking regulations
- the contract was large enough to make business sense for the contractor
- it saved the Council money from the outset
- the pricing mechanisms built into the contract ensured that as the Council continued to change shape, the contract price varied accordingly.

These are just two case studies of white collar services and how they have been contracted for Berkshire.

Berkshire has placed many more 'white collar' contracts. Notable services that have been subject to some form of externalisation are:

- architectural design
- estates and valuation
- facilities management
- mainframe computer services.

Contracting for these sorts of services requires skilful specification and contract management. Although in many ways white collar contracts are very different from blue collar contracts, the skills and techniques required for successful contracting for both types of contract are very similar. The following section summarises the lessons that Berkshire has learnt from both kinds of contractual experience.

General lessons from Berkshire's learning experience

With so much experience of contracting, it is not surprising that Berkshire has a check list of lessons to be learnt. The following section summarises the key lessons and issues to be borne in mind.

❏ Preparing for the contract – the specification

You need to know what you want before you can contract for it. It is, perhaps, surprising that this simple intent can be so difficult to achieve and needs so much attention. There are two golden rules:

- review your services prior to transfer
- specify what you want for the future, not what you may have been doing in the past.

Very early on Berkshire moved away from procedural specifications to a focus on output related specifications. This is a big leap for management and staff and, crucially, it needs clear thinking from the clients or recipients of the service to be contracted. In the case of white collar services and support services there is often organisational confusion about who does what for whom and why. Berkshire has learnt that unless you answer these questions clearly before you write the specification you will be contracting for a muddle. It is hard to achieve this and it needs:

- clear and objective thinking about service trends and directions
- attitudal change within the staff and managers of the service to be contracted and the client side or service recipients
- a hard look at old systems, practices and management structures.

In order to facilitate this work, it is essential to establish a client side team early. This stage is a very fine balance between being sure that the client side is thinking clearly and with a fresh mind and utilising all of the critically important service information available from staff and managers likely to be within the contract whose experience will be invaluable.

In the fast moving world of local government contracts and contract specifications it is essential to build in flexibility. A clearer or more independent look may therefore be required to challenge old practices and establish future needs. Often this is where an external consultant can be used, not to draw up the specifications, but to facilitate discussions with the client side and the potential contractor side which will allow important issues to emerge.

Organisational change is hard and attitudal change is still harder, but it is important that the contractual specification and relationship untangles past behaviour and clarifies roles and responsibility. There is a tendency to avoid this stage not only because it is hard but because some believe contractors will be able to 'sort out the service'. Actually, nothing could be more dangerous.

Putting all of this information together into the form of good specifications and clear organisational relationships between client and contractor is hard, and is likely to be the hardest part of the whole process.

❑ Involving staff and managers

Throughout the process, but particularly in the early stages, it is essential to work closely with the staff and managers. The attitudes of both will need to change if a good specification is to be improved and the right relationships established. In particular staff will need an understanding of what the change will mean for them, then they can contribute to the process.

The Berkshire experience shows that it is by far the best strategy to include and inform staff all the way through the process. Berkshire staff are encouraged to participate in assessment of potential contractors. For example, in both the Highways and Planning and Finance exercises, staff met with potential contractors, visited the companies' other sites and received formal presentations from contractors. Staff then reported directly to the Member Panel considering the bids to pass on their views. The Council, for its part, made it clear in each case that the externalisation would only take place if the majority of staff were willing participants. This level of involvement and trust has paid off.

Staff have acted very responsibly, and have clearly been aware that the Council must assess potential contractors on the basis of price and quality of their bids. In most cases where staff have expressed severe reservations about a potential contractor these reservations have been echoed in the more objective assessment of quality undertaken by the formal assessment team.

All of the externalisations in Berkshire have only been possible through including staff in the process. Keeping staff informed, being clear about the options and clear about where staff participate in the decision making process are all essential.

To summarise, putting together a good specification requires:

- clear forward thinking and planning by managers
- workshops and involvement of staff and managers to help them accept the need for change
- clear specification of future service requirements
- tough decisions on rationalisation and value for money prior to privatisation
- clear project planning, it always takes longer than you think.

❏ The market testing process

Use the pre-qualification stage to your advantage. Once you have clarified your aims and have a draft specification it may be appropriate to ask the market for any ideas you may have missed. This can be done in the pre-qualification phases when potential contractors may well be prepared to talk about how to build in flexibility. Always leave room for innovative ideas. Be as transparent as possible with potential bidders. Bidders may be able to propose quality processes that are new and could be helpful. Many local authorities are traditionally very nervous of talking openly to contractors but if you know what you want or what the options are you can have confidence in talking to the market.

❏ The bidding processes

During the formal bidding process, it is also essential to be as clear and open as possible. As much information should be made available to bidders as possible. Special arrangements should be made to ensure that the client side has sufficient time and resources to answer questions and resolve key issues. The important thing to remember is that this is the beginning of a partnership in the delivery of services. As noted in Chapter 15 partnerships can only be built if both parties are clear about the objectives and outcomes.

❏ The assessment process

Contract assessment has to be about price and quality viewed as two sides of the same equation. Even the proscriptive Government legislation allows for this. In order to make as complete a judgement as possible and avoid mistakes, it is very important to allow sufficient time for assessment. Ideally the process should include :

- full analysis of the tenders. If the specifications and tender documentation have been properly prepared, then a great deal of information about how the contractor will run the contract and the quality mechanisms to be used will be available and will require full consideration

- contractor presentation to decision makers. In the case of local authorities, Councillors must be involved. These presentations provide a good opportunity to pick up on the culture of the potential contractors and may well lead into some of the toughest questioning of quality
- staff feedback and views about potential contractors is essential and extremely useful.

❏ Establishing the partnership

Whatever views there might be about the rights and wrongs of contracting for services, once a contract has been let then in the interests of the customers of the service a good working relationship must be developed between the contractor and the client. Of course, it is very little use to attempt to begin to try to establish a good relationship with the potential contractor at this stage if none of the proper preparatory work has been undertaken in the lead up to the awarding of the contract. A good client contractor relationship is based on the client having been clear about roles and responsibilities right from the start. If the specification is good and clear, then there is a sound basis for proceeding with this stage.

One good mechanism for fine tuning responsibilities and checking on outputs is to allow time during the first three months of the contract for establishing a detailed service level agreement. This agreement can take each output specified of the contractor and turn it into a series of critical success factors which are clearly understood by both client and contractor. This process has the benefit of establishing further detailed discussions between clients and contractors to refine the day to day activities into routines that are well known and established. If any errors have been made in the specification there is room for slight modification. This room can be allowed for in the contract documentation.

The other most important aspect to remember in establishing the client side is that the emerging relationship between client and contractors must be businesslike and complementary, not combative. Client sides should not be over large or attempt to second guess the contractor. This simply wastes money and leads to duplication. By this stage the contractor should have been employed to undertake specified outputs to clear quality standards, this should have been backed up by the establishment of clear critical success factors. Much of the running of the contract should therefore be self regulatory, relying on the quality assurance mechanisms put in place.

This philosophy does not give contractors an easy time. On the contrary, if all of the prior stages have been properly set up, then a very tough contractual regime will have been established.

Implications of contracting for the organisation as a whole

There can be no doubt that following the contracting out route changes the nature and style of the organisation. It has a profound influence on staff, both those who move out with contracts and those who stay behind. In the early days of contracting in Berkshire, the full organisational implications were probably not fully grasped. But several years into the policy, as the extract from the Support Services Review quoted earlier shows, the organisation was having to adjust and plan, having realised that the implications of contracting out several thousands of staff were enormous.

Whatever strategic response authorities have taken to the challenges facing local government there has been a general move away from self contained departments delivering individual services and towards a more corporate approach. The commercial approach tends to lead authorities faster down this route because each contracted or potentially contracted service has had to think through their strategic and operational roles in preparing these specifications for contracts.

Operating in an increasingly contracted environment therefore leads to a changing focus for the authority. Output focused measures of performance provide:

- emphasis on output or customer oriented performance information
- concentration on strategic objectives (overall goal setting)
- focus on new accountability through user views/feedback
- new roles for Members and Officers.

This, in turn, leads to a re-thinking of the way in which the organisation works.

Figure 21.3. illustrates the new roles and relationships which can develop in a local authority. This is a far cry from the departmental management structures of the past.

The real effect of the organisational changes is to create a very small, multi-disciplinary centre working in close partnership with elected Members. The organisation is now typified by a form of matrix management whereby multi-disciplinary groupings work together to deliver specific goods and objectives.

The most visible outward show of change was the County's change last year to the employment of a County Manager rather than a Chief Executive. The County Manager's role is to co-ordinate key policies ensuring that sufficient resources

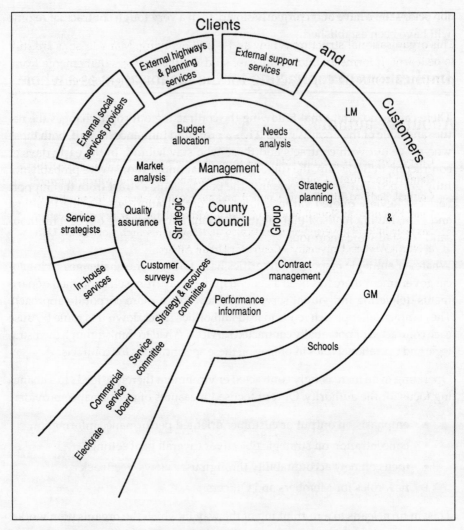

Figure 21.3. Core roles and function.

are available for their delivery. He is no longer seen as being the top of a hierarchical officer structure but as the main facilitator of close Member and officer policy development activity.

This view of the organisation could only have emerged following the establishment of strong and resilient business planning mechanisms within the service areas. Service delivery areas, like contractors, are now seen as having responsibility for delivering a set of functions that have been well specified, are subject to internal quality control mechanisms and are influenced by the strategic direction set by the centre of the organisation.

This organisational structure is new and is still evolving. Many lessons are still to be learnt. It forms an interesting case study in the changes that emerge from pursuing a contractual approach as part of an overall strategic objective.

About the author

Cheryl Coppell is a Senior Manager in local government. Starting work with Cambridge County Council she has also worked for Wandsworth Borough Council, Bedfordshire County Council, and has recently taken up the position of Chief Executive at Slough Borough Council. Although the majority of her career has been in local government she has also undertaken research work in the USA at North Western University's Centre for Urban Affairs.

Chapter 22

Contract management in the Department of Employment

Wilf Styles, John Cavanagh and Bob Mandy

The central theme for this chapter is how contract managers must change in order to meet the challenges set by the new Government policies to improve the quality of service provided by the public sector. It was necessary to begin the process within the then Management Services Branch (MSB) which, at that time, was a fragmented organisation based on three sites with three cultures with three sets of working practices. The contract management of this MSB work later became part of the newly formed Contracts Branch with the delivery of this work on the supplier side. Thus contract management incrementally developed within MSB, beginning at the end of 1992, culminating in the formation of Contracts Branch in January 1994. This process of change united the branch in a single culture through achieving BS5750 in October 1992. Having read the White Paper *Competing for Quality* it was apparent that BS5750 was the way forward for the branch. At the time the main drivers for the quality initiative were to improve the efficiency and effectiveness of the branch, and the professional desire to be the first Consultancy, Inspection and Review service in Whitehall to achieve this standard. Our quality initiative showed us the value of working with the private sector and also the benefits to be gained in sharing experiences with others to improve our business processes. Other initiatives such as the Investors in People standard have helped to build on the foundations laid by our quality initiative.

The lessons learned from the culture change are now being put into practice in managing the changes sweeping through the Business Services Division (BSD) of our Department. The role of the Contract Manager in Contracts Branch is very different to that previously used in the civil service, with the emphasis firmly based on working in partnership with suppliers, using quality principles to underpin the approach. The rest of this chapter is devoted to the approach that is being taken to develop Contracts Branch into an organisation that can truly manage contracts in a modern and forward thinking way.

The civil service has evolved into its present form over the last one hundred and fifty years. Cultural and working practice changes have in the main been gradual and inwardly focused. This means that the civil service has not had to face three of the most demanding challenges that have always faced their private sector counterparts. These are direct competition from others, the rapid change that is required to keep up with the competition and of course the need to make a profit. This situation is rapidly changing with the old values and norms that have in the past shaped the civil service in the past disappearing, possibly for ever, swept away by the Market Testing initiative and the need for all managers to produce the best value for money possible.

Business services division – an agenda for change

Market testing is affecting a great many areas of work throughout the Civil Service and is expanded upon in Chapters 14, 15 and 21. These effects have been felt particularly in the BSD of the Employment Department where, prior to reorganisation, 1200 staff delivered core services to the rest of the department through its four branches. The organisation chart is detailed in Figure 22.1.

These four branches were:

- Estates Branch which delivered estates related services
- Corporate Services Branch which delivered printing, stationery, security, messenger and typing services amongst others
- Management Services Branch which delivered Inspection Consultancy and Review services
- Information Systems Branch which delivered IT related services. (This branch is being market tested in its entirety. As such it will be dealt with separately and does not form part of this chapter although the principles described are equally valid.)

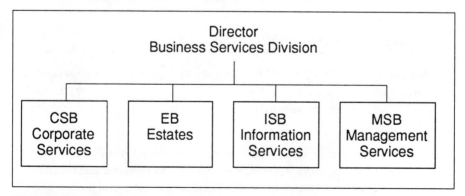

Figure 22.1. Business Services Division: organisation 1993.

It was apparent that virtually all the services provided by BSD could potentially be market tested and there was a requirement to see how we could successfully manage the external and internal service providers. Therefore, some research was needed to decide how this could be done after the market test programme was complete. This new approach was necessary regardless of whether the in–house bid won or the service was contracted out to the private sector. The in–house bid winner or external winners are treated in the same way after the market test except that the in–house bid winner would be managed under a service level agreement rather than through a legally binding contract.

Market testing soon became a major catalyst for change in BSD. Late in 1992 a team from MSB was established to examine the likely effect of market testing and to advise on how best to manage services in the future. This review in reality turned out to be phase one in what became an ongoing process of research, analysis, planning and action. The review and subsequent study on contract management took into account how similar work was carried out in the private sector and across Whitehall. The team were keen to capture good practice and to ensure that BSD could continue to manage a high quality service in a strategic alliance with providers, rather than in the previous arrangement of delivering services through the vertical management of staff across the division.

The study established that in future BSD would be sharply focused on two distinct areas. These were services supplied by the in–house bid winners and contract management of internal and external service providers. The new organisation would have to develop new procedures, skills and training in order to become the competent contract managers that the Employment Department and indeed service users would demand. The study identified the generic contract management activities and then established the skills that typical contract managers would need to discharge their duties. Although drawing up the specification for the contract and the competitive tendering process is currently outside the scope of the contract managers this may be required when services are re–tendered.

Defining contract management

So what is contract management? In one sense of this term the civil service has been managing contracts since its formation. However, it is necessary to understand what we mean by the role in this new scenario. Contract management was defined as:

> The active management of all aspects of the relationship between the service provider and the departmental customers and users to provide a cost effective and reliable service, consistent with legal requirements, financial probity and managerial accountability.

It was clear that a new culture would have to be developed to change the attitudes that surrounded contract management in the past. The review analyzed the way contracts were currently managed, how the private sector managed contracts and determined the way BSD should manage them in the future. The model for this new approach is detailed in Figure 22.2. Contract management is a much clearer and easier form of management than the direct management of a service. Suppliers have a clearly defined contract that sets out what they will deliver and the contract manager ensures that they stick to it! However, whilst this model ensures that the Department gets an efficient service it is important to recognise customer requirements and the opportunity to work together to build a relationship with the supplier to make the service even more efficient. Over and above the relationships between the contract manager, the supplier and the customer the contract manager has a duty to ensure that the tax payer receives the best value for money possible, therefore the contract manager has a duty to the fourth stakeholder in the model, the client i.e. the Department.

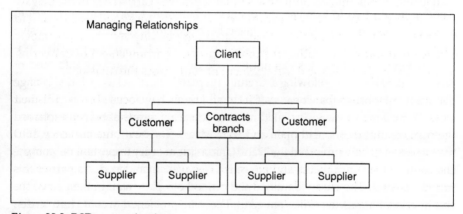

Figure 22.2. BSD reorganisation.

The focus on customer requirements means that the new approach to contract management should include strong quality principles. To this end, Contracts Branch is registered to BS5750 and incorporates the Investors in People principles in its training and development of staff.

What became phase two of the review of the organisation of BSD later in 1993 worked out the detailed points of the future structure of the division, and confirmed the need for a branch focused on contract management. The report also highlighted the huge cultural and organisational changes that would be required to transform BSD into this new organisation. Not least amongst the changes was the conversion of four branches with their separate identities into a new organisation supplying services or managing them, to agreed customer requirements.

The review examined all of the posts in the division (excluding those in ISB) to decide where they belonged in the new structure as either client side or supplier side activities. This created problems in itself, when it became apparent that some posts were split between the supplier side and client side activities. This meant that in some instances not just branches within the division but individual posts had to be redesigned. The new organisation would require a complete redesign of its structure, processes, roles and responsibilities.

The change management process

It was clear that the changes required in BSD would have to be very carefully managed to ensure a smooth transition from the traditional style of service delivery to this new approach. This approach had to ensure that there was no disruption to the delivery of services to customers and that the changes took account of the needs of BSD staff.

Another action was to examine the dangers inherent in rapid change and try to avoid the traps. To this end, staff at all levels have been involved in a comprehensive change management process. Where possible they have helped to advise the decision making and where this has not been possible have been kept informed of progress. BSD has been following a carefully prepared plan that has included change management workshops where staff from all grades have been able to give their views. A BSD roadshow visited all three sites where the heads of branch explained the changes ahead and held open and frank discussions with the audience. BSD management has also involved the Trade Union side at every important point in the change management process and active interest was appreciated. As part of this process, a preference exercise was carried out to help place staff in the part of the organisation that they were best suited to. The main problem that could have arisen from this exercise was that there may have been an imbalance between the profile of staff preference and the posts that were available. Research into the change management process in BSD indicated that staff were more worried by the possible change to a new function than the threat of market testing to their existing area of work. Staff were keen to devote their energies to their current areas of work. With this in mind, the transition to the new structure was started as soon as practically possible. This transition is still in its early stages, Contracts Branch having formally come into existence at the end of January 1994. The start date was driven by the need to manage contracts and Service Level Agreements that had already been let.

Contracts Branch is on a very steep learning curve and has been running monthly 'contract management workshops ' to train staff and inform stakeholders on contract management developments. Initially these were aimed at BSD, but as the expertise has developed they have expanded their scope to include interested parties throughout the Department and beyond. As the branch has learnt about contract management it has cascaded information outwards and is perceived by some as being at the leading edge of contract management, whilst still learning about the process itself. As we built up knowledge on a monthly basis participants became expectant for the next instalment and yet we were still getting up to speed on that knowledge ourselves. This in itself posed a challenge! It seemed at all times like the one eyed man leading the blind. The branch has also produced a contract management policy guide to encourage a consistent approach in contracts management across Employment Department Headquarters (EDHQ).

A new approach to contracts management

The challenge of Market Testing had demonstrated to us that a new way of doing things was required. In fact new concepts were developed out of necessity in Contracts Branch. This approach was needed for setting up and managing contracts and service level agreements for the delivery of goods and services between external customers, suppliers and successful market test in–house suppliers.

This new way of working involved differing approaches to thinking, managing processes, and to the contract management culture, than those that existed before. This meant extensive research to understand what best practice existed and which was the most appropriate for us. It began to emerge that key elements for the success of this new approach in Contracts Branch should include Business Process Re–engineering, Benchmarking, continuous improvement, effective partnerships, Total Quality Management and BS5750 for quality management systems, investors in people (IIP) a complex mosaic indeed.

It was clear that this new way would require the empowerment of management to drive the initiative forward. Many talk about 'empowering people' which in itself is fine, but all too often this can be at the expense of depowering management at the sharp end especially, in our terms, at Grade 7 level. This can lead to a lack of strategic direction for the business, and ultimately inefficiency. Our focus was to empower our people through a strategy of putting power in middle managers' hands. Our approach to this complex issue is detailed later in the chapter.

In setting out our experience it is useful to start in our recent past. Earlier we examined the structure of Business Services Division and how it consisted of four branches with four cultures. A closer examination revealed business activities with at least twelve cultures in existence on three sites. These complexities were futher complicated by previous reorganisations and led to differing approaches to:

- customer satisfaction
- quality initiatives, standards, and systems (BS5750, IIP)

- people management and leadership
- training and development including NVQs
- communications
- contract management and supplier relationships.

To be successful in an ever changing and more competitive world things would need to be different.

The blueprint is for a single contract management culture with business activities pulling in the same direction. This will be needed to manage efficiently the complex stakeholder relationships involved. These relationships, outlined earlier (see Figure 22.2.) are those between ourselves, the suppliers (external and internal), customers, end users and our client (the Permanent Secretary in his role as Principal Accounting Officer). This culture will be achieved through a common approach to business activities built on:

- customer focus
- common quality principles and standards
- effective partnerships.

We compared the business activities within the functions brought together in the newly formed Contracts Branch (see Figure 22.3) against those in the European Quality Award (EQA) model for TQM (see Figure 22.4). We found many different ways of doing these activities. If this were to continue with no clear continuous improvement strategy, then it would have the potential for the business to pull in different directions with incompatible policies, systems and procedures (see Figure 22.5).

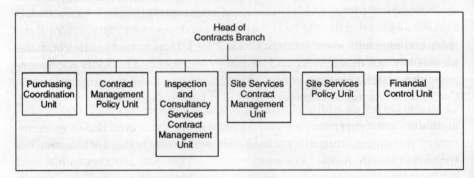

Figure 22.3. Contracts Branch.

In fact if one widens the scope of the comparison of these business activities to include all the stakeholders (and their business activities) involved in the delivery of the services we are managing (see Figure 22. 6), the position becomes far

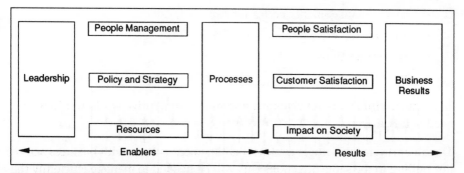

Figure 22.4. The European TQM model.

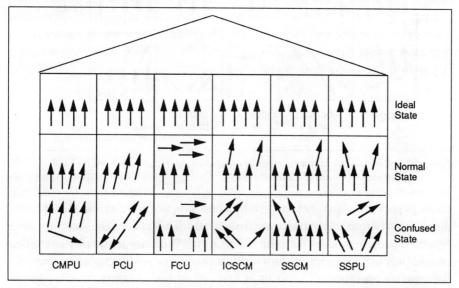

Figure 22.5. Continuous improvement in CB business functions. (Reproduced by kind permission of PA Consultants.)

more complex with even greater potential for lack of harmony, direction and inefficiency and ineffectiveness. This places an increasing importance on managing the relationships effectively.

Contracts Branch, in addition to its policy and intelligent customer role, increasingly does not deliver the service. Rather it ensures that quality and value for money are consistently delivered by the internal or external supplier within the contracted requirements.

Benchmarking

Expertise existed in Management Services Branch as a result of research under-

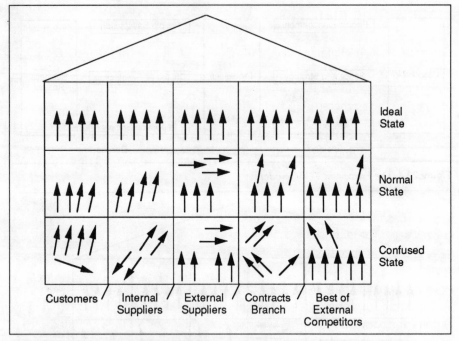

Figure 22.6. Continuous iumprovement in all stakeholders. (Reproduced by kind permission of PA Consultants.)

taken as part of its quality initiative into best practice and during efficiency reviews by visiting comparator organisations. This led to the decision that Benchmarking would be the vehicle for Contracts Branch to identify strengths, provide opportunities for continuous improvement and direct planned innovation into its operations. The focus at first would be Contracts Branch internal operations but later this would extend the involvement by all stakeholders in partnership towards continuous improvement of services.

Benchmarking is a powerful technique to many companies and has been shown to reap large rewards if conducted properly. Thus, credibility and cooperation from external benchmarking partners is quickly lost if they detect the lack of seriousness and disorganisation which results from an uncoordinated approach to benchmarking.

Research told us that Benchmarking needs to be tailored to each business around some common frameworks. But one thing that every authority agrees on is that one should understand fully the process to be benchmarked, its critical success factors and measures before doing any benchmark external visits. In order to gain maximum advantage and retain credibility from benchmarking clubs/focus groups and visits from and to external benchmarking partners, coordination is essential.

Empowering management

Contracts Branch managers and staff will work together in Business Development Teams (BDTs) to benchmark their processes. These teams led by Grade 7s will be a focal point for benchmarking and TQM within each business unit by comparing their processes against:

- the EQA Total Quality Management model: to understand our strengths and identify opportunities for improvement to become the best
- each other's function: to harmonise business activity and systems
- best in class organisations: to learn and innovate from the best
- other comparator organisations: to understand innovations taking place in specific relevant processes.

After analysis the data from the benchmarks form the basis of a self appraisal performance improvement report. This contains recommended improvement action from each BDT which when agreed is the process which as stated earlier empowers management and staff. These form an aggregated Branch plan with the resultant action taken forward across the branch by the management team. A consensus and appraisal system has been developed by the quality team to give a scoring to the whole of a business unit operation based on the EQA model for TQM. This detailed output will allow the Branch to appraise itself against an independent internationally recognised quality model and in a structured way improve towards Total Quality Management.

Benchmarking will be built into the Branch business planning process. This process will have five stages (see Figure 22.7).

Stage one: seek out relevant data and information.

Stage two: assess and analyse the data – decide relevance.

Stage three: decide what improvements to make and targets to set.

Stage four: draw up action plan.

Stage five: implement, monitor and take control.

The plans will be drawn up by each Grade 7 led function and will form the basis of a composite Branch plan for implementation by the functionally based Business Development Teams.

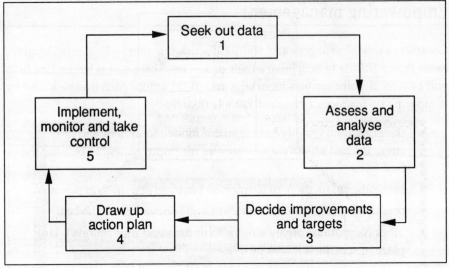

Figure 22.7. Benchmarking: five stage business planning.

The benchmarking process which we are using is an eight stage process (see Figure 22.8).

Stage one: select process to benchmark.

Stage two: identify appropriate measures and information.

Stage three: identify benchmarking partners.

Stage four: measure and describe performance.

Stage five: measure and describe partners performance.

Stage six: compare performance and identify gaps.

Stage seven: decide appropriate changes, develop and implement action plans.

Stage eight: review results, monitor and recalibrate.

Benchmarking as a form of quality improvement research needs to take account of existing quality initiatives in an organisation if it is to build on current good practice. Within the new branch a great deal of work had been done in BS5750 and IIP which has helped the branch develop high quality systems and people skills and will continue to play an important role in its approach to quality. BS5750 and IIP have helped to introduce the branch to continuous improvement through review and self appraisal of the businesses strengths and continue to improve the consistency of operations as we seek to broaden the scope of application. When striving to improve quality and reach a pinnacle of performance, we have found that develop-

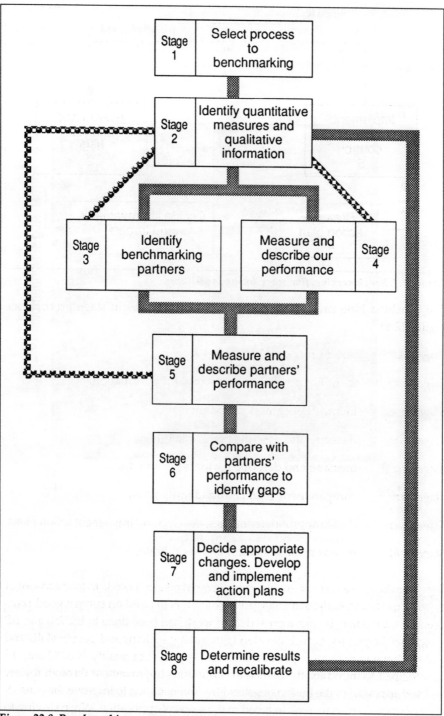

Figure 22.8. Benchmarking – process overview.

ing a high performance team is a prerequisite. To do this, improvement in systems and the development of people in a balanced way will give good results (see Figure 22.9.) Failure to do this with care will result in a build up in people stress or systems stress as development in one outstrips the other.

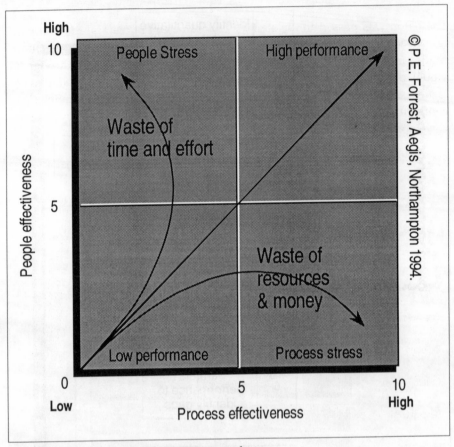

Figure 22.9. Quality management systems performance.

Clearly the required culture change would only happen by design. This design was based on P. E. Forrester's unpublished culture change model (see Figure 22.10). At a culture change workshop the Branch outlined its vision of a one stop contracts/ facilities management unit. The management team worked down through the model to flesh out the vision by producing as outputs from the workshop:

- a description statement of the work: outlining the branches raison-d'être
- an aspiration statement, describing what the branch aspires to
- a set of core values: these give priority to the way we do our work in the branch. They are built on the BSD culture values.

Many culture changes fall by the wayside because of a lack of action plans and local ownership of implementation. This lesson has been learnt in Contracts Branch and it was important therefore that this good work was not lost as so often can happen as strategic ideas evaporate through lack of action. We were determined that, by full application of the model, the core values would be turned into action.

The baton was passed to the staff by the management team at the inaugural branch conference where all staff in syndicates continued to work on the culture change model (see Figure 22.10). They worked downwards in steps through the model, prioritised the core values, produced policies, objectives, strategies and tactics (action plans) to deliver the core values. These were further refined post conference, tailored and implemented within each business unit by Business Development Teams.

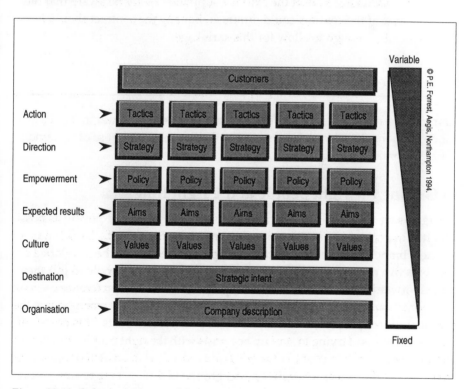

Figure 22.10. Culture change model.

Lessons to be learnt from this experience

This cultural change started in BSD a number of years ago and is still continuing. We have learnt a number of things that we feel will be of use to others who will be faced with similar challenges in managing contracts in the future:

- ideally the contract manager designate should be involved in ensuring that the specification for the future contract is correct
- contracts should be managed as partnerships with suppliers – contracts are there to be developed
- customers should be made aware of the service that is to be provided and all stakeholders should be aware of their responsibilities in ensuring that this is carried out
- financial control, the supplier should only be paid for what they deliver and strict controls should ensure that this happens. Equally the contract manager should ensure that the supplier is paid on time in an agreed way
- in a shrinking market the external suppliers should be aware that the value of the contract could diminish. Equally the contract should be flexible enough to allow for this shrinkage.

Conclusions

Our change management experience meant that certain issues and problems emerged along the way and awareness of these might help those of you undertaking a similar course.

❏ Getting the right people at the right time

Reorganising meant getting the right people into key posts as quickly as possible. It is important to put these people in much earlier than the launch date of the new branch because new systems and procedures need to be developed before effective operation can take place. One cannot rely on people to put themselves forward and be released at the appropriate time. The preference exercise mentioned earlier in the chapter was part of that process and it emerged that the vast majority of people were keen to stay in their present posts. This posed difficulties in terms of trying to staff up key posts with the right people who in turn did not wish to move posts. A further risk is an initial mismatch of skills and experience. All this was set against a background of diminishing resources, previous and existing responsibilities and new ones coming on stream.

❏ Equal opportunities

The evolving new culture was made up, as outlined earlier, from a number of cultures and geographical locations. This presented us with an ideal opportunity to conduct an equal opportunity health check. The subsequent study endorsed the existing Employment Department Group Equal Opportunities policies and the considerable efforts being made by management to consult with staff. An action plan was produced to build on this good practice with the intention of maintaining and continuously improving Equal Opportunities within our business culture.

❑ Communication and commitment

There is a need to spell out clearly what contract management is at an early stage in the change process. If this is not done and communicated effectively to staff a misunderstanding will exist as people in the existing organisation will be working from a different premise to each other based on their past experience of contract management. The first step of this communication is to gain the commitment and support of top management by convincing them that this is the right approach to contract management. Equally important is to involve the Trade Union side at an early stage in order to forge a mutual and understanding partnership.

❑ Delivering the work during the transition

It is also vital to put transition arrangements in place at an early stage to deliver the existing work whilst market testing in-house bid preparation continues satisfactorily while bringing the new branch up to speed. This will ensure that the in-house supplier does not allow the standard of service to slip. If this were to happen then the market test in-house bid would find it difficult to mount a credible bid.

❑ A learning organisation

The process of change is just the beginning of our journey and the preparations we have made to map out clearly a new direction. One cannot just decide to do TQM and then it happens, as Chapter 19 reinforces. There is a need to have dedicated, motivated and skilled individuals with the expertise required to make it happen. To this end the BSD review recommended the formation of a Quality Team to drive the initiative forward, acquiring the required expertise and from time to time reminding management of the stage the branch is at in the process. This is particularly important when managers are under pressure and there is an increased danger of the initiative's stalling by their taking their eye off the ball. It has been about establishing a learning organisation which will work in partnership with all the key stakeholders. We conclude that the successful outcome to this endeavour is not a soft option and will deliver greater efficiency and effectiveness and value for money for the taxpayer.

Contracts branch is at the cutting edge of the changes that are sweeping through Government and the way we handle this is crucial. It is important not just to the success of the Employment Department's efficiency but to the overall effectiveness of the civil service in general. We now have to compete to survive by ensuring ever increasing value for money and quality of service.

Within BSD, the management recognised the benefits of a proactive TQM approach to developing expertise in contract management rather than regarding it as a threat to its existence. Already the benefits of this proactive approach are clear and we are now on the way towards achieving this goal. This means not just surviving in this dynamic market place but making a significant contribution to the evolutionary progress of the public service.

About the authors

Wilf Styles

Head of Contracts Branch since its formation at the beginning of 1994. He has been a champion of TQM, benchmarking and Business Process Re-engineering for a number of years and sees these techniques as an ideal vehicle for becoming a centre of expertise in contracts management in the public sector. Prior to Contracts Branch, Wilf was Head of Management Services Branch which delivered Staff Inspection and Consultancy work. Management Services was the first branch of its type in Whitehall to achieve BS5750 in October 1992.

Bob Mandy

As a member of the Contracts Branch Quality Team, Bob manages the BS5750 quality system and coordinates Investors in People. He has been with the Department for 17 years and involved in quality initiatives for three years. Prior to this, he worked in training as a manager in the Employment Service. Before joining the Civil Service, Bob was a comprehensive school teacher and worked as an industrial chemist.

John Cavanagh

As part of the quality team, John is the Contracts Branch Quality Development and Benchmarking Manager. He is responsible for developing and implementing the branch quality policy, strategy and benchmarking. He has been with the Department 19 years with roles in personnel, training and operational management as well as being involved in quality initiatives in numerous organisations in both the public and private sectors. Prior to joining the Department he worked as a work study engineer in the private sector.

Reference and suggested reading

Cabinet Office (1991) *Competing for Quality: Buying Better Public Services.* Cm 1730 London, HMSO

Chapter 23

The Patient's Charter: fact or fiction?

Roger Lovell

Chapter 13 looked at some of the issues surrounding the Citizen's Charter. This chapter provides a brief description of some research carried out between October 1992 and January 1993, which examined how the Patient's Charter had been implemented in six hospitals within the National Health Service (NHS), during the first six months of its existence.

The introduction of the Charter in April 1992 detailed 24 rights and standards that patients could expect from hospitals within the service. Seven of the rights were already in existence. Others, for example the standard for some clinical activity to commence within 30 minutes of an outpatient appointment, were not only new but also more easily measured. On the surface therefore objective comparisons could be made between the levels of service in similar units.

The objective of the study was twofold. In the first place, it considered the distinction between automatic adherence to the Charter and internalising its philosophy into the normal day to day running of the unit. In other words, how far was the patient focus ethos of the Charter being adopted by the unit, or was it being accepted at face value as a result of political pressure? This was achieved by looking not only at the results of the standards but also the approach taken to them and the attitude adopted towards their implementation. Secondly, the study then widened the investigation to consider what organisational conditions would be expected in a unit geared to the provision of empowering staff to provide better patient care and compared units against those criteria.

Tracer conditions

The six units studied were all within the same NHS Region, thereby giving a degree of consistency at one level of management. In theory therefore we were faced with instituting similar changes within the same overall management command. The units studied included four general acute hospitals and two priority service units concerned with areas such as learning disabilities and mental health.

In view of the length of time available for the study, it was decided to use six of the 24 rights and standards, all of which were easily observable, to make comparisons across the units. The six tracer conditions were the following.

- New Right 2
  To be guaranteed admission for virtually all treatments by a specific date no later than two years from the date when your consultant places you on a waiting list.
- National Standard 6
  When you go to an outpatient clinic, you will be given a specific appointment time and will be seen within 30 minutes.
- Local Standard 1
  Within all specialties, patients will be given dates for outpatient's appointments within a certain time of referral of routine cases.
- National Standard 7
  Your operation should not be cancelled on the day you are due to arrive in hospital. If, exceptionally, your operation has to be postponed twice you will be admitted to hospital within one month of the second cancelled operation.
- National Standard 9
  A decision should be made about any continuing health or social needs you may have, before you are discharged from hospital.
- In-patient Information
  Certain rights and standards are concerned with giving information to patients. The study therefore included an examination of the information received by a patient receiving elective surgery from admission to discharge.

❏ Methods of study

The methods of study were as follows:

One to one interviews

with senior staff, including Board members; charter co-ordinators; nursing managers; business managers; outpatient managers and information managers;

Attitude Survey

of nursing staff;

Sensing meetings

with between six and eight nurses from a variety of grades;

Documentation

in particular business plans, applications for Trust status, discharge plans, nursing plans, general and specific written material for patients and customer satisfaction surveys.

Results of tracer conditions

The results of looking at the tracer conditions are given below.

❏ Two year waiting list and cancelled operations

Both standards depend to a large extent on the optimum usage of theatre and treatment facilities. Given the absence of additional resources in many cases, resort needs to be made to improving procedures. These include reducing the number of do not attends (DNAs) and ensuring that those attending are fit for the operation at the time.

The best performing units

The best performing units had taken a fundamental look at procedures aimed at optimum theatre usage. These:

- ensured that the patient was kept fully informed of what was happening from the time of referral to admission for the operation
- controlled the waiting list by carrying out regular validation of the list by writing to the patient asking whether treatment was still required and, at the same time, updating him or her of the latest estimate of admission; if the patient did not respond within a specific period, the GP was asked to confirm the need, if this was not forthcoming the patient was informed that they had been removed from the list
- established short notice lists giving patients the choice of attending within a matter of hours if the opportunity arose
- provided up to four weeks notice of the date of the operation, thereby allowing patients to arrange their affairs to suit; or, in an increasing number of cases, provided patients with a date of admission at the time of consultation through a diary booking system
- ensured patients were fit for the operation by carrying out pre-operative clerking/examination one week before the operation was due
- established a multi-disciplinary team to monitor the situation closely
- sought confirmation from the patient that they would attend for the operation.

In view of these measures, fewer DNAs occurred and cancellations were kept to a minimum. If they did occur however, patient's were given an adequate reason immediately by a member of the medical staff and re-booking was very strictly monitored to ensure that the patient would be operated on at the earliest opportunity. Above all, such units saw the standard as a continuing downward process and, in one case, had already obtained the 18 month mark.

Poor practice units

Poor practice units on the other hand:

- had not evaluated procedures
- provided little or no information to patient's from the time of consultation until they were called for operation
- carried out no validation of waiting list
- gave as little as one week's notice for the operation, sometimes after a wait of two years without communication
- failed to ask for confirmation of attendance and did not carry out pre-operative clerking, resulting in patient's attending unfit for the operation
- had up to 15% DNAs
- cancelled operations frequently without adequate explanation to the patient
- failed to monitor cancellations closely and, in consequence, failed to achieve the cancellation 'standard'
- had to 'farm out' cases to other hospitals in order to meet the government's target of reducing the list to two years by April 1992, and, since neither resources nor procedures had changed, found themselves creeping up to 27 months by August 1992.

❑ First outpatient appointment

The standard at the time for first outpatient appointment was within 13 weeks of a consultant receiving a letter from the GP. Performance against the standard depended upon the type of complaint, some of which were consistently well inside the standard, while others were some way outside. It was possible however to compare results between units.

Good practice

The better units were fully computerised and provided specific information to patients. In some cases patients could be informed of the date of their appointment five days after receipt of the letter from the GP. The Charter standard was also clearly set out in the letter which not only drew it to the patient's attention but also showed whether or not it had been met.

Poor practice

The poorer performing units were in most cases still tied to outdated manual appointment systems with correspondence designed for general usage. Indeed pro-forma letters were still being used in one case. The average time for patients to receive details of their appointment was between two and three weeks with delays of up to five weeks not uncommon. Needless to say, no mention of Charter standards appeared in the correspondence.

❏ Outpatient clinic

Apart from the length of waiting times for operations, nowhere is the Charter more obviously observed than in performance at outpatient clinics.

Good practice

The best clinics:

- provided specific appointments
- recorded time of arrival, time of appointment and time seen
- continually monitored performance throughout the clinic
- provided individual explanations to patients if delays occurred
- analysed reasons for delays and held multi-disciplinary meetings to consider how these could be minimised in future
- displayed the names of all staff serving a particular clinic, including reasons why a regular member might be absent
- displayed clearly details of Charter standards in various languages in the waiting room
- believed that normal practice should be for the patient to be seen at the time of the appointment.

Intermediate practice

Within this standard an intermediate level of performance was observed as follows:

- appointments were made for specific times
- monitoring of performance took place once an hour
- the names of staff serving the clinic were not displayed
- individual patient's were not told of delays, the time of delay was merely marked on a white board
- no explanations for delays were given
- no evaluation of the reasons for delays took place
- little evidence of Charter standards was displayed
- the prevailing ethos was that if patients were seen within 30 minutes they were 'seen on time.'

Poor practice

Despite the generally unsatisfactory nature of the intermediate practice, worse was observed:

- block bookings were still in operation
- no effective monitoring was taking place
- patients were unaware of the staff serving the clinic
- no mention of the Charter was displayed in the clinic
- one consultant insisted on a block booking system to commence 40 minutes before his arrival
- the overall ethos appeared to be that the consultant's time was more valuable than that of several patients.

❑ Discharge procedures

Discharge procedures particularly looked at the concept of seamless care between the hospital and the community.

Good practice

In the best units there was:

- a discharge policy supplemented by specific standards on each ward
- staff dedicated to managing the interface were employed
- close links with the community existed, including interchange of staff between District and ward nurses
- close monitoring and evaluation of the service was carried out and suggestions adopted.

Poor practice

In the absence of an overall policy individual wards were left to their own devices. Little direct contact took place between the hospital and community staff and there was a feeling that staff saw the hospital service as somewhat self contained.

❑ In-patient information

In order to achieve a measure of consistency the information received by hernia patients was examined.

Good practice

In the best units:

- general information about the unit and its facilities was professionally produced and sent to the patient before admission

- a clear explanation of the particular complaint was given including details of post-operative treatment and guidance
- patients were actively engaged in the preparation of their own nursing plan
- patients were aware of their named nurse and often which team of nurses was looking after them
- nursing standards and ward philosophies were monitored, evaluated and updated by the staff.

Poor practice

In the poorer units:

- little, if any, written information was provided detailing hospital facilities
- pre-admission information consisted of a standard letter
- written details of the complaint and post-operative information were not provided
- patient's had little knowledge of who was their named nurse
- nursing standards and ward philosophies barely existed and many of those that did were out of date and rarely referred to.

Empowerment conditions

Examination of performance against the tracer conditions allowed comparisons to be drawn between the units. While good and poor practice was being carried out in pockets across all units, the data showed clearly that certain units were some way ahead of others in most areas. In order to be transformed into patient care, the tracer conditions needed to pass through the organisational systems operating within the units as shown in Figure 23.1.

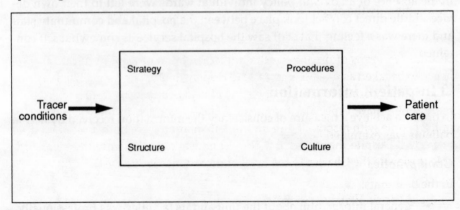

Figure 23.1. Path of the tracer conditions.

As Walker notes (1990):

> staff cannot provide good service to customers (patients), if they themselves are not getting good service from the organisation.

The study therefore compared the strategy process, structure, procedures and culture operating within the units to determine any relationship between the way these were operating and performance of the tracer conditions.

❏ Organisation of the implementation

Before considering the individual aspects of organisation, it is worth considering how units went about implementing the Charter.

How

In discussing how to manage change, Chapter 3 considers when to establish project teams and when to carry out change as part of day to day business. The better performing units all recognised the Charter as a change which needed to be managed, initially at least, by a dedicated resource, either through a project manager or a project team. While this approach can isolate other members of staff not directly involved in the team, making them believe that it is of no concern to them, it does provide a platform for the changes around which a specific strategy can be planned.

In comparison, those units who attempted to implement the Charter as part of day to day business were, by and large, those who had made the least satisfactory progress. This may have been due to the problem of more routine work taking priority as it often does in such situations, but also had much to do with attitude. Indeed such units exuded the impression of 'initiative fatigue,' seeing the Charter as yet one more change. In practice this was largely due to the reactive nature of the units. By continuously reacting, they had lost control of the change. Sadly this was in most cases a symptom. The causes lay much deeper within the way the organisations were being run.

Who

Secondly in terms of organising the implementation of the Charter itself, care needs to be taken as to who is given lead responsibility. The more effective units gave charge not only to senior people but also to people who were respected by more senior staff, especially the medical staff. Too often in the less successful units, people with responsibility for implementation were both junior and little respected. Despite their hard and earnest endeavours therefore they were unable to elevate the Charter to the level of importance it deserved.

❏ The New Environment

One way of looking at the changes currently enveloping the NHS might be to consider them from the viewpoint of the Myers-Briggs personality type which was discussed in Chapter 5. Traditionally, the overall culture of the service could be seen as being ESFJ. In other words, extroverted or outgoing; sensing and viewing things in a sequential manner; feeling and caring for others; carried out in a structured manner.

This type of personality has a high emphasis on caring, avoiding conflict and enjoying harmony. As such it prefers a collegiate style of management which places considerable emphasis on the integrity of professional practice. The intense desire for harmony and avoidance of conflict also results in a high degree of deference within the system, especially toward senior medical staff, which at times can be unhealthy and counter-productive.

This needs to be compared with the overall personality of the Anglo-American business world, which tends to be ESTJ and is primarily behind the new market orientation of the service. On the surface the fact that three letters are the same might indicate little problem about compatibility. The critical difference of 'thinking' as opposed to 'feeling' however, means that the general value systems are at odds. The thinking type makes decisions on an objective basis, influenced primarily by the facts. As such, it is a type quite at home with performance targets, budgeting, value for money and, above all, measurable inputs and outcomes. Looked at this way, it can be seen why so many health professionals are having difficulty in coming to terms with a different way of looking at their world.

It is however the bringing together of these two cultures which provides the main challenge behind the reforms. Likewise, the drive for improved customer service and better value for money behind the Patient's Charter is complimentary with this movement. Perhaps not surprisingly therefore, the better performing units under the tracer conditions all appeared to be on the way to embracing the two cultures.

❏ Strategy

Strategic and business planning requirements have obviously changed considerably since the introduction of the purchaser/provider split, where, by and large, District Health Authorities and Fund Holding General Practitioners are the purchasers and hospitals the providers. Even the most advanced units however appeared to have some way to go in the area of establishing long term measurable goals.

Application for Trust status provided a focus as well as an awareness of the need to become more pro-active in establishing future direction. Sadly in many cases, proposals for the future consisted of grand sounding intentions like:

... to be amongst the top 10% of providers in the NHS...,

without supporting information as to how this might be achieved. This approach also tended to emphasise espoused values which showed little relationship to theories in use. For example, claims that the unit provided, '...post-qualification nurse training of the highest quality...,' were hardly substantiated by a current annual budget of £3000 for 1600 nurses. Having said that, the better performing units were in the throes of introducing strategic planning systems although, with one exception, ideas had been generated primarily in the Boardroom. The exceptional unit however had carried out a series of one-day workshops with staff at all grades giving them the opportunity to consider the future direction of the unit.

❑ Structure

The strong professional ethos, noted above, appears to work well in crisis situations and at other times within their own disciplinary areas. The vertical nature of such structures however can be incompatible with the journey of the patient, as shown in Figure 23.2, who passes across the organisation.

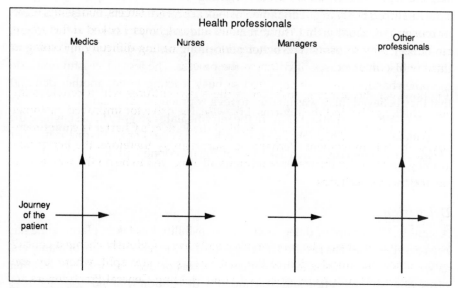

Figure 23.2. The patient's journey.

Two particular attempts to start to overcome this were noticed. Clinical Directorates had been introduced in the better performing units. These consisted of a day to day management team of medical, business and nursing functions for each clinical specialism, with the clinical director reporting to the management board. The key to success of such an arrangement appeared to be the willingness of medical staff to invest non-clinical authority in the clinical director and to submit themselves to this. Interestingly, the relationship between medical staff and other professionals in the better performing units appeared considerably less deferential, with nurses often claiming that they now had a greater self-belief in their own professional ability and were, in consequence, moving away from being the doctor's handmaiden.

Primary Nursing is another area of structural change in the move to improve patient service. This concept, which aims to give an individual nurse primary responsibility for the patient's episode of care during his or her stay in hospital, was proving difficult to introduce in most units for a variety of reasons. In practice, the concept of team nursing was more prevalent where patients were looked after by a particular nursing team, with a named nurse in charge of the patient's care for a particular shift. This approach was reinforced in one unit by senior sisters who elected to wear staff nurse uniforms in order to avoid giving patients the impression that they were overriding the authority of the named nurse.

❏ Procedures

The illustration noted above of how waiting lists for operations were significantly reduced by taking a fundamental look at procedures emphasises the need to ensure continually that these remain relevant, or, in the current vogue, reengineer the processes. The better performing units were not only aware of this but also devoted specific time to the process. The less successful units, on the other hand, frequently appeared so busy reacting to yet another demand that they believed there was no time to review practices. An example of this was at a unit with an outpatient clinic in the intermediate category at best, where the Outpatient Manager had religiously collected data over 12 months on the number of clinics running late. When asked what she had done with it, she stated:

> nothing, I haven't the time.

Delegation

A significant amount of delegation of responsibility has taken place. Some has been excellent and has resulted in the opportunity to reduce layers of managers, as well as getting closer to the patient in terms of decision making. In other cases, physical delegation and psychological delegation were not consistent, as noted in Chapter 11. This was particularly so in poorer performing units where the staff undoubtedly felt that they had responsibility without authority. There were also instances where senior managers believed that delegation amounted to abdication of responsibility on their part.

Nursing standards

In general there appeared to be a significant gap between any strategic planning at the top of the organisation and nursing standards and ward philosophies at ward level. In other words, there was little evidence of tactical planning and staff frequently complained that they had little or no idea of the objectives of the unit in general or their area in particular.

Many examples were discovered of extremely impressive work being carried out at the ward level, either facilitated by practice development nurses or initiated by the staff themselves. The feeling of senior management throughout appeared to be that nursing standards were more likely to be adhered to and owned if they grew from the bottom and were initiated by the staff themselves.

Despite the sterling work in many areas, however, there were even more examples where no standards whatsoever existed and others where standards had fallen into disuse and become outdated when less enthusiastic staff took over. While even in the better performing units nursing standards were not total, they were far more in evidence and the ability to be able to measure performance was present.

Staff awareness of the Charter

Hardly surprisingly, staff were more aware of the Charter and its provisions and demands in the better performing units. This had been achieved through workshops explaining general principles and the establishment of working parties on specific issues. Staff in one unit even received details of the Charter with their pay slips. Team briefing schemes had also been used but the general complaint of staff to these was that they were more interested in providing top-down information, than listening to suggestions from the bottom.

Patient needs

A significant amount of work was being carried out in endeavouring to assess patient needs and opinions. This was being done mainly by survey but also included in-patient groups and, in one case, the use of a patient advocate for mental health patients. In another case a questionnaire was sent to the District nurse on discharge of each patient asking for comments, suggestions etc. Replies were then strictly monitored, evaluated and suggestions implemented.

Despite the wealth of information being collected however, there was little evidence that it was being fed into the strategy making process which still appeared to be driven by providing a service 'to' patients rather than 'for' them. Work needed to be carried out therefore to co-ordinate the information and ensure that data was evaluated and considered.

❏ Culture

The results of the attitude survey showed that staff in better performing units felt more empowered in their work. They believed that their suggestions were actively sought, encouraged and acted upon. They believed that they operated in an atmosphere of trust where mistakes were learned from rather than punished. One nurse commented:

> in the past we worked as well as we could with what we had. Now we work to produce a service that the patients want.

In the poorer performing units staff felt less supported and encouraged.

Above all else, in any endeavour to change there must be a readiness for it. Changes can be specified, designed and communicated to perfection but if there is no willingness to change little will be achieved. What was noticeable above all else in the better performing units was a drive for change from the top of the organisation. From this, staff appeared energised and encouraged throughout the organisation. That said, the Charter has provided a lever for change which has enabled staff in all units to initiate and implement imaginative changes for the ultimate benefit of the patient. In practice, if a genuine readiness and desire for change exists the ethos behind the Charter becomes a reality. To remain in the world of fiction means paying lip service to superficial targets which lack substance and in the end will deeive not only the unit but also, and more importantly, the patients themselves.

References and suggested reading

Ham, C. (1991) *The New National Health Service* Oxford, Radcliffe Medical Press

Spurgeon, P. and Barwell, F. (1991) *Implementing Change in the NHS* London, Chapman Hall

Walker, D. (1990) *Customer First* Aldershot, Gower

Index

D

N

O

P

W

Y